Frontier and Overseas Expeditions from India

Frontier and Overseas Expeditions from India

(in 7 Volumes)

Compiled in the
Intelligence Branch,
Army Headquarters, India

Vol. II
North-West Frontier Tribes between the
Kabul and Guaml Rivers

Low Price Publications
Delhi-110052

Distributed by
D.K. Publishers Distributors (P) Ltd.
4834/24, Ansari Road, Darya Ganj,
New Delhi-110002
Phones: 23278584, 23278368, 23261465
e-mail: dkpd@del3.vsnl.net.in
url: www.dkpd.com

First Published 1907-11

Reprinted in **LPP** 2004

ISBN 81-7536-323-1 (Set)
ISBN 81-7536-325-8 (Vol.2)

Published by
Low Price Publications
A-6, Nimri Commercial Centre,
Near Ashok Vihar Phase-IV,
Delhi-110052
Phones: 27401672, 27452453
e-mail: lpp@nde.vsnl.net.in
url: www.lppindia.com

Printed at
D K Fine Art Press P Ltd.
Delhi-110052

PRINTED IN INDIA

CONTENTS.

CHAPTER I.

CHAPTER II.

CHAPTER III.

CHAPTER IV.

THE ORAKZAI TRIBE.

CHAPTER V.

THE ZAIMUKHT TRIBE.

CHAPTER VI.

THE TURI AND BANGASH TRIBES.

CHAPTER VII.

DARWESH KHEL WAZIRS.

CHAPTER VIII.

MAHSUD WAZIRS AND BHITTANIS.

CHAPTER IX.

MAHSUD AND DARWESH KHEL WAZIRS—(contd.).

CHAPTER X.

THE DAWARIS.

LIST OF MAPS.

CHAPTER I.

THE AFRIDI TRIBE.

Khaibar and Aka Khel Afridis.

THE Afridis are a large tribe, inhabiting the lower and easternmost spurs of the Safed Koh range, to the west and south of the Peshawar district, including the Bazar and Bara valleys. On their east they are bounded by British territory; on their north they have the Mohmands; west, the Shinwaris; and south, the Orakzais and Bangash.

The origin of this tribe, owing to want of written records, is very obscure, but all authorities are agreed to divide them into the following clans:—

1. Kuki Khel.	5. Zakha Khel.
2. Malikdin Khel.	6. Sipah.
3. Kambar Khel.	7. Aka Khel.
4. Kamrai.	8. Adam Khel.

The first six of these clans are known collectively as the Khaibar Afridis. The Aka Khels have no connection with the Khaibar, and are located to the south of the Bara river. The Adam Khels inhabit the hills between the districts of Kohat and Peshawar, and cannot be regarded as a part of the Afridi tribe in any other than an ethnological point of view; for, whether they are viewed with reference to their position, their interests, or their habits, they are a distinct community. The consideration of this clan will therefore be reserved for a separate chapter, the subject of the present chapter being the Khaibar and Aka Khel Afridis.

The Afridi in appearance is generally a fine, tall, athletic highlander, whose springy step, even in traversing the dusty streets of Peshawar, at once denotes his mountain origin. They are lean but muscular men, with long, gaunt faces, high noses and cheek-bones, and rather fair complexions. Brave and hardy, they make good soldiers, but are apt to be somewhat homesick withal. They are careful shots and skirmishers, waiting with the greatest patience for the chance of an easy shot at an enemy. This quality is less shown when, as soldiers of the British Government, they are supplied with unlimited ammunition, but still their *spécialité* is hill fighting. Generally speaking, there is no doubt that the Afridis are now better armed than they have ever been; almost every fighting man possesses a rifle of some sort, and a great number have weapons of the very latest pattern.

Fighting qualities of the Afridi.

The sources of supply of these rifles are various. The best in their possession are Government rifles stolen from our troops, of which, in spite of all precautions, a considerable number find their way across the frontier every year. Every kind of ingenious device has been used to smuggle the stolen weapons across the border. Some years ago a coffin, in which apparently some Pathans were taking the remains of a dead fellow-countryman back to his native land for interment, became an object of suspicion to the police. In spite of the protestations of the heart-broken relatives, the police insisted upon opening it, and found that, instead of a corpse, it was full of stolen rifles. According to official returns, no less than 1,250 breech-loading rifles (of which only $\frac{1}{5}$ have been recovered) were stolen from our troops in the fifteen years ending in 1900; and there is every reason to believe that the great majority of these found their way into the hands of the Afridis and other tribes on the Peshawar border. In addition to the above, a few Kabul-made weapons have been stolen from the Amir's regular troops; and the factories at Maidan in Tirah, at Ilamgudar, in the Sipah country, a short distance beyond Fort Bara, and in the Kohat pass, (where the Adam Khel have half a dozen factories), annually turn out a number of rifles, which, though inferior to those of English manufacture, are far better than the *jezails* and matchlocks of long ago. Of 1,497 rifles surrendered in 1897-98, 245 were classed as "stolen" (*i.e.*, stolen complete), 130 as "foreign" (of which 87 were from Kabul, 77 being Sniders), and 1,122 as "made up".

Rifle stealing.

The great skill shown of recent years in the use of fire-arms by the tribesmen may be accounted for by the very large number of pensioners and reservists who have served in our own regiments; the higher standard of skill and knowledge now demanded in our army being naturally disseminated to a greater extent than formerly amongst the tribesmen by these pensioners and reservists on their return to their own country on the conclusion of their military service. The establishments of our native regiments contain over 2,000 men recruited from the Afridi tribes alone, and as the Pathan is notoriously restless and dislikes expatriation, the average length of individual service is shorter than in the case of our other native soldiers; the result being that a larger number of trained soldiers from Pathan squadrons and companies annually pass back to their homes than is the case with a proportionately large establishment of any other race. The loyalty and conduct of Pathan troops actually serving with the colours has usually been all that could be desired during frontier expeditions; but, on the other hand, it can hardly be expected that men who have become merged again into their tribe, and who, according to their own ideas, are no longer bound to us by any obligation, should maintain an attitude of complete aloofness from any tribal movement prompted by racial feeling and religious excitement. In the Tirah Expedition of 1897-98, the participation of pensioners and reservists in armed resistance to our troops had attained to such proportions, and was regarded as so serious a matter, that the Lieutenant-Governor of the Punjab found it necessary to address the Government of India on the subject, pointing out how numerous these pensioners were, and suggesting drastic measures in regard to them.

Although the fighting powers of the Afridis, from the causes mentioned above, have increased to a very formidable extent, the increase in our own powers of dealing with them have increased in a still greater ratio. Greater efficiency and more perfect armament; the more complete and extensive organization of the services of transport and supply; the greater knowledge of the independent territory beyond our border, gained partly during expeditions and partly by the accumulation of intelligence at other times; the moral effect of the expeditions, uniformly successful, into the most inaccessible fastnesses of the tribe, bringing home to them the fact of their complete helplessness when Government puts out its strength against them, are all factors which more than counterbalance any accession of strength which the last twenty years have given to the tribesmen. In addition we have to consider the immense advantages which the advance of railway construction in recent years has given to Government for the rapid and certain concentration of its resources at any given point.

Previous to the Afghan War of 1878-80, the point of railway nearest to the most formidable of the frontier tribes was Jhelum. The railway has since then been pushed on to Peshawar, and through Peshawar to Jamrud; a branch line runs for hundreds of miles along the left bank of the Indus; Kushalgarh is connected up, through Golra, with Rawalpindi; and from Kushalgarh West, on the right bank of the Indus, the line of light railway running through Kohat and Hangu to Thal, along the flank of the Orakzai and Afridi country, gives enormously extended powers of offensive action against Orakzais, Afridis, and Wazirs.

The approaching completion of the railway bridge at Kushalgarh, the conversion of the existing Kushalgarh-Kohat-Thal light railway to broad gauge, and its further extension to the head of the Kurram valley, will give still more perfect communication beween the frontier and the heart of the Indian Empire. The comparatively few main lines existing twenty years ago have since been extended in every direction, and the network of railways now covering India cannot fail to be of the utmost value in facilitating the concentration of troops and stores in the event of military operations. There is no doubt that these facts are gradually becoming better known and appreciated by the tribesmen. The additional facilities given them for travel outside of their own country are more and more used by them; and numbers of Afridis and other Pathans extend their travels, not only all over British India, but across the seas to our colonies, more particularly to Australia. They are not wanting in natural shrewdness and intelligence; and such intercourse can hardly fail to increase their appreciation of the vast resources at the disposal of their powerful neighbour, and of the uselessness of an armed conflict with Government.

Of the moral attributes of the Afridis, it is quite impossible to say anything in praise. Mackeson, writing of them, says: "The Afridis are a most avaricious race, desperately fond of money. Their fidelity is measured by the length of the purse of the seducer, and they transfer their obedience and support from one party to another of their own clansmen, according to the comparative liberality of the donation." Unlike Muhammadans in general, the Afridis are said to have but little regard for the sanctity of marriage rights, although in other respects strict observers of the precepts of the *Koran*; and such is their shameless and unnatural avarice, that frequent cases occur of a man in good circumstances in the first instance marrying a good-looking girl, but, as times get harder, exchanging her for one of fewer personal attractions and a bag of money. Their women appear at all times unveiled in public, and it is a custom among them to marry the widows of their deceased brothers.

Character and customs of the Afridis.

Ruthless, cowardly robbery, and cold-blooded, treacherous murder, are to an Afridi the salt of life. Brought up from his earliest childhood amid scenes of appalling treachery and merciless revenge, nothing can ever change him: as he has lived—a shameless, cruel savage—so he dies. And it would seem that, notwithstanding their long intercourse with the British, and that very large numbers of them are, or have been, in our service, and must have learnt in some poor way what faith, and mercy, and justice are, yet the Afridi's character to-day is no better than it was in the days of his fathers.

Yet he is reputed brave by those who have seen him fighting. Hardy he is in his own hills, but he is very impatient of heat, and does not like work in the plains, but immediately longs for the cool breezes of Tirah. As soldiers of the British Government, they have gained a greater reputation for fidelity than in any other career. Much has been said of their fidelity in fighting against their own people for us; but when it is remembered that an Afridi generally has a blood-feud with nine out of ten of his own people, the beauty of this attachment fades. They have always been more noted in action for a readiness to plunder than fight, as was the case with Shah Sujah at the battle of Ispahan.

"On the whole," says Elphinstone (generally so eager to record anything good of Afghans), "they are the greatest robbers among the Afghans, and, I imagine, have no faith or sense of honour; for I never heard of anybody hiring an escort of Khaibaris to secure his passage through their country,—a step which always ensures a traveller's safety in the lands of any other tribe."

Notwithstanding this estimate, which MacGregor says some will consider harsh, the Afridi is, on the whole, one of the finest of the Pathan races on our border. His appearance, too, is much in his favour, and he is really braver, more open, and not more treacherous than many other Pathans. This much is certain, that he has the power of prejudicing Englishmen in his favour, and there are few brought into contact with him who do not at least begin with an enthusiastic admiration of his manliness. Again, with a tight hand over him, many of his faults remain dormant, and he soon developes into a valuable soldier.

Hospitality is said to be one of the virtues of an Afridi, and it is possible that if there was no chance of robbing, if not of murdering, a traveller before he came to his door, he would offer such cheer as was forthcoming; but the wanderer who breaks bread wi an Afridi must be cautious; for his host, even while providing his best, will surely be concocting some devilry to entrap his guest as soon as he has left the confines of his lands, or even the shelter of his roof. Still, there are not wanting instances of their giving refuge to a fugitive, and laying down their lives in his defence.

The Afridis are very ignorant, and, although nominally under the rule of their *maliks*, have but very little respect for anything like authority. The men who have most influence amongst them are their *mullas* and *saiyids*. They are all of the Sunni persuasion of the Muhammadan faith.

The Afridis are seldom at feud with their neighbours, as a tribe against tribe, whatever may be the relations of individual members with those of neighbouring tribes. For some years past their extra-tribal feuds have been in a state of quiescence; but amongst themselves they are eternally at feud. Generally the quarrel is confined to the two sections between whom the dispute happens to be; but in cases where the general interests of the whole tribe are concerned, the clans range themselves in the two great factions of Samil and Gar,[1]—the Samil faction including the Malikdin Khel, Zakha Khel, Aka Khel, Sipah, and Kamrai clans; and the Gar, the Kambar Khel, and Kuki Khel. The Adam Khel belong to neither faction, but side with one or the other, as their interests may dictate.[2]

Though in themselves the most disunited of people, in the event of a threatened invasion of their country their *mullas* and *maliks* induce them to lay aside their petty animosities, and unite to face the common danger and defend their common faith. On such occasions it is usual to assemble a council composed of the heads of villages in each clan, and, through the medium of priests, to patch up their internal disputes. They manage this in rather a primitive manner; each negotiator takes a stone, and, placing it on the top of that of his clansman, swears a solemn vow, that, until the common cause be finally settled and these stones removed, the feud between the two parties shall be dormant; and their oaths on these occasions are seldom violated. These councils also arrange all the plans of the campaign and the number of men required from each branch of the tribe, which are furnished in quotas from villages in proportion to their numerical strength, and each party is headed by its own *malik*. On taking the field, each man brings with him a sheep-skin full of flour, and the amount of ammunition that he can manage to collect; but, should hostilities be protracted beyond the time that the supply of provisions will last, the clans are either kept together and fed by contributions from villages in the neighbourhood, or disperse for a few days to collect ammunition and to replenish their commissariat; but, should the latter contingency be adopted, it frequently happens that mistrust of each other, and the fear of treachery in their neighbours, prevent their again uniting.

When no external enemy is in the field, the different clans of this great tribe are continually warring amongst themselves, and it

1 These are the political factions on the Peshawar and Kohat borders. They are said to be derived from two brothers named Gar and Samil, who many years ago had a quarrel, one brother being aided by one party of Pathans, the other by a separate party, whence arose a feud, and now not a year passes that some men are not killed on this old story. The Gar and Samil parties are confined to the Kohat and Peshawar borders. This faction feeling has, however, not sufficient hold on the different sections of a tribe to make them side against their own tribe with outsiders, and with the Afridis the feeling has not so strong a hold as with some other tribes.

2 The Adam Khel are now said to belong to the Gar Faction.

is no uncommon occurrence to find even one-half of a village carrying on a skirmish with the other half; and this may be carried on for two or three consecutive days, the parties firing from towers, or from behind rocks, or any other shelter, upon each other. After seven or eight casualties have occurred on either side, or all their ammunition is exhausted, the point at issue is generally settled by an interchange of marriages.

When not engaged in plundering, the Afridis do simply nothing; time hangs heavily on their hands; for all the common necessary duties of daily life are performed by their women, while the men sleep, or talk of the last midnight murder or robbery. All such domestic labours as fetching wood and water, and cooking, fall to the lot of women, as they do in more civilized countries; but to the Afridi women, in addition, falls nearly all the outdoor labour in the fields. The consequence is, that they are anything but womanly in appearance, habits, or manner; indeed, they are said to be deadly shots with stones, and to frequently distinguish themselves in the defence of their homes. But the Afridis round the Kohat pass are different. Their minds have become more open to the beauties and the results of industry. They are great traders, or rather carriers, and convey the salt from the mines in the Kohat district to Swat, Bajaur, and even Chitral. They also cut and sell the firewood of their hills to the British garrisons of Peshawar and Kohat. By these means they are relieved from the old necessity of robbing and procure a comfortable subsistence.

Between 3,000 and 4,000 Afridis are scattered over India in the military service of the British Government, and of native chiefs. All the clans are represented in these emigrants, except the Zakha Khel, who, according to report, do not leave their own hills.

The Afridis have nothing to give, save fuel, in exchange for our commodities, and so there is no trade properly so called; yet intercourse with us is necessary to them, as their own country does not produce sufficient to feed them, and consequently a strict blockade is a serious measure to most of the clans, especially the Adam Khels and Aka Khels.

Trade is much in the hands of Hindus, who hold a fairly comfortable and respectable position. But they are obliged to wear trousers vertically striped with red, to distinguish them from the faithful, and, idolatry being sternly forbidden on pain of death, are of necessity all Sikhs. *Dharmsalas* with the *Granth* are permitted. Every Hindu is the *hamsaya* of some Afridi *naik* or patron, to whom he pays fines on the birth, death, or marriage of a member of his family. In return, the *naik* is bound to look after his *hamsaya*, and protect his interests. This is not merely a nominal charge, and an Afridi will not accept Hindu *hamsayas* without the consent of his family to the new responsibility undertaken. The Hindus state they immigrated many generations ago from the Punjab. They have adopted many of the wild habits and martial qualities of their Muhammadan lords, and are singularly careless of restrictions about food and drink.

With the insecurity of life and general lawlessness among the Afridis, it is curious to find that sales of land should be constantly effected, and deeds be drawn up which are afterwards produced as proof of the sale. Mortgages, too, are not uncommon, and are scrupulously respected. A quarrel (what we should call a civil suit) is settled by *jirga*, or, according to Muhammadan law, by the *mullas* ; but if both fail, or the parties so prefer it, there is no other means of coming to a conclusion than by arms.

Blood-feuds arise on the slightest occasion, but are spasmodically pursued, often with great bitterness ; at other times the feud is, by mutual consent, allowed to slumber for years, especially if the enemies are not near neighbours. But it is a point of pride and honour to go on as long as possible with the feud. Doubtless many an Afridi who has had violent ancestors, finds his life such a burden to him, and the constant anxiety and watchfulness entailed by a handful of blood-feuds so harassing, that he willingly escapes to the haven of India, and the comparative rest obtained by service in the army ; hoping that time will, before he returns home, have buried many wrongs in oblivion. In addition to private feuds, it is common to have, simultaneously, tribal feuds, when perfectly innocent strangers who happen to belong to the implicated tribes are liable to be shot.

The great security of the Afridis lies in the strength of their country for defence. Their chief point of weakness lies in the facilities with which they can be shut up in their own hills, and cut off from communication with the outer world, provided adequate measures are adopted to effect such a purpose.

The Afridis derive their importance from their geographical position, which gives them command of the Khaibar and Kohat roads; and the history of the British connection with them has been almost entirely with reference to these two passes. Their history before the date of their connection with us can have no interest for any one. Whatever the dynasty has been—whether Jangez, Timur, Babar, Nadar, Ahmad Shah, the Sikh, or the *Farangi* has reigned—it has ever been a record of broken faith.

The Afridis in their mountains, which they inhabit for the most part in the summer, have movable huts made of mats. They come down to the low hills in the winter, where they chiefly live in caves cut out of the earthy part of the hills. They are migratory in their habits. In the autumn months they descend from the pasture grounds about Maidan and Upper Bara with their families and flocks, and pass the winter in the Khaibar, Bazar, Kajurai, and Lower Bara districts. In these several localities, each clan has its own apportioned limits, and in all they generally live in caves, which are formed in long galleries in the cliffs and sides of the ravines in all parts of the hills. None of the sections live in tents. They have a few villages formed by a collection of houses close together. As a rule, each family has its own separate dwelling, proportioned in size to the numbers of the household and their cattle and flocks. Generally, a family of brothers, with their respective children and blood relations, constitute the little communities of these separate dwellings, which are always fortified by walls and towers, and are located on commanding sites on the hills. Sometimes these little forts contain thirty or more separate houses within the enclosure. In April and May the Afridis again move up to their higher hills. A portion, however, of the Kuki Khels, Malikdin Khels, Sipahs, and nearly all the Adam Khels remain in their lower settlements throughout the year.

The area of the country inhabited by the Afridis is about nine hundred square miles. The principal streams that drain their hills are, the northern branch of the Bara river, or Bara proper, the Bazar or Chura river, and the Khaibar stream, all flowing into the Peshawar valley. The valleys lying near the sources of the Bara river are included in the general name of Tirah, which comprises an area of

Geography.

600 to 700 square miles. The greater part of Tirah is inhabited by different sections of the Orakzai tribe, but the valleys known as Rajgal and Maidan are occupied by the Afridis.

The Rajgal valley is drained by one main stream, into which fall some lesser streams from the surrounding hills. Its length is about ten miles, and the breadth of the open country lying on either side of the central stream about four to five miles where widest, its elevation here being over 5,000 feet. Rajgal is inhabited by Kuki Khel Afridis, and their hamlets lie near the stream in the centre of the valley. Temporary sheds are erected by the shepherds among the pine forests which clothe the sides of the surrounding mountains. On the south, Rajgal is separated from Maidan by a steep, rocky, but well-wooded, spur, eight to nine thousand feet in elevation.

Maidan is a circular valley, or basin, about ten miles in diameter, surrounded by mountains, rising to about seven thousand feet in elevation. The northern slopes of these are covered with firs and holly oak, while the southern slopes are generally bare. The climate is described as excellent, the heat of summer being tempered by frequent thunder-storms. In winter the absence of wind makes the cold less severe; but snow lies for three months and more, and sometimes to great depth. The valley is well drained by three or four large watercourses; that to the west, where the Malikdin Khel hamlets stand, is known as the Shaloba, which name is also applied to the entire stream after the others have joined it, *viz.*, the Sher Darra, occupied by the Zakha Khels from the east; the Manakas, occupied by some families of the Jawaki and Ashu Khel sections of the Adam Khels; and the Kahu, occupied by the Kambar Khels. These converging, form the Shaloba Toi, which, leaving Maidan, enters a narrow, rocky gorge three miles long, commanded by heights rising 1,000 feet above it on either side. After emerging from this defile, the torrent flows through open country for two or three miles, then joins the Rajgal stream at Dwa Toi, after which the united stream receives the name of Bara. The open lands between the watercourses are covered with wheat and barley fields, and studded with numerous isolated dwellings which, though loopholed, were apparently not made for defensive purposes. The banks of the streams are honeycombed with caves. It is difficult to ascertain how many Afridis stay during the winter in Maidan,—probably not more than one-fifth of its summer inhabitants. In a warm winter, or if troubles were apprehended towards Peshawar, no doubt more would remain.

After the junction of the Rajgal and Maidan drainage, the united stream, as already mentioned, receives the name of Bara, and the valley through which it flows down to its exit in the Peshawar valley is also known by this name. The elevation of this valley is from 5,000 feet at Dwa Toi to 2,000 at Kajurai; on the north side it is hemmed in by the Surghar range, which divides it from the Bazar valley. This range averages from 6,000 to 7,000 feet in elevation. Its crest and sides are steep and rocky, fairly well wooded with ilex and wild olive, but few timber trees; grass covers much of the slopes, and affords excellent grazing for the cattle during the winter months. Closing in the Bara valley to the south is a range rising to 8,500 feet near Maidan, but falling gradually as it runs east. This range is also very rough and rocky, but has a few timber forests above Waran and Maidan. The slopes of these ranges north and south of the Bara valley close inwards on the stream in the centre, sometimes leaving only a narrow, difficult defile between; at other places their bases are a mile or so on either side from the bank, leaving flat or terraced ground between. In these small basins lie the hamlets and the splendid rice-fields of the various clans who inhabit the valley. The heat in summer is excessive, fevers prevalent, and mosquitoes very troublesome; hence the hamlets are deserted during the hottest months, even by the families that do not resort to Tirah; these take their flocks and herds with them, and live in sheds on the mountain slopes and crests. The valley is portioned out between several clans. Starting from Dwa Toi, in succession come the Malikdin Khel, the Kamrai, the Kambar Khel, the Sipah, the Zakha Khel, the Aka Khel, and the Sturi Khel (Orakzais); then again at its exit into the Kajurai plain, the Malikdin Khel, the Kambar Khel, the Kamrai, and the Sipah clans. The principal villages in the valley are Barwan and Barkai, of the Sturi Khel Orakzais, and the numerous hamlets known as Torabela of the Zakha Khel Afridis.

Shortly after entering the Kajurai plain, the Bara river is joined by the Mastura, which runs south of the main branch and parallel to it. To the north of the Mastura, and not far from Maidan, is the Waran valley. This valley, inhabited by the Aka Khel Afridis, is a basin about ten miles long and four or five miles broad, surrounded by mountains about 8,000 feet in elevation.

Kajurai, into which the united waters of the Bara river flow, is a basin of about thirty square miles in extent. The country is undulating and open, and is covered with long grass. This tract forms the winter resort of the Malikdin Khel, Kambar Khel, Kamrai, and Sipah Afridis, who live in cave dwellings. There is a considerable village with several towers, on the left bank of the Bara river, about three miles from Fort Bara, called Ilamgudar. This village, famous for its rifle factory, is occupied all the year round by Sipah Afridis. There is generally a good supply of water in the Bara river; and in ordinary years the rush of water is so heavy during the melting of the snows above Rajgal and Maidan, that the low country near Peshawar on the banks of the river is flooded.

The summer and winter settlements of the Afridi clans (exclusive of the Adam Khel) are as follows :—

Kuki Khel ..	.. Summer.—Rajgal valley.
	Winter.—Jamrud and neighbouring hills.
	Summer.—Maidan and Upper Bara.
Malikdin Khel	Winter.—Kajurai, Chura, and Khaibar.
Kambar Khel	.. Summer.—Maidan and Upper Bara.
	Winter.—Kajurai.
Kamrai	.. Summer.—Maidan and Upper Bara.
	Winter.—Kajurai.
Zakha Khel	.. Summer.—Maidan and Bara.
	Winter.—Khaibar and Bazar.
Sipah ..	.. Summer.—Bara.
	Winter.—Lower Bara and Kajurai.
Aka Khel	.. Summer.—Waran and Bara.
	Winter.—Hills between Kajurai and Kohat pass.

During the summer months, the winter habitations of the Khaibar Afridis, including Bazar, are quite deserted, if one excepts a few Kuki Khel villages around Jamrud and the Malikdin Khel villages of Chora, which are inhabited all the year round. The Zakha Khels have a great hold over the other clans, not so much from the extent of ground they occupy—for much of it in the Khaibar and Bazar is sterile—as from their position lying between the winter and summer homes of the other sections. They alone can move from Bazar and the Khaibar to Bara, and thence along the crest of the Torghar, without having to pass through the lands of any other clan; every other section, unless prepared and able to make a wide détour, is obliged semi-annually to take its families, cattle, and household goods through Zakha Khel territory in any circumstances, if not also through that of other clans. Naturally, in consequence, the other clans are very shy of incurring the resentment of the Zakha Khels, as a body, and, unless greatly exasperated, will endeavour to remain collectively on good terms with them. Thus, for instance, the Kuki Khels have occasionally been obliged to reach Rajgal from the Khaibar by going round Tartara, through Mohmand and Shinwari country. Other tribes have reached Maidan from Kajurai, *viâ* Orakzai and Aka Khel limits, when at enmity with the Zakha Khels. And for a clan of one tribe to migrate through tribes not connected with it, or its parent tribe, is a delicate experiment. So, upon the whole, by virtue of their position, the Zakha Khels enjoy pre-eminent consideration in Afridi councils. They are less amenable, too, to our control, as their winter settlements are a long way from the border, and their trade with British territory is small.

Next to the Zakha Khels, the Malikdin Khels and Kuki Khels possess the most compact settlements in the Chora and Khaibar valleys, parts of which, as mentioned above, are held summer and winter by portions of these tribes, at Chora itself, and near Jamrud.

The road through the Khaibar, as far as it passes through Afridi limits, is held by the six clans known as the Khaibar Afridis. The road is divided into six sections, which, commencing from Jamrud, are guarded as follows:—The first section is in the hands of the Kuki Khels, the second in charge of the Sipahs, the third is held by the Kuki Khels again, the fourth by the Kambar Khels and the Kamrai, the fifth by the Malikdin Khels, and the sixth by the Zakha Khels. The present arrangements with reference to the Khaibar will be referred to again further on.

Before proceeding to an account of the routes in Afridi country, it may not be out of place briefly to sketch the lines that are taken by Afridi raiders in attacking the road through the Khaibar or the Peshawar district. When, for whatever reason, it is determined that a raid is to be made, a few experienced old raiders, respected either for their skill in planning forays, or for their large personal following, consult together and fix upon a plan, after hearing the reports of spies, who have returned from the threatened localities. Having made up their minds what to do, a summons is sent round to well-known raiders and other young men of their tribe, giving notice that a raid is appointed for a certain date, and all willing to join are to come, with so many days' supplies, to a rendezvous. These preliminaries are always held at as great a distance as possible from the point to be attacked, in order to prevent the news from leaking out; and all particulars are kept a profound secret by the chief raiders. Thus, in summer, raids are concocted in Tirah; in winter, in Upper Bara and Bazar; and though the fact that a raid in some direction is contemplated becomes known, no one but the leaders can tell where the raid will strike till it has begun to move. Very often false reports are carefully spread to mislead informers. A sufficient number of armed raiders having collected at the rendezvous, the raid moves with the utmost rapidity on the objective, timing itself to arrive in its immediate vicinity during the night. The raiders having probably walked continuously thirty or forty miles, lie down for a few hours' rest, and spies are thrown out to give warning of counter-attacks, or of the approaching booty. At daybreak, or as soon as practicable after it, they swoop down on their prey; whatever animals they can lay hands on are rapidly collected, the retreat begins, the cattle or beasts of burden are urged to their highest speed, and the band retires as swiftly as it came, walking or running for many miles, till beyond all danger of pursuit. If pursued, the lagging cattle are cut down, and a show of resistance is made; if the pursuit is hot, the plunder is abandoned, for to lose lives is not the object of the raid. But should the raiders succeed in carrying off their booty, they halt on reaching a place of safety, and, if it is prudent to do so, divide their spoil, break up, and go home to recruit after their exertions. Occasionally, however, it is thought expedient to get rid of the loot at once, in which case the chief raiders arrange with friendly tribes to pass on the cattle

Afridi raids.

that have been robbed to distant valleys, where they are kept for a time, and then disposed of when matters have quieted down.

With regard to the roads in Afridi territory, there are two main routes from Peshawar to Maidan and Rajgal, one through the Khaibar and Bazar valleys, and the other up the Bara valley.

All routes and tracks leading from Jamrud, Ali Musjid, Landi Kotal, and Dakka to Bazar converge at China in Bazar, and have all been traversed at different times by our troops; they are, therefore, sufficiently well known. It is enough to say, taking the roads which constitute the lateral communications between the Khaibar and Bazar, that the road by Shudanna to Chora is fair, and that the passes from Ali Musjid and Shagai over the Chora Kandao and thence to China are the best, and are practicable for cavalry and laden camels. The road from Ali Musjid to Alachi and thence to Karamna is a mule track. From Garhi Lalabeg, the Bori pass, practicable for Afridi pack-bullocks and mules, gives access to Bazar; this is the usual route for the Zakha Khels of the Khaibar when going to Bazar. From Chora to Walai and China, in Bazar, elevation 4,200 feet, the main road follows the bed of the stream.

The route from China continues westward up the Bazar valley for six or eight miles more, and then crosses the Jarobi, or Mangol Bagh, pass, elevation over 5,500 feet, the ascent to and from which is said to be very easy and the road broad. It then descends into the Bara valley at the Sipah village of Sandana, on the bank of the river, in open country.

The main route from Sandana follows the course of the Bara river upwards, six or eight miles, through open, level country, to Dwa Toi, the junction of the Rajgal and Maidan streams, up the banks of which there are roads leading to the valleys of these names. In addition to the main road just mentioned, three or four difficult paths cross from Chora and Bazar over the Surghar range at the Inzari, and the Bokar, or Halwai, passes. These pathways are difficult, and seldom used except for raiding purposes.

The other route to Maidan from Peshawar, *viâ* the Bara valley, is fit for camels the whole way and is much used by the Afridis in their annual migrations from Tirah to their cave villages on the eastern slopes of the hills which form the western border of the Peshawar plain. As far as the Gandao pass this route is fit for carts. Beyond the pass it follows the be[illegible] the Bara river to Maidan, and a cart-road could be made along the right bank of the river without much difficulty. At present the march up stream is an arduous task, as the stream is swift and full of large stones, and has to be crossed and recrossed an innumerable number of times.

For troops approaching Maidan, the Bara route would afford more water and forage than that through the Khaibar and Bazar. What would be the approximate number of men they would probably meet it is difficult to say, as that depends not only on local Afridi politics and feelings, but also on the attitude of the neighbouring tribes, more especially the Orakzais.

From Kohat a route to Maidan branches off the Kohat–Kurram road at Muhammad Khwaja, which place is 36 miles from Kohat and 37½ from Maidan. This route is fit for carts as far as Shinawari, and from thence to Maidan a camel-road was constructed in 1897.

The seven clans of the Afridi tribe, which form the subject of the present chapter, will now be briefly described.

The Kuki Khels.

The Kuki Khels are an important and powerful clan. They keep rather aloof from the other Khaibar Afridis, and boast that they are capable of holding their own, if necessary, against the rest of the Khaibar. This is, however, mere boasting: they could not count on help from any except the Sipahs, and it would be dangerous for the latter to give it. They are mortal foes with the Zakha Khels and also with the Mullagoris.[1] They bear a bad character, but are courageous and warlike, and have supplied many good recruits to the Native

[1] The origin of the Mullagoris is wrapped in obscurity and they are not acknowledged by any of the surrounding tribes. Whatever their origin may be, the tribe is now widely scattered, for, in addition to those who dwell north of and between the Khaibar and the Kabul river, there are others who live about Sapri, in the Mohmand hills, in the Sisobi glen, on the western slopes of the Pandperi range, and along the banks of the Kunar river. With all the surrounding tribes, except the Afridis, they are on friendly terms, but with the latter they are at deadly feud. The Mullagoris, reverting to those north of the Khaibar, muster barely 500 fighting men and are but ill-equipped with fire-arms. They have, however, an excellent reputation for courage, and, being a small tribe, have the good sense to keep united, and as mountaineers excel every tribe of the Khaibar range. With these qualities, notwithstanding their inferior armament, they have been able, not only to hold their own against the Zakha Khel and Kuki Khel Afridis, but even to take the aggressive and to harry the Khusrogis of Bazar. As far as we are concerned, we have had but little trouble with the tribe; and the only occasion on which it has been necessary to coerce them was in 1866 when, for a series of minor offences, they were blockaded until they paid a fine of Rs. 600.

Army. They number about 4,500 fighting men, and are extremely well armed, a large number of their rifles having been stolen from the troops at Peshawar. They trade largely with Peshawar in firewood, grass, etc., and are more dependent on British territory than other tribes, and are notorious for robbery and other offences.

The Malikdin Khels.

The Malikdin Khels are the Khan Khel, or head clan, of the Khaibar Afridis. The clan has lost much of its former influence owing to a succession of bad *maliks*; and whereas all the Khaibar Afridis, with the one exception of the Kuki Khels, would probably gladly have followed the lead of the Malikdin Khels in former days, the Zakha Khel and Kuki Khel now claim to be able to meet them single handed, even though they be backed by all the other Afridi clans.

Although this clan belongs to the Samil faction, whilst the Kambar Khels are Gar, still the fact that these two are descended from one ancestor, by name Mir Ahmad, seems to have induced them to keep up a somewhat close relationship. A combination between the Malikdin Khels and Kambar Khels, who, when united, are called Mir Ahmad Khels, is looked upon as most probable in the event of any large tribal disturbance. The friendship between these two clans is also strengthened by the fact that they live near each other, both in Maidan and in Kajurai, and can therefore combine easily to resist a common enemy.

The Malikdin Khels are well armed, and are also well versed in the use of arms, owing to large numbers of them having passed through the ranks of the regular native army. They are more civilised than the other Khaibar Afridis, and possess a large number of English and Kabul rifles. They number about 4,000 fighting men.

The Kambar Khels.

The Kambar Khels belong to the Gar faction, like the Kuki Khels, but, notwithstanding this, there is mortal enmity between these two clans. On the other hand, the Kambar Khels are proud of being descended from the same ancestor, Mir Ahmad, as the Malikdin Khels, and are disposed to join with them in tribal disputes, although the latter belong to the Samil faction.

They are well known for their warlike disposition. A considerable number take service in our army, and, owing to these circumstances, they are generally well armed, and possess a large number of English rifles. Their fighting strength is about 4,500.

The Kambar Khels come into Peshawar and Kohat to trade during the winter, but they keep more apart from intercourse with British territory than any of the other Khaibar Afridis, except wild Nasrud-din Zakha Khels; and, owing to this, they are little dependent on the British Government.

The Kamrai or Kamar Khel, is the smallest of all the clans, their armed strength consisting of barely 600 men. The clan is a peaceable one, and interferes very little with the concerns of its neighbours; and, in fact, they would be altogether insignificant were it not for the circumstance that they hold possession of the Tsaok route between Bara and Maidan. Nearly all the Khaibar Afridis use this pass, which is defensible by a few men against great odds. The Kamrai, though ill-armed, are thus able to hold it easily, and consequently to seriously inconvenience any clan which may not be on friendly terms with them, and to whom free access is an object.

The Kamrai.

They trade a good deal with Peshawar, bringing in wood and grass during the winter. They would feel the loss of this trade severely in the event of a blockade, and this, combined with the fact that their winter settlements are within easy reach of the Peshawar garrison, makes them naturally anxious to keep on good terms with the British Government.

The Zakha Khels are the most important and most powerful clan of all the Khaibar Afridis. Their importance is chiefly due, as already explained, to their position. In politics they are Samil, but as clan against clan, they are on fairly good terms with all the other Afridis, except the Kuki Khel, with whom they are at deadly feud. They are the most turbulent of all the tribe, and number about 4,500 fighting men, most of whom are well armed; but their reputation for courage does not stand so high as that of some of the other clans. They cultivate as little as they possibly can, and despise the fuel and grass trade with Peshawar, and, in addition, levy tolls on their neighbours.

The Zakha Khels.

Most of the troubles that occur between us and the Afridis are caused by this clan.

The Sipahs.

The Sipahs though small in point of numbers—they only possess about 1,200 fighting men—have a very high reputation for bravery, and, being well armed, are able to give a good account of themselves. They are Samil in politics, and are friendly with the Malikdin Khel and Kamrai.

The Aka Khels.

The Aka Khels are one of the most troublesome of the Afridi clans, and are perhaps the most discontented, owing to the fact that they have no voice in the Afridi *jirgas* in matters relating to the Khaibar and Kohat passes. They number about 1,800 fighting men, and are fairly well off, as they own some good land in the Bara and Waran valleys, and are rich in cattle.

The fighting strength of the Khaibar and Aka Khel Afridis is therefore as follows :—

Kuki Khel	4,500
Malikdin Khel	4,000
Kambar Khel	4,500
Kamrai	600
Zakha Khel	4,500
Sipah	1,200
Aka Khel	1,800
Total ..	21,100

This, added to the number of fighting men of the Adam Khel clan, estimated at 5,900, gives a total of 27,000 as the fighting strength of the Afridis, which is probably nearly correct.

Expedition against the Aka Khel Afridis by a force under Lieutenant-Colonel J. H. Craigie, C.B., in March 1855.

British connection with the Afridis began in 1839, when Colonel Wade, with a contingent of Sikh troops, forced the Khaibar.

The first occasion, however, after the annexation of the Peshawar valley, in which we came into actual conflict with any of the Afridi clans which form the subject of the present chapter, was at the end of 1854.

In that year the Basi Khel section of the Aka Khels, not finding themselves admitted to a share in the allowances of the Kohat pass commenced a series of annoyances and depredations on the Peshawar border, with a view of extorting from Government a participation in those allowances. Amongst other acts, they murdered a syce belonging to the force at Matanni, threatened that village, and finally filled up a well which was being dug at Aimal Chabutra.

On this, Major J. H. Craigie, C.B., commanding a detachment at Bazid Khel, went in pursuit. This party was fired at by the Basi Khels, but was too late to catch them in the plain. On the 9th of December 1854, a Khattak British subject was murdered near Akhor by them, in order to implicate the Adam Khels, with whom they were at feud, and it became necessary to institute a blockade of the clan.

At this time the camp of Lieutenant W. Hamilton, Bengal Artillery, Assistant Civil Engineer, together with his office and treasure chest, happened to be pitched near Badabir, about ten miles from the foot of the hills; and on the night of the 9th of February 1855, the Basi Khels descended on his camp to kill and rob. Lieutenant Hamilton fought bravely for his life, and escaped with some wounds, after shooting one of his assailants; but sixteen of his people were killed and thirty wounded, the Basi Khels carrying off some Rs. 10,000 of Government treasure and property, besides some private effects.

Soon after this, Captain H. R. James, Deputy Commissioner, who was out on the frontier, reported that those branches of the tribe whose winter settlements are between Jani-ka-Ghari, west of Fort Mackeson, and the Bara river, continued to bring their cattle into the grazing grounds at the foot of the hills, as they felt themselves secure from any sudden attack, in consequence of the broad and stony plain lying between them and the nearest point where troops were located, the crossing of which would give them ample notice of any attack. On this, Major L. P. D. Eld, 9th Native Infantry, commanding a detachment at Fort Bara, attempted to surprise the village of Alam Kili by marching across the plain at night, so as to arrive there at early dawn. The march was made in excellent order and perfect silence; the detachment arrived at a ravine, about a mile from the village, an hour before daybreak; but as it was entering broken ground, it became necessary to halt till daylight, and some scouts were sent on to reconnoitre. When these had advanced a short distance from the head of the column, they suddenly found themselves confronted by a picquet of twenty men in a hollow.

Being surrounded, they were compelled to fire, and the picquet fled to the village, firing signals as they went. The detachment then advanced as soon as the light admitted, and found the Afridis had reached the hills, up which they rapidly retreated. To have pursued them further would have involved the troops in a day's skirmishing on the hills without the prospect of inflicting much injury upon the enemy, and it was therefore considered better to return to camp and await another opportunity.

On the 23rd of February there was a spirited little affair between a force, noted in the margin, under Lieutenant E. Tyrwhitt, 14th Irregular Cavalry, and the Basi Khels.

14th Irregular Cavalry,[1]	70 men.
9th Native Infantry,[2]	62 ,,
Mounted levies,	26 ,,

The cavalry patrol from Fort Mackeson, finding a body of Basi Khels in a ravine under the Akhor hills, pursued them, the Akhor people joining in the pursuit, and setting fire to the first Basi Khel village, when Lieutenant Tyrwhitt, coming up with the infantry, drove the enemy from the hills above. The enemy then came down to a small plateau, about three-quarters of a mile distant; on this, Lieutenant Tyrwhitt charged them with the cavalry, driving them up to the village of Zawa, when he had to retire, coming under the matchlock fire from the hills. The retirement, which was pressed by the enemy, was very steadily covered by the 9th Native Infantry, although the enemy were in considerable numbers.

The enemy lost some seven wounded. Our loss was—two sowars of the 14th Irregular Cavalry, one sepoy of the 9th Native Infantry, and one sowar of the levies, wounded.

After Major Eld's operations, the cattle were not brought out of the hills for some days, but the Aka Khels gradually re-acquired confidence, and every day advanced further into the plain, putting out strong picquets at night. On the 26th of February the scouts brought in the intelligence that the flocks had come down to the grazing grounds near Sadat Garhi. Captain James thought, therefore, that by locating a party in one of the ravines in that neighbourhood he might be enabled to intercept them. He accordingly

[1] Mutinied at Jhansi in 1857. [2] Mutinied at Aligarh in 1857.

arranged a plan for doing so with Major Eld, and, considering it better to carry out the design at once, Major Eld marched from Fort Bara at 3 A.M. with the rifle and light companies, 9th Native Infantry, and a troop of the 16th Irregular Cavalry.[1] The march was performed without the least noise, and the men were located before dawn in a ravine lined with tangled grass and brushwood, scouts being placed in the trees in the vicinity and other places. The detachment remained quiet in this situation for about six hours, and at 11 A.M. the Afridi cattle were seen emerging on to the plain, with a party of armed men in advance, who narrowly inspected the brushwood and broken ground about them, the cattle following at a distance. Had they continued in this way an hour longer, they would have placed the detachment between them and the hills, and a large number of cattle and men would have fallen into its hands. Unfortunately, however, some *doolie*-bearers, who had fallen to the rear, found themselves at daybreak in the plain without a sign of the detachment, and, returning to camp, they set out again under the escort of a few sowars to join it. The Afridis soon observed them, and began to return with their cattle. Seeing this Major Eld determined to pursue them, and took the cavalry towards the hills for that purpose; the infantry also advanced at a rapid pace over the low hills in their front, and all were soon engaged with detached parties of the Afridis. The detachment succeeded in capturing 100 head of cattle, killing three of the Afridis, and wounding five. Major Eld then arranged for the retirement of the force; this was effected in excellent order, the skirmishers holding the Afridis, who had gathered to the number of upwards of 300, in check. The detachment returned to camp at 4-30 P.M., with a loss of only one man wounded.

After this raid the cattle of the Aka Khels were taken further south, to the village of Mandan, which appeared to offer a perfectly safe retreat, as it is situated close to the Basi Khel villages, is strongly placed between two hills, and is approached only by a stony road, passing over much broken ground and several ravines with eminences, upon which their picquets were placed to guard against surprise. For some days the cattle went into the ravines

[1] Now the 7th Hariana Lancers.

to graze, but on the 5th of March Captain H. R. James arranged with Major L. P. D. Eld to attempt another surprise.

Accordingly, at 11 P.M., that officer moved out of camp with 300 men of the 9th Native Infantry and a troop of the 16th Irregular Cavalry; the party was conducted by Captain James in the direction of Matanni, and up a ravine which leads to the Basi Khel villages. At about a mile from Mandan a good place for concealment was found, where the detachment remained till the break of day. Scouts were placed on all the commanding points, and the approach of the cattle awaited; at about 11 A.M., strong guards came out of the village, and carefully examined every bush and ravine in their front, picquets were placed on various hills upon which low breastworks had been erected, and a party even came down a portion of the ravine in which the detachment was concealed. It was evident that they only anticipated attack from the direction of the camp, and they did not suspect that by making a circuitous march the detachment could get in rear of them.

The above precautions having been taken by the Afridis, their cattle emerged from the village, and were soon grazing on the low hills in front of it. It was not deemed advisable to wait much longer, for the neighing of a horse might now have discovered the detachment, which was not in a position to receive a large party in case of attack. It therefore moved a little further up the ravine, and then, gaining the high ground, advanced rapidly towards the village, thus intercepting the party that had gone out with the cattle.

Major Eld obtained a commanding position in front of the village, and parties were sent to collect the cattle, the whole of which was soon on the road to camp. The Afridis were taken so much by surprise, that they fled precipitately until they gained the hills in the vicinity of the village, where they rallied, and, their numbers increasing with incredible speed, they attempted to cut off some of the parties returning with the cattle. A company was detached to cover the latter, and, when the animals had been all secured, the detachments were called in, the cavalry sent to the rear, and the retirement covered by the riflemen of the 9th Native Infantry. All was effected in perfect order; but the Afridis pressed the detachment warmly for about three miles, till it had cleared the broken ground.

On this occasion Major Eld secured 1,000 animals, including bullocks, cows, donkeys, sheep, and milch-goats. Three of the Aka Khels were killed, one of whom, Gul Khan, was a man of much influence and wealth, and three others were wounded. The loss sustained by the detachment was very trifling—one sepoy slightly wounded and one horse killed.

After this, those sections of the clan against which these efforts had been directed evinced their submission in a mode most humiliating to Pathans, by sending in a deputation of their chief women to sue for peace on any terms. Captain James informed them that he would allow the elders of their portion of the clan to come to him and state their willingness or otherwise to conform to what might be dictated to them, including of course the restitution of the property plundered at Badabir, and the furtherance of the punishment of the remaining portion of the clan.

On the 25th of March 1855, intelligence having reached Captain James that the Aka Khels had returned with their cattle to the villages of Alam Kili and Mir Kili for the purpose of grazing, he suggested to Lieutenant-Colonel J. H. Craigie, C.B., who had succeeded to the command of the troops, the expediency of driving them out of those places, and compelling them to give up the idea of resettling in the low hills without permission.

Accordingly, at midnight on the 26th of March, Lieut.-Colonel Craigie moved off from his camp at Mashu Khel, with the force marginally noted.

Peshawar Mountain Train Battery.
Two troops, 16th Irregular Cavalry.
Detachment, 4th Native Infantry.[1]
9th Native Infantry.
20th Native Infantry.[2]

To engage the Basi Khels, and to prevent their coming to the assistance of the other sections of the Aka Khels, a force of 500 infantry were to move from Fort Mackeson at 2 A.M., towards the village of Zawa, whilst the Akhor men were to act on the left of this detachment above Akhor.

On arriving, at half-past 6 A.M., on the crest of a ridge of hills overlooking those occupied by the enemy, Lieut.-Colonel Craigie, who was accompanied by Captain H. R. James, the Deputy Commissioner, detached 300 men of the 4th Native Infantry, under the command of Major C. Patterson, to the village of Alam Kili, with

[1] Disbanded in 1861.

[2] Mutinied at Meerut in 1857.

instructions to destroy it, and then rejoin; which was successfully, accomplished.

A party of similar strength from the 20th Native Infantry, under the command of Lieutenant A. I. Shuldham, followed after a short interval by the main column, was directed on Mir Kili, a village on the Bara river, the occupants of which fled on the approach of the troops, when the village was destroyed, as also a number of wood stacks.

The main column then proceeded towards the hills, on which the enemy had posted themselves, covered by the rifle and light companies of the 9th and 20th Regiments, under the command of Major L. P. D. Eld.

The hills over which the troops had to advance were steep, and afforded complete cover to the enemy, whose numbers amounted to 1,000 men. Lieut.-Colonel Craigie was obliged to throw out additional skirmishers, both to the front and flanks, so much so that two-thirds of the infantry were thus employed. The force then advanced about a mile and a half, driving back the enemy from hill to hill,—the sepoys behaving most gallantly; and as, in their eagerness to close with the enemy, they neglected to take full advantage of the cover afforded by the nature of the ground, they suffered more loss than they would otherwise have done.

At 8 A.M., seeing that the country in front was apparently much stronger than that over which the troops had passed, Lieut.-Colonel Craigie decided upon retiring. The crest of the hills in the rear was accordingly occupied successively by skirmishers, and the mountain guns sent back to take up a position on the range of hills from which the column had in the first instance descended.

The main body then began slowly to retire; on which the enemy returned in large numbers, and were enabled, from their knowledge of the ground, to press on the troops, their matchlock fire continuing to be heavy until the troops neared, at half-past 10 A.M., the ridge of hills where the mountain guns were in position.

The return march towards camp was begun at 11 A.M., skirmishers having been previously thrown out to the rear and right flank of the column, until the ground became suitable for cavalry, when the 16th Irregular Cavalry, under Lieutenant F. H. Smith, formed the rear-guard.

Our losses in this affair were nine killed and twenty-one wounded.

The principal object of the expedition had thus been fully attained; the Aka Khels had been driven out of an apparently secure retreat, which they could never re-occupy so long as they were under blockade, and which would cause them great distress.

The Indian Medal, with a clasp for the "North West Frontier," was granted in 1869 to all survivors of the troops engaged in the above operations.

After this the clan was forced to seek a temporary settlement amongst the Sipahs at a spot higher up the river, where there was but little pasturage for their cattle, and they were therefore soon forced to return to Waran.

Throughout the ensuing hot weather but little went on, the Aka Khels being in their summer settlements. On the return of the cold season they came down again to the plains; but the Commissioner, Lieutenant-Colonel H. B. Edwardes, C.B., obtained orders to keep up the blockade till the clan surrendered at discretion.

The blockade was accordingly resumed, and not a man of the Aka Khel clan could venture into the Peshawar market; their wood trade fell into the hands of other clans; and unusually large demands for wood for the public works raised the price of that article to an unprecedented height. About December the loss of annual profits began to be intolerable, and the Aka Khel *jirga* took into their serious consideration the question whether it would be better to make another burst of devilry upon the frontier, in hopes of being bought off, or to give in, and accept any terms that might be imposed. In consequence, all the police posts were strengthened and put on the alert while this point was under debate. Deputations from the Aka Khels went about from hill to hill beseeching the co-operation of the neighbouring clans in one more campaign, but their neighbours had got the wood trade, and declined. All this time the flocks and herds of the Aka Khels could not be grazed upon the open plain for fear of being surprised by the police, and another hungry winter was setting in. The case being hopeless, in the middle of December the Aka Khels sent in to make overtures of submission.

But, looking back to the origin of these annoyances, the Commissioner now determined to transfer the charge of the Aka Khel relation to Kohat, so that one Deputy Commissioner should not be played off against another. The Aka Khel *jirga* were therefore referred to Captain B. Henderson, commanding the 3rd Punjab Infantry, and Assistant Commissioner at Kohat, to whom instructions were sent to accept their overtures of peace on the following conditions :—

1st.—A fine of Rs. 2,500.

2nd.—Forfeiture of all blackmail for the future. (The Basi Khels received Rs. 600 from the Kohat pass allowances.)

3rd.—Refund to Government of all rewards paid for capturing members of the clan.

After the usual number of deputations, and excuses, and evasions, the terms dictated by Captain Henderson at Kohat were agreed to by the clan.

Still, Lieutenant-Colonel Edwardes refused to take off the blockade until the payment of the fine. The clan urged that, if allowed to bring their wood to the market at Peshawar, they would realize the amount immediately; but that officer replied that justice required the fine to be paid before the slightest kindness was shown to them.

They then proposed to pay in wood, and, as the Executive Engineer required all he could get, it was settled that they might deliver wood to the amount of the fine at two outposts—one being Badabir, the scene of the outrage.

The Aka Khels estimated their losses during the blockade at Rs. 77,120.

An agreement was then entered into with the Aka Khels by which they bound themselves, in addition to paying the above fine, to abstain from raids ; not to harbour refugees and criminals ; in disputes with British subjects to refer the matter to our tribunals, etc.

Thus, said Lieutenant-Colonel Edwardes, ended the struggle of the Aka Khel Afridis with a settled Government. Instead of haughtily exacting blackmail from the British for the safety of the Kohat road, they paid a judicial fine for a highway robbery.

The reasons of the Basi Khels having been originally admitted to a share in the Kohat pass allowances will be given in Chapter III, when describing the arrangements with regard to that pass; but it may be here briefly stated that it was in consequence of their claiming a portion of land called Kalamsada, extending from Kotkai to Aimal Chabutra, at the mouth of the pass. Our subsequent dealings with the Basi Khels with regard to this piece of land will also be given in Chapter III.

Our next dealings of importance with the Afridis forming the subject of the present chapter, was with the Kuki Khel clan. In January 1857, when the Amir Dost Muhammad was encamped at Jamrud after his interview with Sir John Lawrence, whose camp was a few miles nearer Peshawar, a party of young officers rode beyond the Amir's camp towards the Khaibar pass, and were fired on by the Kuki Khels. One of the number, Lieutenant T. M. Hand, was so severely wounded that he died during the night. The crime having been brought home to the clan, they were blockaded, and many of their members fell into our hands. During these hostilities the Mutiny broke out, but the blockade was continued in full force, and was so injurious to the interests of the clan, that they paid down a fine of Rs. 3,000, and entered into the following agreement, *viz.*, not to harbour criminals; to resort to our courts in regard to quarrels with British subjects; and to send, when required, an agent to the Deputy Commissioner.

On the outbreak of the Mutiny the Zakha Khel clan was also under blockade for innumerable highway robberies, but, strange to say, they did not take advantage of the opportunity afforded them of troubling us, and on the 14th of August they made their submission, and entered into an agreement similar to that made by the Kuki Khels.

In the early part of 1861 a party of Zakha Khels made a raid on British territory in the neighbourhood of Kajurai. This tract of country is occupied, as already stated, during the winter months by the Malikdin Khel, Kambar Khel, Kamrai, and Sipah clans, and these clans had for a long time refused, on various pretexts, to become jointly responsible for this part of the border.

On the occurrence, however, of this raid, in which one man was killed and three wounded, some of the Kajurai men were seized, and further proceedings threatened unless immediate reparation was made, and an agreement entered into of joint responsibility for the future. The clans concerned sent their representatives to Peshawar, paid a fine of Rs. 1,000, and entered into the desired agreement, which closed that corner of the district against Zakha Khel and other robbers. The agreement with the Sipah and Kamrai clans was made on the 24th of April 1861; that with the Malikdin Khel and Kambar Khel shortly afterwards, and was of the same tenor, *viz.*—

> We agree on our own parts, and in behalf of our respective clans, of our own free will and accord, as follows:—
>
> (I) During the six months of the cold weather, when we reside in the lands called Kajurai, we will be responsible that no theft or crime is committed on any British subject by any member of our clans, or by any member or the Zakha Khel or other clans passing through the said lands of Kajurai.
>
> (II) So long as the Zakha Khels may remain at feud with the Government, we will not allow members of that clan to take up their residence in the Kajurai settlements.

The clans concerned acted fairly up to the engagements entered upon, but it was found necessary to enforce their responsibility by making reprisals on them in 1874, when they allowed some Zakha Khel robbers a passage through their lands. Accordingly, 113 persons and 360 head of cattle were seized, the latter being restored when the Kajurai clans paid the small fine which had been imposed upon them.

The Zakha Khel, and also the Kuki Khel clan, continued to give trouble on our border, and maintained their reputation as the most inveterate and audacious robbers, whose depredations up to the very walls of Peshawar, and even within the city and cantonments, have been notorious since the days of the Sikh rule. On the night of the 4th December 1874, the bandmaster of the 72nd Highlanders, stationed at Peshawar, was carried off by a party of raiders belonging to the Zakha Khel clan, and taken to the Khaibar pass, when he was released uninjured, after a short detention, through the instrumentality of Arbab Abdul Majid Khan. Subsequently the representatives of the clan repudiated the acts of the robbers, and in token thereof burnt the house of the leader of the gang, and returned the small amount of property taken from the bandmaster. At the beginning of 1875 attempts were made, with some success, to conciliate the Zakha Khels by inducing them to send in representatives to Peshawar. In January 1877 the Khalil *arbab*,[1] Abdul Majid Khan, who, under the direction of the Deputy Commissioner, had held the management of the Khaibar Afridis for many years past, died, and was succeeded in his duties by his son, Fateh Muhammad Khan, who, however, did not carry them on for long. Since 1878 our dealings with the Khaibar Afridis have been carried on direct with the tribes, through the officer in charge of the Khaibar. During the Jawaki complications, to be described in Chapter III, the Zakha Khels sent a contingent of 400 men to their help, but these did not go further than the Kohat pass, when they turned back. None of the other Afridi clans responded to the appeal of the Jawakis for help.

Expedition against the Zakha Khel Afridis of the Bazar valley, December 1878.

From the time that the British army advanced into Afghanistan, on the 21st of November 1878, the Afridis of the Khaibar pass began to give trouble. On the 28th of November a signalling party, consisting of a few men under Major H. P. Pearson, Deputy Assistant Quarter Master General, on the Shagai hill, overlooking the Khaibar, was attacked by Afridis. Major Pearson's horse and grasscutter, with one man of the 81st Regiment, were killed, while another man of the same regiment and five mules were wounded.

In order to punish the perpetrators of this outrage, who were traced to the village of Kadam, two guns, supported by detachments of the 9th Foot and 45th Sikhs, accompanied the Political Officer, on the 1st December, to assist the *maliks* of the Kuki Khel clan in attacking the village of Kadam. Some of the marauders gave in at once, while others opened fire on the *jirga*. The supporting party on the heights above the village sent a shell amongst these, which dispersed them at once. The *jirga* then fired the towers and houses of the parties opposed to them. The punishment inflicted was purely a tribal affair, as our troops acted only as a support to the headmen.

[1] The *Khalils* are a tribe who inhabit a portion of the Peshawar district between the Khaibar hills and Peshawar. Their chiefs are styled *arbabs*.

The Afridis after this continued to harass our troops on the line of communications in the Khaibar, and firing into our camp at Ali Musjid was a thing of nightly occurrence. The marauders belonged chiefly to the Zakha Khel clan.

On the 1st of December, Major P. L. N. Cavagnari, C.S.I., the Political Officer on the Khaibar line, led an armed body of Kuki Khels, supported by mountain guns, against the Zakha Khels, and took them by surprise. Punishment was inflicted by burning some of their towers and houses, and it was hoped that the hostile combination was broken up ; but on the 9th of December Major Cavagnari expressed his opinion that the conduct of the Zakha Khels of Bazar and Bara necessitated their being punished as soon as military arrangements for doing so could be completed. An expedition in the Bazar valley was therefore determined upon. A force composed of troops from the 2nd Division, Peshawar Valley Field Force, the head-quarters of which were then established at Jamrud, was to carry out this operation, while troops of the 2nd Brigade of the 1st Division were to co-operate with the movement from Dakka.

Jamrud Column.		
D-A, Royal Horse Artillery ..	3	guns.
1-5th Fusiliers ..	300	men.
51st King's Own Light Infantry	200	„
11th Bengal Lancers ..	1	troop.
13th Bengal Lancers ..	1	„
2nd Gurkha Regiment ..	500	men.
Mhairwara Battalion[1] ..	400	„
Dakka Column.		
11-9th Royal Artillery ..	2	guns.
1-17th Foot	300	men.
8th Company Bengal S. and M.	41	„
27th Punjab Native Infantry	263	„
45th (Rattray's) Sikhs ..	114	„

The force consisted of the troops noted in the margin. The column from Dakka was under the command of Brigadier-General J. A. Tytler, V.C., C.B., the whole force being directed by Lieut.-General F. F. Maude, V.C., C.B., commanding the 2nd Division.

As it was important to cut off the enemy's retreat by the Sisobi pass, the troops from Dakka were to move into the Bazar valley by that route.

At five o'clock on the evening of the 19th of December the troops of the Jamrud column assembled a short distance below Ali Musjid, and, taking the road by the Chora Kandao, the column marched forward during the night. The night was dark, while the mountain road was only a pathway. The head of the column

1 Now the 44th Merwara Infantry.

had not consequently reached further at four o'clock on the morning of the 20th than within half a mile of Chora.

Captain L. H. E. Tucker, the Political Officer with the column, then reported that he had been misinformed as to the distance to Chora. Bazar was still at least eight miles further on, and the road to it lay through the bed of the Chora stream, which had to be forded constantly, about knee-deep, by the infantry.

There was consequently no longer any hope of surprising the enemy at daybreak. As the troops from Jamrud had already been under arms since nine o'clock on the morning of the previous day, and as no advantage was to be gained by advancing any further until daylight broke, a halt was ordered until daybreak at the place where the column had arrived, so that the men might get something to eat. The column then moved on, passing the village of Chora, inhabited by the friendly Malikdin Khels, up the bed of the river.

After passing Chora, the heights on both sides of the river were crowned by flanking parties of the 2nd Gurkhas. Lieut.-Colonel M. H. Heathcote, with a troop of the 13th Bengal Lancers, was sent forward to reconnoitre, and reported that there were no signs of an enemy.

The column moved forward without opposition, except a few long shots fired from the surrounding hills, and reached Walai, the first village of Bazar, soon after noon, but found it deserted.

The first object now was to open communication with the Dakka column, and a letter was accordingly forwarded to Brig.-General J. A. Tytler, and a reply to it received before the evening, stating that though the road he had advanced by had proved very difficult, he had reached the Sisobi pass, and would effect his junction with Lieut.-General Maude on the following day. The troops of the Jamrud column bivouacked for the night at Walai.

Captain Tucker having offered certain terms to the Zakha Khels of the Bazar valley, to be complied with by nine o'clock on the following morning, it was arranged that, in the event of these not having been accepted by the time fixed, the troops should move forward to destroy their towers and villages.

The terms offered were:—

1st.—The payment of a fine of Rs. 1,000.

2nd.—The surrender of six hostages, to be named by the Political Officer.

3rd.—The acceptance of Khawas, the chief of the friendly sections of the Zakha Khel, as the chief of the whole clan.

Meanwhile, the column under Brigadier-General Tytler marched from Dakka at 12-30 A.M., on the 19th, with two days' rations, and bivouacked in a grassy plain about eight miles distant from that place, resuming its march at five o'clock on the morning of the 20th of December. By sunrise the column had reached the village of Chenar.[1] The headman came out to make his submission, and he and another villager accompanied the troops as guides.

From Chenar the road runs in a south-easterly direction to the Sisobi villages,[2] against which the Dakka column had been directed to operate. After a march of three or four miles along a valley of moderate breadth, the villages became visible over the slightly rising ground on the right.

As soon the Brigadier-General had reconnoitred this position, he lined the heights on either side of the villages, and then sent on the Chenar guides to bring in the headmen. They shortly returned with the *maliks* of all the five villages, who tendered their submission and made offers of assistance to the troops. They were accordingly promised protection from damage, and the two most intelligent of the headmen were directed to attend the column as guides on its further advance.

The march was resumed about 12-30 A.M., in a south-easterly direction, through a well-cultivated valley, which here began to be wooded. After moving for a mile and a half through this valley, the column turned to the right, up a zig-zag path, where it could advance in single file only, to the top of the Sisobi pass. This ascent was estimated at 1,200 feet up a hillside covered with oak forest.

[1] This is a Shinwari village which had recently received punishment at our hands. A party of grasscutters, under the escort of some men of the Guide Cavalry, had been surprised on the 8th of December by marauders, who were subsequently traced to this village, and had lost three men and one horse of the escort killed, and one man and one horse wounded. In consequence of this outrage, the fort of Chenar had been destroyed on the 10th of December by a small force from Dakka, under the command of Brigadier-General J. A. Tytler, V.C., C.B.

[2] These are inhabited by Mullagoris.

Continuing in a south-easterly direction, the march was directed towards the largest tower at the foot of the opposite hills, about four miles distant. This place was reached at four o'clock in the afternoon, and was found to consist of a large cave village of about sixty dwellings, which was entirely deserted. Here the column was halted for the night, and here the communication from Lieut.-General Maude, above alluded to, reached Brigadier-General Tytler, as the camp of the Jamrud column was only about three miles to the east.

The troops of the Jamrud column paraded at nine o'clock on the morning of the 21st of December, when the Political Officer reported that the terms offered had not been complied with. At the same hour, Brigadier-General Tytler, having ridden over from his bivouac, reported himself in person to Lieut.-General Maude. His opportune appearance at that particular time excited in no small degree the admiration of the friendly chiefs. He received instructions to destroy the village of Nikai, four or five miles to the westward of his bivouac, and any towers near his position. After destroying Nikai, Brigadier-General Tytler was directed to return to Dakka.

Shortly afterwards, the Jamrud column, having detached a guard for the camp, marched for the village of China. A troop of the 13th Bengal Lancers, under Major W. H. Macnaghten, was sent forward by a different route to the village of Halwai, with orders to destroy that village and to cut off any of the enemy who might be driven out of China.

When the column arrived at China it was found to be deserted; the 2nd Gurkhas therefore, under Lieut.-Colonel D. Macintyre, V.C., were detached to the south of the valley, while a detachment of the Mhairwara Battalion, under Captain O'M. Creagh, was ordered to the east of China. In this manner, every village in the valley of any importance was visited and its towers destroyed. The troops then returned to Walai.

The enemy had everywhere escaped with all his cattle and moveable property, which was not altogether to be regretted, as the destruction of the towers and the capture of a large quantity of grain sufficiently punished them, as well as adequately marked their inability to cope with our troops.

On the 22nd the Jamrud column returned to Ali Musjid. On the return march, the inhabitants of the small Zakha Khel village of Barar Kats succeeded in carrying off several mules. To punish this robbery a company of the 5th Foot and one of the 2nd Gurkhas were detached to burn their tower. While doing this, a small party of Zakha Khels was observed in a narrow gorge near the road. They were very soon dislodged, and two or three of their number killed.

In the meanwhile, the Dakka column, after destroying three villages and two of the towers in the vicinity of their bivouac, marched at 11 A.M. on the 21st for Nikai. This village was also burnt, after which it was too late to reach the Sisobi pass before nightfall, and there was no water nearer than the Sisobi villages. Learning, however, that there was water and a camping-ground some few miles off in another pass, called the Tibai pass, the General resolved to halt the force there for the night, and to move on to Dakka the next day by this new route. The road followed by the column shortly entered a wooded valley with a gradual ascent for about four miles. At half-past four o'clock in the afternoon the column reached the camping-ground, which consisted of several grassy plots in wooded ground.

The ground was commanded on all sides by hills, which were at once occupied by outlying picquets. It soon became evident that the enemy were assembling round the camp. The head of the column had scarcely reached the camping-ground when it was reported that the rear-guard had been attacked; several shots were fired into it close to the camping-ground, and one man of the 17th Foot was shot.

The force having all arrived, strong picquets were posted, and owing to the careful disposition of these numerous posts, the troops were undisturbed during the night. There was little doubt, however, that the enemy were gathering to molest the retirement of the column.

The top of the pass was about a mile distant, and from there one road diverged to the left to Pesh Bolak, while the other turned to the right to Dakka. The road up to the pass was overhung on the left by a high, precipitous mountain, inaccessible on that side, while to the right it was commanded by a series of low hills.

The guides stated that there was little risk of attack from the left, but that the right should be carefully guarded.

The Afridis notoriously attack the baggage guard in preference to any other part of a force, and it was therefore determined to change the usual order of march. Orders were consequently issued for each corps to take its own baggage with it. The artillery and sappers, being most encumbered with mules, were to follow close to the advanced guard. A very strong rear-guard was to be left behind, which, being quite unencumbered with the charge of baggage, would be able to resist the pressure from the rear.

Shortly after daybreak on the morning of the 22nd, a detachment of the 45th Sikhs, under Lieutenant H. N. M'Rae, was ordered to occupy the heights to the right of the pass in advance, and to join the rear-guard as it passed.

Two companies of the 27th Punjab Native Infantry, under Captain J. Cook, were sent to the top of the pass to examine and secure the road leading in from the left, and to check any enemy who might hold the high hill on that side.

These dispositions had not been completed when two signal shots were fired from above the water gorge to the right of the position. A company of the 17th Foot was at once despatched up the gorge, with orders to drive back any enemy it met with, and to rejoin the column further on, under the protection of the flanking parties. The column commenced its march at half-past eight o'clock in the morning. The road was winding, steep, and very difficult for mules, the ascent being about 1,000 feet, and the distance to the top of the pass about a mile and a quarter. The troops had scarcely begun to move when a lively but ineffective fusilade was opened from the high hill on the left.

As the column neared the top of the pass, the positions of the enemy became more exposed, and the flanking parties on the right fired across the valley, but, owing to the great range, with little effect. At the same time the two companies of the 27th Punjab Native Infantry had gone some distance along the road to the left, to examine and secure it. Seeing the Afridis on the top of the steep hill becoming troublesome, Captain J. Cook directed Lieutenant H. P. Leach, R.E., with his half company of sappers, who had just reached the crest of the pass, along with a party of the 27th Punjab Native Infantry under Lieutenant G. A. Williams, to capture the summit. The position was gallantly carried, with the loss of one man wounded. This hill was then occupied and held by a detachment of the 27th Punjab Native Infantry, until the whole force had passed. Meanwhile, the advanced guard, guns, and the different corps, each as compact as possible, with the baggage animals in the centre, had pushed down the pass at a steady pace.

Before ten o'clock the rear-guard, consisting of one company of the 17th Foot and of the 27th Punjab Native Infantry respectively, under the command of Captain W. Lonsdale, of the former regiment, had become hotly engaged, and was reinforced by a second company of the 17th, which had now descended from the hill. Even then it had much trouble in keeping back the enemy, owing to the dense forest and consequent difficulty in seeing them. It was 11 A.M. before the rear-guard reached the summit of the pass. Captain Lonsdale was then directed to hold the crest of the pass with one company of the 17th Foot, and two companies of the 27th Punjab Native Infantry, until the flanking parties were withdrawn, when the rear-guard was to follow the column. The hills on the flanks had been occupied by parties of the 45th Sikhs; but notwithstanding this, the main body had been more or less molested in several places.

About three miles below the top of the pass the road passed through a narrow defile about five or six feet broad, with high, perpendicular walls of rock on either side. The water of the stream was there frozen into thick masses of ice, over which it was found difficult for the mules to travel. The entrance, as well as the outlet of this defile, was commanded from the heights by the flanking parties of the 45th Sikhs; nevertheless, a deep and narrow gorge from the right enabled a party of the enemy, estimated at about 100 men, to creep down unperceived, and to occupy a sheltered position about 200 yards from the outlet. As the 17th Foot and the 27th Punjab Native Infantry successively emerged in some confusion, they were met by a heavy fire from the enemy. Half a company of the 17th Foot moved up the hill and dislodged the tribesmen; but so dangerous did the place appear, that the Brigadier-General left his Orderly Officer, Captain G. W. Rogers, 4th Gurkhas, with a detachment of thirty men of the 45th Sikhs, to hold this position until the rear-guard should have passed.

The enemy, as had been anticipated, returned, but were kept in check by the fire of this party.

About four miles from the top of the pass the valley opens out into a plain with cultivated land, owned by the then friendly Shinwaris [1]. Here the column halted for the rear-guard, which shortly afterwards joined it. It had been a continuous skirmish with the enemy from the top of the pass to the mouth of the gorge, where the party, under Captain Rogers, had been posted. The enemy seized the positions of the rear-guard and of the flanking parties as soon as they were abandoned; but when the cultivated ground was reached, all opposition ceased.

The troops were now mustered, and it was found that no man and no property whatever were missing, while the casualties only amounted to one man killed and seven wounded. The column then resumed its march, and Dakka was reached by the advanced guard shortly after 9 P.M.; but a difficult pass about three miles from that place so lengthened out the column, that it was half-past eleven before the whole force arrived in camp. The distance traversed in this day's march was estimated at twenty-two miles.

The number and losses of the enemy could not be estimated, but several of the Afridis were seen to fall. The total British casualties in the Dakka column during the expedition, amounted to two killed and twenty wounded.

Second Expedition against the Zakha Khel Afridis of the Bazar valley, January 1879.

After the expedition into the Bazar valley in December 1878, the Afridis of the Khaibar pass continued to give trouble.

Efforts were then made by the Political Officers to break up the tribal combination of the Afridis, and on the 8th of January it was reported that the pass was perfectly quiet. The Kuki Khels and the Kambar Khels came in and tendered their submission, but the attitude of the Zakha Khels continued to be unsatisfactory; and the Political Officer, Major P. L. N. Cavagnari, C.S.I., reported that he thought a good effect would be produced by a temporary occupation of the Bazar valley, and by deliberately visiting in rotation recusant villages in the Bazar and Bara

[1] See footnote, page 51.

districts. He further considered that any measures adopted for the punishment of the refractory sections would not be calculated to interfere with the political arrangements entered into with the Khaibar clans. In consequence of these opinions, Lieut.-General Maude, commanding the 2nd Division, Peshawar Valley Field Force, applied on the 16th of January for the sanction of the Commander-in-Chief in India to the proposed expedition, in co-operation with a force from the 1st Division.

The plan of operation proposed by General Maude was to send a column from Jamrud by the direct road to the Bazar valley, and a second column, also from the 2nd Division, from Ali Musjid, by the Alachai route to the same destination. When these two columns had effected a junction, they were to proceed to join the column of the 1st Division from Basawal, at the head of the Bazar valley. The three columns having united, were to be employed for three days in scouring the Bazar valley from this central position, but no opposition was expected during this part of the operations. Enough information had not been obtained to mature a plan of operations in Bara, but General Maude, who was to take the command himself of the whole force, anticipated that the troops which would then be under his orders would suffice to carry out successfully any operations decided on in that direction.

The expedition was sanctioned, but owing to a misapprehension of the proposed plan of operations, its duration was limited to ten days. This time was insufficient to carry out General Maude's original proposals, as he had contemplated a concentration of the whole force in the Bazar valley on the fifth day, and an advance to Bara till at least the ninth day; but the Lieut.-General considered that it would be out of place for him to question the decision of Government, and he therefore issued the necessary orders for the march of the different columns.

Jamrud Column.

	All ranks.
D-A, Royal Horse Artillery, (2 guns on elephants) ..	28
11-9th Royal Artillery (2 guns)..	22
5th Fusiliers	313
25th Foot	316
13th Bengal Cavalry ..	145
Madras Sappers and Miners ..	55
24th Punjab Native Infantry ..	356

The Jamrud Column, consisting of the troops detailed in the margin, marched from Jamrud on the 24th January, and, taking the road by the Khaibar stream, passed the Kuki Khel villages of Kadam, Gagrai, and Jabagai.

This column halted for the night in the bed of the river below Shudanna. As orders had been previously given by the Political Officer accompanying the troops (Captain L. H. E. Tucker) that no armed men were to appear, none were seen, and the attitude of this section of the Afridis was perfectly peaceful.

The following morning this column continued its march by Taoda Mela and the Chora Kandao to Barar Kats, arriving there without opposition at four o'clock on the same afternoon. That part of the baggage of the Ali Musjid column which was on camels came also by the Chora Kandao, but did not reach Barar Kats till half-past eight o'clock in the evening, having been fired on about a mile before reaching camp. Almost immediately after dark, a few of the enemy opened fire on the troops, but, being replied to by the picquets, they soon desisted.

On the same day, the 25th of January, Brig.-General F. E. Appleyard, C.B., marched from Ali Musjid by the Alachai route to Karamna, where, at noon, the column under his command effected a junction with the 6th Native Infantry, under Colonel G. H. Thompson, who had marched the same morning from Landi Kotal by the Bori pass. The rest of the day was occupied in blowing up the towers of Karamna.

Ali Musjid Column.

	All ranks.
11-9th Royal Artillery (2 guns) ..	18
51st Foot	213
Madras Sappers and Miners ..	31
2nd Gurkha Regiment ..	312
Mhairwara Battalion ..	320
From Landi Kotal.	
6th Native Infantry ..	311

At seven o'clock on the morning of this day, the troops from the 1st Division, strength as in margin, under the command of Brig.-General J. A. Tytler, V.C., C.B., marched from Basawal. Four companies, under Colonel H. R. L. Newdigate, 4th Battalion, Rifle Brigade, were detached *en route* to destroy a cave village inhabited by robbers. The inhabitants had fled from it, but the village was, as far as possible, destroyed.

Basawal Column.

	All ranks.
11-9th Royal Artillery (2 guns) ..	25
1-17th Foot	361
4th Battalion Rifle Brigade ..	210
Guide Cavalry	32
Bengal Sappers and Miners ..	43
4th Gurkha Regiment ..	201

This column reached Chenar at three o'clock in the afternoon, where it was joined by a force, strength as in margin, from Dakka, under Lieut.-Colonel F. M. Armstrong, commanding 45th Sikhs. Chenar was deserted by its inhabitants, but, as the villagers of this place had been concerned in cattle robberies from Dakka, their two towers were blown up, and the village destroyed.

Dakka Column.	*All ranks.*
1-17th Foot	52
27th Punjab Native Infantry ..	104
45th (Rattray's) Sikhs ..	257

On the 26th this column continued its march. Five hundred infantry with a party of sappers were detached under Lieut.-Colonel Armstrong to attack and destroy the village of Kasaba.[1] This was effected with slight resistance, the villagers taking to the mountains. Their tower was blown up, and the detachment rejoined the main column.

A short march of four miles brought the column to the Sisobi villages, the inhabitants of which had also been concerned in cattle stealing. The villages were found deserted, and the inhabitants refused to come in when invited to do so by the Brigadier-General. The villages were therefore destroyed, but the towers were left standing, out of consideration for the services rendered by some of the people as guides during the former expedition.

Meanwhile, the Ali Musjid column marched on the morning of this day, the 26th of January, on Barg, to which place some troops were detached from the Jamrud column at Barar Kats to effect a junction with it. These two columns, having united at Barg and blown up the towers of that place, continued their march to the Bazar valley.

The remainder of the Jamrud column had meanwhile continued its advance, but, during the march, the rear-guard was attacked by the enemy near the Obcha Tangi,[2] and two Gurkhas were wounded.

On the 27th of January, four companies of infantry, with a party of sappers, were detached from the Basawal column at seven o'clock in the morning, to seize and repair the Sisobi pass, which had been partly blocked. It was occupied

[1] This, as well as the Sisobi villages, belongs to the Mullagoris.
[2] A ravine between Barar Kats and China.

without opposition, and the road made practicable for camels. This column resumed its march at half-past nine in the morning, and, on arriving at the summit of the pass, was met by a detachment of 400 men, under Colonel C. M. MacGregor, from the Jamrud force. The further advance of this column was entirely unopposed, so that at four o'clock in the afternoon the three columns were united in the Bazar valley under Lieut.-General Maude.

At daybreak on this date, 300 men, under Colonel J. A. Ruddell, 25th Foot, were detached from the Jamrud column to scour the China hill, while a party of cavalry, under Lieut.-Colonel R. C. Low, 13th Bengal Lancers, was sent round to the west of the hill to cut off the retreat of any of the enemy in that direction. These measures were so far successful that some seven or eight of the enemy who remained on the hill were killed.

There could be no doubt of the hostile feelings of the Zakha Khel Afridis towards the troops, as, directly the force entered their country, it was fired on by day and also by night. The inhabitants had also deserted their villages, and set fire to them, although the Political Officer had told them that they would not be molested. None of these people showed themselves in the daytime to the troops, but they kept prowling about the hills and ravines, and fired at small parties. This sort of warfare was not formidable, and; though somewhat harassing to the troops, was more so to the enemy.

On the 27th, the Lieutenant-General determined the following day to reconnoitre in force the Bokar pass towards Bara. There seemed every chance of this step being resisted, and the country was quite unknown to any one with the column. A force of 1,000 men with two mountain guns was therefore detailed, under the command of Brig.-General Tytler, to accompany Lieut.-General Maude whilst carrying out this reconnaissance.

On the arrival of the force at Halwai, two miles from camp, the enemy opened fire from a hill opposite that village, and the advance was contested from that point till within 1,100 yards of the Bokar pass. The enemy was, however, forced to abandon each successive position, and a good view of the pass and of the surrounding hills was obtained before returning. The rear-guard reached camp just at dusk, the enemy not venturing to follow up the column beyond the high ground near Halwai. The casualties on this occasion were, one sepoy of the 4th Gurkhas killed, Lieutenant H. R. L. Holmes, 45th Sikhs, one sergeant, 11-9th Royal Artillery, and two *kahars* wounded. The loss of the enemy was admitted to be fifteen killed.

The following day a detachment of 450 bayonets, under Colonel G. H. Thompson, commanding 6th Native Infantry, was detached to blow up the towers of Halwai, where fire had been first opened on the troops the day before. The towers were demolished, but, on the return march of this detachment through the low hills to the south of the camp, the whole country at once became alive with the enemy. The detachment threw out skirmishers, as it fell back, and inflicted a loss, estimated at twenty men, on the Afridis, while the casualties on our side were one killed and five wounded.

It was now becoming apparent that an Afridi war might develop itself if the troops forced their way into Bara. Should this further complication arise, a grave responsibility would be incurred by the Lieut.-General Commanding the force, in the absence of specific instructions from Government, notwithstanding the assurance of the Political Officer that any combination of other clans with the Zakha Khels was altogether improbable.

Those officers with the column, such as Brig.-General J. A. Tytler and Colonel C. M. MacGregor, who had had experience of the hill tribes, fully concurred in the opinion that an Afridi war would be started should the troops make any further advance. Lieut.-General Maude felt, therefore, that in what appeared to him a question of great delicacy, he required, before he pushed on into Bara, the opinion of a political officer of higher standing than Captain Tucker, although nothing could exceed the energy displayed by that officer in endeavouring to get the best information, and to settle matters satisfactorily.

The Political Officer on the Khaibar and Jalalabad line, Major P. L. N. Cavagnari, was therefore requested by telegraph to join the column if possible, the reason for this request being at the same time explained to him; but he was unable at that time to leave Jalalabad, where he then was with the 1st Division, Peshawar Valley Field Force.

On the evening of this day, the 29th of January, a circular was received from Army Head-Quarters addressed to officers commanding columns in Afghanistan, in which the Commander-in-Chief reminded them of the Viceroy's proclamation of the 21st of November 1878, and requested them to bear in mind that the British Government had declared war, not against the people of Afghanistan or adjoining tribes, but against the Amir, Sher Ali, and his troops. The letter further directed them individually to use their utmost endeavours to avoid provoking unnecessary collisions with the tribes and other inhabitants of the country, and to render its occupation as little burdensome to them as possible. As this communication, though in the form of a circular, was addressed to the General Officer Commanding by name, and was dated four days subsequent to the telegram according sanction to the expedition, while there was nothing to show that its contents were not applicable to the existing state of things with the expeditionary force, Lieut.-General Maude felt, upon its receipt, more than ever the responsibility attached to his position.

This position on the 30th of January was as follows:—A limit of ten days, of which that day was the fourth, had been fixed by Government for the expedition; conciliation, in accordance with the wishes of Government, as appeared from the above-mentioned circular, was to be adopted; the hostile attitude of the tribesmen rendered an advance impossible without encountering the resistance of a combination of clans; the conviction of the General Officer Commanding was that it was not the time when Government would wish to risk the commencement of an Afridi war.

Lieut.-General Maude, therefore, determined to ask for more explicit orders, and he accordingly telegraphed to Army Head-Quarters on that day (the 30th), and, having explained the situation, asked for specific instructions as to his future proceedings, and whether he was to force his way into the Bara valley against such opposition as he might meet.

On the evening of the 30th of January, Captain Tucker reported that although on the previous day he had informed the Lieut.-General that sections of the Zakha Khels alone were assembled to dispute the advance of the troops, he had since learned that members of other clans had assembled, some from a considerable distance, and were still assembling, to combine with the Zakha Khels to oppose the advance of the column.

Lieut.-General Maude instructed the Political Officer to endeavour to break up this combination, and, in reporting the circumstances by telegraph to Army Head-Quarters, he suggested that, if Major Cavagnari could not join the column, either he himself or Colonel C. M. MacGregor should be invested with full political power to settle the question as might appear best for the interests of Government in the existing juncture of affairs.

Lieut.-General Maude considered himself quite able to force his way with the troops at his disposal into Bara and out again, but he did not disguise from Government that such a step would undoubtedly lead to an Afridi war.

It subsequently transpired that detachments from the Kuki Khel, Aka Khel, Kambar Khel, Malikdin Khel, and Sipah Afridis, as well as from the Sangu Khel Shinwaris, and the Orakzais, were assembled in the Bara passes to hold them.

On the 31st of January a convoy of provisions arrived in camp. It was on this occasion that Lieutenant R. C. Hart, Royal Engineers, distinguished himself by an act of conspicuous gallantry. This officer took the initiative in running some 1,200 yards to the rescue of a sowar of the 13th Bengal Lancers, who had fallen wounded, and was about to be despatched by a party of Afridis. Lieutenant Hart ran along a river-bed exposed to the fire of the enemy from both flanks and also from a party in the river-bed itself, and, having reached the wounded man, drove off the enemy, and, with the aid of some sepoys of the 24th Punjab Native Infantry and 45th Sikhs, who had followed him, brought him under cover. The sowar subsequently died, but for this act of gallantry Lieutenant Hart was awarded the Victoria Cross.

On the same day a telegram was received from Lieut.-General Sir S. J. Browne, commanding the 1st Division, urgently calling for the return of Brig.-General Tytler's force, as he had received information that an attack on Jalalabad and Dakka by Mohmands and Bajauris might be expected on the 7th of February. Just at this time it transpired that the enemy had suffered severely in the skirmishes of the past few days, and that, in consequence of the protracted occupation of their valley by the troops, the inhabitants of this district were well disposed to open negotiations,

This was followed by the arrival in camp, on the first of February, of a deputation from all the sections of the Bara Zakha Khels. They expressed themselves desirous of opening friendly relations, attesting their sincerity on this point by bringing in with them some of the camels which had been stolen from the troops some time before in the Khaibar pass.

On the 2nd of February the Political Officer reported that he had come to terms with the *jirga*, which he considered to be satisfactory; and it then became possible for orders to be issued for the return of the three columns to their respective stations on the following day.

The same evening the Lieutenant-General received a telegram in reply to his of the 30th and 31st, informing him that the instructions of Government regarding avoiding unnecessary collisions with the people of Afghanistan were to be accepted as general, and applicable more particularly to tribes which had hitherto been directly under Afghan rule, and that there was nothing, in the instructions referred to, to prevent Lieut.-General Maude carrying out the expedition into the Bara valley. He was also informed that he was left free, in consultation with Mr. D. C. Macnabb, the Commissioner of Peshawar, who had been invested with full political powers, and had been directed to join him at once, to act on his own judgment in carrying out the intention for which the expedition was planned.

On the receipt of these instructions the Lieutenant-General decided to adhere to the orders he had previously issued for the whole force to commence its return march on the following day. This decision was chiefly caused by the sudden recall of Brig.-General Tytler's force, as it was necessary for it to march the following morning if it was to arrive in time at Jalalabad and Dakka to meet the expected attack upon these places. In addition to this, the Political Officer stated that he was satisfied with the terms to which the Bara Zakha Khels had agreed. He was also of opinion that a more lengthened occupation of the valley would cause much irritation, and lead to a risk of collision with other tribes with whom the Government had no quarrel. General Maude was inclined to agree with this view, as there was no doubt that considerable detachments from various tribes were massed in the

Bara passes. Nor could there be any two opinions on this head, that though the troops were perfectly able to force their way into the Bara valley, such a step would bring on a war in which all the tribes from the Bazar valley to Kurram would join; while to stay in the Bazar valley longer would be very likely to cause the representatives of these tribes to commit acts of hostility which would call for immediate retaliation by the troops.

On the 3rd of February, therefore, the different columns left the Bazar valley—Brig.-General Tytler by the Sisobi pass for Dakka, the troops of the 2nd Division by Chora for Jamrud and Ali Musjid respectively.

The Political Officer with the column was expressly informed that no settlement of the case would be considered satisfactory if the columns were fired at on their return march. He was directed to inform the Zakha Khels that if shots were fired, the troops would, sooner or later, to a certainty, return. That none of the columns, contrary to Afridi custom, were molested during their withdrawal, may be taken as a proof of the sincerity of their submission.

The British casualties in the above operations amounted to five killed, and thirteen wounded.

After this expedition the Zakha Khel Afridis showed a disposition for a time to remain friendly, but at the end of March they again began to give trouble, and continued to do so until the termination of the first phase of the operations in Afghanistan by the Treaty of Gandamak in May.

On the withdrawal of the British army in June, the Afridis of the Khaibar pass did not attempt to molest the troops, except in one instance, in which they made an attack on the baggage of the 9th Lancers on the 6th of June, when two cartmen were killed, and some property of the officers stolen.

After the termination of the first campaign in June 1879, arrangements for the safety of the Khaibar were made with the Afridis. The leading representatives of the clans were summoned to Peshawar from Tirah, and, after long negotiations, consented to serve under the British Government for the same allowances which they had been wont to receive, though somewhat irregularly, from the Kabul Durbar. A large force of *jazailchis*, under a selected officer, was appointed to patrol the road, escort convoys, and relieve the military of the onerous duties of watch and ward. These arrangements worked very satisfactorily, and from the beginning of the second campaign to April 1880 the security and quiet of the Khaibar pass were almost unbroken. Two raids attempted by Zakha Khel Afridis, in October 1879, were punished by the Afridis themselves; the Khusrogis, the offending section, were compelled to pay a fine of Rs. 800, and to surrender hostages for good behaviour.

In April 1880 the misconduct of the Nasr-ud-din Khel and Annai sections of the Zakha Khels gave some trouble, and the hostages who had been taken as security for the good behaviour of these, the most turbulent sections of the Khaibar Afridis, absconded. Shortly after, a *saiyid*, named Mir Bashir, of Tirah, with the countenance of Mulla Wali Khan, a devotee of great influence among all the Afridis, took advantage of the discontent which existed among certain sections of the Zakha Khels, and proclaimed himself *Badshah* of Tirah. He found followers principally among the Malikdin Khels and Kambar Khels, and levied money and grain contributions as tribute, and for the supplies of the army which he endeavoured to raise and drill in his support.

Under his influence, and at the instigation of an ex-*malik* of the Sipah clan, several raids were committed in the month of June, and an expedition to Tirah was proposed; but the emergency was not considered to be sufficiently grave to call for so important a movement, and shortly after this the influence of Mir Bashir died away. The Afridis were never seriously inclined to exchange their democratic freedom for the rule of a priest who demanded revenue and took tithe of their crops and herds, and this, combined with doubts of the sincerity of his religious pretensions, caused his popularity to wane as fast as it had risen.

The British army which had been in occupation of Northern Afghanistan returned through the Khaibar at the end of August and beginning of September 1880. The pass remained quiet, and there were no attempts, even on the part of isolated fanatics or bad characters, to plunder stores or molest the camps at night. The positions at Ali Musjid and Landi Kotal continued to be held by our troops, but in the month of September the Government of India announced its determination to withdraw the regular forces stationed in the Khaibar, if satisfactory arrangements could be made to keep the pass open under the independent and exclusive charge of the clans. No time was accordingly lost in summoning the representative headmen of the Khaibar clans, of whom more than 300 assembled in Peshawar towards the end of that month. It was found necessary to give the headmen time to discuss matters among themselves, and to secure the consent of sections still absent in Tirah and Bara to the arrangements which were proposed. They had also, before any agreement could be made, to undertake the coercion of the Khusrogis and Paindai Zakha Khels. In this they succeeded, and in January 1881 a complete *jirga* of all the Khaibar clans was collected at Peshawar, where their headmen affixed their seals to a final agreement with the British Government on the 17th February 1881.

The terms of this agreement were as follows :—

(1) Independence of Afridis to be recognized, but no interference by any other power than Great Britain to be allowed.

(2) In consideration of certain allowances, the Afridis to undertake to maintain order throughout the Khaibar.

(3) All matters concerning pass arrangements to be submitted to a general meeting of representatives from all the clans.

(4) No traveller to enter the pass without an order.

(5) The clans not to require military aid from India, for the defence of the pass, but the Government of India to be allowed to re-occupy the pass at pleasure.

(6) The clans to furnish such a number of *jazailchis* as the Government might direct, with head-quarters at Jamrud ; to be subject to the political inspection, and to be paid by the British Government, but not to constitute a government force.

(7) All tolls, etc., to belong to the Government.

(8) Offences on the road to be dealt with by a general *jirga* reporting to the Government.

(9) The clans to abstain from committing outrages in British territory.

(10—15) Minor arrangements with reference to the custody of Ali Masjid and other Government buildings in the pass ; to undertakings to forward posts and expresses at any time ; and to the territorial limits of tribal responsibility, *viz.*, Landi Khana on the west, and Jamrud on the east.

The British Government engaged to continue the subsidies which had hitherto been paid on the following scale:—

			Rs.	
Afridis ..	Kuki Khel	.. .. ..	1,300	*per mensem.*
	Malikdin Khel	.. .. ..	1,300	" "
	Kambar Khel	.. .. ..	500	" "
	Kamrai	.. .. ..	250	" "
	Zakha Khel	.. .. ..	1,700	" "
	Sipah	.. .. ..	1,300	" "
[1] *Shinwaris of Loargai*		.. .. ..	805	" "
	Total	..	7,155	" "
			or 85,860	per annum.

Besides the above, there were small special allowances to minor headmen, who rendered service in the first campaign, but had to give place to the old tribal chiefs when they made submission after the peace of Gandamak. These allowances raised the annual subsidies to a total of Rs. 87,540.

The position of the *jazailchis* was entirely changed in the new arrangement. The British Government now merely paid the cost of their maintenance, a sum amounting to about Rs. 87,160 per annum; but they were to be appointed and dismissed by the chiefs of the clans concerned, who were solely responsible for their management, reporting their arrangements to the Political Officer at Jamrud. The strength of this body was about 550 men, with the usual complement of subadars, jemadars, and subordinate officers.

[1] The *Shinwaris* are a powerful tribe, numbering between 11,000 and 12,000 fighting men, who reside in Ningrahar. With the exception of one small section, they have in ordinary times no dealings with the British, and therefore do not come within the scope of the present work. The only occasions on which we have come into contact with them were during the first Afghan war, and during the operations in 1878-80. In November 1841 this tribe attacked the British post at Pesh Bolak, and in the following year an expedition was sent into their country to inflict punishment. In the last campaign in Afghanistan they caused considerable annoyance on our line of communications, and several punitive expeditions were sent against them. The Shinwaris are divided into four clans—(I) Mandehzai; (II) Sangu Khel; (III) Ali Sher Khel; and (IV) Sipah. Members of the Ali Sher Khel clan inhabit the Loargai valley about Landi Kotal in the Khaibar, and are known as the Loargai Shinwaris. This is the only portion of the tribe within the British sphere of influence.

The Loargai Shinwaris number about 850 fairly well-armed fighting men. They retain close relations with their kinsmen across the border and can, at all times, count on the latter coming to their assistance. They are fairly well off, and cultivate all the available land in the Loargai plain; their habitations are substantial fortified homesteads.

When these arrangements were complete and in working order, the British troops were withdrawn, on the 21st of March 1881, from the positions they had held at Ali Musjid and Landi Kotal.

The pass was after that date entirely protected by *jazailchis*; and the arrangements made with the Khaibar Afridis were found to work satisfactorily. Tolls on caravans commenced to be levied on the 15th September 1881, and the income from this source was estimated at about 60,000 rupees per annum. The first occasion on which the traffic in the Khaibar was molested was on the 21st of February 1882, when, as a demonstration, a body of Zakha Khels, chiefly belonging to the Annai section, attempted an unsuccessful raid on a caravan about three miles from Ali Musjid. Due warning of their intention had been previously received, and the two Zakha Khel companies of the *jazailchis*, with half of the Malikdin Khel company, repulsed the marauders with a loss of four men killed and ten wounded, before they could attack the travellers on the road. Shortly afterwards the offending section of the Zakha Khels submitted. It seems that they had reason to be discontented with the conduct of the Zakha Khel *maliks* in the distribution of the tribal subsidy, and their action is to be attributed more to this cause than to a desire to break the treaty which provided for the management of the pass by the Afridis. Measures were taken to remove their causes for discontent by a re-allotment of the Zakha Khel subsidy. At the same time the opportunity was taken to bring the distant section of the Zia-ud-din, which inhabits a tract in the Bara valley, detached from the main settlements of the Zakha Khels, into closer connection with the responsibility of the clan for all its sub-divisions.

Unconnected with the affairs of the Khaibar and our general relations with the Afridis were the two night attacks by Kamal, Malikdin Khel, and his gang, on picquets of native cavalry at Peshawar and Kohat. In the first, which occurred on the night of the 19th of July 1881, Kamal, with eight associates, surprised a post on the road leading from the Peshawar cantonment to Jamrud. Of the duffadar and six men who formed the picquet, three were killed and three badly wounded, and four of their carbines were carried off. The raiders escaped unpunished, owing to the darkness of the night, the rugged and broken nature of the ground they traversed, and the precaution they took of cutting the telegraph wire to Jamrud. On the night of the 20th of September 1881 a similar carefully planned and boldly executed attack was delivered on the quarter-guard of the 3rd Punjab Cavalry at Kohat, by Kamal and eight or nine companions belonging to the Malikdin Khel clan. On this occasion three sowars were killed and four wounded, and two carbines were taken Of the raiders, two were wounded, of whom one was abandoned by his comrades, and was captured near the *kotal* of the Kohat pass the next morning. He subsequently died of his wounds.

The audacity of these raids brought them into conspicuous notice, but it was clear that they were not the outcome of collective tribal ill-feeling against the British, nor prompted by any expectation of plunder, but were the acts of individual border ruffians who were actuated by personal motives of revenge. Kamal himself, who had served in our army, where he acquired a knowledge of military routine which materially facilitated the execution of his plans, lost a brother, and two near relatives of his associates were killed, in a raid which they attempted, in February 1881, on cattle of Peshawar villages grazing on the Aka Khel border. Nevertheless, these raids constituted a breach of the engagement by which the Khaibar clans had bound themselves to prevent such outrages. It was therefore required of them either to surrender the raiders to justice, or to pay a fine of Rs. 7,000, and to exclude Kamal from the Afridi country. Both the demands involved in the second alternative were obeyed without hesitation, and a heavy reward was offered for the capture of Kamal. Fines were also levied from the clans who permitted him to pass through their limits to Kohat.

On the 6th of January 1883, the outlaw Kamal, with the assistance of some men of his own clan and of the Basi Khel section of the Aka Khels, having returned to Basi Khel territory, made a raid on British territory and carried off four horses and a mule belonging to a British officer marching from Peshawar towards Matanni, and the stolen animals were given a passage through the Aka Khel limits to the Orakzai country. The horses were, however, brought back in the following March by the Aka Khels. The Malikdin Khels were also to some extent implicated in this offence, as, contrary to the express agreement with Government into which they had entered, they had permitted Kamal to return to the tribal settlement in Maidan, whence he had started to commit this raid. The Malikdin Khels were accordingly fined Rs. 780, and the Basi Khels Rs. 750.

Meanwhile the Aka Khels, since the punishment they had received in 1855, had been generally well behaved; and the most important offence committed by them of late years had been the destruction of a police post in course of construction on their border in October 1880. For this offence a fine of Rs. 1,000, with Rs. 1,200 compensation, was recovered from the clan.

Our further dealings with the Khaibar and Aka Khel Afridis will be reserved for a fresh chapter.

APPENDIX A.

Genealogy of the Zakha Khel Afridis.

Clans.	Divisions.	Sub-divisions.	Sections.
ZAKHA KHEL ..	NASR-UD-DIN ..	Habib Khel or Paindai	Wasul Khel.
			Dreplari.
		Khusrogi	Durar.
			Dreplari.
	BUDAI	Pakhai	Walli Khel.
			Saddo Khel.
			Hassan Khel.
			Shekawal.
			Sikandar Khel.
			Miri Khel.
		Ziauddin	Surat Kor.
			Kakai Kor.
		Annai	Shekhai.
			Bash Khel.
			Umar Khel.
	SHANAI OR SHAN KHEL.	Balajhoi	Sultan Khel.
		Usman Khel ..	Moghal Khel.
			Tarki Khel.
		Umar Beg Khel ..	....

APPENDIX B.

Genealogy of the Aka Khel Afridis.

Clans.	Divisions.	Sub-divisions.	Sections.
AKA KHEL ..	SAHIB JAN	Kamal Khel	Sanzal Khel or Sanial Khel.
			Basi Khel.
			Ashraf Khel.
	SHER GULLA ..	Madda Khel ..	Darri Khel.
			Mir Khan Khel.
		Sultan Khel.. ..	Shinki Khel.
			Kob Khel.
			Utam Khel.
			Azad Khel.
	MIRI KHEL	....	....

APPENDIX C.

Genealogy of the Malikdin Khel and Sipah Afridis.

Clans.	Divisions.	Sub-divisions.	Sections.
MALIKDIN KHEL ..	DAULAT KHEL ..	Lar Daulat Khel ..	Umar Khel.
			Mohmand Khel.
		Bar Daulat Khel ..	....
		Wand Khel	....
	UMAR KHAN KHEL ..	Umar Khan Khel ..	Kuddi Khel.
			Sher Khan Khel.
	KULA KARNA KHEL ..	Kula Khel	....
		Karna Khel	....
SIPAH	URMUZ KHEL ..	Landi Khel	Wand Garhai, Ali Khel.
			Abdul Rahim Khel.
			Ibrahim Khel.
		Keimal Khel ..	Hilal Khel.
			Baghdad Khel.
			Babur Khel.
		Abdul Khel.. ..	Buzr Khel.
			Nazi Khel.
			Auli Khel.
			Tor Khel.
			Bahadur Khel.
			Lal Khel.
			Sultan Khel.
	BABAKRI KHEL ..	Suran Khel	Mamil Khel.
			Kasim Khel.
			Kaim Khel.
			Sultan Khel.
			Miri Khel.
		Ghaibi Khel ..	Karra Khel.
			Zangi Khel.
			Khal Khel.
			Piru Khel.
			Surkha Khel.
		Jawakai	Ali Khel.
			Khumari Khel.

APPENDIX D.

Genealogy of the Kamrai Afridis.

Clans.	Divisions.	Sub-divisions.	Sections.
KAMRAI OR KAMAR KHEL.	KHWAIDAD KHEL OR (BAR KAMRAIS).	Sob Khel ..	Gawar Khel.
			Sarwar Khel.
			Shamsher Khel.
			Shudil Khel.
		Azad Khel ..	Hukdad Khel.
			Khanzad Khel.
			Amir Khan Khel.
			Mirdad Khel.
	MUGHAL KHEL ..	Mughul Khel ..	Khujal Khel.
			Tarkial Khel.
		Khwas Khel ..	....
		Painda Khel ..	....
		Amal Khel	....
	BARMI KHEL ..	....	....
	YAR ALI KHEL ..	Ikhtyar Khel ..	....
		Ayub Khel	....
		Musa Khel	....
	SHEIKH ALI KHEL ..	Tor Khel	....
		Kulli Khel	....
		Hassan Khel	....
		Kuzi Khel	....

APPENDIX E.

Genealogy of the Kuki Khel Afridis.

CLANS.	Divisions.	Sub-divisions.	Sections.
KUKI KHEL ..	SIKANDAR KHEL ..	Usman Khel ..	Mir Kalan Khel.
		Zakku Khel	Multani Khel.
	MITHA KHAN KHEL ..	Assad Khel	Walli Khel.
			Maddu Khel.
			Karun Khel.
			Tor Khel.
		Hassan Khel ..	Kattia Khel.
			Mannia Khel.
	ABDAL KHEL ..	Fateh Khel	Yari Khel.
		Umar Khel	Sheri Khel.
		Khadak Khel ..	....
		Madar Khel	....

APPENDIX F.

Genealogy of the Kambar Khel Afridis.

Clans.	Divisions.	Sub-divisions.	Sections.
KAMBAR KHEL	KAMBAR KHEL	Masti-Khel (Dreplari)	Zamia Khel.
KAMBAR KHEL	KAMBAR KHEL	Masti-Khel (Dreplari)	Umar Khel.
KAMBAR KHEL	KAMBAR KHEL	Pabbi Khel (Dreplari)	Jan Beg Khel.
KAMBAR KHEL	KAMBAR KHEL	Pabbi Khel (Dreplari)	Yargul Khel.
KAMBAR KHEL	KAMBAR KHEL	Sheikhmal Khel	Miran Khel.
KAMBAR KHEL	KAMBAR KHEL	Sheikhmal Khel	Yaran Khel.
KAMBAR KHEL	KAMBAR KHEL	Sheikhmal Khel	Kaim Khel.
KAMBAR KHEL	KAMBAR KHEL	Sheikhmal Khel	Ali Khel.
KAMBAR KHEL	KAMBAR KHEL	Sheikhmal Khel	Suliman Khel.
KAMBAR KHEL	KAMBAR KHEL	Durbi Khel (Dreplari)	Wardurbi Khel.
KAMBAR KHEL	KAMBAR KHEL	Durbi Khel (Dreplari)	Aziz Khel.
KAMBAR KHEL	KAMBAR KHEL	Durbi Khel (Dreplari)	Gohar Khel.
KAMBAR KHEL	KAMBAR KHEL	Durbi Khel (Dreplari)	Azar Khel.
KAMBAR KHEL	KAMBAR KHEL	Durbi Khel (Dreplari)	Jalil Khel.
KAMBAR KHEL	KAMBAR KHEL	Durbi Khel (Dreplari)	Ramsher Khel.
KAMBAR KHEL	MAT KHAN KHEL	Sher Khel	....
KAMBAR KHEL	MAT KHAN KHEL	Walli Beg Khel	....
KAMBAR KHEL	MAT KHAN KHEL	Bash Khel	....
KAMBAR KHEL	MAT KHAN KHEL	Mirza Beg Khel	....
KAMBAR KHEL	MAT KHAN KHEL	Sarbadar Khel	....
KAMBAR KHEL	MAT KHAN KHEL	Khojal Khel	....
KAMBAR KHEL	MAT KHAN KHEL	Ambar Khel	Guli Khel.

CHAPTER II.

THE AFRIDI TRIBE.—(Continued.)

Operations of the Tirah Expeditionary Force against the Khaibar and Aka Khel Afridis, in 1897-98.

AFTER the events described in the last chapter the conduct of the Afridis as a whole was good, and they kept faithfully to their treaty obligations. Certain specific cases of misconduct by individuals occurred, but received no support or encouragement from the bulk of the tribe; and no punitive measures were required up to the time of the outbreak in 1897. The most noteworthy minor case of misconduct occurred in July 1892, when Malik Amin Khan, Kuki Khel, aggrieved at having been deprived of half his *maliki* allowances on account of repeated misconduct, collected a *lashkar* of some 500 or 600 men and attacked the Khaibar. This *lashkar* occupied a hill above Shadi Bagiar to the south of the east entrance of the Khaibar on the evening of the 4th July 1892, and during the ensuing night made attacks on Shadi Bagiar, Jehangira, and Fort Maude just inside the pass. The *mullas* in Tirah combined to try and persuade the other Afridi clans to join, but without success. As soon as news of the approach of this *lashkar* became known, reinforcements, consisting of 200 men of the 14th Sikhs, 100 men of the Royal Scots Fusiliers, and 2 field guns, were despatched to Jamrud.

Hearing of the arrival of these troops Amin Khan's gathering dispersed early on the morning of the 5th July, without a man of the Jamrud garrison advancing a yard beyond that place.

Before proceeding to describe the part played by the Afridi tribe in the rising of 1897, it may be of advantage to give a brief resumé of the causes which are put forward as the most important factors in explanation of that sudden and, at the time, almost unaccountable display of hostility towards the British Government.

Probable causes of the rising.

As was narrated in the last chapter, on the 17th February 1881, the independence of the Khaibar clans was recognized, whilst they, on their part, accepted entire and exclusive responsibility for the safeguarding of the Khaibar pass, and bound themselves to commit no offences in British territory, to levy no tolls, and to have no political dealings with Kabul. Article No. 5 of the Afridis' agreement expressly states—"Our responsibility for the security of the road is independent of aid from Government in the form of troops. It lies with the discretion of Government to retain its troops within the Pass or to withdraw them and to re-occupy at pleasure." The terms of this agreement should be borne in mind when estimating the sincerity and truthfulness of their petitions to the Amir of Afghanistan, subsequent to the outbreak of 1897, to the effect that our hold on the Khaibar was an act of tyranny on the part of Government and an infringement of their treaty rights. The only change introduced into the management of the Pass was the gradual development of the corps of *jezailchis* into the "Khaibar Rifles," their armament being improved by the provision of Snider rifles at Government expense, and a British officer (the late Captain Barton of the Guides) being appointed Commandant in 1896. But neither on this point nor on any other did they give any sign of discontent, and our relations with them continued to be most friendly, until the sudden and wholly unlooked for outbreak in August 1897 again forced us into hostilities with almost the whole of the Khaibar Afridis.

The relative importance of the different causes predisposing to this outbreak is a point upon which authorities greatly differ. This much is certain, that the reasons put forward by the tribes themselves do not embody the real causes which formed the mainspring of their action, nor, even if well grounded, would such comparatively trivial grievances as the enhancement of the salt-tax, the non-restitution of certain runaway women, etc., have proved sufficient motive for so violent and universal an uprising and so widespread a combination amongst tribes separated by such bitter feuds, mutually jealous and suspicious of one another, and so difficult to arouse to common and concerted action. The various reasons given for their action, including their own pretexts subsequently alleged, will be given in detail; but which of them formed the most direct and powerful incentive is a matter that is never likely to be known. Religious fanaticism, however it may have been originally aroused and inflamed, was undoubtedly the immediate incentive. The preaching of the *mullas* can always be relied upon to fan an incipient flame of the kind: they are always, amongst the Pathan tribes, ill-disposed towards a settled form of government, as their own power and prestige suffer in proportion to the growth of a strong and respected central authority. They are impartially hostile to any form of government, Muhammadan included, which attempts to substitute any code of law and order for a régime in which their own powers are so extensive.

At first sight, the theory that the successes of the Turkish troops against the Greeks, in the campaign which immediately preceded the risings of 1897, had a marked effect in rousing their dormant fanaticism, might seem somewhat far-fetched. But if we consider the ignorance and credulity of these tribesmen, and how wholly dependent they are for news of the outside world upon *mullas*, and others directly interested in misleading them, it becomes apparent that such an event as the war in question—in which the true believer undoubtedly did get much the better of the infidel Greek, as could be proved to the satisfaction of the tribesmen from our own newspaper accounts—might form a most powerful weapon in the hands of the *mullas*, who could place their own interpretation upon events, and colour them to their liking, without the tribesmen being able to detect the slenderness of the foundations upon which the huge structure of misrepresentation was raised. To what an extraordinary extent garbled and exaggerated accounts of current events passed for facts amongst them, can be understood from the letter, found in Mulla Saiyid Akbar's house, quoted in full in Appendix A.

To us, of course, it is quite evident that a war between Greece and Turkey may be carried to any conclusion without affecting relations between England and the Sultan. To the Afridi, such nice distinctions as the difference between a Greek and an Englishman are hardly worthy of consideration. The infidels had made war upon Islam; the Almighty had given victory to the true believer; all infidels are alike "tarred with the same brush"; now, when the Musalman was everywhere victorious, was the auspicious time: now the tide might be taken at the flood. The noisy sentimentality of some few English partisans and sympathisers with the Greeks, and the much advertised departure of certain volunteers to their assistance, duly recorded, with more prominence and detail than their importance merited, in all our newspapers, may have proved, in the hands of the *mullas*, incontestible evidence that the English as a whole not only sympathised with the Greeks, but were fighting on their side.

Allusion has been made above to the Musalman being everywhere victorious. The Afridi was told, and believed, that the victory of his co-religionists all along the Indian Frontier was as brilliant and complete as it had been in Europe. That the treacherous attack on Colonel Bunny and his party in the Tochi was successful, that many British officers had been killed, and that Government had not been able, up to the time of the Afridi outbreak, to avenge the outrage, lost nothing in the telling when told in Tirah. On the top of this came the news of the attack on the Malakand, distorted by the *mullas* to represent a brilliant and complete victory for the tribesmen, and a crushing defeat for the British.

Another motive which probably, in conjunction with religious fanaticism, had some effect on the action of the tribesmen, and which is put forward by some writers as the principal incentive for their hostility, was suspicion of the motives prompting us to delimit the frontier between Afghanistan and independent territory by the Durand Line. Ignorant, fanatical, and fiercely jealous of their independence, the tribesmen had always looked askance at the frontier delimitation proceedings, and with misgivings as to our ultimate intentions. Even the Amir himself was suspicious of our motives, and his hostility to the whole proceeding—to the necessity of which he had in the beginning reluctantly agreed—became so pronounced and unmistakable towards the end of the delimitation, that demarkation of the boundary through the Mohmand country had to be abandoned. That many of the tribesmen regarded the delimitation and parcelling out of their country as the first preliminary to the destruction, or at any rate, the curtailment, of their independence, was marked by them in a very decided manner by the attack of the Mahsud Wazirs upon the Boundary Commission and its escort at Wana on the 3rd November 1894, as will be related when dealing with that tribe. At a time of unrest and excitement, this feeling, skilfully worked on, was in all probability another lever in the hands of the malcontents.

Yet another factor, and one of whose importance we have the most ample proof, was the universal feeling amongst the tribesmen that they could rely not only upon the approval and moral support, but also upon the active intervention in their favour, of the Amir of Afghanistan. His attitude towards them was persistently misrepresented. The *mullas* were preaching a *jehad*; and the Amir had just written a book on the same subject, and had also assumed the title of "Light of Union and of the Faith." In the minds of the more primitive Muhammadans, religious activity and violence are always rather closely connected: and the Amir's book undoubtedly was used as a proof that His Majesty was with them heart and hand.

Whilst the Amir's name was being thus freely used, and every endeavour was being made to involve, or at any rate to compromise, him in the struggle, His Majesty maintained a perfectly correct attitude towards his ally. His position, however, was extremely difficult and delicate; and in letters to the Government of India he dwelt upon the immense difficulties he had himself had in dealing with religious fanaticism, and maintained that the Hadda Mulla, the chief instigator of the troubles, was just as much an enemy to himself as to the British, and had been active in stirring up the Afghans on former occasions to rebel against him. He promised to use his utmost endeavours to prevent his own subjects from taking any part in the risings, but pointed out his inability to disarm or arrest independent tribesmen taking refuge with their families in his dominions, as they were closely allied to his own subjects by blood and marriage, and any such action on his part would result in a universal outburst of indignation against him. He pointed out that whereas the British Government had at its disposal Sikhs and Hindus, as well as British soldiers, for dealing with fanatics of this kind, he himself had no soldiers but those drawn from these very tribesmen, who would never consent to take action against their own kith and kin; but he promised to prevent his territories being used as a base of operations by the Afridis. On the 13th August he issued a proclamation in Pushtu, to the effect that he would not help or countenance any action hostile to the British Government. On the 17th August 1897, immediately after the Afridi outbreak, in public durbar at Kabul, he assured the whole assembly that he had always adhered to his promises to the British Government, and that he had never instigated his subjects against it. A contingent of the Amir's subjects who had started to join the Afridis, from Tagao, north-west of Jalalabad, were stopped by his orders at the latter place: and a *lashkar* of several thousands of Afghans from Ningrahar, Kunar, and Jalalabad, on their way to join the *jehad*, were dispersed by his orders on the 1st September 1897. In the middle of September, a deputation of eighteen leading *maliks*, etc., of the Afridi and Orakzai tribes, on their way to make a petition to the Amir at Kabul, were stopped at Jalalabad by His Majesty's orders and sent back, their petition for assistance in money, guns, and troops being peremptorily refused. On the 17th October His Majesty received the Afridi and Orakzai *jirgas* in a brief interview, but refused to change his attitude.

His Excellency the Viceroy accepted the assurances of the Amir and thanked him for his friendly attitude.

With regard to the Amir's book on *jehad*, and his assumption in 1896 of the title "Light of Union and the Faith," his action appears to have been prompted by self defence, with a view to silencing the machinations of the *mullas* against him. The nature of the struggle between him and them has already been alluded to: and he seems to have taken this course with a view to strengthening his own position by proclaiming himself the leader of religion in his own country. The admission in the letter of the Afridi *jirga*, given in Appendix A, that "His Highness advised us not to fight with the British Government, and this was and has been his advice ever since," bears independent witness to his sincerity.

Either from secret sympathy with the organizers of the outbreak,—for he had been for years a personal friend of the Hadda Mulla,—from a supposition that in assisting the tribesmen he would be strengthening the position of the Amir at the expense of the British Government, from fanaticism, or from a mixture of all three motives, the *Sipah Salar*,[1] Ghulam Haidar, took up a different attitude from the Amir; and his total neglect to restrain the subjects of the Amir under his immediate control, and even the regular troops, from joining the insurgents, formed the subject of vigorous protests from the Government of India.

[1] Afghan Commander-in-Chief.

In conclusion the following reasons for their action, given by the Chamkannis in reply to Sir W. Lockart's proclamation, probably embodied the most compelling causes for the action of all the tribes.

Friendship and enmity are not in our choice; whatever orders we may receive from the *Fakir Sahib* of Swat, the *Mulla Sahib* of Hadda or the Aka Khel Mulla, and from all Islam, we cannot refuse to obey them; if we lose our lives, no matter.

The following is a brief resumé of the events which immediately preceded the Afridi outbreak, and which are dealt with at length in other parts of this work:—

Events which preceded the Afridi outbreak.

On the 10th June 1897, without the slightest warning being given of any discontent amongst the tribes concerned, the escort to the Political Officer in the Tochi, who was engaged in collecting a small fine for admitted misconduct by the Madda Khel sub-division of the Darwesh Khel Wazirs, was treacherously attacked, the British officers shot down, and the escort forced to retire, with considerable loss, on Datta Khel.[1]

On the 26th July, with almost equal suddenness, the Malakand and Chakdara posts were assailed by vast numbers of tribesmen.[2] A few days before the attack on the Malakand, Major Deane, the Political Officer for Swat and Dir, had heard that a mad *fakir*, with a following of a few boys, was preaching against Government and trying to create trouble: a few hours only before the attack came, he learnt that the rising had spread like wild fire, that the tribesmen had joined in thousands, and that an attack was imminent. After a struggle lasting several days and nights, during which the tribesmen, in ever-increasing numbers, attacked with the most reckless courage, they were finally beaten off with losses estimated to exceed 3,000 men in killed, the total strength of the hostile gathering being estimated at 20,000 men.

On the 7th August, the Hadda Mulla, descending the Gandab valley, burnt the British frontier village of Shankargarh, and attacked the Shabkadar post, with a following of about 5,000 men, mostly Mohmands.[3] Warning had been given of the

[1] See Chapter IX. [2] See Chapter IX, Volume I.
[3] See Chapter XI, Volume I.

impending danger, and when the attack came, a force was already marching from Peshawar to Shabkadar. This force arrived next morning, and, on the 9th, attacked the tribesmen and eventually defeated and drove them off with heavy loss.

As will be easily understood, the gravity of these events, and the knowledge that further risings amongst tribes not yet implicated were to be feared, imposed on Government the necessity of taking measures of precaution on a large scale, besides making immediate preparations to punish the offending tribesmen. The movements of the Afridis and Orakzais, the most powerful of the frontier tribes, were watched with anxiety, and the normal garrison of Peshawar was considerably strengthened, in order to safeguard that border.

2nd Reserve Brigade.
2nd Bn., Oxfordshire L. I.
2nd Bn., Royal Irish Regt.
1st Bn., 3rd Gurkhas.
12th Bengal Infantry.
No. 3 Mountain Battery.
18th Bengal Lancers.
No. 4 Coy., Bombay S. and M.

3rd Reserve Brigade.
1st Bn., Northampton Regt.
1st Bn., Dorset Regiment.
9th Gurkhas.
1st Bn., 2nd Gurkhas.
3rd Field Battery.
3rd Bengal Cavalry.
No. 4 Coy., Madras S. and M.

As it had now become evident that very considerable forces would be required to cope with the situation created by these formidable and widespread outbreaks, as well as to deal with any fresh developments which might be caused by the rising spreading to the Afridis and Orakzais, orders were issued on the 14th August for the concentration at Rawalpindi of a 2nd and 3rd Reserve Brigade, as shown in the margin, under the command respectively of Brig.-General R. Westmacott, C.B., and Brig.-General A. G. Yeatman-Biggs, C.B. A 1st Reserve Brigade had already been formed in support of the column from the Malakand about to march into Swat under Sir Bindon Blood.

"K" Battery, R. H. A.
4th Dragoon Guards.
2 squadrons, 9th B. L.
A wing, Devonshire Regt.
A wing, Gordon Highlanders.
2nd Battalion, 1st Gurkhas.
26th Punjab Infantry.

In addition to these concentrations, Brig.-General Elles, commanding at Peshawar, formed a second moveable column as shown in the margin, for the general protection of the border against the Afridis, with the special idea of its moving out to protect Jamrud, or the head of the Peshawar water-supply from the Bara river. It was intended that it should be available for any portion of the frontier in the vicinity of Peshawar not protected by the Shabkadar column, but not for any operations in the Khaibar pass. The garrison of regular troops in Jamrud, ordinarily consisting of 100 rifles and 50 sabres, in addition to the Khaibar Rifles, was doubled, garrisons of regular troops being also placed in Forts Michni (50 carbines) and Abazai (100 rifles), in place of the Border Military Police.

Although these precautions were taken to prevent raiding into our territory, and the general situation as regards the Afridis was looked upon as disquieting, no very serious apprehension was felt for the safety of the Khaibar, which had now been for sixteen years held by the tribal levies with uniform good faith. It was expected that any trouble given by the turbulent members of that tribe would take the more normal form of raiding in force; and that, if they ventured into the plains, the striking force at Peshawar would be quite strong enough to deal with them.

The first definite news of unrest amongst the Afridis was received on the 4th August, when a telegram was received from the Deputy Commissioner of Kohat to the effect that Mulla Saiyid Akbar had succeeded in persuading the Orakzais to unite against Government, and was in Tirah endeavouring to persuade the Afridis to do the same.

The Commissioner of Peshawar (Sir Richard Udny) had, however, received other information from Tirah, which he considered reliable, to the effect that affairs there were fairly quiet; and he was consequently inclined to believe that the above report from Kohat gave an exaggerated idea of the situation. On the 15th August the Deputy Commissioner of Kohat again telegraphed to the effect that an Afridi *lashkar* had collected with the intention of attacking Jamrud, and that such action on the part of the Afridis would be followed by the Orakzais; but Sir Richard still declined to believe that the situation was as threatening as represented and telegraphed to Government that reports from reliable sources informed him that there was no serious or general movement either among Orakzais or Afridis.

As there was nothing so far to show in what direction an attack by the tribesmen, if it actually took place, might be delivered, the Government of the Punjab recommended the reinforcement of the garrison of Kohat, to provide for the eventuality of the Afridis and Orakzais breaking out to the south and south-east of their country. The advisability of this precaution is evident from a glance at the map, Kohat being isolated and, at the time, unconnected by rail with Kushalgarh; whereas in and about Peshawar there was already a force of from 5,000 to 6,000 men, exclusive of the Shabkadar column, numbering about 2,500 more; in addition to this Peshawar could be rapidly reinforced by rail, if necessary, from the reserve brigades at Rawalpindi. The Government of India accordingly sanctioned the immediate despatch to Kohat of the reinforcements in the margin, and also notified its intention to still further strengthen the forces in the Peshawar district.

9th Field Battery, R. A.
A wing, 1st Royal Scots Fus.
18th Bengal Lancers.
15th Sikhs.

On the evening of the 17th August, Colonel Aslam Khan, Officiating Political Officer in the Khaibar, arrived in Peshawar, bringing with him Malik Amin Khan, Kuki Khel, with the information that an Afridi *lashkar*, reported to be 10,000 strong, accompanied by 1,500 *mullas* from Ningrahar, had started from Bagh in Tirah on the 16th, with the intention of attacking the Khaibar posts, and that they might be expected there on the 18th. Sir Richard Udny and Brig.-General Elles decided against occupying Landi Kotal or other posts in the Khaibar with regular troops, not only because the question of supply, at short notice, would present great difficulties, but also because such a course would imply distrust in the intention of the tribesmen to keep to their treaty obligations, and in the loyalty of the Khaibar Rifles. The garrisons of the latter at the various posts had recently been strengthened: Landi Kotal, the most advanced and important post, had in particular had its garrison increased from 200 to 354 rifles, amply supplied with all stores, including 50,000 rounds of reserve ammunition.

Captain Barton, Commandant of the Khaibar Rifles, was at Landi Kotal at this time. Hearing of the advance of the Afridi *lashkar*, he had written to Sir Richard Udny, asking for a small detachment of regular troops, he being of opinion that this course would encourage the Khaibar Rifles, by making them feel that they had Government support behind them. But before this letter arrived, Sir Richard had already despatched an order to Captain Barton to return to Jamrud; as, in the event of an attack upon Landi Kotal, the Commissioner considered that his presence there might hamper the action of Government to the extent of committing it to the despatch of a relief force for his rescue.

The garrisons at Ali Musjid and Fort Maude were now strengthened by 100 tribesmen each; and urgent orders were issued to the Zakha Khel *maliks* to reinforce Landi Kotal with contingents; the Shinwari *maliks* were also reminded of their responsibility for the safety of the Pass, and on the early morning of the 18th, a column, as shown in the margin, was despatched to Jamrud; Bara Fort being at the same time strengthened by the addition of one company, 2-1st Gurkhas, and fifty men of the 9th Bengal Lancers.

"K" Battery, R. H. A.
No. 3 Mountain Battery.
4th Dragoon Guards.
Wing of the Gordons (386 men).
7 companies, 2-1st Gurkhas (732 men).
Wing, 26th Punjab Infantry (280 men).

Two or three days passed away without anything happening. On his way down the Khaibar, Captain Barton had seen no signs of any gathering; *kafilas* were passing up and down the Pass as usual without meeting the *lashkar*; and the Commissioner at last began to think that either he had been misled by exaggerated rumours, or that the Afridis, overawed by the display of force, had abandoned all idea of an attack upon the Khaibar posts.

On the 21st, reliable news was obtained that the Afridi *laskhar* of 10,000 men had really moved, with the intention of attacking the Khaibar posts if held by Government troops; but that, if they were held by the Khaibar Rifles alone, they would only attack Jamrud and Bara. To meet this eventuality, Bara and Jamrud were both still further reinforced, the former by two squadrons, 9th Bengal Lancers, the 57th Field Battery, and a wing, 30th Punjab Infantry; the latter by a wing of the Gordons and a wing of the 28th Bombay Pioneers. Any active operations into the Khaibar were rendered impossible by scarcity of transport, all transport immediately available having been requisitioned for military operations in progress in other parts of the frontier. The transport on this date in the Peshawar valley consisted of only 553 camels, 714 mules, and 190 bullocks, most of which were required for the supply of the troops at Shabkadar, Bara, and Jamrud, and for various station duties.

Attack on the Khaibar posts.

In the early morning of the 23rd, the attack on the Khaibar posts began. On that date, the distribution of the Khaibar Rifles was as follows:—Jamrud, 271; Bagiar, 13; Jehangira, 7; Fort Maude, 42 (reinforced by 100 tribesmen); Ali Musjid, 80 (reinforced by 100 tribesmen, only 40 of whom were present at the time of attack); Kata Kushtia, 7; Gurgura, 10; Landi Kotal, 374; Fort Tytler, 20. Fort Maude, the nearest important post to British territory, was the first to be seriously attacked; this was probably due to the Afridis, hearing on their arrival of the strength of the garrisons then in Jamrud and Fort Bara, having wisely abandoned their first intention of attacking these places, and diverted their attention to the easier task of attacking the Khaibar posts.

At about 8 A.M., Brig.-General Westmacott, who had been appointed to command at Jamrud, heard that firing had been going on at Ali Musjid since early morning; and shortly afterwards news arrived that the bulk of the Afridi forces had moved off to Fort Maude, the attack on which began in earnest about 10 A.M. Soon after 3 P.M., hearing that the latter place was being pressed, General Westmacott moved out, as a demonstration, to Bagiar, at the entrance to the Pass, whence "K" Battery opened fire on the enemy near Fort Maude, over 3,000 yards distant.

This action quickly caused the retirement of the attacking force; but no sooner had the troops been withdrawn than the garrison evacuated the post, which was at once seized and destroyed by the enemy. The Bagiar and Jehangira posts were evacuated at the same time. Of the Fort Maude garrison, eleven Zakha Khels deserted with their rifles: the remainder came into Jamrud.

Ali Musjid was next attacked. By 7 P.M., the garrison, finding their ammunition was running out, and seeing that Fort Maude had fallen, escaped to Jamrud, with a loss of two killed and one wounded; the enemy's loss being estimated at twelve killed. Nineteen of the garrison, with their rifles, were missing.

On the morning of the 24th, the *lashkar*, which had passed the night at Ali Musjid, started for Landi Kotal, the garrisons of the small posts at Kata Kushtia and Gurgura taking to the hills on their approach. As the *lashkar* marched up the Pass, it was joined by all the neighbouring villagers, and, arriving at Landi Kotal about 8 A.M., began the attack forthwith.

Subadar Mursil Khan commanded the fort. Subadar-Major Mir Akbar was also present, but did not assume command, as he was there as the representative of his father, the Zakha Khel Malik Khwas Khan, and not in his military capacity. Khwas Khan had already joined the *lashkar*, and sent word to his son to admit him—

which he eventually succeeded in doing. All through the 24th and the ensuing night the defence was resolutely maintained; but in the early morning of the 25th, urged by their fellow clansmen outside, the Shinwaris of the garrison, who numbered about seventy men, jumped down from the northern wall of the fort and made for their homes, being fired upon by some other tribesmen of the garrison as they went. A nephew of Khwas Khan now appeared, waving a flag of truce. On being admitted to the fort, he stated that he was authorized to make terms, and informed the garrison that the British had abandoned Jamrud, and that it was doubtful if they could hold Peshawar. The native officers, knowing that Forts Maude and Ali Musjid had fallen without any attempt to relieve them, and believing themselves abandoned to their fate, decided to make terms; and agreed to evacuate the fort on the understanding that the *lashkar* would move from the vicinity till evening.

Fall of Landi Kotal.

Subadar-Major Mir Akbar now ordered "cease fire" to be sounded, and the garrison to pack their baggage. As they quitted the walls to do so, some Zakha Khels and Shinwaris from outside scaled the low bastion at the north-east corner of the fort and began to loot; the rest of the *lashkar*, which had begun to move away, swarming back to their assistance. The garrison at once manned the walls again, and Subadar Mursil Khan himself proceeded to the north-east corner and cleared the enemy out, but was unfortunately shot dead whilst doing so. Mir Akbar then divided the reserve ammunition amongst his own following, who numbered about fifty men, and released two Zakha Khels who had been made prisoners.

All was now confusion inside the fort, and about 11 A.M. the end came, the gate being opened from within, and the *lashkar* swarming into the post. The Mullagori and Shilmani sepoys, numbering about ninety men, fought their way out, and escaped to the Shilmani country, with a loss of two killed and two wounded; the remainder of the garrison joined the *lashkar*. The post was then looted and burnt. Of the garrison, one native officer, five sepoys and nine followers were killed, one native officer and six sepoys wounded. The losses of the enemy were said to be from 200 to 250.

In spite of all that their *mullas* could do to keep them together, the tribesmen then began to disperse to their homes, carrying their dead and wounded, while picquets of the Zakha Khels guarded the approaches from Jamrud.

During September, 134 of the garrison of Landi Kotal rejoined at Jamrud with their rifles; but, at the end of that month, of the 836 rifles in the hands of the corps, 274 were still unaccounted for. All men of the corps who rejoined were disarmed and given leave to their homes, while pensions were bestowed on the families of those who had died fighting on our side.

On the 3rd September, orders were issued for the concentration of troops for an advance into Tirah. But the extremely difficult nature of the country to be invaded, the formidable extent of the hostile combination against Government, their armament, and the transport difficulty already mentioned, all made it evident that no forward movement could take place until very extensive preparations had been made. Still, notwithstanding the fact that the expedition promised to be a larger and more difficult military operation than any that had previously taken place on the frontier, Government had determined that it should take place, even though the tribes might show a disposition to submit before it began. This unprovoked aggression on the part of the Afridis and Orakzais had, in the opinion of the Government, created a situation so grave and so subversive of our dominant position on the frontier, that nothing short of humbling the pride of the tribesmen by dictating our own terms in the heart of their country would meet the occasion. It was also regarded as a matter of primary importance that the punitive operations should take place with as little delay as possible; *bis dat qui cito dat* being peculiarly applicable in punitive measures against Pathans.

Plan of campaign.

By starting our operations in the late autumn we could not hope to do the same amount of material damage to the enemy as would be the case were the expedition deferred until the spring, when the crops, being young, could not be cut in anticipation of our approach; moreover, by waiting till the spring we should have avoided exposing our troops to the hardships of a rigorous winter. But the necessity of striking at once outweighed all other considerations, and every possible endeavour was made to hurry on the preparations, so as to get the expedition over before the most severe cold should set in. The 12th October was originally fixed upon as the date for the expedition to start, it being hoped that all might be ready by then, and that the conclusion of operations in Bajaur and the Mohmand country would set free large numbers of troops and transport animals for use in Tirah. These operations, however, proved longer than anticipated; and only one brigade with its transport, instead of two, became available from the troops under Sir Bindon Blood's command.

It was decided to make Kohat, and not Peshawar, the base of operations, for the following reasons:—The Kohat route was shorter: Shinawari, our advanced base, would be only thirty miles from Maidan, whereas Peshawar was over sixty, and the road, though difficult, was better than anything we could use from the Peshawar side; the roads into Tirah along the courses of the Bara, Mastura, and Khanki rivers, were known to be in places unfit even for mule transport, and to contain most difficult defiles, defensible by an almost inaccessible enemy, against whom we should have great difficulty in protecting our long line of communications; finally, it was hoped that at either the Sampagha or Arhanga pass, their two really strong and defensible positions, the enemy would make a resolute stand, and enable a decisive victory to be obtained, instead of successively occupying one strong position after another, after having taken each of which we should be obliged to wait again until the road behind was made practicable for transport. The main objection to the Kohat route lay in the fact of there being no railway nearer than Kushalgarh, on the Indus, over thirty miles to the east of Kohat.

The total force assembled for the invasion of Tirah was about 44,000 fighting men, details of which, with the staff, will be found in the Appendix. Lieut.-General Sir William Lockhart, Commanding the Punjab, was appointed to the supreme command. He was on furlough in England at the time, and was recalled by telegram. The troops were divided into a main column, consisting of two divisions, each composed of two brigades of infantry with divisional troops, and two subsidiary columns; besides troops to hold the lines of communications, and a mixed brigade held in reserve at Rawalpindi. The main column, under the personal command of Sir William

Distribution of troops.

Lockhart, was intended for the actual invasion of Tirah, from Kohat, *viâ* the Sampagha and Arhanga passes: the two subsidiary columns, operating from Peshawar and along the Hangu-Thal-Parachinar line, respectively, were to support the advance of the main column in such manner as circumstances might require.

Pending the arrival of Sir William Lockhart, the actual preparations for the advance were made by Major-General Yeatman-Biggs. Sir William Lockhart did not reach Kohat until the 4th October.

Transport.

Everything was now ready but the transport, which was a question of paramount difficulty. The very greatest exertions had to be made to improvise what was required, and officers were despatched to scour the Punjab in quest of camels, mules, bullock carts, ponies, pack-bullocks, and even donkeys. The total number of transport animals in use by Government for the purposes of the Tirah Expedition reached, in round numbers, nearly 60,000, in addition to some 12,000 to 13,000 in use with other expeditions proceeding simultaneously on the frontier. From Kushalgarh to Shinawari, *viâ* Kohat and Muhammad Khwaja, the road was practicable for carts; but for the invasion of Tirah, nothing but pack transport could accompany the troops actually entering the country: and, camel transport being too slow and cumbersome, mules, ponies, and donkeys were alone suitable.

Whilst the necessary troops, supplies, and transport were being collected, no military operations of importance against the Afridis were undertaken. Such preliminary measures as were necessary against the Orakzais will be found detailed in Chapter IV. Some skirmishing between our reconnoitring parties and the enemy occurred in October.

Preliminary operations.

On the 1st, near Sadda in the Kurram, a patrol of the 3rd Bengal Cavalry was ambuscaded, a duffadar being killed and two sowars severely wounded: whether their assailants were Afridis or Orakzais did not transpire. On the 10th Captain Jones and a corporal, 4th Dragoon Guards, were killed whilst reconnoitring the Sam Ghakhe pass, three miles from Jamrud, towards Kajurai. On the 18th, two squadrons, 9th Bengal Lancers, under Captain Brazier-Creagh, reconnoitring up the Bara valley towards Mamanai, were ambuscaded on their return by 500 Aka Khel Afridis and Sturi Khel Orakzais, losing one non-commissioned officer, four sowars and eighteen horses killed, four sowars and ten horses wounded, and four sowars missing. In addition to the above, sniping into camp and cutting of telegraph wires was, as usual, indulged in by the hostile tribesmen.

By the 16th October the concentration of the main column on the Hangu-Shinawari line was far enough advanced to enable Sir William Lockhart to decide on moving into the Khanki valley on the 20th, and to issue his orders to that effect.

As a preliminary to this advance arrangements were made to improve the road leading from Shinawari over the Chagru Kotal towards Kharappa, so as to make it fit for transport. By the 15th October this work had been completed to the top of the pass; but as further work was necessary on the north side of the *kotal*, it became necessary to dislodge the enemy from the village of Dargai and the ridges in the vicinity, from which they could open effective fire on our working-parties as soon as the latter crossed the summit.

Accordingly, Sir Power Palmer, who, in the temporary absence of Major-General Yeatman-Biggs, had succeeded to the command at Shinawari, arranged to move out to the attack in the early morning of the 18th October.

Main Column.

1st Bn. Gordon Highlanders.
1st " Dorset Regiment.
1st " 2nd Gurkhas.
15th Sikhs.
No. 4 Co. Madras S. and M.
No. 8 M. B., R. A.
Machine Gun Det. 16th Lcrs.
Scouts, 5th Gurkhas.

2nd Column.

2nd Battalion K. O. S. B.
1st " 3rd Gurkhas.
No. 5 M. B., R. A.
Rocket Detachment R. A.

The troops detailed for the attack were distributed into two columns as detailed in the margin. The main column, under the command of Brig.-General F. J. Kempster, was accompanied by Sir Power Palmer in person, and the 2nd Column was under the command of Brig.-General R. Westmacott. In addition, one company 3rd Sikhs accompanied Sir Power Palmer as personal escort. Sir William Lockhart watched the operations from the vicinity of the Samana Sukh.

The main column left Shinawari Camp at 4-30 A.M. It was directed to proceed up a long rugged spur on the north-west of Shinawari, and then to execute a turning movement against the right flank of the enemy in the vicinity of Dargai. The 2nd Column, which had been detailed for the frontal attack on Dargai from the Chagru Kotal, started at 5 A.M., and reached the latter place without opposition at about 8-30 A.M., where it was joined by the 1st Battalion, Northamptonshire Regiment, and No. 9 Mountain Battery, Royal

First capture of Dargai.

Artillery, who had marched that morning from Fort Lockhart to the Samana Sukh, to reconnoitre and protect the right flank of the advance up the defile. From the Chagru Kotal very few of the enemy were to be seen on the Dargai position; it was accordingly decided that the 2nd Column should at once advance against it. At 9 A.M. the advance began, 3rd Gurkhas leading, King's Own Scottish Borderers in support, Northamptons in reserve; two companies Northamptons being left as escort to the Mountain Batteries, which, from the *kotal*, covered the advance of the infantry with their fire. The enemy now began to show in ever-increasing numbers on the high cliffs south of Dargai, overlooking the line of advance of the troops; and as the leading infantry reached Mama Khan, fire was opened upon them from the heights. From Mama Khan, by deviating to the south of the spur along the top of which the track runs, the troops were covered for about 900 yards by a deep fold in the ground; but on arriving at the point marked B on the plan all cover for a further advance ceased.

The small plateau upon which the village of Dargai is situated terminates abruptly to the south in a line of almost sheer cliffs, the ascent of which is made by a track, which climbs up at a point where the cliff is more broken and shelving than elsewhere. Connecting this point with B is a narrow neck along which, as far as point A, there is no cover whatever. Point A is too close in under the cliffs to be reached by fire from the summit, and the neck here broadens out owing to the fall of débris from above. The summit, where the path crosses it, is about 250 feet above B; while a little to the west a steep rocky knoll rises another 150 feet.

At 11 A.M. the infantry opened fire from the point B. Under cover of their fire and that of the two batteries, the Gurkhas, advancing by alternate rushes, gained the dead ground at the foot of the cliffs; and, just before noon, closely supported by the King's Own Scottish Borderers, they swarmed up the steep ascent, and took the position, headed by Lieutenant W. G. L. Beynon. The enemy, who now had news of the advance of the strong column under Brig.-General Kempster on their right flank, made only a half-hearted stand against the assault, and fled north-west towards the Khanki valley, leaving twenty dead. The Narikh Sukh was then occupied by the British, and the defences round Dargai destroyed. Our losses amounted to two men killed and thirteen wounded.

Meanwhile the advance of the main column had been unexpectedly slow, owing to the difficult nature of the path. By the time the 5th mile was reached, the track was found to be impassable for mules, and No. 8 Mountain Battery, and all laden animals, had consequently to return to Shinawari, escorted by the Dorsets and two companies 15th Sikhs. The remainder of the column then advanced, headed by the 1-2nd Gurkhas, and the scouts of the 5th Gurkhas. At about 11 A.M., heliographic communication was opened between the two columns, and just before noon the advanced guard were in a commanding position at Khand Talao, about 2½ miles west of Dargai. No opposition had been met with, the appearance of a column from this quarter being wholly unexpected. A halt had to be made at this point to admit of the column closing up; but the 1-2nd Gurkhas were enabled to inflict considerable loss on a body of the enemy flying from Dargai. It was 2-30 P.M., before the column was able to move on again towards Dargai, and by this time considerable bodies of the enemy had collected on the heights to the north of the line of advance, and harassed the rear-guard; while about 4,000 Afridis were seen to be approaching Dargai from the Khanki valley.

By 3-10 P.M., before these reinforcements could reach the scene of action, the advanced guard of the main column had effected a junction with the 2nd column at Dargai, and Brig.-General Westmacott then immediately began to withdraw his brigade. Leaving No. 5 Mountain Battery at the Chagru Kotal, he sent No. 9 Mountain Battery to occupy a position on the Samana Sukh, under escort of the Northamptons, so as to cover the retirement from that place.

The enemy now began to press the rear-guard closely, and the difficult operation of withdrawing from the heights of Dargai was attended with considerable loss; Major R. D. Jennings Bramly and two men being killed, and Captain D. R. Sladen, Lieutenant M. L. Pears, 2nd-Lieutenant T. H. Keyes and ten men wounded. The rear-guard, however, showed so steady a front, and were so well supported by the accurate fire of the mountain guns, that the advance of the enemy was soon checked, and the further retirement of the main column to Shinawari *viâ* the Chagru Kotal was unmolested. The total British casualties on this day amounted to one officer and seven men killed, five officers and twenty-nine men wounded.

If it had been possible to hold the Dargai position, instead of returning from it, the heavy casualties incurred in retaking it two days later might have been avoided; but the difficulties of making adequate arrangements for holding it, at the late hour when the concentration of the two columns had been effected, appeared insurmountable. The nearest water was at Talao,—three miles distant—the road to which place was impassable for transport animals, and was commanded throughout its entire length by high rugged hills, upon which the enemy were then beginning to arrive in force. Dargai is over 6,000 feet high, and there was neither firewood nor warm clothing for the troops; nor, at that hour, could arrangements have been made for sending supplies of any kind to them, over a track all but impracticable for laden animals even in daylight. Besides this the force would have been exposed, throughout the night, to attack from vast numbers of the Afridis; and the losses which would certainly have been incurred then may be set against those which we suffered on the 20th.

Second advance on Dargai.

The actual advance from Shinawari for the invasion of Tirah took place on the 20th, as previously arranged. As the enemy was known to have re-occupied the Dargai ridge in great force, and it was necessary to dislodge him from that position before the road north of the Chagru Kotal could be safely traversed by the transport of the force, the 3rd Sikhs, the Derbyshire Regiment, and No. 1 (Kohat) Mountain Battery, were placed at the disposal of Major-General Yeatman-Biggs, in addition to the troops of the 2nd Division. On the previous day, Yeatman-Biggs had proposed that, owing to the return of the Afridis to Dargai, the advance should be made to Kharappa *viâ* Fort Gulistan, the Samana Sukh, and the Talai spur, instead of down the Chagru defile, thus turning the enemy's position; and orders had been issued on the night of the 19th to this effect. Sir W. Lockhart, however, was unable to accept this change in his plans, and about midnight Yeatman-Biggs was directed to adhere to the original plan of movement. Sir William Lockhart considered that the enemy would probably retire from Dargai as soon as troops had been pushed on to the junction of the Narikh and Chagru ravines as their flanks would then be threatened. In the end, however, troops were not advanced beyond the Chagru Kotal until the Dargai heights had been taken by a frontal attack.

Further to distract the enemy's attention and weaken his defence at Dargai, a report, given out as a dead secret to natives whom he knew would divulge it, was circulated by Mr. Donald, Political Officer, to the effect that a flanking attack would be made along the line taken by the main column on the 18th. Under the impression that they had obtained reliable information of our intentions, a large contingent of the enemy remained out on their right flank all day on the 20th, and gave no assistance to the tribesmen in front of Dargai, at the actual point of attack.

At 4-30 A.M. on the 20th, the advanced guard moved off, followed by the remainder of the troops, as per margin; the baggage train was immediately in rear of the main body. The block on the road, however, due to the check caused by the enemy's opposition, was so great that the rear-guard was not able to get out of Shinawari Camp by nightfall.

Advanced Guard.

3rd Gurkha Scouts.
1-2nd Gurkhas.
1st Battalion Dorsets.
No. 4 Company Madras Sappers and Miners.
No. 8 Mountain Battery.
No. 5 Mountain Battery.
Maxim Gun Detachment, 16th Lancers.
1st Battalion Gordons.
15th Sikhs.

Main Body.

No. 1 (Kohat) Mountain Battery.
2nd Battalion Derbyshire.
3rd Sikhs.
21st Madras Pioneers.
Sirmur Imperial Service Sappers.
Rocket Battery Jhind Infantry.

Rear-guard.

K. O. S. Borderers.
3rd Gurkhas.

The advanced guard, under Brig.-General Kempster, reached the Chagru Kotal about 8 A.M., without opposition; No. 9 Mountain Battery, escorted by the Northamptons, who were to protect the right flank, arriving in position on the Samana Sukh at the same hour. The enemy, with whom twenty-nine standards were counted, were in great strength at Dargai and Narikh Sukh, and on the hills to the west. A reliable spy brought information that they included Ali Khel, Mamuzai, and Alisherzai Orakzais and Malikdin Khel, Kambar Khel, Kamrai, Zakha Khel, Sipah, and Kuki Khel Afridis. Subsequent information put the gathering at over 12,000 men, more than half of them Afridis.

At about 9 A.M., Major-General Yeatman-Biggs, arriving at the head of the main body, ordered Brig.-General Kempster to clear the Dargai ridge. The rest of the troops and baggage were meanwhile halted, as the enemy's fire commanded the line of advance. The infantry detailed for the attack were ordered to advance by the route taken by Brig.-General Westmacott's Brigade on the 18th, and moved off at 9-30 A.M., the 1-2nd Gurkhas and 1-3rd Gurkha scouts in 1st Line, Dorsets support, and Derbyshires in reserve. The Gordons and Maxim detachment were ordered to support the attack by long-range fire at about 1,100 yards, from the Mama Khan ridge; whilst Nos. 1, 5 and 8 Mountain Batteries, massed at Madhu Gurhi on the northern slope of the Chagru Kotal (range 1,800 yards), and No. 9 Mountain Battery at Samana Sukh (range 3,300 yards), afforded the artillery preparation. At 10 A.M., the artillery opened an accurate and well-sustained fire, which enabled the troops to form up behind cover about 500 yards from the cliffs, with the exposed neck, B to A, in front of them. At 11-45 A.M., the Gurkha scouts, led by Lieutenant Tillard, and a portion of the 1-2nd Gurkhas, led by Lieutenant-Colonel Travers, dashed out from under cover and made for the nearest broken ground 100 yards away towards the cliffs.

The enemy had evidently been waiting for this moment, and instantly poured an extremely rapid and accurate fire upon the exposed space. Undaunted by the heavy casualties sustained by the first party, a second rush was made by the Gurkhas, led by Major Judge, who was shot through the head, neck, and chest just before reaching cover. A third rush was led by Captain Robinson, who reached cover with a wound in his ankle. Seeing that all available cover to the west was fully occupied, Captain Robinson now returned to point out a more sheltered line of advance on the east, and was mortally wounded in so doing.

When the Gurkhas attempted to advance beyond the point they had now reached, they came under a heavy flanking fire from the cliffs to the west, in addition to the fire from the front, and further advance was completely checked. Some attempts were made by small parties to rush forward; but the fire was annihilating. Up to this the Gurkhas had lost three officers and over fifty men; the Dorsets, accordingly, at about 2-15 P.M., advanced in support. Captain Arnold of that regiment, followed by a small party from his company, attempted to rush across the fire-swept zone, but fell dangerously wounded, almost every man with him being also hit. Lieutenant Hewitt then tried to lead a few Dorsets across: with the exception of their leader, who got across with a graze, all the party was accounted for by the Afridis. Small parties of Dorsets and Derbyshires continued to try to rush across the ridge, but the proportion of casualties was very high, between forty and fifty of the Dorsets and a dozen or so of the Derbys being hit in these attempts.

Meanwhile small groups of the enemy, from the Khanki valley, had crept round and opened fire on the troops on our right on the Samana Sukh, but were driven off by the 36th Sikhs under Lieut.-Colonel Haughton, who had reinforced that flank from the Samana.

At about 2-20 P.M., Major-General Yeatman-Biggs received a heliogram from Lieut.-Colonel Piercy, commanding the Dorsets, that further advance was impossible without reinforcements. Brig.-General Kempster was then directed to order up the Gordons and 3rd Sikhs to the scene of action, a wing of the 21st Madras Pioneers taking the place of the Gordons at Mama Khan, and the Jhind Infantry becoming escort to the guns at the *kotal*. Arrangements were made with the artillery to open a rapid concentrated fire, on a given signal, to be maintained for three minutes; at the end of which the Gordons would assault the position.

Storming of the Dargai heights.

At 2-45 P.M., on the conclusion of this artillery preparation, Lieut.-Colonel Mathias, commanding the Gordons, communicated the General's order to his men, and gave the word to attack. Headed by Lieut.-Colonel Mathias, the pipers playing, the leading party of the Gordons dashed across the exposed space, followed by the rest of the regiment, by the 3rd Sikhs, and by all the other troops in the position, the whole swarming up the steep slope without a pause. The enemy did not await the final assault, but fled in all directions towards the Khanki valley, followed by long range valleys from the troops. Their losses would have been heavier but for the skilful construction of the *sangars*, which were in some cases provided with head-cover of stones and beams of wood.

For his gallant leading and splendid example on this occasion, Lieut.-Colonel Mathias was recommended for the Victoria Cross, the same distinction being conferred upon Lance-Corporal Milne, who headed the pipers, upon Piper Findlater, for continuing to play when shot through the feet and unable to stand, and upon Private Lawson—all of the Gordons. Lieutenant Pennell, Derbyshire Regiment, and Private Vickery were also awarded the Victoria Cross.

The British casualties on this occasion amounted to 4 officers and 34 men killed, 14 officers and 147 men wounded. Major-General Yeatman-Biggs published a complimentary order the following morning, in which he made special allusion to the conduct of the Gordons; and Her Majesty the Queen was graciously pleased to send the following telegram, which was published in Force Orders :—

Balmoral, 22nd October 1897.

Please express my congratulations to all ranks, British and Native troops, on their gallant conduct in actions 18th and 20th. Deeply deplore loss of precious lives among officers and men of my army. Pray report condition of wounded, and assure them of my true sympathy.

No further advance towards Kharappa being possible that evening, the following dispositions were made for the night. The Dargai heights were held by the Dorsets, Derbys, and 3rd Sikhs, the ridge by the Gordons, the Samana Sukh by the 21st Madras Pioneers. The rest of the troops bivouacked on or near the Chagru Kotal; except the Northamptons, 36th Sikhs, and No. 9 Mountain Battery, who all returned to the Samana forts.

Advanced Guard.
15th Sikhs.
No. 8 Mountain Battery.
Main Body.
No. 5 Mountain Battery.
Gordon Highlanders.
Jhind Infantry.

The night of the 20th–21st having passed without any event of note, the advance was resumed on the 21st; Brig.-General Westmacott, with the marginally named troops, moving off at 9-30 A.M. The Dargai heights were held by the Derbys and 3rd Sikhs; and no opposition was met with until the Khanki river was reached, when a few shots were fired. Camp was pitched on the left bank of the river, in a position of considerable natural strength.

No. 9 Mountain Battery.
Northampton Regt.
36th Sikhs.
No. 3 Company, Bombay Sappers and Miners.

During the afternoon Sir William Lockhart, with the troops as per margin, joined at Kharappa, marching *viâ* Fort Cavagnari and the Talai spur. The track was so bad that the last of the baggage of this column did not reach camp until midday on the 23rd. Very little of the baggage of Brig.-General Kempster's force arrived on the night of the 21st; its security being provided for by parking at the village of Taikhana, in the Chagru valley, all transport which had not passed that point by 6 P.M. No attack was made on the troops or transport in the Chagru valley, either on this occasion or subsequently, though a good deal of firing into Kharappa camp took place this night,—an attempt to rush the west side of the camp being repelled without casualties on our side.

No forward move was made from Kharappa until the 28th, the intervening time being occupied by road-making, strengthening camps on the line of communications, completing the concentration of troops and supplies, and daily foraging operations up and down the Khanki river. On the 22nd a reconnaissance towards the Sampagha found that pass held by about 1,000 men with four standards. On the 24th Brig.-General R. Hart, V.C., assumed command of the 1st Brigade, 1st Division, in place of Brig.-General I. Hamilton, who had broken his leg. On the 25th a foraging party, as shown in the margin, under Lieut.-Colonel Yule (Devons), which had gone 3½ miles up the Khanki valley, was attacked by large numbers of the enemy when retiring; and, although reinforced, they were followed up closely, and by 4-30 P.M. the enemy were firing into camp, causing many casualties amongst troops and transport animals. Captain F. F. Badcock, D.S.O., 1-5th Gurkhas, was dangerously, and Lieutenant G. D. Crocker, Royal Munster Fusiliers, slightly wounded, both from this sniping. In addition to these officers, our total losses on this date were one man killed and thirty-six wounded, thirteen of these casualties having occurred during the retirement of the foraging party. In consequence of the losses caused by this sniping, picquets, in strong *sangars*, were placed on all the neighbouring heights the next morning, with excellent results.

No. 1 Mountain Battery.
½ Battalion Devonshire Regt.
¼ Battalion Derby. Regt.
⅜ Battalion 2-1st Gurkhas.

On the 28th, the force, which in round numbers now amounted to 17,600 fighting men, an almost equal number of followers, and 24,000 animals, marched to Ghandaki. Moving out at 5 A.M. the Northamptons and 36th Sikhs, under Lieut.-Colonel Chaytor, seized the heights north of Khangarbur, which commanded the line of advance. The rest of the troops marched in two columns, the 1st Division starting at 7 A.M., and the 2nd Division an hour later. In the afternoon, whilst the troops and transport were concentrating at Ghandaki camp, a reconnaissance by Brig.-General Hart, V.C., and his brigade was pushed to the foot of the Sampagha pass. Large numbers of the enemy were seen holding the pass and adjoining spurs; and during the subsequent retirement they inflicted several casualties upon the British force, Lieut.-Colonel Sage, 2-1st Gurkhas, being among the wounded. They also made several determined attacks on the picquet during the night.

The following morning, the 1st Brigade, with the whole of the Artillery, left camp at 5 A.M., the Devons moving to the right against the village of Nazeno and adjoining spurs, the Derbys and artillery against an isolated hill at the foot of the pass, and the 2-1st Gurkhas against the Kandi-Mishti villages on the left. When daylight broke, the enemy appeared to be in greater force on the west of the pass than on the pass itself; they had already made up their minds that we would attempt to turn their position by an attack on that flank, and the move of the 2-1st Gurkhas against the Kandi-Mishti villages confirmed them in the belief that our assault was coming there. As a matter of fact, there was no intention on our part to attack the flanks of the pass, the heights on both sides being precipitous.

Capture of the Sampagha pass.

At 7-30 A.M. the concentrated batteries of the 1st Division, under Lieut.-Colonel Duthy, came into action on the isolated hill at the foot of the pass against the enemy's advanced *sangars* on a round knoll half-way up to the *kotal*, range 1,850. The other three batteries pushed on with the main body and, occupying this knoll, which had now been evacuated by the enemy, they continued to shell the summit of the pass until the advance of the infantry began to mask their fire. The summit of the pass was now seized by the Queen's Regiment, but the enemy still held obstinately to their *sangars* on some ridges to the north-east and north-west, from whence they kept up a heavy cross fire on the *kotal* path. The 5th and 9th Mountain Batteries were accordingly ordered up to the summit, and, under cover of their fire, these remaining *sangars* were gallantly stormed by the infantry,—the Queen's and the 3rd Sikhs on the right, and the King's Own Scottish Borderers and

36th Sikhs on the left,—and by half past eleven all opposition had ceased.

Our total casualties amounted to one officer (Captain F. R. McC. DeButts, Commanding No. 5 Mountain Battery) killed, one (Major Hanford Flood, Queen's) wounded; one man killed and twenty-nine wounded.

After the capture of the pass, a short halt was made to rest the troops; the advance was then resumed, the 3rd Brigade leading, with the 15th Sikhs as advanced guard. Four companies Yorkshire Regiment and five companies 3rd Sikhs occupied the heights on either side of the top of the pass, whilst the 1st Brigade and 28th Bombay Pioneers, under Brig.-General Hart, remained at the south foot until all the baggage had crossed. Meanwhile the rest of the troops pushed on to the bivouac in the Mastura valley, about two miles north of the *kotal*. Very little transport was got over that night, the ascent to the pass being excessively steep and difficult; the force therefore halted during the following day (30th) to allow the baggage to close up. Sir William Lockhart, with the 3rd Brigade, reconnoitred the Arhanga pass, about five miles distant, which was found to be only lightly held by the enemy. A considerable amount of forage was obtained in the Mastura valley, although some of the houses had been burned by the inhabitants before evacuating them. As this part of the country had never been visited by any force, nor by any individual European, it was all carefully mapped and surveyed as the troops advanced.

On the 31st, the force moved against the Arhanga pass. At 6 A.M. the 4th Brigade (Brig.-General Westmacott), strength as shown in the margin, left camp for the frontal attack. The village of Unai, situated on a small round hill at the foot of the pass, which had been selected as a position for the artillery, was captured by the King's Own Scottish Borderers after slight opposition, and the artillery of the 2nd Division immediately opened fire from it upon the enemy's main position at the summit of the pass: range 1,350 yards. Although the flanks of the position were not so inaccessible as in the case of the Sampagha pass, the position was nevertheless a very strong one; the heights on either side completely commanded the approaches, and the *kotal* path

Gurkha scouts.
K. O. S. Borderers.
1-3rd Gurkhas.
Northampton Regiment.
36th Sikhs.
1. Coy. S. and M.

was reported by Sir William Lockhart as the steepest and worst yet encountered. Whilst the 4th Brigade, under cover of the artillery fire (which was shortly reinforced by the three batteries of the 1st Division), moved directly against the front of the position, the 2nd Brigade marched up a ravine to the east of the pass to attack the enemy's left, and the 3rd Brigade on the west threatened their right. Very little opposition was offered, and before 10 A.M. the whole position was in our hands. Our losses in this engagement were Captain C. T. A. Searle, 36th Sikhs, and one man, 3rd Sikhs wounded, and one driver, No. 8 Mountain Battery, killed.

The hills on the far side, commanding the pass, having been secured and picqueted, the advance to Maidan was resumed, camp being reached by the advanced guard about 3 P.M., without opposition. Every effort was made to hurry forward the transport during daylight, and strong escorts accompanied the baggage; but in spite of this, an attack was made on the column at about 9 P.M., during which three drivers were killed and two wounded, and two boxes of Martini-Henry ammunition were lost. On the following night the enemy again made a daring and successful attack on a convoy, capturing thirteen boxes of Lee-Metford ammunition and a treasure chest of "The Queen's," and inflicting a loss of three men killed and three wounded on the small escort. After this, no baggage was allowed out of Mastura camp after 3 P.M.

K. O. S. Borderers.
1-3rd Gurkhas.
No. 8 Mountain Battery.

From Camp Maidan, on the morning after the capture of the Arhanga pass, the marginally named force marched at 10 A.M., under Lieut.-Colonel H. G. Dixon, C.B., King's Own Scottish Borderers, to Bagh, about three miles west of camp; this being the political centre of Tirah, and the meeting place of the Afridi *jirgas*. The mosque, being a sacred edifice, was not touched by our troops, but the small grove of trees surrounding it was destroyed. In the afternoon, a large body of the enemy having been seen moving down from the Saran Sar hill, north-east of camp, to obtain supplies from their deserted houses, a force was sent out to oppose them. In the slight skirmish which ensued, Lieutenant E. G. Caffin, Yorkshire Regiment, was severely wounded.

On the 2nd November, a telegram was received from Her Majesty the Queen, containing congratulations on the capture of the Sampagha pass, and enquiries for the wounded.

Upon our arrival in Maidan, the Political Officers with the force had sent out in all directions to summon the tribes to send in their *jirgas*, informing them that it was only by accepting the terms imposed by Government that they could hope to escape further ruin and destruction of property. During the first week of November, negotiations were opened with most of the Afridi clans, though it was some time longer before they submitted.

Submission of the Orakzais.

Little or no trouble had, however, been given by the Orakzais during our advance, subsequent to the actions at Dargai; and it was evident that they had no more fight in them. On the 12th November they accepted our terms of peace; by the 20th, they had paid up the whole fine imposed on them both in rifles and money; and except that it was still considered advisable to watch them, they did not further affect the course of the campaign. Of the Afridi clans, the Zakha Khel were irreconcilably hostile, and succeeded in forcing the Aka Khel, a weaker and far less numerous tribe, to adopt the same attitude.

Meanwhile, skirmishes and attacks on convoys were of almost daily occurrence. Fighting was, however, confined to the immediate vicinity of the main column, the whole of the long line of communications (now 100 miles, from Kushalgarh to Maidan) being unmolested, with the exception of the section north of Mastura. Foraging parties were almost invariably fired on, and camp was constantly sniped at night, Captain E. Y. Watson of the Commissariat, and Lieutenant C. L. Gifford of the Northamptons being killed, and Captain E. L. Sullivan, 36th Sikhs, severely wounded by this desultory fire, besides drivers and transport animals.

The first serious action, after Maidan was entered, occurred

Saran Sar reconnaissance.

on the 9th, during the reconnaissance of Saran Sar, a pass into the Bara valley, at a height of about 2,500 feet above camp Maidan. To make a thorough survey of this pass, which was about five miles from camp, and to punish the Zakha Khels by destroying their villages, a reconnaissance in force by the troops shown in the margin, under Brig.-General Westmacott, moved out about 7 A.M. The crest of the *kotal* was reached about 11-30 A.M. after a sharp skirmish, in which the enemy suffered severely and the Northamptons and Dorsets lost two or three men wounded. The retirement began about two o'clock in the afternoon, the defences of a large number of Khusrogi Zakha Khel villages having been first destroyed and their stores of grain and forage carried off.

No. 8 Mountain Battery.
No. 5 " "
1st Bn. Dorset Regiment.
1st Bn. Northampton Regt.
15th Sikhs.
36th "
No. 4 Company, Madras Sappers and Miners.

At the time the retirement began, not an Afridi was visible, nor did any appear until the Northamptons, who were covering the retirement, had left the crest of the hill and were well on their way down. But the enemy, following their usual practice, had meantime been creeping up unseen from every side; and a close and heavy fire was suddenly opened, one of the Northamptons being killed and some half a dozen wounded. As the ground was too steep and difficult for stretchers, each man who was hit required four men to carry him down the craggy cliffs: a process which was not only exceedingly slow and tiring, but also exposed the carriers to further casualties. At 4 P.M. the 36th Sikhs, under Lieut.-Colonel Haughton, were ordered some way back to assist the Northamptons, now encumbered with ten or twelve wounded, and to take over the rear-guard duties. At the foot of the hill the 36th overtook the Northamptons, and again halted to cover their further retirement. The ground from here back to camp is much intersected by deep *nalas.* The Northamptons had originally advanced along the bed of the main *nala*; and, considering it the quickest and easiest way to transport their wounded back to camp, they decided to retire by the same route. When Lieut.-Colonel Haughton heard that they were fairly started, assuming that they were in line and touch with the Dorsets and the two companies 15th Sikhs, who were protecting the right flank, he withdrew across the open country, keeping clear of the main ravine, his regiment having been detailed to protect the left flank of the retirement. In the gathering darkness the different companies of the Northamptons now lost touch of one another and of the flanking troops; the leading companies being close to camp, whilst the rearmost had been able to move only so slowly that they were nearly two miles behind. Unfortunately, these rearmost troops did not themselves throw out the strong flanking parties on the edges of the *nala* which would alone have made them secure at the bottom of it, now that touch had been lost with other corps. The Afridis, who had all the time been following them up and watching for a chance to attack them at a disadvantage, now poured in a heavy fire from the edges of the *nala*, the Northamptons losing heavily without being in a position to retaliate. Hearing the firing, a detached company of the 36th, under Lieutenant Van Someren, went back to their assistance, and, attacking the flank and rear of the enemy, succeeded in extricating them; a wing, 2-4th Gurkhas, and a company, 3rd Sikhs, were also sent back from camp to assist in bringing them in. The total casualties for the day were two British officers, seventeen British and one native rank and file killed, three British and one native officer, thirty-five British and seven native rank and file wounded. The behaviour of the Northamptons, in defending their wounded when themselves in a desperate position and assailed by overwhelming force, was warmly praised by the Brig.-General Commanding.

On the 11th, Sir William Lockhart made another reconnaissance in force to the top of Saran Sar, to complete the survey and inflict further punishment on the Zakha Khels. The enemy again attempted to press the retirement, but were driven off with heavy loss; our casualties being 2nd-Lieutenant W. D. Wright, Royal West Surrey Regiment, wounded, and one man killed. Large quantities of grain and fodder were brought in on this day.

On the 13th, a small foraging party of five weak companies of various regiments, under Major Smith-Dorrien (Derbys), from Mastura camp, was attacked about 2½ miles west of camp, by several hundred Orakzais. In the ensuing action and retirement our losses were two officers and four men wounded. The Orakzais, by their *jirgas*, had accepted the terms of peace on the preceding day; but it was explained that news of this had not yet reached the tribesmen scattered on the hills, and that they were unaware that their representatives had concluded peace.

As already stated, the Zakha Khels, themselves numbering 4,500 fighting men, well armed, and irreconcilably hostile, had coerced the Aka Khels, numbering not above 1,800 fighting men, comparatively poorly armed, and quite willing to accept terms, into following their lead. To overawe the Aka Khels and detach them, if possible, from their alliance with the Zakha Khels, and also to punish the Zya-ud-Din Zakha Khels by destroying their village defences near the Tseri Kandao, a force as per margin, under Brig.-General Kempster, left Camp Maidan on the 13th, and encamped in an open defensible site near the Sher Khel villages in the Waran valley. They met with no opposition on their way from camp, communication with which was maintained by the 36th Sikhs, detached to hold the Tseri Kandao. On the previous day, the Aka Khel *jirga* had come in, saying that their clan desired peace, and, that they had no objection to the proposed reconnaissance of their valley. Opposition from them was consequently not anticipated; nor, until the 15th, was any offered, though large numbers of armed Aka Khels on the neighbouring hills watched the proceedings of our troops, which included the destruction of the house of the notorious Aka Khel *mulla*, Saiyid Akbar. During the evening of the 14th, however, numbers of Zakha Khels came over into the Waran valley, to incite the Aka Khels to fight. It was their intention, in any case, to fire into our camp from the Aka Khel villages, in the hope that we should lay the blame on the Aka Khels, and begin a wholesale destruction of the villages in the valley, thus goading the Aka Khels into opposition. This course of action on the part of the Zakha Khels had fortunately been foreseen by the Political Officer, and consequently, when, during the reconnaissance and subsequent retirement to camp on the 15th, we were attacked and followed up, the blame was apportioned in the right quarter, and the Aka Khel villages were not damaged.

No. 8 Mountain Battery.
No. 5 " "
1st Bn. Gordon Highlanders.
1st " Dorset Regiment.
1-2nd Gurkhas.
15th Sikhs.
36th "
No. 4 Company, Madras Sappers and Miners.
No. 4 Company, Bombay Sappers and Miners.

The action of the Zakha Khels on this occasion may be compared to the similar course taken by the Boer irreconcilables after Lord Roberts' proclamation in the summer of 1900, when those who had determined to continue the fighting visited the districts of those who had surrendered, and forced them back on commando.

On the 16th, General Kempster with his force marched for Camp Maidan. The transport reached camp unmolested during the afternoon; and the rear-guard, for the first mile and a half of the homeward journey, was also not attacked. The arrangements for the withdrawal of the rear-guard were as follows: the 36th Sikhs were to take up a position on the Maidan side of the pass, whilst the 15th Sikhs, who now relieved the above regiment on the summit, held the heights on either side of the Tseri Kandao until the rear-guard (consisting of the 1-2nd Gurkhas), had passed through them. The 15th Sikhs were then to take up the duties of rear-guard, passing in their turn through the 36th Sikhs, who would form the rear-guard for the rest of the march to Camp Maidan.

As the 1-2nd Gurkhas approached the pass, they were vigorously attacked in rear by ever-increasing numbers; and by the time they had reached the *kotal* they had lost Lieutenant Wylie and three men killed, and four wounded. After they had passed through the 15th Sikhs, the latter regiment was disposed as follows:—two companies on the south of the pass; two on the north of it; and, further north again, two more companies, under Captain N. A. Lewarne and Lieutenant C. A. Vivian, who held the south edge of the pinewoods which covered the summits of the long spur running down from the Saran Sar. Lieut.-Colonel Abbott himself, with one company, held the actual *kotal*; while the remaining company, under Captain G. F. Rowcroft, was on a commanding spot 800 yards in rear, to cover the general retirement. These companies were all very weak from twenty to thirty men each.

The retirement was proceeding satisfactorily until it came to Captain Lewarne's turn. The moment he began to retire, a hot fire was opened on him from the wood above; several men were immediately hit, and a large number of the enemy charged down upon him sword in hand. Waiting until they were close up, he opened a steady and rapid fire upon them; and the other company under Lieutenant Vivian coming promptly to his assistance, the enemy were driven back with very heavy loss. It was, however, impossible, without incurring further heavy casualties, to remove the wounded from the *sangar*.

Meanwhile an attack in force had also been made upon Lieut.-Colonel Abbott in the main *sangar* below, where he had been joined by several others of his companies. As he also had numerous wounded in his *sangar*, whom he could not get away without assistance, he signalled to Brig.-General Kempster to this effect; and the 36th Sikhs and two companies of Dorsets were immediately ordered back to his assistance. A detached company of the 36th, under Captain Custance, had, however, arrived already, and Lieut.-Colonel Haughton, 36th Sikhs, in anticipation of the order, was moving up with all he had been able to collect of his regiment. On his arrival he found both Colonel Abbott and Captain Custance wounded. He was shortly joined by Major Des Vœux, who brought up the remainder of the 36th and a weak company of the Dorsets, under Captain Hammond; the other company of the Dorsets having been posted in a house close by, which commanded the road, to cover the eventual retirement of the rear-guard. This company was under command of Lieutenant Crooke, Suffolk Regiment, with Lieutenant Hales, East Yorkshire Regiment, both attached to the Dorsets.

Under the heavy fire poured in by these reinforcements, the rear-guard was withdrawn to the foot of the hill without further casualties. The dead and wounded were then sent on to Camp Maidan, and the remainder of the troops halted to collect stragglers, it being now quite dark. The enemy now tried to cut off the whole of this little force, numbering only some 200 men; and they opened a withering fire from some ruined houses on the line of retreat, and also from every coign of vantage in the vicinity. Lieut.-Colonel Haughton instantly fixed bayonets and charged the houses, killing several of the enemy, and putting the remainder to flight; but the ruins, which had only been set on fire that morning, were too hot to occupy. In this charge the troops had become divided into two parties, part remaining under Haughton, the remainder under Des Vœux. Two companies under Major Des Vœux succeeded in finding a house which had cooled down enough to admit of it being occupied; but before the party under Lieut.-Colonel Haughton could throw up any defences, Captain Lewarne had been killed, and Lieutenant Munn (Adjutant, 36th Sikhs) and half a dozen men wounded. After a trying night Colonel Haughton rejoined Major Des Vœux at dawn, and began to retire on camp, the enemy contenting themselves with firing a few parting shots. The little party was met by a relieving force and reached Camp Maidan in safety.

Meanwhile disaster had overtaken the Dorsets left behind under Lieutenants Crooke and Hales. What actually happened is never likely to be known; but it would appear that, hearing men on the road below, and believing them in the darkness to be Sikhs, they abandoned the house, and were instantly overwhelmed by the Afridis. Lieutenants Crooke and Hales and nine men were killed, and many others wounded; the remainder made their way back to camp, Lieutenant Hale's half company being brought in intact by the senior Sergeant.

Brig.-General Kempster, considering that to send any more troops back to the assistance of the Sikhs would only result in further confusion and loss in such intricate and difficult country, had arrived with the rest of his brigade in Camp Maidan about 8-30 P.M.

Our total casualties in this affair were four British officers and twenty-five men killed, three British and three Native officers and thirty-eight men wounded. The enemy's losses were estimated at 300. Zakha Khels, Aka Khels, Kamrai, and Sipah were reported to have taken part in the action. The Waran valley was subsequently visited on the 10th December and the Aka Khels severely punished.

Meanwhile, in Maidan, an attempt to establish more peaceable relations, by purchasing fodder from the Malikdin and Kambar Khels, had proved a failure, and was taken advantage of by the enemy to make treacherous attacks. Firing into camp also continued.

On the 17th, Sir William Lockhart addressed some of the troops in camp, giving useful hints for the conduct of the particular kind of mountain warfare in which the force was engaged. The substance of the remarks were published for general information and guidance on the 18th, and will be found in Appendix D.

On the 18th November, preparations were made to move the camp to Bagh. This step was considered advisable both from the political effect to be obtained from occupying the religious centre of the country, and from the strategical advantage of being nearer to certain other districts, the Rajgul valley in particular, as yet unvisited by our troops.

On this day the only troops to move out were the 2nd Brigade and Divisional troops of the 1st Division under Major-General Symons. Under the impression that the movement was only for reconnaissance or foraging, and that their own opportunity would come later in the day, when the force began to retire, the tribesmen offered no serious opposition to the advance. But when they became aware, from our preparations, that it was intended to place a permanent camp at Bagh, they mustered in force and opened fire from every side, occupying towers and fortified houses, of which there were a large number in the vicinity. Some stubborn fighting ensued, our total losses for the day amounting to five killed, and a native officer and eighteen men wounded. The camp and picquets were heavily fired into throughout the night, and some transport animals were hit; the men, well entrenched, had no casualties.

During the 19th, 20th and 21st, all the stores at Camp Maidan, and the whole of the troops, were moved to the new camp.

On the 20th the 15th Sikhs, now reduced by casualties and sickness to a fraction of its original strength, was sent back to Shinawari, being considered too weak for duty. Their departure from the force was marked by a special complimentary order by Sir William Lockhart, in which he expressed in the warmest terms his appreciation of their gallantry and endurance.

The same day terms were made known to such of the *jirgas* as had come in, and proclamations setting forth the terms were also despatched to the clans who had not yet sent in their *jirgas*.

The terms were :—

A fine of Rs. 50,000.
Surrender of 800 breech-loading rifles.
Restoration of all Government Rifles and property.
Forfeiture of all allowances.

The tribes were given a week in which to comply with these terms. On their requesting that no more of their towers and fortifications should be destroyed pending their reply, they were informed that such measures would depend upon their own conduct, but that if firing into camp and upon foraging parties ceased, their wishes would be met.

To punish the recalcitrant Kuki Khels, and to explore the approaches to the Bara valley with a view to future operations in that direction, Sir William Lockhart, with the troops named in the margin, under Brig.-General Westmacott, started on the 22nd for Dwa Toi, on a three-days' reconnaissance. The route lay along the difficult and dangerous Shaloba defile, about six miles in length.

King's Own Scottish Borderers.
1st Bn. Yorkshire Regiment.
36th Sikhs.
1-2nd Gurkhas.
1-3rd „
28th Bombay Pioneers.
No. 3 Company, Bombay Sappers and Miners.
No. 4 Company, Madras Sappers and Miners.
No. 5 Mountain Battery.
Gurkha scouts.

Before dawn the two flanking battalions moved off to crown the heights on either side of the defile, and remained there throughout the three days: the Yorkshires on the right bank, the 1-2nd Gurkhas on the left.

The main body marched at 9 A.M., but, owing to the difficulties of the route, they did not reach Dwa Toi until 4 P.M. On arriving at that place the 28th Pioneers, who formed the advanced guard, came under fire from the hills to the north, which they immediately stormed. Hardly any baggage got through to Dwa Toi that night, the bulk of it, on the approach of darkness, being parked and surrounded by strong picquets by Lieut.-Colonel Haughton, commanding the rear-guard.

The following day was spent in destroying Kuki Khel fortifications, and in improving the pathway, and, on the 24th, at daybreak, the force started its return journey to Bagh. At that early hour the enemy were not yet astir, and all the picquets round camp were withdrawn without loss. The rear-guard was, however, soon hotly engaged. Some casualties having occurred amongst the 36th Sikhs, who again furnished it, a few hospital mules were sent back to bring on the less severely wounded. A number of the enemy made an attempt to carry off these mules, but were surprised and cornered in the river-bed by the 36th Sikhs, and suffered heavily. The flanking battalions on the heights, especially the 1-2nd Gurkhas, were also attacked during retirement, but neither they nor the Yorkshires had any casualties.

Our losses during these three days were :—one British officer and four men killed; two British officers and twenty-eight wounded.

On arrival in camp Sir William Lockhart found a letter awaiting him from the Kambar Khels and Malikdin Khels, objecting to the severity of the terms, especially in the matter of rifles, in which our demand, they stated, exceeded their powers of compliance. They also requested that the value of all damage done to them might be deducted from their fine, and concluded with a warning that there would be trouble if we attempted to make a road down the Bara valley. They stated, however, that they would give hostages pending compliance. In reply, they were told that no abatement would be made, and no hostages received, until large instalments of money and rifles were paid.

Although the attitude of the bulk of the Orakzais, as already stated, was by now satisfactory, there were certain sections of that tribe who had not yet complied with the terms—namely, the Massuzais, Alisherzais, and Mamuzais, the most westerly of the tribe. With these may be included the Chamkannis who, though not belonging to the Orakzais, are their near neighbours. The reply of the Chamkannis to the Political Officers, on a fine being demanded, was a flat and defiant refusal. As, from Bagh, he was now within reach of their country, Sir William Lockhart determined to bring all these sections to terms; and accordingly, on the 26th November, he marched against them. An account of this expedition will be found in the chapter dealing with the Orakzai tribe.

Before leaving Bagh on this expedition, Sir William Lockhart had determined upon evacuating Tirah and proceeding to the winter settlements of the Afridis nearer Peshawar. He issued a proclamation to the Afridis, warning them that he was only going lower down on account of the cold in Tirah, and that he had by no means done with them, and advising them, for their own sake, to submit without further delay.

On the 6th December, Sir William Lockhart returned to Bagh from his expedition against the Orakzais and Chamkannis. During his absence preparations had been going forward for the evacuation of Tirah, all heavy baggage having been sent back to Shinawari *en route* to Bara *viâ* Kushalgarh, to meet the troops of the 1st and 2nd Divisions, who were to march there *viâ* the Mastura and Bara valleys respectively. The Commissariat-Transport Department had also been busy replacing all weakly and unfit animals, as far as possible, by fresh ones from the base or line of communications.

Advanced Guard.

1-3rd Gurkhas and scouts.
28th Bombay Pioneers.
Two companies, Sappers and Miners.
Half battalion, 2nd Punjab Infantry.

Main Body.

K. O. S. Borderers (6 companies).
No. 8 Mountain Battery.
No. 5 Mountain Battery (4 guns).
Royal Scots Fusiliers.
Dorset Regiment.
Hospitals.
Baggage.

Rear-guard.

Two companies, K. O. S. B.
No. 5 Mountain Battery (2 guns).
36th Sikhs.

On the 7th and 8th December the Maidan valley was evacuated. Brig.-General Gaselee's brigade marched *viâ* the Arhanga pass to join Major-General Symons, detailed to march down through the Mastura valley; Brig.-General Westmacott's force, as detailed in the margin, proceeded through the Shaloba defile to Dwa Toi. The fortunes of the 2nd Division, which, on its march down the Bara valley, experienced some of the heaviest rear-guard fighting ever encountered in an Indian frontier campaign, will be followed first.

Advanced Guard.

1-2nd Gurkhas.
Two guns, No 9 Mountain Battery.
One company, Northamptons.

Main Body.

Three companies, Northamptons.
Transport.
Hospitals.
Two guns, No. 9 Mountain Battery.
Four companies, Northamptons.

Rear-guard.

Two guns, No. 9 Mountain Battery.
Half battalion, Gordons.
Two companies, 2nd Punjab Infantry.

The leading troops of Brig.-General Westmacott's force (henceforward known as the 4th Brigade) reached Dwa Toi, unopposed, before noon on the 7th. On the following day the force remained halted, whilst the 3rd Brigade—which had been occupied on the 7th in the further destruction of Kambar Khel and Malikdin Khel fortifications—marched from Bagh to join them. The latter brigade, in the marginally named order, made slow progress. The road was so slippery from drizzling rain and traffic, that they were blocked until 1 P.M. by the rear-guard, 4th Brigade, which had not reached camp the previous day, and had to halt for the night in the defile. The march was resumed next morning, and all were in by dusk on the 9th, though a good many animals had succumbed on the road. On this day (the 9th) Sir William Lockhart, with 1,000 rifles and a battery, all from the 4th Brigade, reconnoitred five miles up the Rajgul valley from Dwa Toi, foraging and destroying fortifications.

On the following day the 4th Brigade marched for camp Sandana, and the 3rd Brigade for Karana, three miles in rear of the first named place. The whole of the strongly fortified villages passed *en route* were destroyed after slight opposition. On the morning of the 11th the whole force started for Sher Khel, ten miles from Sandana. Rain had been falling steadily all night and continued throughout the day, thus adding to the difficulties of the 3rd Brigade in leaving their camp at Karana. The pathways leading out of camp were very steep, and were soon deep in mud; and though all units had started working on ramps at daybreak, the heavy rain made the going so slippery that the animals could only be brought down with the greatest difficulty, thereby causing a delay and dislocation of plans which had the most serious consequences. The orders originally issued were for the 3rd Brigade to start at 7-30 A.M., the 4th Brigade at 8-15 A.M., so as to enable the 3rd Brigade to close up on the troops in front; the baggage and hospitals were intended to be massed between the two brigades. As it was, the rear-guard of the 3rd Brigade was not out of camp till about eleven o'clock, nor, owing to a thick mist, could the news of this delay be signalled on to General Westmacott.

The Afridi's instincts, seldom at fault in guerilla warfare, made him immediately aware that all these factors would tell in his favour, and that he would now have a chance to meet us on more even terms than hitherto; and the 3rd Brigade had no sooner begun to leave camp than the enemy, favoured by the mist and by abundant cover, directed a heavy and telling fire upon the crowded and helpless transport animals and followers, who became more and more unmanageable as the march continued. Meanwhile, seeing no signs of the rear brigade and being uncertain of its movements, General Westmacott drew in all his picquets as soon as his rear-guard had passed on, instead of leaving them out to safeguard the 3rd Brigade as had usually been done. Owing to the enemy concentrating his main efforts against the latter brigade, the one in front had no very serious opposition to encounter, and reached Sher Khel in safety about 4 P.M.

In the meantime the 3rd Brigade had had to re-picquet the heights on either flank, and the consequent delay kept bringing the transport to a halt under a fire from which they would have been comparatively secure had they been passing along a road the flanks of which were already picqueted. Terrified of remaining with the bulk of the transport, which, herded together at these checks, afforded an excellent target, many of the mule drivers and *doolie*-bearers now attempted to make their own way to camp, and their animals were soon in difficulties in the boggy fields and rough rocky *nalas* running down to the river-bed. As they approached camp—which did not happen till long after nightfall—things became worse, and all semblance of control was at an end. Some of the drivers broached kegs of rum and became helplessly drunk, while others, deserting their animals, and seized by an ungovernable panic, made straight for the Sher Khel camp fires.

On the arrival of the leading brigade in camp, a message had been sent back to Brig.-General Kempster informing him that he could use his discretion as to whether he would come on to Sher Khel that night, or halt in any suitable position a couple of miles in rear. Not knowing how far behind the rearmost portion of his force was, and hoping to save his troops the heavy extra picquet duties of a separate camp, he decided to push on, in the belief that camp was quite near. Most of his force got safely in; but the rear portion of the rear-guard, consisting of a company Gordons, a company Dorsets, a half company 2nd Punjab Infantry and two or three companies 1-2nd Gurkhas, the whole under the command of Major Downman, Gordon Highlanders, were left behind, about three miles from Sher Khel. On arrival at this point, Major Downman had found a large number of transport animals hopelessly entangled in the rice-fields, and mostly abandoned by their drivers. As it would have been impossible for his tired men to reach camp that night without abandoning this transport, Major Downman established himself for the night in some houses a little further on, which were rushed by the Gordons.

On the morning of the 12th Brig.-General Kempster, with two battalions and a battery, went back and brought in Major Downman's rear-guard, who had been fired on all night by the enemy. The rest of the force remained halted for the day. The total losses on the 11th and 12th (combatants only) were seven killed and thirty-five wounded.

On the 13th, the march was resumed, 3rd Brigade leading, 4th Brigade rear-guard. On this occasion the picquets thrown out by the leading brigade were left out until the rear-guard of the whole division had passed. One battalion picqueted both flanks as long as there were sufficient men, after which another battalion continued the work; battalions being thus kept together. Special guards were also detailed to prevent *doolie*-bearers leaving the *doolies*, and for the transport. The distance from Sher Khel to Shinkamar, the point fixed for the next camp, was supposed to be seven miles, but it turned out to be a great deal more, and neither brigade succeeded in reaching it that day, although the leading troops met with hardly any opposition.

For the first three miles, as far as Gallai Khel, the track lay in the river-bed, thence passing north to the Lakarai Kotal and down to Sawaikot. The enemy, looking on this march as almost their last chance of inflicting heavy losses before the force, joined the Peshawar column, as arranged, at Barkai, attacked with great boldness as soon as the rear-guard of the 4th Brigade left camp; and the fighting was incessant throughout the day. In spite of the careful dispositions made for the covering of the retirement with infantry and artillery fire, our casualties soon became very numerous, and the fighting line was still further weakened through nearly all wounded men having to be carried by the troops, the *doolie*-bearers being utterly incapable of any work.

At Gallai Khel, as the transport was blocked by the narrowness of the steep track leading out of the river-bed, the rear brigade had to make a long halt. At this point the enemy swarmed across the river, in their eagerness to get at the baggage; but, coming under a cross-fire of artillery, infantry, and machine guns, they were repulsed with great slaughter. Nothing daunted, they pressed the retirement as vigorously as ever; and when, on the approach of darkness, Brig.-General Westmacott decided to halt for the night on a ridge running across the line of march—for he saw that it was hopeless to attempt to join the leading brigade, which had camped a couple of miles ahead of him, about half a mile west of the Lakarai Kotal—they made a most determined rush. They were, however, again driven off with loss; and though they fired into the camp during the night, little harm was done. Our casualties during the day's fighting were severe, over seventy men having been hit.

There was no water-supply at either of the camps on this night, and the troops had to depend on what they carried with them.

This was unfortunately very little, for so terrified had the mule drivers been during the day's fighting that they had neglected to fill their *pakhals*. In addition, owing to the panic amongst the drivers, much of the 4th Brigade transport had been inextricably mixed up with the leading brigade's, and had pressed forward into the latter's camp, with the result that the 4th Brigade had a very trying night after their hard day's work.

The Peshawar Column, under Brig.-General Hammond, had already arrived, practically unopposed, at Sawaikot. Hearing by heliograph that the 2nd Division were encumbered with many wounded and sick, the transport of whom was causing great difficulty, General Hammond at once came out with 8 *doolies*, and 300 *doolie*-bearers for the leading brigade, after which he returned to Sawaikot.

On the 14th at daybreak the 3rd Brigade marched for Sawaikot (seven miles) and encamped at Mamanai, unopposed, sending back their water-mules from Barkai to the 4th Brigade. The latter were again attacked from daybreak, but the enemy did not follow up in any numbers beyond the Lakarai Kotal; and after meeting the advanced picquets of the Peshawar column about four miles from Sawaikot, the brigade was unmolested during the rest of its march to Mamanai.

On the 17th the 3rd Brigade marched for Bara, where it remained until the 12th February 1898. The 4th Brigade halted at Mamanai.

We will now turn to the operation of the 1st Division.

On the 7th December (the same day on which Brig.-General Westmacott, with the 4th Brigade, marched for Dwa Toi) a portion of the 2nd Brigade marched from Camp Bagh to join Major-General Symons' force for the march down the Mastura valley. On the same day Brig.-General Hart marched out of Camp Mastura with the 2-1st Gurkhas, Derbys, Maler Kotla Sappers, a mountain battery, and hospitals, to Thagasam, about three miles down the Mastura river, where he was joined by the troops from Camp Kharappa and the Sampagha pass, which positions were now evacuated. The remainder of Major-General Symons' force meanwhile stayed at Camp Mastura.

Operations of the 1st Division.

On the 8th, the whole force, under the orders of Major-General Symons, (with the exception of the troops still with Brig.-General Gaselee, as per margin, at Bagh), marched to Camp Haider Khel, about ten miles. They advanced in two columns; the larger, under Brig.-General Hart, proceeding *viâ* the Mishti valley and Sangra pass, north of the river; the smaller column, accompanied by Major-General Symons, keeping to the river-bed. The weather was bad, but no opposition was met with.

1st Bn. Yorkshire Regiment.
3rd Sikhs.
2-4th Gurkhas.
No. 2 Mountain Battery.

On the same day the evacuation of Maidan was completed by Brig.-General Kempster's brigade marching north to join the 4th Brigade at Dwa Toi (as already narrated) whilst Brig.-General Gaselee marched south to join Major-General Symons' force in the Mastura valley. Brig.-General Gaselee's force was thus one march behind the rest of the 1st Division.

The camp at Haider Khel was directly south of the Aka Khel country, and within a few miles of it; and as it was now beyond question that the Aka Khels had thrown in their lot with the Zakha Khels and other irreconcilables, and were actively hostile to us, it was decided to take the opportunity of inflicting signal punishment on them, whilst they were within such easy reach of our troops. Two passes lead from Haider Khel to their settlements in the Waran valley; of these the Chora was known to be very difficult, but the other, the Khokanni, was reconnoitred and found practicable for mules, though rough.

On the 9th, all the baggage, and all troops not detailed for the punitive operations, marched to Hissar, at the junction of the Waran and Mastura valleys. The remainder of the force, as per margin, under Brig.-General R. C. Hart, V.C., C.B., taking with them one day's cooked rations, field stretchers, and half 1st reserve ammunition, moved off for the Waran valley at 8 A.M., the crest of the Khokanni pass having been seized by the 2-1st Gurkhas an hour earlier. No opposition was at first encountered, the Aka Khels being taken by surprise. The destruction of fortified houses began at once, and

Four companies, 2-1st Gurkhas.
Six companies, Derbys.
Three companies, Devons.
Three companies, Nabha Regt.
Six companies, 21st Madras Pioneers.
Six companies, 30th Punjab Infantry.
No. 1 Mountain Battery.
Kohat Mountain Battery.
No. 1 Company, Bengal Sappers and Miners.

about 150 were destroyed, including those of the Sanzal Khel, Sultan Khel, and Miri Khel sections: the Madda Khel and Basi Khel were too far off to be reached in time. The house of Mulla Saiyid Akbar, now partially repaired, was also again destroyed; and the total loss inflicted was estimated at Rs. 50,000.

When the force began to retire down the valley towards Hissar, numbers of Aka Khels and Zakha Khels, having meanwhile collected, pressed on the rear-guard, but were kept at a distance by artillery and infantry fire. Our total casualties were one killed, and four wounded.

No further opposition was encountered by the division during its march. On the 13th, the 1st brigade reached Mamanai, and the whole division concentrated at Ilamgudar on the 17th. It is worthy of note that out of 8,533 transport animals, not a mule nor a load was lost, with the exception of three mules killed by falling over a precipice.

Operation in the Khaibar and Bazar valleys.

As the 1st Division and Peshawar column had seen little of the recent fighting, whereas the 2nd Division had had some very severe engagements, it was decided that the latter should remain to guard the Bara valley line, whilst the two former forces advanced into the Bazar and Khaibar valleys. The objects to be accomplished by the troops detailed for the forthcoming operations were:—

(1) The reopening of the road through the Khaibar pass.
(2) Destruction of Zakha Khel defences in the Khaibar.
(3) Re-occupation and repair of Khaibar forts.
(4) Restoration of Landi Kotal water-supply.
(5) A punitive visit to the Zakha Khel and Malikdin settlements in the Bazar valley.

The first four of these measures were allotted to the Peshawar column, the last to the 1st Division.

In accordance with this programme, the 4th Brigade remained at Mamanai and the 3rd Brigade moved to Fort Bara, as already narrated, while the Peshawar Column and the 1st Division concentrated at Jamrud, where they remained until the 23rd. Major-General Yeatman-Biggs having been placed on the sick list,[1] Sir Power Palmer assumed command of the 2nd Division, in addition to the command of the lines of communication.

On the 18th December the Officer Commanding the Peshawar Column made a reconnaissance to Fort Maude, which was found deserted; Ali Musjid also appeared to be empty, and no trace of the enemy was seen. On the 23rd Ali Musjid was occupied by the Peshawar Column without opposition, and on the following day the 1st Division concentrated at Lala China, where large quantities of fuel and fodder were found. The composition of the Division, whose strength amounted to about 7,500 fighting men, 5,600 followers, and 9,000 animals, was as before, except that the Maler Kotla Sappers and Nabha Infantry were now struck off the strength, and a wing of the Royal Scots Fusiliers was left at Jamrud.

On the 25th, the Division entered the Bazar valley in two columns, the 1st Brigade (Major-General Symons), marching *viâ* the Alachi pass to Karamna, and the 2nd Brigade (Brig - General Gaselee), accompanied by Sir William Lockhart, to Chora, *viâ* the Chora pass. No opposition was encountered by the 2nd Brigade; and the 1st Brigade only had one small encounter with a handful of the enemy at Karamna. The Alachi Kandao itself was difficult, and the transport was seriously delayed, a portion of it having to pass the night at the eastern foot of the *kotal*: but it was not attacked during the night.

Next day (26th) the 1st Brigade moved from Karamna to Barg, a distance of only $2\frac{1}{2}$ miles, but an exceedingly difficult march. The track lay through a narrow gorge strewn with huge boulders, and the heights on each side were very steep, and hard to picquet. All the troops were not in until 9-15 P.M., as the Sappers and Pioneers had to break a path practically the whole way.

The march of the 1st Brigade was unopposed throughout, but the 2nd Brigade, which on this day marched from Chora to China, had its rear-guard followed up persistently, losing two men killed and four wounded. The route lay along the bed of the Chora stream until it issues from the hills at Gabagai, when it left the river-bed and ascended by a rather steep path on to the Bazar valley plateau.

[1] He died on 4th January 1898.

On the 27th, after destroying the houses and towers which composed China, the 2nd Brigade returned to Chora. Their retirement was followed up on both flanks, but on arrival opposite Barar Kats, the heights above which were held by picquets furnished by the Sussex Regiment from Barg, the enemy transferred all their attention to the latter, following them up boldly and persistently from the moment they began to retire upon their own brigade camp at Barg.

On the 28th, the 2nd Brigade marched back from Chora to the Khaibar, unopposed, after destroying the defences. The 1st Brigade, making a very early start, marched from Barg to Karamna, where they hoped to surprise a party of the enemy reported to be passing the night there; but the village was found deserted. The rear-guard was, as usual, closely followed up, losing one killed and seven wounded.

On the 29th, the 2nd Brigade marched unmolested to Jamrud and the 1st Brigade from Karamna to Lala China. The withdrawal of the picquets of the latter was rendered exceptionally difficult by a dense mist on the hilltops; but the retirement was successfully carried out by Major Smith-Dorrien (Derbys) with a total loss of fifteen wounded, the enemy having likewise numerous casualties.

Whilst these operations were in progress in the Bazar valley, the Peshawar Column moved up the Khaibar to fulfil the part allotted to it in the general scheme. After assisting the 1st Brigade in its advance into the Bazar valley on the 25th December, by covering its flank, it returned to Ali Musjid, and, the following morning, marched to Landi Kotal, leaving a wing of Oxfords, the 45th Sikhs, and two guns, at the former place. The villages between Ali Musjid and Landi Kotal were found deserted, and Landi Kotal itself was a ruin, everything of value having been either carried away or destroyed. The water-pipes leading from the wells into the fort had been badly damaged, but the large open tanks outside the fortified *serai*, which had been originally constructed at a cost of nearly three lakhs of rupees, were undamaged. As the Shinwaris, who live in the vicinity of Landi Kotal, had already submitted and paid up the fine imposed on them, Brig.-General Hammond utilized their services in picqueting the hills in the vicinity to keep off the raiders: this duty was faithfully performed by them, Zakha Khel raiding parties being attacked unhesitatingly, although they knew that this would lead to reprisals. They also brought back quantities of beams, roofing, etc., which had been carried off when Landi Kotal was looted.

As the Zakha Khels had been given up to the 28th to pay the portion of the fine due from them, and as it was wished to give them every chance of compliance before renewing coercive measures, Brig.-General Hammond, on the day after his arrival, moved out to reconnoitre the Bori pass from its north end, Sir William Lockhart having intended to withdraw the 1st Brigade by that route if found to be practicable for transport. The track was comparatively easy at first, though commanded by precipitous hills. At 1½ miles, however, it was found that the cliffs suddenly close in, and the track goes through a deep chasm in the rock, in many places only three feet wide. The sides of this passage are sheer walls of rock, 100 feet to 150 feet high. The passage is about 100 yards long, and was paved with slippery rocks in which rough steps had been worn. No laden mule could possibly get through the defile until the track had been considerably improved, and it was estimated that to make the place passable would take at least a week's work. On the way to this defile the headmen of the Saddu Khel villages passed *en route* sent a message to say that if their villages were approached, they had 400 or 500 men in them who would fight. Seeing the hills crowned on either side, however, they thought better of it; and no resistance was offered to the column in either advance or retirement, though a couple of messengers despatched to the Bazar valley were intercepted. On the 29th, the Zakha Khels having shown no signs of submission, punitive measures were resumed against them, forage being carried off, and towers demolished. On the following day the same process was continued; but in the retirement the enemy showed more boldness than he had hitherto displayed in the Khaibar, and our casualties were considerable. A wing of the Oxfords, who had been on picquet duty round the Sultan Khel villages during these operations, began to retire late in the afternoon, and were soon heavily engaged with the enemy. Assisted by a neighbouring picquet of the 9th Gurkhas and a section of the Inniskillings, they took refuge in the neighbouring Sultan Khel villages; and, news of the fighting having reached Brig.-General Hammond, he immediately came out with reinforcements, and the whole party were withdrawn without further casualties. Their losses had been three killed and fourteen wounded, the latter number including three officers.

An unfortunate incident occurred on this day. Sir Henry Havelock-Allan, V.C., K.C.B., M.P., had been permitted to accompany Sir William Lockhart, as his guest, in the Bazar valley. As he was returning to Jamrud, he left his escort near Ali Musjid and entered a ravine alone, and was picked off by the enemy and killed. His body was subsequently found and conveyed to Peshawar.

Punitive measures, accompanied by desultory and indecisive fighting, continued as before; and, as the submission of the tribe appeared to be as far off as ever, preparations were now undertaken for a spring campaign. Up to date, out of a grand total of 1,097 rifles demanded from the Afridis, 89 only had been given up, towards which the Zakha Khel contributed 5; the money fines were equally in arrears, only Rs. 3,830 having altogether been paid. Meanwhile the two Zakha Khel *maliks*, Khwas Khan and Wali Muhammad Khan, from their secure asylum in Afghan territory, used every endeavour to persuade their countrymen to continue their resistance. Malikdin Khel, Kambar Khel, Sipah, and Kamrai all sent in representative *jirgas*, asking for peace, but professing inability to comply with our terms; but the Zakha Khel remained as defiant as before, and, in spite of the loss inflicted on them, the Afridis as a whole showed no disposition to give in.

On the 1st January 1898, whilst engaged in punitive measures against the Zakha Khels of the Tsera Nala, near the Nikki Khel villages at the Khaibar entrance of the Bori pass, the Peshawar column lost Lieutenant Hammond and one man mortally, and two others severely, wounded. On the 3rd, Major Hickman, 34th Pioneers, was shot dead whilst on convoy duty in the pass; on the 16th, in a skirmish near Kata Kushtia in the pass, a sepoy was killed; on the 25th, near the Bori pass, a party of about fifty of the enemy was surprised and suffered heavy loss. No further fighting of any importance occurred in the Khaibar up to the end of the campaign, and the only remaining engagement of note which took place in 1898 was that at Shinkamar, on the 29th January, now to be related.

After their return from the Bara valley, the 3rd and 4th Brigades had remained encamped at Bara and Mamanai, respectively. Nothing of importance had happened on this line since their arrival, with the exception of raiding and wire-cutting, principally by the Zakha Khels. On two occasions this guerilla warfare had resulted in loss to our troops: on the 16th January, when a day picquet from Mamanai, retiring for the evening, was fired into, and again on the 18th, when a party of four men on their way to picquet a hill near Mamanai in the early morning were ambuscaded by a party of Afridis who had occupied the hill before them. In both cases the troops engaged were the 28th Bombay Pioneers.

Action at Shinkamar.

As reports had been received that the Afridis in large numbers had come down to graze their cattle on the Kajurai plain, Sir William Lockhart, with the object of bringing them to terms by the capture of their flocks and herds, directed that combined operations by the 1st and 2nd Divisions should take place on the 29th January, in order to surround the Kajurai plain and block every egress from it to the north and west. The whole movement was to be under the command of Sir Power Palmer. The plan of operations was that a column from the 1st Brigade, marching from Ali Musjid, should occupy the line of the Chora river from Chora to Tangi, while a second column of the 2nd Brigade, marching from Jamrud, should watch the Sam Ghakhe pass, west of the Besai Hill, and picquet the heights to the west, until they established touch with the troops of the 1st Brigade. The 4th Brigade from Mamanai were to send out a column to block the Shinkamar pass; and into the net formed by these troops the 3rd Brigade from Bara was to sweep the Afridi flocks and herds, marching so as to reach Karawal by 8 A.M., then moving towards the Shinkamar pass, and finally south-east to Gandao Post, where they were to bivouac for the night. The other columns were to co-operate by driving the enemy, if sighted, on to the Bara column, and to act as circumstances might indicate. The greatest secrecy was observed with regard to the proposed movements.

The columns, with the exception of the one from Mamanai, met with little or no opposition, either in advance or retirement. Their orders had directed them to cease all operations by 1 P.M., and as no trace of the enemy was found by the Ali Musjid, Jamrud, or Bara columns by that hour, they returned to the posts from which they had come. Sir Power Palmer, from the position he had taken on the Besai hill, had hoped to be able to establish signalling communication with all his columns; but the state of the weather prevented heliographic communication with any but the one from Bara.

2 guns, No. 5 M. B., R. A.
427 rifles, Yorkshire L. I.
200 rifles, 36th Sikhs.

Meanwhile the column from Mamanai, strength as shown in the margin, had fought one of the hardest actions of the campaign. Starting at 5 A.M., under Lieut.-Colonel T. J. Seppings, Yorkshire Light Infantry, they reached the top of the Shinkamar Kotal by 8 A.M. without serious opposition, the heights on the west of the pass being picqueted by the 36th Sikhs and those on the east by two companies Yorkshire Light Infantry; a company 1-3rd Gurkhas from camp also taking up position further to the west, between the Lakarai Kotal and the line of retreat of the column, to cover its eventual retirement. At about 10-30 A.M., Lieut.-Colonel Haughton, commanding the advanced guard, pushed forward to some caves, about a mile down the north side of the pass, picqueting the heights on either side as he advanced. He then sent back an orderly to bring on some more of the main body of the 36th Sikhs. By some unfortunate misunderstanding, the orderly took this message to the picquet on the heights commanding the pass from the west, with the result that the Native officer at once withdrew his picquet, and, following over the pass, joined the advanced guard, which was then just beginning to retire. The position vacated by the picquet was soon occupied by the enemy, who were able to bring a heavy fire from it on all the troops in the pass.

Lieut.-Colonel Seppings then ordered a company of the Yorkshire Light Infantry, under Lieutenant Dowdall, to re-occupy the position; but the enemy were now on it in force, and the fire brought to bear on the attacking company was so heavy that they were unable to advance more than 150 yards from the *kotal*, to a small knoll about a quarter of the way up the hill: here Lieutenant Dowdall was killed. A second company of the Yorkshire Light Infantry, under Lieutenant Walker, was sent up to their assistance, but could get no further, Lieutenant Walker being killed; and heavy casualties having now occurred in both companies, their withdrawal with their wounded had become a very difficult matter. Meanwhile Lieut.-Colonel Haughton had arrived on the scene. Sending the remainder of his regiment to take up a position to cover his advance, he himself, with his Adjutant (Lieutenant Turing) and one weak company, went forward to help to extricate the two companies of the Yorkshires, upon whom the enemy were now rushing in on every side.

The Sikhs fixed bayonets, and attempted to repel the onslaught by a counter-charge, but Colonel Haughton—now fighting with the rifle of one of his own men, who had just been killed beside him—was here shot through the head and killed, Lieutenant Turing being killed almost immediately afterwards. Under cover of a reinforcement of the Yorkshire Light Infantry, under Major Earle, which now arrived, the two companies were at last withdrawn to the heights on the east of the defile, along which a general retirement began. Owing to the steep and exposed nature of the country it was found impossible to carry away the bodies of the killed, but their rifles and ammunition were almost all saved. At the mouth of the pass the column was met by a force under Brig.-General Westmacott, who had come out as soon as news of heavy fighting reached him; and, covered by the latter, the column withdrew to camp, the enemy not now pressing the retirement in force. The total casualties in this affair were five officers and twenty-eight men killed, three officers and thirty-four men wounded. A man of the Yorkshire Light Infantry, dangerously wounded in this engagement, was restored by the Afridis, but died from the effects of his wounds and subsequent exposure.

No. 8 M. B., R. A.
400 rifles, K. O. S. Bs.
400 rifles, Gor. Highlanders.
250 rifles, K. O. Yorkshire L. I.
400 rifles, 3rd Gurkhas.
250 rifles, 1-2nd Gurkhas.
250 rifles, 36th Sikhs.

On the following day, Brig.-General Westmacott called up enough reinforcements from the 3rd Brigade at Bara to enable him to march out from Mamanai with a strong column, and on the 31st, with the force as per margin, he marched at 5 A.M. for Shinkamar, to recover the bodies of the dead; a second column, under Lieut.-Colonel Sturt, demonstrating against the other side of the pass from the Bara direction. The enemy had constructed *sangars* to defend the pass; but, suspicious of the movements and intentions of Lieut.-Colonel Sturt's column, they did not occupy them, but remained in observation until the retirement began, when they followed up the rear-guard. Twenty-two bodies of those killed on the 29th were recovered. Our casualties during the retirement were Surgeon-Lieutenant M. Dick, 2nd-Lieutenant D. S. Browne, and five men wounded.

This was practically the last fight of the campaign.

The Orakzais, and such sections of the Afridis as had submitted, were all feeling the effects of the blockade acutely; and in an interview with Sir William Lockhart on the 14th February they petitioned that more time might be given them to pay up their fines and that the blockade might be raised for each individual clan as it submitted and complied with the terms. On the 22nd February these requests were granted, but were made conditional on the submission and continued good behaviour of the tribes. As a result of this the Sipahs and Kamrai had all submitted by the 26th; the Malikdin Khels completed the payment of their fine by the 20th; further progress towards settlement was made by the Kambar, Kuki, and Aka Khels; and, towards the end of February, the Zakha Khels themselves began to show signs of contemplating submission. The opening of the Khaibar pass for the free passage of all traffic was a further blow to the latter, as they had imagined that it could never be reopened without their co-operation. *Kafilas* under escort began passing up and down the pass, exactly as before, on the 7th March.

On the 13th March Sir William Lockhart again had an interview with the *jirgas*, and informed them that no further grace would be given, and that if all fines were not paid up by the 17th he would recommence operations against them. In accordance with this pronouncement he again appeared at Jamrud on the 17th, with a large number of transport animals from Peshawar. News also reached the tribesmen that Brig.-General Ian Hamilton's brigade had advanced a couple of miles beyond Barkai up the Bara valley; and now, thoroughly alarmed, they begged for further delay. Sir William Lockhart agreed to this only upon condition that the Kuki Khel and Kambar Khel should give hostages, one man for every two rifles, for all rifles still owing on the evening of the 18th: failing compliance, not only would he begin a forward advance on the 19th, but the blockade would be re-imposed upon the four clans who had already submitted. The hostages were duly delivered and sent to Fort Attock, and within ten days, every rifle from these sections having been paid, they were released. The Aka Khel followed this example by handing over hostages for what they still owed on the 29th March, in consequence of which the 3rd Brigade was withdrawn to Sawaikot, two battalions with two guns being left at Barkai.

The Zakha Khels were now the only clan who had not made complete submission. Their green crops in the Khaibar were being daily cut and carried off for forage; pressure was also being brought to bear upon them by all the other clans; and their *maliks,* Khwas Khan and Wali Muhammad, who from Jalalabad were still urging them to hold out, had been replaced by others more amenable. By the 3rd April they too had fully submitted and given hostages for what they still owed. All hostilities were thereupon ordered to cease, and demobilization at once began; the following forces, however, were still retained with their full complement of transport :—

1st Brigade, under Brig.-General Hart, at Bara.

2nd Brigade, under Brig.-General Gaselee, at Jamrud and Ali Musjid.

3rd Brigade (formerly Peshawar Column, afterwards called the "5th Brigade, Tirah Expeditionary Force") under Brig.-General Hammond, at Landi Kotal.

The whole of the above forces were placed under command of Major-General Symons, who was also given supreme political control, Sir William Lockhart proceeding on the 6th April to England.

Although as a tribe the Afridis had fully submitted, there were still certain raiders from the Zakha Khels who continued to give trouble and do any damage they could. The attitude of the Afridis as a whole was, however, friendly, and has continued fairly satisfactory up to the present time. By the end of June the force in the Khaibar was reduced to a single brigade, with head-quarters at Landi Kotal; and being no longer a Major-General's command, it was handed over to Brig.-General C. C. Egerton, C.B., D.S.O., A.D.C., with the same powers as his predecessor. The force was further reduced later on by the withdrawal of the two British battalions, and finally the remaining regular troops were also recalled in 1900, the safeguarding of the pass being handed back to the Khaibar Rifles as before.

The final settlement with the Afridis did not, however, take place for some months after the conclusion of peace. Early in September 1898 the terms regulating our future relations with the tribe received the formal assent of the British Government; and at the end of that month summonses were sent out to the various clans, directing their representatives to attend at Peshawar on the 22nd October. With the exception of the Kambar Khel—who were not properly represented on account of factional feuds—and the Annai section of the Zakha Khel, the gathering of headmen, numbering 850, was thoroughly representative: and on the 24th the terms were announced to them in durbar by Brig.-General Egerton and Mr. Cunningham, Chief Political Officer. The terms were read over twice in Pushtu, and carefully explained clause by clause; the *jirgas* being then told to go away and discuss the matter thoroughly amongst themselves, and to re-assemble on the 27th to give their answer and submit any petitions they might have to make. They were further informed that the terms were final, and that there could be no change in their essential conditions.

The substance of the terms was as follows:—

1st.—The Afridis by their own acts ruptured all agreements, forfeited all allowances, and forced the British Government to take and hold the Khaibar pass, which, as already announced by Sir William Lockhart, will be managed and controlled as the British Government think most desirable.

2nd.—The pass will be kept open for trade. The British Government will build a fort at Landi Kotal, and posts between that and Jamrud; will keep up a good road or roads, and, if they want it, a railway; and will take such measures as they think fit to punish offences and preserve order.

3rd.—The Afridis will have no dealings with any power but the British. They will be left to manage their own affairs in their own country; but, in the Khaibar pass, they are responsible to the British Government that they will co-operate to preserve order and security of life and property on road and railway and within the limits of the pass.

4th.—The British Government will give allowances as formerly to the Khaibar Afridi clans for discharging this duty, and will maintain a militia, recruited from the Afridi and other tribes, and commanded by British officers. The British Government do not undertake always to keep troops at Landi Kotal, but will make arrangements for supporting the militia if circumstances require.

5th.—Arrangements for trade in the Khaibar will be made by the the British Government, and the militia will be used for guarding traders.

6th.—The allowances granted by the British Government will begin to reckon from the date of the adhesion by the tribes to terms settled by the Government of India: but they are subject to withdrawal for misbehaviour in the pass, in British India, or against the friends or allies of Government.

In explanation of the above terms, the *jirgas* were informed that even if Government should withdraw its regular troops from the pass, it reserved to itself the right to re-occupy all or any part of it, at any time, with regulars. They were further told that the amount of the allowances withheld since the beginning of the disturbances would be taken as discharging some part of their liability for damage to Government buildings, towards which would also be credited the amount realised by the sale of the confiscated property of the Zakha Khel *maliks,* Khwas Khan and Wali Muhammad; and that, in spite of the fact that the forfeited allowances did not nearly cover the amount due for damage done, Government was prepared to grant tribal allowances with effect from three months previous to the date named in the final clause.

On the 27th the *jirgas* again assembled; and as they now numbered 1,200 men, they had selected certain representatives to act for them. They accepted all the terms unconditionally and gave their assent in writing. As the Kambar Khel and Annai section of the Zakha Khel were still absent, the final ratification of the terms did not take place until the 4th November, on which date these clans also agreed unconditionally. The arrears of subsidies were paid on the following day, and the *jirgas* then dispersed to their homes.

The Indian Medal, 1895, was in 1898 awarded to all troops which took part in the above operations in Tirah.

In December 1899, the regular garrison was withdrawn from the Khaibar, and the pass has, since then, been guarded by the Khaibar Rifles, who have been reorganized, and are now a well trained and disciplined regiment, 1,700 strong, with six British officers.

Since 1898 it has not been found necessary to take military action against the tribe. They have, however, especially the Zakha Khels, committed numerous raids and outrages in British territory. These have been, as a rule, punished by forfeiture of allowances, and, in some cases, the clans themselves have been induced to take action against the raiders.

The Afridis have constantly endeavoured to secure the countenance and protection of the Amir of Afghanistan, but without much success. At the present time they are much better armed then they were in 1897, and the number of modern rifles in their possession increases more rapidly every year.

On the whole their attitude towards Government is much the same as it was prior to 1897, while the improvement in their armament has made them more formidable as foes than they were at that time.

APPENDIX A.

Translation of a letter from Kazi Mira Khan, and other Adam Khels composing the Afridi Jirga at Kabul, to Mulla Saiyid Akbar, Aka Khel, dated the 28th Jamadi-ul-awal 1315 = *25th October* 1897.

After compliments.—Let it be known to you that having been appointed by you and other Musalman brethren as a *jirga* to attend on His Highness the Amir, we arrived here and held an interview with His Highness, who advised us not to fight with the British Government, and this was and has been his advice ever since. We said we accepted this advice, but that our wishes ought to be met by the British Government. We were ordered to record them in detail, when His Highness said he would, after consideration, submit them to the British Government, and see what reply they would give. We put down our wishes in detail and presented them to His Highness, who submitted them to the British Government, but no reply has yet been received. We shall see what reply comes.

There is a British Agent at Kabul who has on his establishment many Hindustani Musalmans. One of these became our acquaintance. This man is a good Musalman and a well-wisher of his co-religionists. He has given us a piece of good and correct news which is to the following effect:—

"You, Muhammadans, must take care lest you be deceived by the British, who are at present in distressed circumstances. For instance, Aden, a seaport which was in possession of the British, has been taken from them by the Sultan. The Suez Canal, through which the British forces could easily reach India in 20 days, has also been taken possession of by the Sultan, and has now been granted on lease to Russia. The British forces now require six months to reach India. The friendly alliance between the British and the Germans has also been disturbed on account of some disagreement about trade, which must result in the two nations rising in arms against each other. The Sultan, the Germans, the Russians, and the French are all in arms against the British at all seaports, and fighting is going on in Egypt too against them. In short, the British are disheartened now-a-days. The Viceroy and the Generals who are to advance against you have received distinct orders from London that the operations in the Khaibar and Tirah must be brought to an end in two weeks' time, as the troops are required in Egypt and at other seaports. In the case of the Mohmands and people of Gandab who had killed ten thousand British troops and had inflicted a heavy loss of rifles and property on them, the British in their great dismay, concluded a settlement with them for 24 rifles only, whereas thousands of rifles and lakhs of rupees should have been demanded. This peace with the Mohmands is by way of deceit, and when the British get rid of their other difficulties, they will turn back, and demand from the Mohmands the remaining rifles and compensation for their losses. They will say that, as the Mohmands have become British subjects by surrendering 24 rifles, they must make good the remaining loss too. The British are always giving out that their troops will enter Khaibar and Tirah on such and such dates, but they do not march on those dates, and remain where they are. This is deceitful on the part of the English, who wish to mislead Musalmans by a payment of Rs. 5, and seek for an opportunity to make an attack by surprise. I have thus informed you of the deeds and perplexities of the English."

We, the *jirga* people, consider it necessary to inform you of this, so that you may be aware of the distress, confusion, and deceitfulness of the British and may communicate the information to all the Musalmans of the *lashkar*, in order that they may be on their guard against being cheated by the British in any way. You should also send us daily news for our information, and see that no attacks are made on you by surprise. Also appoint a few clever men as messengers to bring us daily news and letters from you and *vice versâ*. Send us by the bearer all news of that side, and in future, too, send us fresh news daily by other messengers, as it is important that we should know about each other.

APPENDIX B.

Detail of Troops employed in the Tirah Expedition, 1897-98.

A.—THE MAIN COLUMN.

I.—FIRST DIVISION.

(i) First Brigade.

2nd Battalion, the Derbyshire Regiment.
1st „ „ Devonshire „
2nd „ 1st Gurkha Rifles.
30th Punjab Infantry.

(ii) Second Brigade.

2nd Battalion, the Yorkshire Regiment.
1st „ Royal West Surrey Regiment.
2nd „ 4th Gurkha Rifles.
3rd Sikh Infantry (Punjab Frontier Force).

II.—SECOND DIVISION.

(i) First Brigade.

1st Battalion, the Gordon Highlanders.
1st „ „ Dorsetshire Regiment.
1st „ 2nd Gurkha Rifles.
15th Sikhs.

(ii) Second Brigade.

2nd Battalion, the King's Own Scottish Borderers.
1st „ „ Northamptonshire Regiment.
1st „ 3rd Gurkhas.
36th Sikhs.

DIVISIONAL TROOPS.

No. 8 Mountain Battery, Royal Artillery.
„ 9 „ „ „ „
„ 5 „ „ „ „ (Bombay).
Machine Gun Detachment, 16th Lancers.
2 squadrons, 18th Bengal Lancers.
21st Madras Infantry (Pioneers).
No. 4 Company, Madras Sappers and Miners.
1 Printing Section, „ „ „ „

Jhind Imperial Service Infantry.

Sirmur „ „ Sappers.

B.—LINE OF COMMUNICATIONS.

22nd Punjab Infantry.

2nd Battalion, 2nd Gurkha Rifles.

39th Gharwal Rifles.

2nd Punjab Infantry (Punjab Frontier Force).

3rd Bengal Cavalry.

The Jeypore Imperial Service Transport Corps.

The Gwalior „ „ „ „

C.—THE PESHAWAR COLUMN.

2nd Battalion, Royal Inniskilling Fusiliers.

2nd „ Oxfordshire Light Infantry.

9th Gurkha Rifles.

45th Sikhs.

57th Field Battery, Royal Artillery.

No. 3 Mountain Battery, Royal Artillery.

9th Bengal Lancers.

No. 5 Company, Bengal Sappers and Miners.

D.—THE KURRAM MOVEABLE COLUMN.

12th Bengal Infantry.

The Nabha Imperial Service Infantry.

4 guns, 3rd Field Battery, Royal Artillery.

6th Bengal Cavalry.

1 Regiment, Central India Horse.

E.—THE RAWAL PINDI RESERVE BRIGADE.

2nd Battalion, King's Own Yorkshire Light Infantry.

1st „ Duke of Cornwall's Light Infantry.

27th Bombay Light Infantry (Baluchis).

2nd Infantry, Hyderabad Contingent.

Jodhpur Imperial Service Lancers.

In addition to the above, the following troops were ordered to concentrate at Peshawar on the conclusion of the Mohmand operations, to be employed as might be required in support of the operations in Tirah:—

13th Bengal Lancers.

37th Dogras.

4 Companies, 1st Battalion, Somersetshire Light Infantry.

No. 1 Mountain Battery, Royal Artillery.

28th Bombay Pioneers.

No. 3 Company, Bombay Sappers and Miners.

APPENDIX C.

COMMANDS AND STAFF OF THE TIRAH EXPEDITIONARY FORCE.

ARMY STAFF.

Lieutenant-General Commanding	General Sir W. S. A. Lockhart, K.C.B., K.C.S.I.
Aides-de-Camp	Lieutenant F. A. Maxwell, 18th B. L.
	2nd-Lieut. J. H. A. Annesley, 18th Hussars.
D. A. G. and Chief of the Staff	Brigadier-General W. G. Nicholson, C.B.
A. A. G.	Lieutenant-Colonel E. G. Barrow, 7th B. I.
A. Q. M. G.	Major G. H. W. O'Sullivan, R.E.
D. A. A. G.	Captain J. A. L. Haldane.
D. A. Q. M. G. ..	Captain C. O. Swanston, 18th B. L.
A. Q. M. G.	Colonel G. H. More-Molyneux.
D. A. Q. M. G. (I) ..	Captain E. W. Maconchy, D.S.O., 4th Sikhs.
Field Intelligence Officer ..	Captain F. F. Badcock, D.S.O.
Principal Medical Officer ..	Surgeon-Colonel G. Thompson, C.B., I.M.S.
C. R. A.	Brigadier-General C. H. Spragge, R.A.
Ordnance Officer	Colonel C. H. Scott, R.A.
C. R. E.	Brevet Colonel J. E. Broadbent, R.E.
Head Quarter Commandant ..	Captain R. E. Grimston, 6th B. L.
Commissariat Transport Officer	Captain G. W. Palin, Assistant Commissary General.
Inspecting Veterinary Officer ..	Veterinary Lieutenant-Colonel B. L. Glover.
Chief Survey Officer	Brevet Colonel Sir T. H. Holdich, K.C.I.E., C.B., R.E.

MAIN COLUMN.

FIRST DIVISION.

Commanding	Brigadier-General W. P. Symons, C.B.
Aide-de-Camp	Captain A. G. Dallas, 16th Lancers.
A. A. G.	Lieutenant-Colonel C. W. Muir, C.I.E., 17th Bengal Cavalry.
A. Q. M. G.	Major E. A. G. Gosset, 2nd Derbys.

D. A. Q. M. G. (I) .. .. Captain A Nicholls, 2nd Punjab Infantry.
Field Intelligence Officer .. Lieut. C. E. Macquoid, 1st Lancers H.C.
Principal Medical Officer .. Surgeon-Colonel E. Townsend, A.M.S.
C. R. A. .. .. Lieutenant-Colonel A. E. Duthy, R.A.
Divisional Ordnance Officer Captain A. R. Braid, R.A.
Commanding Royal Engineer .. Lieutenant-Colonel H. H. Hart, R.E.
Divisional Commissariat Officer Major W. R. Yielding, C.I.E., D.S.O.
Divisional Transport Officer .. Captain F. C. W. Rideout.

FIRST BRIGADE OF FIRST DIVISION.

Commanding .. .. Colonel I. M. S. Hamilton, C.B., D.S.O. (with the temporary rank of Brigadier-General; invalided and replaced by Brigadier-General R. C. Hart, C.B., V.C.).
Orderly Officer .. .. Captain C. O. Swanston, 18th B. L.
D. A. Q. M. G. .. .. Captain A. G. H. Kemball, 1-5th Gurkhas.
D. A. A. G. .. .. Captain H. R. B. Donne, 1st Norfolk Regt.
Brigade Commissariat Officer .. Captain A. Mullaly.
Brigade Transport Officer .. Captain E. de V. Wintle, 15th B. L.

SECOND BRIGADE OF FIRST DIVISION.

Commanding .. .. Brigadier-General A. Gaselee, C.B., A.D.C.
Orderly Officer .. .. Lieutenant A. N. D. Fagan, 1st Lancers.
D. A. A. G. .. .. Major W. Aldworth, D.S.O., 1st Bedfords.
D. A. Q. M. G. .. .. Major A. A. Barrett, 2–5th Gurkhas.
Brigade Commissariat Officer .. Lieutenant C. S. D. Leslie.
Brigade Transport Officer .. Lieutenant H. Macandrew, 5th B. C.

SECOND DIVISION.

Commanding .. .. Major-General A. G. Yeatman-Biggs, C.B., (invalided and replaced by Lieutenant-General Sir A. P. Palmer, K.C.B.).
Aide-de-Camp .. .. Captain E. St. A. Wake, 10th B. L.
A. A. G. .. .. Lieutenant-Colonel R. K. Ridgeway, V.C.
A. Q. M. G. .. .. Major C. P. Triscott, D.S.O., R.A.
D. A. Q. M. G. (I) .. .. Major R. C. A. Bewicke-Copley, King's Royal Rifle Corps.
Field Intelligence Officer .. Captain H. F. Walters, 24th Bo. I.
P. M. O. .. .. Surgeon-Colonel G. McB. Davis, D.S.O.
C. R. A. .. .. Lieutenant-Colonel R. Purdy, R.A.
C. R. E. .. .. Lieutenant-Colonel C. B. Wilkieson, R.E.
Divisional Commissariat Officer Lieutenant-Colonel B. L. P. Reilly,
Divisional Transport Officer .. Major H. L. Hutchins.

FIRST BRIGADE OF SECOND DIVISION.

Commanding (with temporary rank of Brigadier-General).	Colonel F. J. Kempster, D.S.O., A.D.C. (replaced by Colonel I. Hamilton, C.B., D.S.O.).
Orderly Officer	Lieut. G. D. Crocker, 2nd Roy. Muns. Fus.
D. A. A. G.	Major H. St. Leger-Wood, 1st Dorsets.
D. A. Q. M. G.	Major H. S. Massy, 19th Bengal Lancers.
Brigade Commissariat Officer ..	Lieutenant D. H. Drake-Brockman.
Brigade Transport Officer ..	Lieut. R. A. N. Tytler, 1st Gordons.

SECOND BRIGADE OF SECOND DIVISION.

Commanding ..	Brigadier-General R. Westmacott, C.B., D.S.O.
Orderly Officer ..	Lieutenant R. C. Wellesley, R.H.A.
D. A. A. G.	Captain W. P. Blood, 1st Roy. Irish Fus.
D. A. Q. M. G.	Captain F. J. M. Edwards, 3rd Bo. C.
Brigade Commissariat Officer ..	Captain E. Y. Watson.
Brigade Transport Officer ..	Captain W. H. Armstrong, 1st East Yorks.

LINE OF COMMUNICATIONS.

General Officer Commanding ..	Lieutenant-General Sir A. P. Palmer, K.C.B.
Aide-de-Camp ..	Lieutenant F. C. Galloway, R.A.
A. A. and A. Q. M. G. ..	Captain (temporary Major) J. W. G. Tulloch, 24th Bombay Infantry.
D. A. A. G. and Q. M. G. ..	Captain I. Phillips, 1-5th Gurkhas.
Principal Medical Officer (with temporary rank of Surgeon Colonel).	Brigade-Surgeon Lieutenant-Colonel W. E. Saunders, A.M.S.
Senior Ordnance Officer ..	Colonel C. H. Scott, R.A.
Section Commandants ..	Captain O. B. S. F. Shore, 18th B. L.
	Captain G. St. L. Steel, 2nd B. L.
	Captain F. de B. Young, 6th B. L.
Commissary General ..	Colonel L. W. Christopher.
Chief Transport Officer ..	Major H. Mansfield, A.C.G.

STAFF AT THE BASE.

Base Commandant ..	Colonel W. J. Vousden, V.C., I.S.C.
D. A. A. and Q. M. G. ..	Major A. J. W. Allen, 1st East Kents.
Commandant, British Troops Depôt	Captain A. F. Bundock, 2nd Lancs. R.
Commandant Native Troops Depôt	Captain S. M. Edwards, D.S.O.
Base Ordnance Officer ..	Captain M. W. S. Pasley, R.A.
Base Commissariat Officer ..	Major R. H. Marrett, A.C.G.

THE PESHAWAR COLUMN.

Commanding ..	.. Brigadier-General A. G. Hammond, C.B., V.C., D.S.O., A.D.C.
Orderly Officer ..	.. Lieutenant H. D. Hammond, R.A.
A. A. and Q. M. G. ..	.. Lieut.-Colonel F. S. Gwatkin, 13th B. L.
D. A. A. and Q. M. G.	.. Major C. T. Becker, 2nd K. O. S. B.
Field Intelligence Officer	.. Captain F. A. Hoghton, 1st Bombay Infantry.
P. M. O.	.. Lieut.-Colonel R. G. Thomsett, A.M.S.
C. R. A.	.. Lieut.-Colonel W. M. M. Smith, R.A.
Brigade Commissariat Officer	.. Lieutenant H. H. Jones, D.A.C.G.
Brigade Transport Officer	.. Lieutenant C. Charlton, R.H.A.

THE KURRAM MOVEABLE COLUMN.

Colonel (with rank of Colonel on the Staff).	Colonel W. Hill, I.S.C.
Orderly Officer	.. Captain R. O. C. Hume, 1st Border Regt.
D. A. A. G.	.. Major E. F. H. McSwiney, D.S.O.
D. A. Q. M. G.	.. Captain C. P. Scudamore, D.S.O.
Principal Medical Officer	.. Lieutenant-Colonel W. R. Murphy, D.S.O.
Brigade Commissariat Officer	.. Captain C. F .T. Murray, A.C.G.
Brigade Transport Officer	.. Captain H. W. C. Colghoun.

THE RAWAL PINDI RESERVE BRIGADE.

Commanding	.. Brigadier-General C. R. Macgregor, D.S.O.
Orderly Officer	.. Lieutenant E. W. C. Ridgeway, 29th P. I.
D. A. A. G.	.. Major Sir R. A. W. Colleton, Bart.
D. A. Q. M. G.	.. Captain H. Hudson, 19th Bengal Lancers.
Brigade Commissariat Officer	.. Lieutenant E. G. Vaughan, D.A.C.G.
Brigade Transport Officer	.. Lieutenant K. E. Nangle, 3rd Infantry H.C.

APPENDIX D.

Memorandum by Sir William Lockhart, for guidance of troops campaigning in Tirah.

Camp Maidan, 18th November.

General Sir W. Lockhart desires the following remarks to be communicated to every corps, battery, and company of Sappers and Miners in the Tirah Expeditionary Force:—

1. It must be remembered that the force is opposed to perhaps the best skirmishers and best natural rifle shots in the world; and that the country they inhabit is probably the most difficult on the face of the globe. The enemy's strength lies in his knowledge of the country, which enables him to watch our movements unperceived by us, and to take advantage of every rise in the ground and every ravine. Our strength lies in our discipline, controlled fire, and mutual support.

Our weakness lies in our ignorance of the ground, and the consequent tendency of small bodies to straggle and get detached. The moral of this is, that careful touch must be maintained; and, should small parties become isolated from any cause, instead of seeking shelter in ravines where they offer themselves as sheep to the slaughter, they must stick to the open as far as possible. It is to be hoped that we may have the opportunity of wiping out all old scores with the enemy before many days have elapsed, and meanwhile there is no occasion for us to be depressed because some of us have been outnumbered and overwhelmed by the enemy.

2. Without laying down any hard and fast rules, the General Officer Commanding wishes the following principles to be borne in mind when retiring in the face of the enemy.

(*a*) The retirement should be conducted by lines, or parties, in succession. The rearmost troops that are holding the crests of ridges, spurs, or commanding positions, must retire through the second line or supporting troops, the latter covering the withdrawal with fire, and holding their position until all the troops in rear have passed through them. If there be a third line, fairly close up, the rearmost troops should pass through this line also, and take up a further covering position behind the third line. This operation should be continued by the successive lines or parties so long as the enemy continues to press on the retiring force.

(*b*) Under no circumstances whatever shou'd any of the troops return to camp without direct orders to that effect from the Officer Commanding the force engaged, until the successful withdrawal of the whole force is assured; for, if the troops in the front, or in advanced positions, have reason to think that they are not supported in rear, and will not be backed up until they have passed through the lines covering their withdrawal, they naturally are apt to lose heart, and heavy loss or disaster may result.

(*c*) Bodies of troops holding a crest, knoll, or spur, must show cunning and activity in retiring. A few men, without exposing themselves, must first slip away and get down the hillside, while the remainder extend, and thus lead the enemy to believe that the original number is still present; then more must retire in the same way, and finally those who are left to the last, who ought to be selected for their activity, must get down the hill as rapidly as possible and in an open formation.

(*d*) In all retirements in front of an enemy like the Afridis, extended formations should be made use of. If possible, the enemy should never be given the chance of firing into collected bodies of our troops.

(*e*) The long range of Artillery fire enables the guns, if properly handled, to keep the enemy in check while the rearmost line is withdrawing through the supporting lines.

CHAPTER III.

THE AFRIDI TRIBE—(continued.)

Adam Khel Afridis.

In Chapter I it was stated that the Afridi tribe was divided into eight clans, and these, with one exception, formed the subject of the first two chapters. It is now proposed to consider the remaining clan, the Adam Khel, which, though a branch of the Afridi tribe, cannot, as already stated, be regarded as a part of it in any other than an ethnological point of view.

The Adam Khel Afridis inhabit the hills between the districts of Peshawar and Kohat, and, with the exception of some of the Kalla Khel, who own the Basi glen in Maidan, and who migrate annually, they are permanent settlers. They are one of the most powerful and most numerous of the Afridi clans, with a great reputation for bravery, and derive much importance from the command they hold over the Kohat pass, through which runs the shortest and best route from Kohat to Peshawar. Though cultivators of land to a considerable extent, their chief employment is in the salt trade. This article they obtain from the Bahadur Khel mines and dispose of, not only to British subjects, but to all the trans-border tribes north-east of Kohat. They have always been hostile to any enhancement of the salt-tax. They also employ themselves in the manufacture of Martini rifles, but this trade is centred in the Kohat pass, where there are seven different workshops.

The late Sir Louis Cavagnari said in one of his reports: "The whole of the Adam Khel Afridis are entirely dependent for existence on their trade with British territory, and a protracted blockade would at all times be sufficient to reduce them to terms."

The Adam Khel Afridis are divided into four branches—(1) Galai, (2) Hasan Khel, (3) Jawaki, and (4) Ashu Khel.

The Galai are divided into the following sections—Sheraki, Bosti Khel, Zargun Khel, and Tor-Sapar or Yagi Khel. They live in the Kohat pass and the Torsappar glen, and number about 1,400 fighting men. Their principal dependence is on trade. Their lands yield sufficient for a year's consumption, but there is no surplus. Their chief occupation is carrying salt on camels to Peshawar, and their revenue is assisted by a subsidy from the British Government for the safety of the road leading from Peshawar through the Kohat pass.

The Galai.

The Hasan Khel are divided into two principal sections, the Tatar Khel,[1] and the Janakhwari or Eastern, Hasan Khel. The former live at the northern end of the Kohat pass, near Akhor, while the latter reside below the Cherat hills in the Janakhwari and Musa Darra glens. Their fighting strength is about 1,800, of whom the Tatar Khel furnish 300 and the Janakhwari 1,500.

The Hasan Khel.

Their means of livelihood are bringing in wood and charcoal to Peshawar, and in cultivating some *lalmi* land belonging to Mohmands of Sham Shattu and of Azakhel. They would become very hopeless if blockaded.

The Jawaki Afridis live to the east of the Kohat pass, and for the most part inhabit the valleys forming the southern portion of the Adam Khel country. They also occupy the northern valley of Bori and the country around Pustawani, which connects Bori with the southern Jawaki territory. They are divided into two sections, the Haibat Khel, and the Kimat Khel.

The Jawakis.

The Jawakis are the principal carriers of wood to the Kohat cantonment, and also have a large carrying trade in salt. They possess a number of camels, which are constantly employed in carrying wood, grass, or salt, and the trade they derive in this way is very large. Their fighting strength is estimated at about 1,200 men.

[1] The Tatar Khel, often known as the Akhorwal, or Western, Hasan Khel is one of the pass sections, and is very closely associated with the Galai. They are often included with the latter under the general head of Kohat Pass Afridis. The term Hasan Khel is generally restricted to the Eastern Hasan Khels.

The Ashu Khel. The Ashu Khel Afridis are located to the south of Fort Mackeson, on the first range of hills, and in the Uchalgada valley. They are reported to possess 1,400 fighting men. In 1853 it had been intended to punish the Ashu Khels of Kandao for their share in the depredations on the Peshawar border, for which Bori was destroyed; but they gave in a timely submission, and so avoided punishment. They are an unimportant section, and are hardly recognized in the Adam Khel *jirga*.

The fighting strength of the Adam Khel clan is thus—

Galai	1,400
Hasan Khel	1,800
Jawaki	1,200
Ashu Khel	1,400
Total	5,800

Expedition against the Kohat Pass Afridis, by a force under Brigadier Sir Colin Campbell, K.C.B., in February 1850.

The British connection with the Adam Khel Afridis commenced immediately after the annexation of the Peshawar and Kohat districts. Following the example of all former governors of Peshawar, the British, in April 1849, entered into an agreement with the Kohat Pass Afridis to pay them Rs. 5,700 per annum, for which they were to protect the road through the pass. On the 2nd February 1850 a party of sappers employed in constructing a road from Kohat to the crest of the *kotal*, in British territory, were surprised by a body of Afridis. The assailed had not even time to arm themselves, before twelve were killed and six wounded, the assailants numbering, it was said, about one thousand men.

Lieut.-Colonel G. St. P. Lawrence, the Deputy Commissioner of Peshawar, at first supposed the outrage was no indication of any hostile combination of the hill tribes, but merely an effort of the sections, through whose territory the road was to pass, to prevent our labours, and thus purchase forbearance.

Subsequent information, however, pointed to a coalition between the Galai Afridis and the men of Akhor in particular. The instigator and leader was reported to have been a proscribed freebooter, named Daria Khan; and the avowed object of the aggression was to compel reversion to the rates at which salt was formerly sold at the Kohat mines. In Lieut.-Colonel Lawrence's opinion, however, the chief cause was the making of the Kohat road, which would throw open the fastnesses of the neighbouring tribes, and make them accessible to regular troops.

Two regiments of the Punjab Irregular Force, the 1st Punjab Infantry [1] and the 1st Punjab Cavalry,[2] were at the time of the outrage under orders for Kohat, and their departure was therefore stopped.

About this time the Commander-in-Chief, General Sir Charles J. Napier, G.C.B., had arrived at Peshawar, and on the 7th of February 1850, orders were issued for an advance through the Kohat pass. The force which was detailed for this duty was under the immediate command of Brigadier Sir Colin Campbell, K.C.B., but the Commander-in-Chief was to accompany it in person. Fourteen days' provisions were to accompany the troops, and four officers taken from regiments that did not form part of the force were to accompany it as baggage masters. Any man found plundering would be hanged or flogged. Officers were to march in the lightest order, and no reprisals by the troops were to be allowed without distinct orders.

The object of the expedition was two-fold: first, to strengthen Kohat by the 1st Punjab Cavalry and 1st Punjab Infantry; and, secondly, to punish the offending sections.

- 2nd troop, 2nd Brigade, Horse Artillery, with separate elephant transport.
- 2 5½-inch mortars, carried on one elephant.
- 2 companies, 60th Rifles.
- 2 companies, 61st Foot.
- 2 companies, 98th Foot.
- 15th Irregular Cavalry.[3]
- 1st Punjab Cavalry.
- 23rd Native Infantry (Commander-in-Chief's escort).[4]
- 31st Native Infantry.[5]
- 1st Punjab Infantry.

The force, as per margin, marched on the 9th Feb. to Matanni, entering the Kohat pass on the 10th. The advance was covered by the 1st Punjab Infantry. As the column entered the pass, it was met by a deputation from the village of Akhor, who endeavoured to exculpate themselves; but Lieut.-Colonel Lawrence being

[1] Now the 55th Coke's Rifles (Frontier Force).

[2] Now the 21st Prince Albert Victor's Own Cavalry (Frontier Force).

[3] Disbanded in 1861.

[4] Mutinied at Mhow in 1857.

[5] Now the 2nd Queen's Own Rajput Light Infantry.

assured that this was one of the villages which had taken part in the massacre of the sappers, an answer was returned to the deputation that the villagers must within an hour surrender themselves and their arms. At the end of the hour the *maliks* returned, stating that their companions would not listen to the terms, whereupon the Commander-in-Chief ordered Sir Colin Campbell to crown the heights round the village.

The enemy were posted chiefly on the heights, only a few occupying the village. Lieut.-Colonel Lawrence had assembled about 1,600 levies under their *arbabs*, or chiefs. These were ordered to ascend the heights; those on the right in support of a detachment of the 60th Rifles and 1st Punjab Infantry, under Captain J. Coke, and those on the left in support of detachments of the Guides and 1st Punjab Infantry, under Lieutenant H. B. Lumsden, of the former corps.

The brunt of the skirmishing fell on the 1st Punjab Infantry. Strong opposition was offered by the enemy, who were behind breastworks; but, covered by the fire of two Horse Artillery guns, these breastworks were speedily carried. The levies had gone up boldly enough; but, once there, nothing could induce them to come down until the village had been taken, and it was quickly evident that little assistance was to be expected from them.

The village of Akhor was then partially destroyed, and the obstruction to the entrance of the defile being thus removed, the column moved forward towards the village of Zargun Khel, leaving at the head of the pass a large number of the levies and the 15th Irregular Cavalry, under Major S. Fisher.

On nearing Zargun Khel, the enemy were again found posted on the heights above the village, whence they were driven by detachments of the 60th and 98th Regiments, assisted by the Horse Artillery, when this village was also burnt.

On encamping for the night in the valley, which in this part is commanded from the heights on either side, the enemy crowned the hills, and kept up a desultory fire on the camp immediately below them, killing and wounding several of the force. Two companies of the 31st Native Infantry, under Captain W. P. Hampton, and a company of the 1st Punjab Infantry accordingly cleared the heights on both sides, and held them for the night.

Previous to the column moving forward on the morning of the 11th, a detachment, consisting of two guns on elephants, one company, 61st Regiment, five companies, 1st Punjab Infantry, two troops, 1st Punjab Cavalry, and 600 levies, the whole under the command of Lieut.-Colonel J. Fordyce, proceeded to the village of Khui. The advance was covered by the 1st Punjab Infantry, which had one man wounded. Resistance similiar to that previously experienced was met at Khui, which was also burnt.

On the return of this detachment, the column resumed its march through the pass, which, after leaving Zargun Khel, becomes extremely narrow and difficult, being commanded by the heights which immediately overlook it, and which were held by the enemy. These heights were taken by three companies of the 1st Punjab Infantry on the left, whilst a detachment of the 60th Rifles, supported by one of the 98th Foot, crowned the heights on the right.

Meanwhile the rear-guard, composed of the 23rd Native Infantry and two Horse Artillery guns, under Major J. Platt, met with considerable annoyance from large bodies of the enemy, who pressed heavily on its rear and flanks, and occupied each height as soon as it was vacated by our troops, until the village of Sharaki was reached.

Sharaki was found deserted, and destroyed, and the march of the force was continued to the foot of the Kohat *kotal*, where the force encamped.

At this time, Kohat was held by some irregular troops with artillery, under Lieutenant F. R. Pollock, Assistant Commissioner, and the force was joined at the foot of the *kotal* by two guns and these irregulars.

In the afternoon the 1st Punjab Cavalry continued its march to Kohat.

The heights overlooking the front of the camp were occupied by a company of the 23rd Native Infantry, which, immediately after dark, was attacked by a party of the enemy, who were, however, driven off before the arrival of the in-lying picquet, which had been sent up when the firing was first heard.

About eight o'clock on the following morning, two companies of the 31st Native Infantry, which, under Captain W. R. Dunmore of that regiment, had held the heights overlooking the rear of the camp, were ordered down, as no enemy were in sight, to enable the men to procure water and regular food, it being the third day they had not cooked. As this order was being conveyed to Captain Dunmore, a party of twenty men of the 31st Native Infantry was detached under a native officer, with particular instructions to ascend the heights in a direction pointed out to him as more easy of access, and to hold the position during the temporary absence of the two companies.

This native officer, instead of obeying his orders, proceeded direct upon Captain Dunmore's detachment, at this time in the act of descending the steepest part of the hill by alternate companies. The result was that the rearmost company, under Ensign W. H. Sitwell, still some distance up the hill, as well as the native officer's party, which had just reached him, were suddenly attacked by a body of the enemy, who opened a very severe fire, and rolled down huge stones. Ensign Sitwell and several of his men were struck down by the first discharge; and so sudden and impetuous was the attack of the mountaineers, that it was with the greatest difficulty that certain men of his regiment succeeded in rescuing that officer's body. The retreat of the party was covered by one of the Horse Artillery guns, which prevented the enemy following up their first attack.

At the same time the other picquet of the 23rd Native Infantry was attacked; to reinforce which a company of the same regiment was immediately sent forward, under Lieutenant T. H. Hilliard. The enemy was driven off, but Lieutenant Hilliard was severely wounded in carrying out this operation.

Sir Charles Napier then rode over to inspect Kohat, and during the day two companies of the 98th Regiment, two companies, 31st Native Infantry, and two companies, 1st Punjab Infantry, with the Horse Artillery, the whole under the command of Major E. Haythorne, 98th Foot, were detached to cover a party employed in burning the three villages of Bosti Khel. The enemy offered resistance, as on the previous occasions, but the duty was effected without a single casualty.

On the morning of the 13th, the force was put in motion to return to Peshawar, the baggage being in the centre of the column, and every precaution taken for its protection, as in the advance.

The 1st Punjab Infantry remained on the ground for some time after the force had started, and then proceeded to Kohat without molestation, although a large number of Bizotis (Orakzais) were on the neighbouring hills.

Sir Colin Campbell's column had begun its march about 7 A.M.; on the advanced guard nearing Sharaki, the enemy opened fire from the surrounding heights, and from this point until the rear-guard reached the immediate vicinity of Akhor, nearly the whole length of the defile, the Afridis contested the ground, opposing the force in front, and hanging incessantly on its flanks and rear, with greater perseverance even than they had manifested in our advance.

The loss in these operations was nineteen killed, seventy-four wounded, and one missing, of which thirty were in the 1st Punjab Infantry.

The force encamped outside the pass on the evening of the 13th, and returned to Peshawar the following day.

The Indian Medal, with a clasp for the "North-West Frontier," was granted in 1869 to all survivors of the troops engaged in the operations against the Kohat Pass Afridis.

Soon after the expedition above related, hostilities broke out afresh.

On the 28th of February 1850 a *jirga* assembled among the hillmen, and it was decided to attack the police tower on the summit of the Kohat Kotal. The next day the Afridis of the pass, with the Bizoti and Utman Khel sections of the Orakzais, surrounded the tower and took possession of the road, driving back the detachment of Multani police which had gone to the aid of the men in the tower.

The ammunition of the police was all but expended when Captain J. Coke arrived at the foot of the *kotal* with 450 bayonets of the 1st Punjab Infantry, a squadron of the 1st Punjab Cavalry, and two guns.

There were from 1,500 to 2,000 Orakzais and Afridis on the hill, the road up which was commanded on all sides.

Captain Coke immediately attacked the hill with the 1st Punjab Infantry, leaving the guns at the foot, protected by the cavalry. The enemy were driven back, and a company of the 1st Punjab Infantry put into the tower with a supply of ammunition and food. Our loss had been eleven killed and fourteen wounded, which was severe, considering the number of men engaged.

On the 2nd of March, Daria Khan arrived in the pass with the Hasan Khel Afridis and a number of the Khaibar Afridis, and, being joined by the Bizotis and Utman Khels (Orakzais) and by the men of the pass, he attacked the tower in the evening, but was beaten off. During the night the enemy pushed on close up to the tower, under cover of the rocks, cutting off the water, which was in a small tank about 150 yards down the hill; they then erected breastworks across the road up the hill. The attacking force consisted of some 2,000 men, but the native officer in command of the tower, Subadar Muhammad Khan, defended the place with great spirit.

It was now imperative that a movement should be made for the relief of the tower, and Captain Coke moved out with 450 bayonets and some 500 Bangash levies. After a conference between the Bangash men and the Afridis and Orakzais, the enemy retired from the hill, when Captain Coke withdrew his men and the police from the tower. The enemy soon returned and destroyed the deserted post, and the same evening dispersed to their homes.

On the 22nd of March, Apothecary M. Healy, proceeding *viâ* Khushalgarh to join the 1st Punjab Infantry at Kohat, was attacked by a party of hillmen, believed to have been Galai Afridis. He had gone on in advance of his escort, and was cut down when within about six miles of Kohat, near the village of Togh, dying shortly afterwards from the effects of the wounds.

At the beginning of April several of the headmen of the Galai Afridis came in to the Deputy Commissioner of Peshawar, denying that the murder had been committed by their sections, and suing for terms. On the 24th of April the head-quarters and two squadrons, 1st Punjab Cavalry, marched through the Kohat pass to Peshawar, meeting with no opposition, but, on the contrary, finding the headmen and others offering every facility for their progress.

At the end of April the chief *maliks* of the offending sections came in to Lieut.-Colonel Lawrence of their own accord, and sued for peace. The terms offered by the Government were as follows, and the whole of the clan in British territory were to be ejected in the event of their not being acceded to:—

1st.—The clan to engage to keep the pass open at all times, safe and free.

2nd.—The clan to receive the same allowances as in 1849, and to be admitted to the same terms in respect to salt as other tribes.

3rd.—For the fulfilment of these conditions hostages to be given.

On the 6th June 1850 all the assembled *maliks* of Akhor, Zargun Khel, and Sharaki accepted the conditions, and promised hostages; but it soon became evident that the body of the clan represented by these *maliks* was not prepared for submission. On the 9th of June a native officer returning from Kohat was plundered, the *dâk* papers were torn up, and the carrier beaten, and an intended attack on the Assistant Commissioner of Kohat was reported.

Orders were therefore issued both at Peshawar and Kohat for shutting out the offending sections and seizing such as happened to be in British territory. This was followed by numerous seizures,—some of women,—which gave particular anxiety to the tribe.

As regards the renewal of hostilities, Government prohibited any extensive aggressive movement till after the rains, considering it safer to await the result of the blockade already established.

On the 18th of September the Commissioner of Peshawar brought to the notice of the Board of Administration that the Afridis of the Kohat pass had again sued for terms, offering the headmen of the pass as their security. He pointed out the advisability of entering into a treaty, as there was every reason to believe the present submission was sincere. He also drew attention to the great importance of maintaining permanent possession of the Kohat salt mines, and to the advantages to be gained by having strong outposts at these points; because an exclusion for six months of any tribe habitually frequenting the mines must reduce them to submission or starvation.

The Board, in soliciting the orders of Government, recommended a treaty with the Kohat Pass Afridis, and, though concurring in the necessity for posts at the salt mines, deferred sanctioning them until the sites had been inspected and reported on by some officer of mature experience. The Government of India, willing to treat the clan considerately, consented to renew their old allowances on condition of their being responsible for the security of the pass. In order to strengthen the arrangement, Rahmat Khan, a chief of the neighbouring Orakzais, was admitted to a share of the responsibility, and was granted a personal allowance of Rs. 2,000 per annum, and Rs. 6,000 as the pay of a mounted guard, to be maintained on the crest of the *kotal* near Kohat. These payments, as then (November 1850) revised, aggregated Rs. 13,700 per annum.

From this time till 1853, the pass remained open, occasional robberies only being committed; but the Afridis regarded the share which Rahmat Khan had in the pass arrangements with extreme jealousy, and the ill-feeling thus raised culminated in October of that year, when they attacked and seized Rahmat Khan's post on the *kotal*, in which there were only twenty (instead of the stipulated one hundred) men. The pass was then closed, postal communication stopped, and British officers were fired upon by the Afridis.

The Chief Commissioner soon after this (November 1853) arrived at Peshawar, and directed Captain H. R. James, the Deputy Commissioner, to arrange for the attendance of the *maliks* of the Kohat pass. These men accordingly came in, and had a long conference with the Chief Commissioner, during which Major H. B. Edwardes, the Commissioner, Captain H. R. James, and Captain J. Coke, the officer in charge of Kohat, were present.

There were four modes of arranging for the reopening of the Kohat pass which appeared feasible—1*st*, to restore matters to the *status quo*, *viz*., to give Rahmat Khan (Orakzai) Rs. 13,700 per annum for himself and the Afridis, making them responsible, as formerly, for the security of the pass; 2*nd*, to give the Afridis for the pass (but only as their own share of the old allowances) Rs. 5,700; 3*rd*, to divide the pass into sections, making separate arrangements with the heads of those tribes who held each portion; and 4*th*, to hold the *kotal*, or summit of the pass, ourselves, and make an arrangement with the Afridis for the remainder.

To the first plan all our officers were opposed. They felt that the Afridis were opposed to further connection with Rahmat Khan, who had proved his incapacity to conciliate and control them. The second plan was that to which Captain James inclined as most acceptable to the Afridis themselves; the third was the proposition of Captain Coke; and the last, that of Lieut.-Colonel F. Mackeson, the late Commissioner of Peshawar, to which the Chief Commissioner himself inclined. This last was eventually given up, not simply because it entailed considerable expense, but because it did not appear probable that any reasonable number of the undisciplined irregulars, unconnected with the tribes in the vicinity of the pass, could hold the *kotal*.

The discussion was therefore narrowed to the second and third plans, and though Captain James still inclined to his former views, it was agreed that the one of making separate arrangements promised the best security and the greatest permanence. Our officers were unanimously of opinion that it was out of the question to give the Afridis a rupee in excess of their former emoluments. Rahmat Khan was their own selection. He may have treated them ill, but it was not right to allow them to benefit by their own wrongful acts. They had repeatedly broken their engagements and shut the pass. They had even, when enjoying our allowances, permitted travellers to be murdered and robbed close to their villages, which offered a refuge to the outlaws and ruffians of our districts, from whence they sallied out to plunder.

The Afridis had finally crowned a series of misdeeds by attacking the posts of their chosen leader, and expelling his men.

The following, therefore, were the propositions which it was decided should be offered to the Afridis:—*1st*, that the whole crest of the *kotal* and the side of the hill towards Kohat down to Captain Coke's first post at the Kohat entrance of the pass should be made over to the Bangash tribe[1] who, out of their allowances, should satisfy and be responsible for the good conduct of the Bizoti, Utman Khel, Firoz Khel, and other minor sections, and that the allowance for this duty should be Rs. 7,700 per annum; *2nd*, that from below the *kotal* (on the Peshawar side) down to the Akhor and the Basi Khel boundary, should be made over to the Afridis on Rs. 5,400 per annum; *3rd*, with the Basi Khel Afridis an arrangement should be made for the rest of the road (being

[1] For a description of this tribe and our dealings with them, see Chapter VI.

the broken ground outside the pass on the Peshawar side) for Rs. 600.

A conference accordingly took place on the 5th of November with the Galai and Hasan Khel Afridis, who, with Rahmat Khan (Orakzais), had hitherto engaged for the whole pass. The Chief Commissioner on this occasion carefully recapitulated the past history of our engagements, showing how great had been their perfidy, ingratitude, and inconstancy. They replied that they were prepared to be faithful to their promises for the future; that, in fact, they had never broken them, but that Rahmat Khan had defrauded them; and that for the future they wished to have no chief over them.

The Chief Commissioner then told them the arrangements which he proposed, by which they would be responsible only for that portion of the pass which was within the lands of their own tribes. This they refused, saying they would alone engage for the whole pass and take all the allowances; and added, that rather than not have the whole pass to themselves, they would accept the responsibility on their former share of the allowances, *viz.*, Rs. 5,700.

The Afridis positively refusing our terms, the Chief Commissioner broke up the conference, and desired them to withdraw and consider the matter over quietly among themselves, and return in the space of two hours with their final resolve. Half an hour afterwards he was told that they had left Peshawar for their homes. On hearing this, though the Chief Commissioner felt that no faith could be placed in these Afridis, though he did not believe that they would accept the engagement, or that, if they did, they would adhere to it, still he was sorry that the *maliks* had left Peshawar while a prospect of an arrangement existed. He therefore sent after them, on the plea that their final answer should be formally given. On their return, Captain James was empowered to offer them the engagement they had desired, *viz.*, the responsibility of the whole pass on the allowance of Rs. 5,700 per annum. This might be thought so far a concession, that it gave up to the charge of the Afridis the *kotal* which we had hitherto held at our own disposal, and which they had never occupied. But, on the other hand, it was a punishment, inasmuch as it doubled their responsibility without increasing their allowance.

The Afridis, however, refused Captain James's offer, saying that nothing but the full allowance would satisfy them, and thus proving that their first offer was not sincere. On this they received their dismissal, and set off for the pass. They had not, however, reached the pass before they again desired to negotiate, and sent in a message, proposing to return next day and endeavour to effect an arrangement. This the Chief Commissioner refused. The fact was, that had the Afridis accepted the terms, there was not the slightest security that they would fulfil them. No tribe or party would go bail for them, and they could give no pledges of any real value for their sincerity. The system among hill tribes of giving hostages is little check on them when dealing with us, for they know that we shall not oppress their people. Under native rule, the hostages of a tribe who grossly infringed a treaty would have been put to death, or at least mutilated.

It may, perhaps, be asked why the Afridis of the pass were anxious to enter into engagements which they would not maintain. The reply is, that since the closing of the pass, a number of their tribe had been arrested at Kohat, whom they were anxious to see released ; and, moreover, this was the height of the salt season, and the closing of the pass at this time to them was a great blow, for it stopped their carrying trade. If, therefore, we had to force the Afridis of the Kohat pass into terms which, however distasteful to them, they would have great difficulty in breaking, this was the best time for effecting our object.

By the old arrangement, Rahmat Khan received Rs. 8,000 per annum, Rs. 2,000 as his personal allowance, and Rs. 6,000 for the pay of 100 men to hold the *kotal*. He appears to have kept up twenty men in two small posts below the summit on the Kohat side of the hill, spent a few rupees among the *maliks* of the section, and appropriated the rest. The Galai and Hasan Khel Afridis received Rs. 5,700, out of which they had to satisfy the Basi Khels. The latter were at feud with the Afridis of the pass, and, from their position outside on the left of the road leading to Peshawar, possessed great facilities for plundering, of which they never failed to avail themselves. It was useless, therefore, including them in any arrangement with the Galai and Hasan Khel Afridis. The very smallest sum which the Kohat Pass Afridis could pay the Basi Khel was Rs. 300 per annum, and this sum was accordingly deducted from the allowances of the former, and added to an equal sum out of that which Rahmat Khan formerly enjoyed. Thus, Rs. 7,700 remained for the Bangash tribe.

It has been remarked that it was the wish of Lieut.-Colonel F. Mackeson, the late Commissioner of Peshawar, not to make over the *kotal* to any tribe, whether Afridis or Bangash; and the Chief Commissioner inclined to the same view. The latter did not wish, however, as Lieut.-Colonel Mackeson proposed, to place there a body of undisciplined irregulars collected from distant places, as he believed that, with no cover and no water, they could not have held their position; his idea was that Captain Coke should select men from the Bangash, the Bizoti, and Utman Khel Orakzais, and other tribes in the vicinity of the pass, and place them in charge. Captain Coke, however, assured him that the men of these tribes would not enlist for such employment. The Chief Commissioner then sent Captain Coke back to Kohat, and empowered him to make an arrangement with the Bangash tribe, and to repair the two old towers, and to build three new ones on the *kotal*. If successful, this step must place the Afridis entirely at our mercy. Their hills did not afford them sufficient subsistence; they existed mainly by carrying salt from the Kohat mines into the Peshawar valley, and thus it would be impossible for them to do anything against our consent in the face of the Bangash tribe, backed by our troops. Shut out from Kohat, and blockaded by a force in front of the pass on the Peshawar side, they might emerge from their defile as individuals, to steal and to plunder, as they formerly did when enjoying the bounty of Government, but they could do nothing more.

It had long been contemplated to build a fort on the Peshawar side of the pass, near its mouth; accordingly a force was now moved out to that point, and the work on the post, known as Fort Mackeson, was commenced.

On his return to Kohat, Captain Coke assembled all the Bangash *maliks*, and asked them if they were ready to undertake the holding of the *kotal* against the Afridis on the allowances granted by Government. As they almost all agreed to do so, Captain Coke ordered them to furnish their separate quota of men, and on the 11th he moved out with them to the *kotal*, taking a wing of the 1st

Punjab Infantry and of the 3rd Punjab Infantry,[1] with two guns, to be kept in reserve at the foot of the pass.

The top of the *kotal* was gained without an Afridi being seen or a shot being fired. There being no water of any kind, it was necessary to make immediate arrangements for its supply, not only for the use of the men, but also for building the towers. These arrangements being completed, on the morning of the 12th the party had just started work, when, about ten o'clock, the alarm was given that the Afridis were coming down. They pushed boldly up the *kotal* from the glen on their own side, and got above the Bangash men on the left, where they had entrenched themselves with loose stones on the summits of a hill. The picquet of the Bangash on this hill now gave way and ran in on the others. Captain Coke was on the hill with ten or twelve men of the 1st Punjab Infantry, by one of whom the leading Afridi was cut down; but there was a general panic among the Bangash, who made a rush down the hill, evacuating all the strong positions before the force from below could support them. Having covered their retreat, and brought them out into the plain, Captain Coke found they were too disheartened to attempt anything again that day, and he therefore strengthened the camp at the foot of the *kotal* with another regiment of infantry and two more guns, and sent Khwaja Muhammad Khan to bring up his Khattaks, hoping, with the aid of the Bizotis and Jawaki Afridis, to carry out the work.

Captain Coke and three of his men were wounded in this skirmish, and three of the Bangash *maliks* were killed, as well as other casualties.

An arrangement was subsequently entered into by which the Bizoti and Sipaya Orakzais and the Jawaki Afridis agreed to aid the Bangash tribe in the defence of the *kotal*; and to receive as follows, *viz.*, Bangash, Rs. 3,200; Jawakis, Rs. 2,000; Bizotis, Rs. 2,000; and Sipayas, Rs. 500.

Meanwhile the Afridis of the pass were suffering from the blockade. The British authorities had acted on the principle that if the Afridis would not keep the pass open, the doors of the pass must be shut upon them. Eventually, therefore, the Galai and Hasan Khel Afridis tendered their submission, and offered

[1] Disbanded in 1882.

to reopen the pass. This offer was accepted, except that they were to receive only Rs. 5,400 instead of the Rs. 5,700 formerly given, the remaining Rs. 300 being given from the allowances of the Akhor Hasan Khel to the Basi Khel, Aka Khel Afridis. This last sum was afterwards increased to Rs. 600. This arrangement was concluded before the end of 1853.

The aggregate allowances of the pass were thus divided as follows:—

				Rs.
Bangash tribe	..	..	..	3,200
Orakzai tribe	..	..	..	2,500
Jawaki Afridis	..	..	..	2,000
Kohat Pass Afridis	..	..	..	5,400
Basi Khel Afridis	..	..	..	600
		Total	..	13,700

This total was subsequently increased to Rs. 14,600; the Bangash allowance being increased to Rs. 4,400 (Rs. 2,400 to Bahadur Sher Khan, for charge of the pass, and Rs. 2,000 to the Bangash tribe), and the allowance to the Pass Afridis being reduced to Rs. 5,100. This last amount was distributed as follows:—For guards furnished by the Akhor Hasan Khels, Rs. 1,200; for the *maliks* of this section, Rs. 1,050—total, Rs. 2,250; to the villages of Sherakai and Bosti Khel, Rs. 950; to Torsappar, Rs. 950; and to Zargun Khel, Rs. 950—total, Rs. 2,850.

Expedition against the Bori villages of the Jawaki Afridis, by a force under Colonel S. B. Boileau, in November 1853.

When the Afridis of the Kohat pass misbehaved in 1850, the Jawaki section offered to engage for that pass, or to conduct communications through their own, the Jamu and Bori passes, and to carry the *dâk* regularly. The Jawaki route was actually used for a short time, but the Jawaki Afridis soon proved themselves to be worse even than their neighbours. They committed numerous raids and murders in the Kohat and Peshawar districts, robbed boats on the Indus, and were also concerned in the murder of Apothecary Healy.

In 1851 Lieutenant H. B. Lumsden reported that several serious raids had been committed on Kohat and Khushalgarh by the Jawakis of Paia and Ghariba, who had also attacked one of the Khattak villages; and he recommended that these villages should be destroyed by Khwaja Muhammad Khan, the Khattak chief, whilst Captain J. Coke, with a force, prevented any co-operation from the villages of Turki and Shindih. Nothing, however, seems to have come of these proposals.

The conduct of the Jawakis continued during the next two years to be bad, more especially that of the men of the Bori villages. These villages had, during the first year of our rule, given a great deal of trouble to the authorities; and on the 8th of June 1853, Captain H. R. James, the Deputy Commissioner of Peshawar, reported that the boldness and frequency with which the Bori Afridis committed raids in the Peshawar district called for serious notice, as their villages had become an asylum for every noted robber.

The Commissioner, Lieut.-Colonel F. Mackeson C.B., stated that in most of these raids and outrages, the gang of Afridis had not exceeded more than thirty in number, and had not averaged more than twelve, and he considered that these disorders were of a nature that could be put down by police arrangements; he accordingly urged the establishment of police posts along the Afridi and Khattak borders, but at the same time advised that at a convenient season a severe example should be made of the Boriwals.

In September 1853, Lieut.-Colonel Mackeson was assassinated, and was succeeded by Major H. B. Edwardes, C.B.; and in November 1853, Mr. John Lawrence, the Chief Commissioner, having proceeded to Peshawar, held a conference on the 15th of that month with the *maliks* of the villages connected with the Jawaki pass. Desiring, if possible, to avoid hostilities, the Chief Commissioner arranged with all the villages of the Jawaki pass, except Bori, that the interdict to their resort to the salt mines and to the markets of Kohat and Peshawar should be withdrawn on the following conditions:—

1*st*.—That neither they, not any person living in their villages, should commit crimes for the future in British territory, in return for which they should have full permission to trade and to cultivate within our boundaries.

2nd.—That they should not give a passage through their lands to depredators coming into British territory, or to criminals passing therefrom.

3rd.—That they should on no account afford an asylum to criminals and outlaws flying from justice.

The Chief Commissioner was most anxious to get these Afridis to agree to seize and surrender such criminals as had taken refuge in their villages; but this they stoutly refused, simply stipulating that they would send them away. To the third condition they also evinced great repugnance, and it was only on their seeing that a refusal on this point would lead to a continuance of the blockade that they gave a reluctant consent.

These Afridis stated, with truth, that it was the immemorial custom of their clans never to refuse an asylum to anyone demanding it, and that to surrender an individual who had obtained refuge with them, or even to deny him their hospitality, was a great disgrace. The Chief Commissioner was impressed with the belief, from the conduct and bearing of these Afridis, that they were sincerely desirous as a body for peace. The fact, however, that it was for their interest to be on good terms with us, was doubtless the strongest lien on their good faith.

The Chief Commissioner was even willing to make terms with the Bori men. The desire of Government to avoid a recourse to hostilities, the unsatisfactory state of affairs with the Afridis of the Kohat pass, and the extraordinary sickness among the troops at Peshawar,—all pointed to the advantage of this course. The terms offered were—

1st.—That they should make restitution for all property proved to have been stolen or plundered during the past year; on their pleading their poverty, this point was modified to the surrender of the horses of the mounted robbers.

2nd.—That they should release any prisoners detained for ransom.

3rd.—That they should surrender certain outlaws of the cis-Indus districts who had found refuge with them.

Each and all these propositions, however, they rejected; and nothing, therefore, remained but to send a force against them.

The Bori valley is about twelve miles long, and has an entrance at each extremity; but as they are both narrow and very defensible defiles, it was determined to cross the outer range at the most favourable point. It had been ascertained that a practicable path ascended through the village of Kandao, and a second was known to exist to the south of that village; but general information represented the Sarghasha pass, which crosses the outer range between Kandao and Taruni, to be the most practicable road, and it was therefore chosen. It had also been decided to avoid the Kandao pass in entering the Bori valley, so as not to alarm the Ashu Khel Afridis of Kandao, who were then at peace with us. But Lieut.-Colonel R. Napier, Bengal Engineers, having reconnoitred the grounds on the day preceding the advance of the force, had advised that the heights should be occupied from this point, so as to turn the flank of all opposition at the Sarghasha pass.

Advanced Guard.
Corps of Guides.
Mountain Train Battery.
Main Body.
66th Gurkhas.[1]
22nd Foot.
20th Native Infantry.[2]
Two 9-pounder guns.
Sappers and Miners.
Rear-guard.
66th Gurkhas (200 men).
7th Irregular Cav. (1 squadron).[3]

At 4 A.M. on the 29th November the force covering the erection of Fort Mackeson, under the command of Colonel S. B. Boileau, and accompanied by Captain H. R. James, the Deputy Commissioner, marched from the camp at Bazid Khel, in the order noted in the margin.

The first part of the road, which was some five or six miles in all, was over a good hard plain, but the approach to the Sarghasha pass, for the distance of about a mile, lay through ravines and low hills.

The Guide Infantry, under Lieutenant W. S. R. Hodson, was detached to ascend the path leading through Kandao, and to crown the outer range of hills to prevent the enemy defending the Sarghasha pass. Captain James had taken the precaution of having the *maliks* of all the friendly Afridi villages in attendance on him, and a *malik* of Kandao was now sent on to his own people to assure them of our peaceable intentions; nevertheless, though they abstained from hostilities, they could not rely on our good faith, and numbers fled up the hill with such property as they could hastily carry off.

[1] Now the 1st Gurkhas. [2] Mutinied at Meerut in 1857.
[3] Now the 5th Cavalry.

Although the road had been good, and there had been a faint moon between five and six o'clock, it was seven o'clock before the foot of the Sarghasha pass was reached. Here a reserve of two companies of infantry and the cavalry were left, the main body reaching the summit of the pass at 10-30 A.M., where the Guide Corps had already arrived, having found a good and easy road from Kandao leading to Bori, the existence of which was not previously known to us.

The Sarghasha is the proper pass of the men of Bori. It was found to be steep, winding, narrow, and long, and though quite practicable for horses and any beasts of burden, it only admitted of troops ascending in single file. If, therefore, it had been disputed by the Afridis, Lieut.-Colonel Napier's manœuvre would have been essential to the success of the main column; but there was no indication of any opposition having been contemplated here.

The sappers, who with the materials for blowing up the towers of the Bori villages had been left with the reserve, were now ordered up; but as some delay occurred in their advance up the hill, it was determined to go on without them, and to abandon the idea of blowing up the towers. Leaving a picquet of a company of Her Majesty's 22nd Regiment, under Captain W. H. Poulett, and a company of the Guides, under Ensign J. H. Tyler, 20th Native Infantry, on the crest of the outer range, the force descended into the valley of Bori and advanced across the plain, covered by the light company of Her Majesty's 22nd Regiment. As the furthest Bori villages lay near the Taruni entrance of the valley; and as Colonel Boileau was assured by the Commissioner of the neutrality of the men of Taruni, whose village is built in the gorge of that defile, it was determined to withdraw from the valley by that route, and the plan of operations was made accordingly.

The spurs commanding the main portion of the Bori villages were crowned in the most brilliant manner by Lieutenant W. S. R. Hodson with three companies of the Guides, and by Lieutenant F. McC. Turner, his second-in-command, with two companies of that regiment and twenty-five men of the 66th Gurkhas. Lieutenant Turner's party had carried the first village *en route*, and swept fifteen or twenty of the Afridis before them up the hill; and when the mountain guns, coming up, played upon the towers, the few remaining defenders abandoned the village to its fate. The enemy being thus removed to a distance, the first village was entered, and its fort set on fire.

In the meantime the 22nd Regiment, under Colonel S. J. Cotton, and two detachments of the Gurkhas, under Captain C. C. G. Ross and Lieutenant J. A. Law, had, covered by the artillery fire, driven the enemy from the other two villages and fired them successively, the Afridis making no stand in the plain, but taking to the hills, from whence they poured down a matchlock fire till driven to a distance by our skirmishers. By twelve o'clock heavy columns of flame and smoke were rising from every Bori village.

While the work of demolition was being thus leisurely carried on below, the contests on the heights above grew warmer every hour, as friends and allies from Pustawani, Torsappar, and Jamu came down the higher ranges to assist their clansmen of Bori.

The struggle of the day was for the peak of the centre hill, where the Afridis had, by erecting a breastwork on an isolated point, made an almost impregnable position. Here Lieutenant F. McC. Turner, with about twenty men, was brought to bay; and such showers of stones and bullets were rained upon them that an advance was impossible, while to retire would have been fatal.

The Afridis in the breastwork were seen from the opposite height to draw their knives, and watch intently for the first movement in retreat, as the signal to leap down upon the Guides. But no wavering was to be found in that little band. They at once sounded the bugle for help, and stood their ground, returning the fire of the Afridis. On seeing Lieutenant Turner's position, Lieutenant Hodson had sent a company of Guides from his own party; but they were unable to reach Lieutenant Turner. A company of the 66th Gurkas was then sent up, and shortly afterwards a second company; and gallantly carried the enemy's stronghold, led by Assistant Surgeon R. Lyell, of the Guide Corps.

It was now nearly three o'clock, the work of the day was done, and it was deemed advisable to retire while there was yet light; the troops were therefore recalled, the main body being drawn up in the centre of the valley. The Guides and Gurkhas were most skilfully withdrawn from the heights by Lieutenant Hodson, a party of Gurkhas, under Captain C. C. G. Ross, and two mountain guns, under Lieutenant T. Pulman, covering the retirement; this detachment of Gurkhas with the Corps of Guides then formed the rear-guard.

A little after 3 P.M. the column was set in motion towards the Taruni pass—the 20th Native Infantry and Mountain Train Battery in advance, followed by the 66th Gurkhas and the 22nd Foot.

The Bor miouth of the Taruni defile is split into two roads by an isolated hill. The main column defiled down the lower one, while two companies of Her Majesty's 22nd, under Captain D. Anderson, skirmished with great steadiness along the upper.

The enemy, in considerable force, attempted to press the rear-guard, but were checked by Lieutenant Hodson, who charged them with a small party of the Guides Cavalry, which had made its way through the Taruni pass during the day; every subsequent attempt was met by so hot a fire from the rear-guard that not the slightest impression was made, and shortly after passing the Taruni all molestation ceased.

Captain Poulett's detachment, which had been left on the crest of the Sarghasha ridge, had, in the meanwhile, conformed to the movements of the main column, and had moved along the crest of the ridge parallel to the march of the force, checking an attempt of the enemy to intercept the line of march, and covering the left flank as far as the Taruni defile, where it joined the main column.

During the attack on Bori, the outer range of hills above Janakhwar, Khui, and Taruni was covered with armed Afridis, quietly watching the progress of events; and as the head of the column neared Taruni, considerable anxiety was felt as to the part which our new Afridi allies in that and the other villages would play. Certainly they had been admitted to treaties with us, and allowed to trade when the salt mines were closed to the other tribes; but it was a great temptation. The "infidels" were in the pass, harassed by a long day's work, and still engaged with an enemy in the rear.

The Afridis sat in hundreds on the hill, and saw that they had only to descend it in front to place the column between two fires ; yet they refrained, and kept their faith, and even sent deputies to the men of Bori to warn them not to come beyond their border ; whilst the Taruni men actually brought water at the Chief Commissioner's request up to the top of the ridge for the Europeans who held the pass.

Thus the force moved out on to the plain, through friends, and by an easy, level road, instead of having to fight its way in darkness over the steep passes of Sarghasha or Kandao.

Night closed upon the column as it emerged from the defile, and the foremost did not reach camp till 8 P.M., the main body not till ten or eleven, after being more than eighteen hours under arms. The European soldiers had food in their haversacks, but the majority of the force had none ; and all were without water, as the springs at Bori, being far up a ravine, were in the hands of the enemy.

The strength of the force actually engaged in the attack on the Bori villages was about 1,700 of all ranks ; the loss on our side had been eight killed and twenty-nine wounded, and that of the Afridis somewhat less.

Of the results, Major H. B. Edwardes said the real loss of the Bori Afridis was not to be found in killed and wounded, or even in the destruction of their homes and stocks of winter fodder for the cattle, but in the loss of prestige, in the violation of their hills as a refuge for proclaimed criminals, in seeing that even our heavy regular army contains, and can produce when need requires, some troops who can take to the hillside as lightly as themselves, and drive them off their roughest crags with weapons of superior range.

The Indian Medal, with a clasp for the "North-West Frontier," was granted in 1869 to all survivors of the troops engaged in the above operations.

A few days after the expedition, the men of Bori made overtures of submission to Major H. B. Edwardes through a holy man named Saiyid Gul Mian, who, however, broke off the negotiations when told that no terms would be made till the refugee criminals were expelled from Bori. This, he said, was hopeless, because it was contrary to the customs of Pathan hospitality.

Early in December 1853 the Boriwals applied to Captain J. Coke, Deputy Commissioner of Kohat, for terms of peace. That officer was authorized to receive their submission and admit them to friendly intercourse on the one condition that they expelled all refugee criminals with them, and promised to receive no more.

On the 11th of January 1854 Captain Coke wrote to Major Edwardes to say that the *maliks* of Bori had come in to him and agreed to everything, except the expulsion of refugees; and as they were willing to admit no more in the future, they hoped this point would be waived. This, however, Major Edwardes refused, because the principle at stake was worth more than peace with Bori.

On the 17th of January Captain Coke reported that the Bori deputies had at last agreed to expel the refugees if two months' grace were given them; but they wished to be allowed free intercourse with British territory at once, and on this understanding they had signed a treaty of submission, which Captain Coke sent for sanction. In reply, Major Edwardes said he regretted to be hard on them, but the treaty of friendship and friendly intercourse could only begin from the date of our enemies being expelled from Bori.

On the 8th of February Captain Coke reported the unconditional submission of the Boriwals to all our terms, and the actual expulsion of the refugee criminals. Accordingly, the following agreement was signed by them on the 24th February 1854:—

1st.—We will abstain hereafter from committing raids, highway robberies, thefts, or other crimes within British territory.

2nd.—If any criminal comes to our settlements from British territory we will promptly eject him; and if we ascertain that he is in possession of stolen property, we will make restitution of the same to Government.

3rd.—If any resident of our settlements is apprehended for crime in British territory, we will not intercede for him; and if such person comes with stolen property to our settlements, we will make restitution of the same, and punish the thief according to our Afghan usage, and not permit him to return to British territory for the perpetration of crime.

4th.—In regard to certain criminals who have taken refuge with us from the other side of the Indus, we agree, within two months, to eject them from our settlement.

5th.—We will associate ourselves with the rest of our tribe in any service which the district officer may call upon them to perform.

6th.—Whereas the Pakhi[1] Afridis have always been associated with us in our former evil deeds, we agree to be responsible for them also.

7th.—We give as our securities Mir Mubarak Shah, Naib Muhammad Saiyid Khan, and Bahadur Sher Khan; if we commit any breach of the above engagements, the Government is free to call them to account.

8th.—In consideration of the above agreements, we shall be allowed to come and go in British territory.

9th.—In consideration of the same, the Government will be asked to release seven men of our section now in prison.

10th.—We will bring no evil-disposed person with us into British territory.

After the settlement with the Kohat Pass Afridis in 1853, the pass remained open till 1866, with the exception of one brief interval of twenty-six days. This interregnum was occasioned by a feud among the Afridis of the pass, during which some robberies were committed. The heads of the confederacy traced the perpetrators to the Bosti Khel villages, and the Deputy Commissioner of Kohat sent the Bangash men down, and compelled the inhabitants of these villages to make good the value of the plundered property, and to pay a fine.

As has been related in Chapter I, the Basi Khel Afridis, in consequence of their misconduct, had forfeited, in 1855, their share in the pass allowances. This section was again concerned in the complications in the Kohat pass in 1866.

The reason of the Basi Khels having been originally admitted to a share in the pass allowances was in consequence of their claiming a portion of land called Kalamsada, extending from Kotkai to Aimal Chabutra, and it was in consequence of the constant fighting on this piece of land between the Basi Khels and Akhorwals that Captain J. Coke made the arrangement that the former should receive Rs. 300 out of the allowances of the latter. This amount was afterwards increased, as already mentioned, to Rs. 600, but was forfeited in 1855 by their misconduct.

In 1859 the Basi Khels again came forward with their claims to the Kalamsada, and consequent share of the allowances. In February 1859 an agreement was made, by which both parties

[1] Pakhi is a village at the eastern extremity of the Uchalgada valley.

bound themselves to refrain from fighting on the road near the disputed ground for five years. This was afterwards extended for one year more, to February 1865.

Disputes had also been going on for some time between the Bolaki and Gaddia Khel sections of the Akhorwals as to the relative proportion in which the shares of each should be paid. These and the Basi Khel dispute had caused fighting in the pass about Akhor, and, the Commissioner being unable to induce them to come to some agreement, the pass was closed and the allowances stopped; and it was not until October 1866 that these differences could be adjusted.

The Basi Khels and Hasan Khels, however, still continued to give trouble, and the former demanded a right of interference in the management of the pass, unwarranted by former usage. For their contumacy they were debarred from access to British territory, when, after a brief interval, they submitted on the 8th of April 1867; and, on consideration of their renouncing their claim to the disputed tract of Kalamsada, an allowance of Rs. 1,000 per annum was granted to them.

The Hasan Khels were also subjected to a strict blockade, but after the institution of the blockade more outrages were perpetrated: a policeman on duty at an outpost was carried off by a band led by a notorious Hasan Khel freebooter; a party of police were fired at while patrolling; shots were fired at our posts; and lastly, the Government mail, *en route* from the Indus to Kohat, was plundered on the high road by men of the Hasan Khel section.

The *jirga* of the section were then summoned to Peshawar, but at the end of ten days they firmly declined, by letter, to give way on the points at issue. Orders were accordingly issued for the assembling of a force to carry out coercive measures against this section.

The force was to consist of 5,001 men of all arms, with 14 guns, and was to be divided into two columns, under the command of Colonel R. O. Bright, 19th Foot, and Colonel S. J. Browne, V.C., C.B., Corps of Guides, respectively. The force was to be ready to march on the 12th or 13th of April.

Colonel Bright's column was to advance from Azakhel on Khui and Janakhwar, while Colonel Browne, having bivouacked on the Cherat hill on the previous night, was to move along the ridge over the Jalala Sar, descending on Janakhwar, and closing the retreat of the enemy towards the latter place.

These preparations, however, soon changed the aspect of affairs. The Hasan Khel Afridis, who had hitherto mistaken forbearance for weakness or indifference, on perceiving the preparations for their chastisement, at once submitted unconditionally to the terms imposed upon them, and gave hostages for their future good conduct.

After the agreement come to in 1866, the Kohat pass remained open till 1876, with the exception of a period of ten days in 1870. In that year Lord Mayo rode through it on his way to Kohat, and a few days after, on the night of the 15th of April 1870, two muleteers and a servant of an officer were murdered in the most cowardly and brutal manner, in cold blood, and all the property they had with them was plundered. The murderers belonged to the Zargun Khel and Bosti Khel villages. Captain C. E. Macaulay, Deputy Commissioner of Kohat, at once seized all the men and property of the Afridis of the pass, and by the evening of the same day had Rs. 10,000 worth of property in his possession, consisting principally of camels laden with salt. The surrender of the criminals was then demanded by the Deputy Commissioner, but not acquiesced in by the Afridis, when in lieu they were offered the following terms: *1st*, the destruction of Malik Bashu's village; *2nd*, the destruction of Sherdil's (one of the murderers) house in Zargun Khel; *3rd*, the destruction of Yasin's (another of the murderers) house in Bosti Khel; *4th*, the prohibition against ever again building these without the permission of Government; *5th*, the expulsion of the three criminals from the pass for one year; *6th*, the payment of Rs. 1,000 by each of the murderers as compensation for the blood of the murdered men. These terms were agreed to after some demur. Security having been taken for the future good behaviour of the criminals, the pass was declared open again, after having been closed for ten days. One of the murderers, however, Nazr Ali, a Zakha Khel Afridi, was not included in this arrangement, and on the 7th of August of the same year he was captured by the villagers of Akhor, brought in, and hanged on the 19th on the crest of the Kohat Kotal.

The cause of the rupture which led to the closing of the pass in 1876 was due to the reopening of a question which had for many years been discussed, *viz.*, the construction of a road practicable for wheeled traffic through the pass. The Afridis, jealous of their independence, had always opposed the construction of this road, but in 1873 the question was again raised by the Commissioner of Peshawar, and all the frontier authorities considered that our relations with the Galai Afridis were now on so friendly a footing that the time had arrived when we might open negotiations for the construction of the road with a fair prospect of success. The Bangash chief, Bahadur Sher Khan, who had for many years been in charge for the pass arrangements, being also of opinion that no active opposition would be made to its construction, the assent of the sections concerned was requested.

The Afridis of the pass generally were willing to agree to the proposals of the Government; and the question would have been amicably settled but for the opposition of one contumacious village—Sharaki—which absolutely refused to agree to the proposals, and endeavoured to embroil the whole tribe. The closing of the pass was therefore forced upon the Government. Afridi trade was not prohibited until the 7th of February 1876, in consequence of distinct insults offered by the Sharaki men to the Government messenger sent to summon the *jirga* to listen to the Government demands.

Hostilities on the part of the Afridis at once began in the usual manner; night attacks and dakaities were made on British territory; cattle and goats carried off; and the towers on the crest of the pass, which were in charge of the Jawaki and Orakzai levies, were burnt on the 16th of February.

Blockade arrangements were instituted in the Peshawar and Kohat districts, and, in the first named, the Afridi crops grown within British territory were, in the spring, ordered to be cut and confiscated. In order to do this, on the 15th April large numbers of men were collected from different villages and assembled at Aimal Chabutra. To protect the men employed in cutting the the crops, troops were ordered out from Peshawar.

B-F Royal Horse Artillery.
Det., 11th Bengal Lancers.
17th Bengal Cavalry.
1 company Sappers and Miners.
20th Punjab Native Infantry.

At 3 A.M. on the 17th April a force, as per margin, under the command of Lieut.-Colonel R. G. Rogers, commanding 20th Punjab Native Infantry, marched from Peshawar towards Aimal Chabutra. After a short halt there, it moved on towards the Kotkai tower at the mouth of the pass, and the villagers then began to cut the crops. The troops were advanced to within 1,000 yards of Kotkai, near which the enemy could be seen, and while they remained in this position the enemy kept up a dropping fire, which was replied to by B-F Royal Horse Artillery and the 20th Punjab Native Infantry.

Several casualties occurred in the 20th Punjab Native Infantry before the troops were withdrawn.

The following day the same force was again moved out, but having been kept at a greater distance from the hills, no further casualties occurred, and the crops in the neighbourhood of the pass were successfully gathered.

At the beginning of the rupture, the Galai Afridis alone were implicated. The Jawakis, who had badly defended the tower entrusted to them, and who had been remiss in allowing thieves to pass through their territory, were punished by a heavy fine, which they paid, and then remained neutral until the termination of the quarrel.

The Hasan Khel and Ashu Khel, the other sections of the Adam Khel clan, were included in the blockade early in August; but no outrage of importance was committed by the former until the 10th of January, when a number of outlaws, sheltered in Hasan Khel territory, committed a very serious dakaiti in the military station of Nowshera, killing a police constable and a havildar, and carrying off arms from the police station, as well as robbing shops in the immediate neighbourhood.

The Hasan Khels were soon weary of the hostile attitude they had assumed, and signified their readiness to come to terms. The Government was quite willing to receive their submission, but only on their acceptance of the original demands which had been made, *viz.*, to consent to the construction of a road through the Hasan Khel section of the pass, and compensation for all offences committed since the beginning of the blockade, a suitable fine, and hostages to ensure compliance with these terms. In February 1877 the Hasan Khels agreed to the conditions, accepting the responsibility for future offences; and their submission was then accepted.

The collapse of the Galai Afridis soon followed, and towards the end of March they sent in their leaders to Kohat and made formal submission, accepting the Government terms, which were the improvement of the rocky portion of the road north of the *kotal* under Government supervision, the surrender of all property belonging to British subjects, and a fine of Rs. 3,000.

These terms were imposed by the Lieutenant-Governor in a public durbar held at Kohat on the 24th of March, and were accepted by the *jirga*. Bahadur Sher Khan, Bangash, received the title of *Nawab* and a *khillat*, and others who had done good service were also rewarded. The pass was then declared open, and, on the 26th the Lieutenant-Governor passed through it on his way to Peshawar.

After the reopening of the pass, the unsatisfactory attitude of the Gaddia Khel section of the Akhorwals threatened to raise fresh complications, and accordingly Captain P. L. N. Cavagnari, the Deputy Commissioner of Peshawar, obtained sanction to coerce them to submit to the Government demands by a prompt display of military force.

It was therefore decided to attempt to capture the Gaddia Khel hamlet on the Kalamsada tract, and close to the Aimal Chabutra post, by a night surprise, before the residents could effect their escape to the hills.

In communication with Colonel J. E. Cordner, R.A., commanding at Peshawar, it was arranged to move out a small force, consisting of two guns Royal Horse Artillery, a troop of cavalry, and fifty bayonets, on the night of the 14th August 1877. The detachment was to leave cantonments so as to reach Aimal Chabutra a little before daybreak. The distance to be traversed being about twenty miles, *ekkas* were to be provided for the infantry, so that the men should arrive at their destination fresh for whatever work they might have to perform.

At about half-past nine o'clock Captain Cavagnari, accompanied by Mr. Christie, District Superintendent of Police, went on ahead of the troops to make arrangements along the road for cutting off all communications with the southern border, and also to provide for the attendance of some village levies. Captain E. R. Conolly, Assistant Commissioner, was told off to accompany the troops, and to conduct them to the rendezvous decided upon.

The troops arrived punctually at the hour fixed, and halted at the place agreed upon till it was light enough to move against the village. It was then about 3-30 A.M., the distance having been accomplished in something over four hours, which, considering the time of year, the extreme darkness of the night, and the fact of the road being intersected in many places with steep ravines, was most creditable.

By the time scouts and picquets of the levies had been posted on the low hills which command the plain in rear of the village, day had begun to dawn, and the troops were moved into position. On reaching Aimal Chabutra, Lieut.-Colonel G. C. Rowcroft, who commanded the detachment, divided the cavalry into two portions, sending them at a smart gallop to the right and left rear of the village, and directing them to prevent any of the residents effecting their retreat to the hills. The guns were posted to the north of the village.

All the arrangements were completed without disturbing the residents of the hamlet, and at first it almost appeared that the village had been deserted. Simultaneously with the movement of troops into position, an agent was deputed to the villagers, warning them of the folly of resistance, and assuring them that under no circumstances would their women or children be harmed. After some delay, a deputation of the leading men came forward and tendered their submission.

Captain Cavagnari then demanded the surrender of all the adult men in the village with their arms, and this was very reluctantly and slowly complied with. The whole of the village cattle were next ordered to be given up as security for whatever fine had to be levied, and as the Afridis were rather slow about this, a feint was made of moving the infantry close up to the village, with the object of sending them in to search the houses. This hastened their movements, and by seven o'clock the troops were marched away, twenty-seven prisoners and a hundred head of oxen having been taken as guarantees for the tribesmen's prompt compliance with the demands of Government.

Expedition against the Jawaki Afridis by a force under Colonel D. Mocatta, in August 1877.

In 1853, as has been seen above, the Jawaki Afridis were admitted to a share in the allowances of the Kohat pass. They then agreed to furnish an outpost on the *kotal* with twelve armed men

to be present in a tower erected there, and to share with the Bangash tribe the responsibility for any injury or loss sustained thereon. For this service a share in the pass allowances of Rs. 2,000 was guaranteed to them, and this they had enjoyed up to the year 1877. For many years past the Jawakis had behaved well. Being the principal carriers of wood to the Kohat cantonments, and also having a large carrying trade in salt, they had amassed considerable wealth, and, their own country being barren, and their very existence depending on a free intercourse with British territory, they had shown far less inclination than other sections to embroil themselves with the Government.

During the disturbances of 1876-77, and the blockade of the Galai Afridis, the Jawakis showed a certain sympathy with their kinsmen who were engaged in hostilities with the British Government, but they themselves took no active part in the matter. They, however, abandoned their tower on the *kotal*, which was destroyed, as already stated, by the Galai Afridis in February 1876, and they failed to keep their portion of the border free from the attacks of thieves belonging to the blockaded sections of the Adam Khel clan. They were therefore proceeded against by seizure of their men and property found in the Kohat district, upon which they at once gave in their submission, adjusted claims to the extent of Rs. 2,000, and gave selected hostages to maintain strict neutrality.

This engagement the Jawakis observed until the close of the Kohat pass difficulties in 1877. At that time the consideration of the re-allotment of the pass allowances was rendered necessary, as it was felt that, as distributed, they were open to objection, as they were in some cases being paid to sections who performed no appreciable service. It was known that it was under consideration to reduce the Jawaki allowance of Rs. 2,000, which was not fairly earned, seeing that no Jawaki villages abutted on the pass, and that during the complications of 1876-77 the tribe had shown that they were not able to render the service which was expected from them. In the event, however, of this allowance being withdrawn from the Jawakis, the Government were prepared to allow them an equivalent for the performance of real duties in guarding the Khushalgarh road and telegraph line, which, running close to the independent hills, were always liable to attack.

The Jawakis, however, did not wait for the decision of the Government, but began to show a spirit of hostility in the month of July 1877, when, on the 15th of that month, they cut the telegraph wire between Kohat and Khushalgarh in several places. The Jawaki *jirga*, who were responsible for its safety, were at once summoned, but refused to come to Kohat, sending an insolent message that the Bangash *jirga* should be sent to discuss the matter with them in their own territory. A *baramta* of those Jawakis and their property found in British territory was at once ordered, which was fairly successful, and ninety-three men and a large number of cattle were seized.

On the 24th July a considerable number of Jawakis, who had hidden themselves in ambush on the Kohat road, rescued two of their men who had been seized and were being escorted by the police to Kohat, three of the guard, together with the prisoners, being carried off into the Jawaki hills. The *jirga* was at once ordered to release the prisoners and to return their arms, but, under the pretence of fearing arrest, they declined to come in to Kohat, though the captives were released on the 27th July. The next night the telegraph wire was cut a second time, and the Deputy Commissioner threatened to forfeit the pension and property of the principal Jawaki *malik* (Babri) in British territory, and to eject the members of the tribe from their hamlets in the Kohat district. The *jirga* came to Kohat on the 30th, where, the case being completely proved against them, they made submission, returned the arms of the police, and paid a fine of Rs. 300.

The matter being thus settled, the *jirga* were ordered to return to their villages. In spite, however, of their submission and the payment of the fine, the Jawakis almost immediately began to show signs of an inclination to give further trouble, and on the 8th of August began to remove their property and grain from their hamlets on the Khushalgarh road. The leading *malik* of the hamlets in British territory was, therefore, summoned, who explained that the reason for this action was the fear of the residents of being again arrested. He promised that the removal of the property should cease.

On the 17th August, on the Khushalgarh road, eleven miles from Kohat, a small party of sepoys, proceeding on leave, were attacked by Jawaki raiders. Three were killed, and the telegraph wire was again cut. For the safety of this important line of communication, cavalry and infantry patrols were ordered to be furnished, during daylight, by the garrison of Kohat. Khattak levies, horse and foot, were also ordered to attend for service, and the police posts were strengthened. Brunswick rifles and ammunition from the Kohat stores were at the same time served out to villages on the Jawaki frontier.

The agents of Nawab Bahadur Sher Khan, Bangash, who had now the entire management of the whole Adam Khel clan, were sent into the hills to summon the *jirga*; but they returned, stating that both the sub-sections of the Jawakis, *viz.*, the Haibat Khel and the Kimat Khel, were engaged in the raids, and that the section demanded that their six requests should be granted, otherwise they would not come in to Kohat.

Nightly attacks on British villages and British subjects were now committed by the Jawakis; on the 27th of August a bridge on the Khushalgarh road was burnt, and two days later an unsuccessful attempt was made to burn a second bridge. It was therefore decided that the immediate punishment of the section was absolutely necessary, but it was considered that the season was unfavourable for prolonged operations. It was accordingly determined to see if a sudden dash into their country, with the object of inflicting as much injury as possible, would bring them to their senses and cause them to submit.

The causes of this outbreak on the part of the Jawakis, as far as can be gathered, appear to have been :—

1st.—The conviction of the Jawakis, founded on information, not officially conveyed to them, but irregularly obtained, and possibly communicated by persons interested in their misbehaviour, that the allowances hitherto given to them for their jointly holding the *kotal* of the Kohat pass were to be withdrawn.

2nd.—The enforcement of the responsibility of the section for damage committed to the road and telegraph without any remuneration for such responsibility.

3rd.—Transfer of the management of the section, which had lately been ordered by the Government, to Nawab Bahadur Sher Khan, who was notoriously hostile to some of its principal members.

At this time the two leading *maliks* among the Jawakis were Babri and Mushki, both belonging to the Kimat Khel Jawakis;

of the Haibat Khel, the leading *malik* was Zal Beg of Paia. All these men were at this time hostile to the British Government, and had done their utmost to incite the section to a rupture with us.

At the end of August secret orders were issued to Brig.-General C. B. Keyes, C.B., commanding the Punjab Frontier Force, to penetrate the Jawaki country in three columns, with the object of cutting off the retreat of a body of raiders, who were lurking about the Khushalgarh road, obstructing traffic and harassing patrol parties.

On the night of the 29th of August, the troops told off for the expedition were all in position, ready for an advance. Brig.-General Keyes, however, owing to a sudden illness, was unable to accompany the force, and the command devolved on Colonel D. Mocatta, commanding the 3rd Sikh Infantry.

The following was the plan of operations. The first column, composed of the troops as per margin, and accompanied by Colonel Mocatta, and also by Colonel Sir F. R. Pollock, K.C.S.I., the Commissioner, was to enter the Jawaki country by the Tortang defile, and to push forward as rapidly as possible until it arrived at a central point, at the northern end of the Gandiali ravine, with a view to cutting off the retreat in that direction of the main body of the enemy, which, it was anticipated, would be opposed to the second column in the Gandiali defile.

No. 1 Mountain Battery.		
2nd Punjab Cavalry	.. 45	sabres.
1st Sikh Infantry	.. 103	bayonets.
3rd Sikh Infantry	.. 278	"
4th Sikh Infantry	.. 245	"

The second column, composed of the troops as per margin, was to advance up the Gandiali pass at daylight, but was to play with the enemy, rather than press them seriously, until time had been given for the arrival of the first column at the other end of the defile.

2nd Punjab Cavalry	.. 104	sabres.
1st Sikh Infantry	.. 220	bayonets.
6th Punjab Infantry	.. 297	"

The third column, composed of troops as per margin, was to advance from Shadipur on the Indus, *viâ* Shekh Aladad Ziarat, with orders to cut off the enemy's retreat along the Tambol Sar range, and to continue its march until it effected a junction with the other two columns, when the entire force would retire to British territory by the Gandiali pass.

Corps of Guides, 201 bayonets.

In accordance with the above plan, the first column reached the entrance of the Tortang defile shortly before daylight on the 30th, and as soon as dawn appeared, the levies of Nawab Bahadur Sher Khan were directed to crown the heights on the right, whilst those on the left were secured by three companies of the 3rd Sikhs, under Lieutenant C. H. M. Smith. The column then advanced up the defile. The enemy opened fire from a strong position on the left, but a few rounds from the mountain guns soon cleared the advance. On emerging from the pass the column had to traverse a valley studded with hamlets, which were burnt by the levies.

At 8-15 A.M. a junction was effected with the second column. This column had begun its march through the Gandiali defile shortly after daybreak, but, although it expected to meet with determined opposition, no resistance had been offered to its advance. On emerging from the pass a few of the enemy were seen near the village of Turki; they were immediately dispersed by the 2nd Punjab Cavalry, under Major F. Lance, with the loss to them of one killed and two taken prisoners.

The first and second columns having now united, it was necessary to effect a junction with the third column Leaving therefore the 6th Punjab Infantry, under Major S. J. Browne, with the Khattak levies, to hold the Gandiali pass, Colonel Mocatta advanced with the rest of the troops along the base of the Tambol hills, the left flank being protected by two companies of the 4th Punjab Infantry, the 2nd Punjab Cavalry forming the rear-guard.

The enemy now began to press the rear-guard, and it was therefore necessary to strengthen it by a company of the 1st Sikhs, and subsequently by the 4th Punjab Infantry. As it was now evident that the original plan of retiring by the Gandiali pass would only be effected with much difficulty, and probably with considerable loss, Colonel Mocatta decided to return to British territory by some other route, and accordingly he sent orders to Major Browne to retire to Gumbat through the Gandiali defile.

At the village of Lashkari Banda, which had been just set on fire by the Guides, Colonel Mocatta effected a junction with the third column. The whole force then retired by the Kuka China pass to British territory. Major R. B. P. P. Campbell, commanding the third column, had, in anticipation of this, posted a portion of his troops on the crest of this pass to protect the retirement to the border village of Talanj. The pass was difficult, but practicable; small parties of the enemy followed closely, and three of our men were wounded. The hamlet of Talanj, at the foot of the hills, was reached about 6-30 P.M., and the force then marched across the plain to Gumbat, which was reached at 9-30 P.M.

Although measures had been taken to ensure the utmost secrecy with regard to the movement of the troops preparatory to this expedition, yet it was subsequently discovered that the Jawakis had information on the 29th which led them to expect that an attack was intended, and this would explain the small amount of opposition met with by the second column.

The British casualties in these operations amounted to one man killed and one officer and nine men wounded.

Expedition against the Jawaki Afridis by a combined force under Brigadiers-General C. P. Keyes, C.B., and C. C. G. Ross, C.B., November to January 1877-78.

Although at first an opinion prevailed that a good effect had been obtained by the expedition into the Jawaki country on the 30th of August, yet the main object of the expedition, in inflicting personal loss on the enemy in killed, wounded, and prisoners, was not attained, and the number of casualties on the side of the enemy was exceedingly small. Property of considerable value was certainly destroyed, but the effect of this does not seem to have been of much importance, and it must also be remembered that all the loss of property had fallen on the Kimat Khel alone, and that the Haibat Khel section had not suffered at all.

Meanwhile the hostile attitude of the Jawakis remained unchanged, and aggressions on British territory did not cease. These continued outrages of the section at last rendered further punitive measures against them absolutely necessary, and it was determined that a joint occupation of the country should be made by Brig.-General C. P. Keyes, C.B., with a force composed of troops belonging to the Punjab Frontier Force, and supported by the 29th Punjab Native Infantry in reserve at Khushalgarh, while Brig.-General C. C. G. Ross, C.B., commanding the Peshawar district, should advance with a column from that direction. The blockade, which had for some time been of a purely military character, was to be made more active, and to be extended by

Brig.-General Keyes's occupation of the villages of Paia and Turki, cutting a line of country through the Jawaki territory.

Before these operations were undertaken the *jirgas* of the non-committed sections of the Adam Khel clan, *viz.*, the Galai, Ashu Khel, and Hassan Khel, were summoned to Peshawar, and were received by the Commissioner on the 28th of October. They were informed of the intention of Government, and were assured that, in the event of their remaining neutral, no injury whatever would be caused to them. The leading men of the *jirgas*, without hesitation, agreed to remain neutral, and selected hostages from the families of each section were given as a guarantee of their good faith. At the same time a proclamation was prepared by the Government of India, which was to be made public after Brig.-General Keyes had entered the Jawaki country and taken up his position.

It had been ascertained that, after the expedition into their country on the 30th of August, the Jawakis had made overtures for help to the Akhund [1] of Swat and to the Amir of Kabul. Both applications were unsuccessful, the *Akhund* strongly condemning the tribes as thieves and rascals, who were only murdering and plundering their unarmed co-religionists (referring to raids on Kohat villages), and the Amir informing them that they were mistaken in supposing that he countenanced or approved of their proceedings.

On the 6th of November orders were issued by Brig.-General C. P. Keyes, for the formation of three columns, as per margin, for offensive operations against the Jawakis. The troops were to carry with them cooked food for two days. At 5 A.M., on the morning of the 9th, the first column marched through the Tortang pass without meeting any opposition, and joined the second column, which had advanced unopposed by the Gandiali defile, near Turki, at

No. I Column at Kohat, under command of Colonel D. Mocatta, 3rd Sikh Infantry.		
No. 1 Mountain Battery.		
2nd Punjab Cavalry	.. 25	sabres.
Corps of Guides	.. 380	bayonets.
1st Sikh Infantry	.. 225	,,
3rd Sikh Infantry	.. 225	,,
No. II Column at Gumbat, under command of Major B. Williams, 2nd Punjab Cavalry.		
2nd Punjab Cavalry	.. 5	sabres.
4th Punjab Infantry	.. 350	bayonets.
6th Punjab Infantry	.. 300	,,
No. III Column at Lukha Talao, under command of Colonel P. F. Gardiner, 5th Gurkhas.		
No. 2 Mountain Battery	2	guns.
5th Punjab Infantry	.. 280	bayonets.
5th Gurkha Regiment	.. 280	,,

[1] For the history of this man see Volume I.

10 A.M. The baggage of both columns having been formed in column of route, a continued movement on Paia was made, and at 1 P.M. the force arrived within 2,000 yards of the highest point commanding the approach to Paia from the west. This was immediately assaulted by the Guides in front, and by the 4th Punjab Infantry in flank, the enemy, after a few shots, taking to flight. It has since been ascertained that Malik Babri was leading the defence, and, being unable to retire quick enough, hid in the ravines below, and thus escaped the Guides, whose skirmishers passed over him. At 3 P.M. the force descended on Paia, and occupied the principal villages.

In the meantime the third column had pushed forward from Shadipur through the Namung pass, and met with no opposition until emerging from the defile, when the enemy was found holding the ridges on the right. They were soon driven off by two companies of the 5th Punjab Infantry, and the advance was continued till the village of Kahkto was reached, where the troops received orders to entrench themselves.

On the following day the 4th and 6th Punjab Infantry were sent to the rear from Paia, to reconnoitre and secure the best line for convoys, and on the 11th of November the first convoy arrived at 10 A.M., unmolested.

On the 12th the enemy having occupied the hills to the south of Colonel Gardiner's position, a company of the 5th Punjab Infantry was sent to dislodge them. Having gained the heights and driven them off, the company began to retire, when they were suddenly attacked by superior numbers of the enemy, who had remained concealed in the ravines on the other side of the crest. A gallant stand was made by Major C. E. Stewart and Lieutenant G. Gaisford and their men, who, from the nature of the ground, were broken up into small parties, and the heights were eventually regained, the enemy being driven off in great confusion, with a loss on our side of three men wounded.

On the 13th Colonel Gardiner's column joined the head-quarters at Paia, but, before doing so, seven towers were blown up and nine burnt, and the village of Zal Beg was completely destroyed.

On the 14th, No. 4 (Hazara) Mountain Battery was added to the strength of Brig.-General Keyes's force.

On the 15th, after blowing up the principal towers in the

Paia valley, the main body retired to Shindih and Turki, with the loss of only one man, wounded. The position occupied by the camp at Shindih was on the lower Jamu lands in front (to the south) of Bagh. Heavy rain fell on the 16th, 17th, and 18th, and again from the 22nd to the 25th. During this period reconnaissances and surveys were actively pushed on, and Brig.-General Keyes returned to Kohat on the 17th, for the purpose of carrying out a reconnaissance in the direction of the Bazid Khel Kotal, with the first column, which moved to Kohat on the 18th. On the 20th the Brig.-General returned to the head-quarters camp, leaving the troops of the first column to proceed on the 21st and 22nd to Turki.

Owing to heavy rain, military operations were now rendered impossible, and nothing of importance occurred till the 1st of December, when it had been decided to advance on Jamu, one of the principal fastnesses of the Jawaki country. As it appeared difficult to retire a force from Jamu without heavy loss, after advancing and capturing that place, Brig.-General Keyes suggested that the operations should be simultaneous with an advance by the Peshawar force on Bori. It will, however, be seen hereafter that, owing to the rain and the breaking of the bridge at Attock, the Peshawar force was not able to occupy the Sarghasha ridge until the 4th December, and the value of this operation in aid of General Keyes's movement on Jamu was therefore in a great measure lost.

Right Column, under Major J. W. McQueen, 5th Punjab Infantry.
5th and 6th Punjab Infantry, reinforced by half No. 2 M. Battery, and the Corps of Guides.
Centre Column, under Colonel P. F. Gardiner, 5th Gurkhas.
No. 4 (Hazara) Mountain Battery, 4th Punjab Infantry, and 5th Gurkhas.
Colonel Mocatta, 3rd Sikh Infantry.
Half No. 1 Mountain Battery, 1st and 3rd Sikh Infantry, and 29th Punjab Native Infantry.

On the morning of the 1st December the troops paraded noiselessly some time before dawn. The force was divided into three columns, as per margin. At 4 A.M. the right column moved to the plateau to the north-east of the camp in the direction of Paia. The left column moved by a high ridge to a point to the north-west of the camp. The centre column advanced in the direction of Bagh and Saparai. The right and left columns having arrived at their respective positions, the general advance began; and, notwithstanding the enemy's breastworks and other preparations, the attack was a complete surprise. The enemy was driven into and beyond the two villages of Shahi Khel, close to the Nara Khula defile, where the Jamu valley is very narrow. These villages were occupied for an hour and then fired.

The troops then fell back on the village of Saparai in the Jamu valley, which was occupied by the head-quarters and the troops marginally noted, the remainder of the force retiring to the camp in front of Bagh. Our loss had been slight, one killed and eight wounded, while the enemy's was estimated at about thirty killed and wounded.

No. 4 (Hazara) Mn. Battery.
Corps of Guides.
1st Sikh Infantry.
4th Punjab Infantry.

As soon as the village of Saparai had been occupied, the proclamation of Government [1] was distributed in all directions, and the enemy allowed to remove and bury their dead.

On the morning of the 3rd, Brig.-General Keyes, with a party of the 3rd Sikhs, proceeded to reconnoitre the Bazid Khel Kotal, which was found to be much less difficult than it had been represented to be, and capable of being turned from the heights on the Kohat side. It would, however, be a formidable obstacle to troops hampered by baggage, if defended by an active enemy. On the 4th, after blowing up the towers, the whole force was withdrawn to the camp in front of Bagh, without casualty, the village of Bagh itself being fired as the troops retired.

It is now necessary to turn to the Peshawar side. On the 12th of November the garrison of Fort Mackeson had a skirmish with raiders between that place and Sham Shatu. On the 16th November Brig.-General C. C. G. Ross, commanding at Peshawar, reported the occupation of the Sarghasha ridge in considerable strength by Jawakis, who came across from the Kohat side under the impression that an invasion of their country from the direction of Peshawar was intended; these men descended nightly on the Sham Shatu road. On the 21st of November the garrison of Fort Mackeson moved out to oppose an intended raid. On this occasion, Captain H. B. Swiney, 17th Bengal Cavalry, was killed.

In the meanwhile the concentration of troops at Fort Mackeson was being pushed on, and it was expected that all arrangements would be ready by the evening of the 1st of December; but

[1] See Appendix A.

unforeseen difficulties arose, and a heavy fall of rain, quite exceptional at that time of the year, caused a flood on the Indus, which destroyed the bridge-of-boats at Attock, and caused a block on the line of communications with Rawal Pindi, so that it was not until the 3rd of December that the whole force was concentrated and ready to move into the Jawaki country.

1st Brigade, under Colonel J. Doran, C.B.
Half 1-C Royal Horse Artillery.
51st Foot.
2 companies, Sappers and Miners.
22nd Punjab Native Infantry.
27th Punjab Native Infantry.

2nd Brigade, under Colonel H. J. Buchanan.
Half 1-C Royal Horse Artillery.
13-9th Royal Artillery (40-prs.).
9th Foot.
4th Battalion, Rifle Brigade.
14th Native Infantry.
29th Punjab Native Infantry.

The force, under the command of Brig.-General C. C. G. Ross, C.B., consisted of 3,959 of all arms and was divided into two brigades, as per margin, one under the command of Colonel J. Doran, C.B., and the other under Colonel H. J. Buchanan, 9th Regiment.

The Bori valley is separated from the plain to the south of the Mackeson–Sham Shatu road by a rocky range of hills, as already described in the account of the operations against the Boriwals in 1853. This range is crossed by a comparatively low pass at Kandao, and by a second more direct pass, known as the Sarghasha pass, over a higher part of the ridge. The plan of operations was to occupy the crest of the ridge with artillery and infantry, and from this position, which entirely commanded the Bori valley, to take such measures as should be found most suitable for attacking the villages and destroying their towers and other defences.

The road *viâ* Kandao was selected for the advance of the 1st Brigade, under Colonel Doran, which was to make its way to the top of the ridge, and turn the Sarghasha pass at the same time as the latter was forced by direct attack by the 2nd Brigade, under Colonel Buchanan. Arrangements had previously been made with the Ashu Khel Afridis for the troops to use the road by Kandao, which lay within their territory.

At dawn on the morning of the 4th of December Colonel Doran's column, the 27th Punjab Native Infantry leading, left camp, and marched towards Kandao, followed by the 2nd Brigade. On arriving in front of Kandao, the latter turned off the road by a track leading to the Sarghasha pass, at the foot of which it arrived about 11 A.M. Colonel Buchanan had received instructions not to advance until he saw the skirmishers of the 27th Punjab Native Infantry on the hill above Kandao. He was then to make his way to the crest of the ridge, and, having dislodged the enemy, to move along the crest to meet his baggage and water, which were to join him *viâ* Kandao.

The advance of Colonel Doran's column was completely successful, and the skirmishers of the 27th Punjab Native Infantry, supported in their advance by the Royal Horse Artillery guns, were soon on the top of the Kandao pass, the small body of the enemy opposed to them being speedily dispersed. The turning movement of this column rendered the crest of the Sarghasha pass untenable by the enemy, who now abandoned their position and retired, partly towards the Bori valley and partly along the Sarghasha ridge towards Khui, keeping up a desultory fire on the advancing troops as they retired. Meanwhile Colonel Buchanan's column, covered by the fire of the heavy guns, had gained the top of the pass, and the ridge was in our hands. It had been intended that the troops under Colonel Doran should return to the plain before Kandao for the night, but it was found necessary to alter this arrangement, and orders were issued for the whole force to bivouac on the ridge.

On the following morning, the 51st Regiment and 22nd Punjab Native Infantry were ordered to return to Kandao, and march thence by the road along the foot of the hills to the ground near the foot of the Sarghasha pass. During the day the road by this pass was improved by the Sappers and Miners, aided by infantry working-parties, and the line of communications with the plains was transferred to this route, that by Kandao being abandoned to prevent any chance of complications with the Ashu Khel Afridis.

On the 6th, 7th, and 8th December the troops were employed in the destruction of the villages and towers in the Bori valley.

The destruction of the villages was carried out by the sappers, covered by infantry and by the fire of the artillery on the ridge. On the first two days the rocky heights above the villages attacked were held by considerable bodies of the enemy, who maintained a brisk, though generally ineffective, fire, until dislodged by the steady advance of the infantry skirmishers, and by the admirably directed shells of the Royal Horse Artillery guns from the top of the Sarghasha ridge. On each occasion, the enemy, as is usually the case, reappeared as soon as we began to retire, but the fire of the guns and the steadiness of our skirmishers, effectually prevented them from pressing on our retirement. On the last day of our operations in the valley two of the strongest villages were occupied without resistance. The Afridis appear to have found that their traditional tactics were useless against the arms and disciplined troops opposed to them, and, with the exception of a few individuals, none of them on this occasion attempted to hold their ground or to fire upon the troops when retiring. During these three days' operations our loss was only one man killed and ten wounded.

The Jawakis of the Bori valley had now taken refuge in the neighbouring villages of the uncommitted sections, or had retreated into the heart of the Jawaki country.

While the operations in the Bori valley were in progress, Brig.-General Keyes, on the 7th December, successfully attacked and destroyed, without loss to ourselves, the village and towers of Ghariba, a place which the Jawakis had long considered secure from attack.

Although the chief places of the Jawakis had now been occupied and destroyed, and the blockade satisfactorily maintained by our forces, yet the enemy shewed no signs of surrender. Had it been possible to ensure the friendliness of the other sections, the maintenance of the blockade, though a tedious proceeding, would certainly have brought the people to terms without the risk of any further advance into their country ; but this friendliness did not appear to be assured, and a further advance, by both forces in combination, into the Pustawani valley was decided upon. For many years past the strategic value of the Pustawani valley, to a force operating against the Adam Khel clan, had been recognized, and it was known that this portion of the Jawaki country was considered impregnable by them. It was also hoped that, by making a sudden combined movement in this direction, a surprise might be effected, and property and cattle seized, which would materially aid the settlement of affairs.

On the Peshawar side the road from the Bori valley to Pustawani leads through the Bori China pass, which, as a result of a reconnaissance carried out on the 25th December, was found to be just practicable for laden mules.

It was accordingly proposed by Brig.-General Ross that his force should bivouac in the Bori valley on the 26th, and advance to Pustawani on the 27th, in co-operation with Brig.-General Keyes; but heavy rain rendered all movements impossible, owing to danger of floods in the pass, and the advance had therefore to be postponed until the 31st of December. It was expected that Brig.-General Keyes's force from the Kohat side would arrive in the Pustawani valley on the same day.

Four days' rations were taken by the Peshawar column, of which two days' supply was carried by the regiments, the remainder by the Commissariat. The force employed consisted of 1-C Royal Horse Artillery, with Infantry detachments, on the Sargha-sha ridge, and two brigades, under Colonels Doran and Buchanan, which were composed of the troops as per margin. No. 4 (Hazara) Mountain Battery, with an escort of 50 bayonets of the 22nd Punjab Native Infantry, was attached to the 2nd Brigade until the crowning of the *kotal* was completed, when it was ordered to join Colonel Doran's column.

1st Brigade, under Colonel J. Doran, C.B.		
9th Regiment	100	bayonets.
4th Battalion, Rifle Brigade	130	"
17th Bengal Cavalry ..	20	sabres.
2 companies, S. and M. ..	160	bayonets.
27th Punjab Native Infantry	484	"
2nd Brigade, under Colonel H. J. Buchanan.		
9th Regiment	300	bayonets.
14th Native Infantry ..	489	"
20th Punjab Native Infantry	369	"

Colonel Doran was directed to detach two companies to the crest of the hills on the left of the pass, and to furnish a strong party as a rear-guard, the remainder of his column being pushed on to the head of the pass, with instructions to await further orders regarding the attack on Pustawani.

On the morning of the 31st December the troops advanced, and the 1st Brigade, under Colonel Buchanan, having crowned the hills to the right, moved along towards the *kotal*. The advance up the pass, as had been anticipated, proved difficult, and much delay occurred in the passage of the baggage. On arrival at the crest, a party under Major H. W. Gordon, 20th Punjab Native Infantry took up a position, with orders to hold the heights on both sides of the road during the stay of the force in the valley.

The advance of the troops to the right and left of the pass was almost entirely unopposed, a few stray shots only being fired at the 27th Punjab Native Infantry, while some small parties who opened fire on the advanced skirmishers of the right column were at once dispersed by the Hazara Mountain Battery.

On the arrival of Colonel Doran's brigade at the top of the pass he received orders to move down the opposite slope, and attack the village of Pustawani. His attack was led by some skirmishers of the 9th Foot and 27th Punjab Native Infantry, with the detachment of the Rifle Brigade and other troops in support. The village of Pustawani consisted of four principal hamlets, with two towers, concealed from the foot of the pass by a low rocky hill in the middle of the valley, on the reverse slopes of which they were built. The village appeared from the *kotal* to be unoccupied, but the skirmishers, on approaching to within five or six hundred yards of it, were received with a rapid, but ill-directed, fire from a small party of about thirty of the enemy. The rocky hill above the village was quickly occupied by the skirmishers, but not before the enemy had time to gain the hills on the southern side of the valley, where they disappeared.

The Brig.-General then pushed on towards Walai with a portion of his force and met Brig.-General Keyes, escorted by a few mounted orderlies, about a mile above Pustawani. After consulting as to future operations, Brig.-General Ross returned to Pustawani and General Keyes to his picquets on the Dargai Sar.

In the meantime, ground had been selected for the bivouacs of the different corps in and near Pustawani, and the greater part of the baggage reached camp during the afternoon.

General Keyes had informed General Ross that he intended to withdraw from the positions occupied by his troops on the Dargai Sar towards Kohat, on the morning of the 1st January. The latter, however, decided to remain in the Pustawani valley another day, in order to send a survey party to the hills above Walai. On the evening of the 1st January all preparations were made for the return of the force at daybreak next morning to the Sarghasha ridge and camp, and a portion of Colonel Buchanan's brigade was marched to the head of the pass.

The following morning at daylight the heights on both sides of the pass were crowned by the same troops as had been employed for this duty on the 31st December, and, when the road was reported clear, the baggage, preceded by an advanced guard of native infantry, left camp and traversed the pass without a check.

Colonel Doran's brigade left Pustawani two hours later, after destroying the towers and setting fire to the villages, and followed the baggage through the pass. The opposition met with was very slight, and the whole of the troops reached the Sarghasha camp without casualties.

It is now necessary to turn to the operations of Brig.-General Keyes's force. After the capture of Ghariba, the force was withdrawn to the camp in front of Bagh, and it was not till the 31st December that the combined advance on Pustawani could be begun.

The troops to take part in these operations were divided into three columns, as per margin.

Advanced Column.		
Corps of Guides	.. 200	bayonets.
5th Punjab Infantry	.. 200	"
Centre Column.		
No. 2 Mountain Battery	.. 2	guns.
4th Punjab Infantry	.. 200	bayonets.
6th Punjab Infantry	.. 200	"
5th Gurkha Regiment	.. 200	"
Rear Column.		
No. 1 Mountain Battery	.. 2	guns.
1st Sikh Infantry	.. 200	bayonets.
3rd Sikh Infantry	.. 200	"
29th Punjab Native Infantry	200	"

The advanced column was under the command of Major J. W. McQueen, 5th Punjab Infantry; the centre column, composed of troops from Shindih, was under the command of Colonel P. F. Gardiner, 5th Gurkhas; and the rear column, composed of troops from Turki, was under the command of Colonel D. Mocatta, 3rd Sikh Infantry.

At 5-30 A.M. on the morning of the 31st of December the advanced column marched from camp, and, proceeding along the convoy route, debouched on the Paia plain, and from there advanced on Ghariba. A few of the enemy were seen retiring as the troops advanced, but not a shot was fired. On gaining the village of Ghariba, the column turned to the left up the spur of the Dargai Sar. The ground was exceedingly difficult, and, had it been defended, even by a few men, the troops could not have advanced without considerable loss. On reaching the summit of the Dargai Sar, two companies of the Guides, under Lieutenant F. D. Battye, were sent to hold the hill overlooking Jamu, and a small party of the Guides was also sent down to the ridge at the head of the pass to await the arrival of the main column.

In the meanwhile, the other two columns left camp at 6-30 A.M., and followed the advanced column to Ghariba. On arriving there, the Brig.-General, with the 4th Punjab Infantry, 5th

Gurkhas, and the guns of No. 2 Mountain Battery, moved on at once to the Dargai pass, leaving the baggage and the 6th Punjab Infantry with the rear column at Ghariba. On reaching the mouth of the pass, a few shots were fired at long distances, and one sepoy of the 5th Gurkhas was wounded. A considerable quantity of grain was found in the ravines, and it was evident that the advance of the troops in this direction was unexpected.

As soon as the leading regiment reached the crest of the pass, the Brig.-General sent a company of the 4th Punjab Infantry to occupy Walai, to which place he himself proceeded. The road proved to be much more difficult than had been expected; and as Walai was found to be an unsuitable position for the force to bivouac, orders were sent back for the troops to remain for the night as nearly as possible in the positions they then held. Leaving the company of infantry to hold the village, Brig.-General Keyes, with a few mounted orderlies, reconnoitred towards Pustawani, which was now occupied by the Peshawar troops, and met Brig.-General Ross, as already narrated.

The retirement of General Keyes's force was begun on the 1st January, and was successfully carried out, in spite of considerable opposition. It was, however, quite dark before the regiments reached their respective positions.

On the following day, the 2nd of January, Brig.-General Keyes visited the Lieutenant-Governor at Kohat, and it was decided that further operations should be undertaken against Jamu for the purpose of exploring the Nara Khula defile, which was the only remaining stronghold of the Jawakis. The operations were delayed, in consequence of the uncertainty as to the attitude of the neutral sections of the Adam Khel clan, but it was finally arranged that a simultaneous advance should be made from the Peshawar and Kohat sides on the morning of the 15th of January, that both columns should, on the evening of that day, occupy the same positions as they held on the 31st of December, and that on the 16th a consultation should be held at Walai as to the measures required for the passage of the Kohat force through the Nara Khula pass, and such further movements as General Keyes might think necessary to complete the occupation of the Jawaki country.

On the morning of the 15th of January Brig.-General Ross's force, composed of the same corps as on the first expedition to Pustawani and divided into two columns, as on that occasion, under the command of Colonels Doran and Buchanan respectively, moved into the Pustawani valley by the Bori China pass. The force occupied Pustawani without resistance at about 11 A.M., and the baggage arrived in camp early in the afternoon. The *kotal* was occupied by Major H. W. Gordon, 20th Punjab Native Infantry, as on the former occasion. Heliographic communication was established with Brig.-General Keyes, who had again occupied the Dargai ridge. At about 1 P.M., a small force, consisting of No. 4 (Hazara) Mountain Battery, the 9th Foot, and the 14th Native Infantry, under Colonel Buchanan, was despatched to reconnoitre in the direction of Walai and towards the Nara Khula defile; the column was fired on during its advance, but a few shells from the Hazara Mountain Battery soon dispersed the enemy. Having effected their object, the force returned to camp. As a result of this reconnaissance it was decided to evacuate Pustawani, and to move the whole force to Walai on the following day.

The troops were under arms at daybreak on the morning of the 16th, and marched shortly afterwards towards Walai, the hills on the left being crowned by the 27th Punjab Native Infantry, Colonel Buchanan's brigade at the same time moving along the spur forming the northern boundary of the valley, by which the reconnoitring party had advanced on the previous day. The village of Walai was occupied without opposition by Colonel Doran's troops, and the 20th Punjab Native Infantry, which formed the advanced guard of the other brigade, was pushed on to the crest of the spur from the main range overlooking the Gulu Tangai.

At 9 A.M. General Ross was joined at Walai by General Keyes, and was requested by the latter to co-operate with him by sending troops to the crest of the Torsappar range, which forms the boundary between the Jawaki and Galai Afridis. Orders were sent to Colonel Buchanan to move his brigade towards the Torsappar watershed, and the 20th Punjab Native Infantry, which formed the advanced guard, began at once to move up the spur. The ascent was long and steep, and, when near the top, the advance was delayed for a short time by a small party of the enemy, who were strongly posted near the crest of the hill. They were, however, soon dislodged, and were pursued by the leading skirmishers across the Galai Afridi frontier. The remainder of Colonel Buchanan's brigade shortly afterwards joined the 20th Punjab Native Infantry on the watershed. The troops returned by the same spur by which they had ascended, and then turned to the right and descended into the Gulu Tangai, where it had been arranged that they should bivouac.

On the following day it was determined that the Peshawar column should abandon its communications by the Sarghasha pass, and should join Brig.-General Keyes's force on the 18th, and retire to the camp below the Sarghasha pass, *viâ* Kohat.

The 17th was spent in survey work and early the next morning, the Peshawar column marched towards the Nara Khula, to join Brig.-General Keyes's force.

It is now necessary to turn to the movements of the Kohat column since the morning of the 15th of January. Early on the morning of that day, the 4th and 5th Punjab Infantry, under the command of Major J. W. McQueen, moved in advance of the main column with orders to march direct on Ghariba, and push on at once, as rapidly as possible, up the Dargai range.

The Corps of Guides (200 bayonets) advanced at the same time by the spur by which Major McQueen's column had ascended on the 31st of December, with orders not to push the advance, if seriously opposed, until the heights on the right were gained by the 4th and 5th Punjab Infantry. The baggage and main column advanced direct by the Dargai pass, halting near the entrance until the skirmishers of the right and left attacks were seen advancing along the heights towards the *kotal*. The 4th Punjab Infantry, which led the right advance, met with some slight opposition near the foot of the spur by which it ascended, but opposition ceased before the difficult ground near the top was reached.

In conjunction with the movement to the crest of the Dargai Sar, above described, a second column had been ordered to occupy the Jamu valley, with the object of forcing the Nara Khula defile. This column, consisting of the troops as per margin, under the command of Colonel D. Mocatta, marched from Turki at 6 A.M. on the 15th, and occupied the Jamu villages by 9 A.M., without opposition. Here Colonel Mocatta received orders from

No. 1 Mountain Battery ..	2	guns.
1st Sikh Infantry ..	230	bayonets.
3rd Sikh Infantry ..	230	"
29th Punjab Native Infy.	230	"

Brig.-General Keyes to make the necessary arrangements for forcing the Nara Khula on the following day.

In accordance with these instructions, on the morning of the 16th, a party of 100 bayonets, 1st Sikh Infantry, was sent forward to seize the ridge which connects the Mandaher Sar with the Zira hill on the west side of the Nara Khula. The party encountered considerable opposition, but, owing to the excellent arrangements made by Major A. G. Ross, who was in command, they succeeded in their object, and picquets were placed which commanded the Nara Khula from the left. An hour later, another party consisting of fifty bayonets of the 3rd Sikh Infantry, under Lieutenant C. H. M. Smith, was sent to seize a conical hill which overlooked the defile throughout almost its entire length. In the meanwhile, the guns of No. 2 Mountain Battery on the Dargai Sar had taken up a position overlooking the Nara Khula on the east side. The right and left flanks being thus secured, Colonel Mocatta, at 10 A.M., gave orders for an advance to be made through the defile. On reaching the further end of the pass, a smart fire was opened on the advanced party, and one man of the 1st Sikh Infantry was wounded. A few of the enemy were occupying a ridge about 500 or 600 yards in advance of the gorge, and it was necessary to dislodge them. This duty was performed by Major H. C. P. Rice with 30 bayonets of the 1st Sikh Infantry, and the heights on the right and left having been secured by parties from the 29th Punjab Native Infantry and 3rd Sikh Infantry respectively, the remainder of the troops were ordered to halt under cover, pending further orders. The guns, however, continued to shell the enemy, who appeared in considerable numbers on the higher ridge facing the gorge, at a distance of about 1,600 yards.

At noon, not having received any orders from General Keyes, and not wishing to delay too long in retiring, as previously directed, to Jamu, Colonel Mocatta ordered the advanced picquets to be withdrawn, and the force to begin its retirement. A small party of the 3rd Sikh Infantry was left in the gorge to keep down the fire of the enemy, who had occupied the hill in front of the gorge directly the picquet of the 1st Sikh Infantry was withdrawn. This party of the 3rd Sikh Infantry kept up a heavy fire on the hill occupied by the enemy, until it was seen that the picquets on the right and left, as well as that of the 1st Sikh Infantry had had time to get down from the heights occupied by them. The delay, which was unavoidable, had, however, given time for the more adventurous amongst the enemy to creep down the hill under cover of the thick jungle in front of the gorge; and almost as soon as the 3rd Sikh Infantry was withdrawn, they occupied the gorge, and kept up a heavy fire upon the road. By this fire a havildar was killed, and Major Rice, commanding the 1st Sikh Infantry, who, with a company of his regiment, had taken up a position about half a mile in rear of the mouth of the gorge to cover the retirement of the 3rd Sikh Infantry, was dangerously wounded. After this, the enemy, coming under the fire of Major Ross's party on the Zira hill, and of Lieutenant Smith's party on the conical hill, ceased to follow, but kept on firing down the ravine until all the covering parties were ultimately withdrawn. Leaving a native officer and forty bayonets on the Zira crest, Major Ross withdrew the remainder of his men from that hill, and the whole force returned to their quarters in the Jamu villages.

On the 17th of January it was decided that General Keyes should abandon his position on the Dargai Sar and take up a new one in the Nara Khula defile; it was also determined, as already mentioned, that the Peshawar column should give up its communications with the Sarghasha camp and join Brig.-General Keyes in the Nara Khula on the morning of the 18th. The combined forces were then to be employed in visiting the valley to the west of the Nara Khula defile, which was the only part of the Jawaki country which was still occupied by the fighting men of the tribe.

On the morning of the 17th, Colonel Mocatta, in obedience to orders received from Brig.-General Keyes, again advanced through the Nara Khula defile. No opposition was experienced in the advance, but, on reconnoitring the hills in front of the gorge, they were found to be occupied by a few of the enemy. A company of the 29th Punjab Native Infantry was therefore directed to occupy these hills. At about 11 A.M. General Keyes arrived from Walai, and, the picquets on the hills in front of the gorge having been relieved, Colonel Mocatta was directed to withdraw his column to Jamu, leaving a picquet of the 3rd Sikh Infantry on the Zira hill to the west of the gorge. On the following day, this column, with the exception of the 1st Sikh Infantry, who remained at Jamu and furnished picquets on the Zira and Dargai hills, returned to Turki.

During the day, parties of the enemy had been observed on the heights in front overlooking the Torsappar valley, and in the evening it was reported that Babri and other leading men were there. General Keyes, therefore, ordered the advanced picquets of the Guides and 5th Punjab Infantry to be pushed forward under cover of the night, and to seize the crest at daybreak. These regiments were supported by the 6th and 4th Punjab Infantry respectively. Unfortunately, the enemy had retreated after dark, and the troops accordingly occupied the crest without opposition at daybreak on the 18th. Major McQueen was then instructed to make arrangements for holding the crest with strong picquets during the time the force remained in the Nara Khula. Having ordered the 6th Punjab Infantry and the 5th Gurkhas to return to their camp at Shindih, General Keyes then proceeded in the direction of Walai to meet Brig.-General Ross, who was advancing with the whole of his force towards the Nara Khula. On meeting, it was arranged that Colonel Doran's brigade should march through the Nara Khula to Jamu, Colonel Buchanan's brigade remaining in the defile.

On the 19th of January, orders were issued by General Keyes, for the march of the whole force to Jamu and Turki on the following morning. On the 20th the troops moved off at daylight, and reached Jamu without a shot having been fired. Colonel Buchanan's brigade was directed to hold Jamu during the 20th and 21st, relieving Colonel Doran's troops, which were ordered to march to Kohat. This place they reached on the 21st, and on the 22nd proceeded through the Kohat pass without meeting with any interruption. The 1st Sikh Infantry and the 5th Punjab Infantry were attached to Colonel Buchanan's brigade for the purpose of holding Bagh and the heights towards Paia and Ghariba. On the 21st Colonel Buchanan received orders to retire to Turki on the following day. Accordingly, on the morning of the 22nd, after blowing up the towers in Jamu and Sultan Khel, he retired his troops through Shindih to Turki, the towers in the village of Bagh being destroyed *en route*. The 1st Sikhs brought up the rear, and accompanied the brigade to their position at Turki, while the 5th Punjab Infantry returned to their camp at Shindih.

On the 23rd, Colonel Buchanan's brigade moved to Kohat, and on the following day, moved back to the Peshawar valley, through the Kohat pass, whence, as already stated, Colonel Doran's brigade had preceded them on the 22nd. The troops, as per margin, were then ordered to occupy the Sarghasha ridge as a force of observation, and the remainder of Brig.-General Ross's troops were withdrawn to Peshawar.

No. 4 (Hazara) Mountain Battery.
17th Bengal Cavalry.
200 bayonets, Rifle Brigade.
14th Native Infantry.
27th Punjab Native Infantry.

Almost immediately after the retirement of our troops, the Jawakis had begun to show signs of a desire to submit, if only the terms were such as, consistently with Afghan honour, they could accept; and on the afternoon of the 23rd of January, their *jirga*, consisting of some sixty of all sections, except that of Malik Mushki, came into Shindih, and subsequently to Kohat to hear the terms which the Government offered. These terms had thus been stated in directions issued to the Commissioner of Peshawar at the commencement of the operations—

(1) Restitution of stolen property.

(2) Fine of Rs. 10,000.

(3) Surrender of all Government arms, and arms of European manufacture. A number of native matchlocks proportional to the number of English arms surrendered to be taken. With reference to these last a proportionate reduction might be made in the fine.

(4) Occupation of Jamu by British troops. (This had already been carried out.)

(5) Construction of a road through Jawaki country, to be left to the decision of Brig.-General Keyes as to the possibility of its execution. During the military occupation the communications to be improved as much as possible.

(6) Survey of the Jawaki country to be made. (This had already been carried out.)

(7) Surrender to be demanded of the persons chiefly concerned in leading or instigating the treacherous attack upon unarmed sepoys on the Khushalgarh road on the 17th of August, and in the Shahkot raid on the 25th of October. If surrendered, a reduction to be made in the amount of the fine and in the number of arms to be demanded. (These persons were four in number, *viz.*, Khaishtu, brother of Malik Mushki of Turki, and Hasan, brother of Malik Zel Beg of Paia, who were the leaders in the attack on the

unarmed sepoys; Malik Rambazai, in whose hamlet the raid on Shahkot had been planned; and Sheru, the leader in that raid. The last, however, was reported to have been killed in the attack.)

(8) Hostages for future good behaviour.

(9) Jawaki pass allowances to be finally withdrawn.

The *jirga* was informed of these terms in the order 7, 3, 1, 2, and 8, no reference being made to the others, as it was considered undesirable to allude to them. After consulting together, they expressed their readiness to pay the fine and restore stolen property. They, however, demurred to the surrender of arms as an impossible condition, and absolutely refused to give up the ringleaders. Their reverses had not yet broken their spirit, and they made the preposterous demand that in estimating the amount of fine the Government should take into account as compensation the losses sustained by them during the expedition. It being impossible to discuss such demands as these, the *jirga* was dismissed.

The principal Jawakis had now taken refuge with the neutral Afridis in the Kohat pass, and pressure was brought to bear upon the latter to induce submission. The Jawakis had expressed themselves ready to abandon their lands and become subordinate holders of land under their pass kinsmen; and, were this not permitted, they expressed their intention of emigrating to the Tirah hills, where an asylum had been offered to them. Either of these alternatives would have been most undesirable, since it would have left the Government with no one against whom their claims, still unsatisfied, could be enforced; the Galai Afridis were, therefore, informed that they would be held responsible for all outrages committed by any members of the Jawaki section in British territory. The Government of India, at length finding that the insistence of the unconditional surrender of the persons demanded would merely maintain the troops in the field, and necessitate the occupation of the Jawaki country for an indefinite period without much hope of a final settlement, and with the danger of the embroilment of the neighbouring clans, so far modified the demand as to accept, in lieu of the surrender of the leaders, their perpetual exclusion from Jawaki territory if the section were absolutely unable to give them up. The compensation to be demanded was, moreover, reduced to any amount which the Lieutenant-Governor might see fit to demand, or might be abandoned altogether if the

Jawakis were unable to pay. The progress of the negotiations need not be noted in detail; but, on the basis of the last mentioned concessions, a settlement with the section was effected. The conditions finally accepted by the Jawakis were the following:—

(1) Complete submission to the Lieutenant-Governor of the Punjab, in public durbar at Peshawar.

(2) Payment of a fine of Rs. 5,000.

(3) Permanent expulsion from the Jawaki territory of the four ringleaders in raids, whose surrender had been at first demanded.

(4) Surrender of twenty-five English rifles and twenty-five native matchlocks.

(5) The giving of hostages for good behaviour in future.

These conditions were ratified at a durbar held at Peshawar on the 4th of March 1878. This was attended by the officers of the garrison, as well as the civil officers, and by the native chiefs and officials. The submission of the Jawaki deputation was received, the fine of Rs. 5,000 was paid in cash, and the stipulated number of arms given up. Deputations from those sections of the Adam Khel Afridis who had remained neutral were also present, and to these suitable presents were made, and the services of those chiefs who had given help during the operations were acknowledged and rewarded.

After this the British troops were withdrawn from Jawaki territory, the prisoners of war and the hostages held by us were released, and the garrisons of the British posts on the Adam Khel frontier were reduced to their normal strength.

The British losses during the operations against the Jawakis, from the 9th of November 1877 to the 19th of January 1878, were eleven killed and fifty-one wounded.

The Indian Medal, with a clasp for "Jawaki," was granted in 1879 to all who took part in the active operations against the Jawaki Afridis, between the 9th November 1877 and the 19th of January 1878, inclusive.

During the operations against the Jawakis, the other sections of the Adam Khel clan fairly acted up to the promises of neutrality they had made, thus showing that the cohesion between the several branches of the Adam Khel was less complete than had hitherto been supposed to be the case. Individual members no doubt joined their kinsmen in opposing the advance of the British force, and several of the uncommitted sections were among the killed and wounded in the first skirmishes with our troops. But this was to be anticipated, and indeed it was hopeless to expect that the main body of the clan could altogether influence the more excitable members when fighting was going on in their immediate neighbourhood. The other Afridi clans, however, although solicited for assistance by the Jawakis in the most urgent manner, never came to the support of their kinsmen in any large numbers. A body of Zakha Khels, some 300 or 400 in number, came as far as the Kohat pass, and there threatened to create additional complications by firing on a party of English officers proceeding along the road; but they did not proceed further, and pressure was brought to bear upon the Galai Afridis to compel their return to their own country.

After the conclusion of the Jawaki campaign in March 1878, the Adam Khel clan continued to behave well, but sent their *jirgas* to Kabul to visit the Amir in the autumn. The malcontent Jawakis, *viz.*, the friends and kinsmen, some fifty in number, of those who had been outlawed, were the first to go; and, on their returning with fifty-two Kabul-made Enfield rifles and Rs. 2,000 in cash, the greed of the Hasan Khel and Galai sections was excited, and they also sent their deputations. The former received Rs. 2,500 in cash, whilst the pass men were given some hundred Kabul-made Enfield rifles, Rs. 2,400 in cash, as well as bayonets caps, and flints.

After the outbreak of the Afghan war, reports were circulated of the intention of the Pass Afridis to close the road; and of emissaries and written messages having been sent to the various sections of the Adam Khel clan by the Amir of Kabul to either do so or furnish him with armed contingents. The *mullas* also threatened to burn the houses of any persons who should frequent British territory for purposes of trade by which our troops might benefit. But neither the Amir's messages, nor the threatenings of *mullas*, were of any avail, and though a few men may have joined the other Afridi clans in the Khaibar, the conduct of the Adam Khels, as a whole, remained satisfactory. The pass was not closed for a single hour; treasure, ordnance stores, troops, and English travellers passed through it without molestation, and it continued to be, throughout the campaign, a valuable military line of communication between Kohat and Peshawar. The Adam Khels also did good service by offering their camels for carrying supplies and stores, and no less than 2,000 of these were employed for this purpose.

After the agreement made with them in 1878, the Jawakis committed several offences on the Khushalgarh road, but a settlement was effected with them in February 1880, and fines amounting to Rs. 3,598 were realized from them.

In August 1880, Nawab Bahadur Sher Khan, Bangash, died, and, as a temporary measure, the charge of our relations with the Adam Khel Afridis was entrusted to his brother, Ata Muhammad Khan. In June 1882, however, the old system of managing the Adam Khels through a middleman was abolished, and on that date the task of dealing with the clan was transferred to the Deputy Commissioner in person. The *jirgas* of all the sections were summoned to Kohat, and the object of Government in directing the change of management was fully explained to them. It was effected without any hindrance, the tribesmen showing little concern in the matter. There is no doubt that an additional element of strength in transactions with the Kohat Pass Afridis was gained by the adoption of direct personal relations with the clan. The allowance of Rs. 2,400 a year, formerly paid to Bahadur Sher Khan for the management of the Kohat pass, was placed at the disposal of the Deputy Commissioner of Kohat, to meet unforeseen and contingent charges arising from its control.

In February 1883 a violent dispute arose between the Gaddia Khel and Bolaki Khel sections of the Akhorwals, regarding a *mela* which the latter proposed to build in the Kalamsada. As this quarrel threatened to disturb the peace of the road and to render it necessary to close the pass, as in 1864, the *jirgas* of the contending sections were summoned to Peshawar, and the dispute was peaceably arranged, the Bolaki Khel being admitted to the Kalamsada. The *mela* was accordingly built, but on the 5th August, taking advantage of the fact that the hamlet was almost deserted by the usual guards, who had gone in to Akhor to keep the *Eed*, the Gaddia Khels attacked and destroyed it. The Galai and Hassan Khel *jirgas* at once repaired to Akhor, and insisted on the quarrel being settled without fighting; but it was some time before this was effected.

In May 1883 an agitation was commenced in the Kohat pass on account of the proposed enhancement of the duty on salt. The price of salt at the five mines open in the Kohat district at that time varied from two to four *annas* a maund (the rates which had been fixed with the sanction of the Government of India in 1850), but for reasons into which it is not necessary here to enter, the Government had decided to raise the duty to eight *annas* a maund at all the mines. The enhancement of this duty had been under consideration for some years, but it was not until 1883 that steps were taken to carry the measure into effect. When it became known that the rates were to be raised from the 1st of July, the Afridis of the Kohat pass decided to offer resistance. The grounds of their objections appear to have been that such a measure would interfere with their profits as carriers; that they had a right to the monopoly of the carrying trade; and that the rates fixed in 1850 were fixed in perpetuity, and the Government had no right to raise them. These grounds were shown to be quite untenable, and the Lieutenant-Governor, in reviewing the question, expressed his opinion that the Pass Afridis could not be permitted for a moment to dictate to the British Government what course it should pursue in a purely domestic matter such as the increase of the salt duty. Of the different sections of the Kohat Pass Afridis, the Bosti Khel and Sheraki were most eager in their opposition; the Zargun Khel and Akhor sections, though siding with the opposition, were comparatively lukewarm; while the men of Torsappar, who had been opposed to the agitation from the beginning, held entirely aloof. At the end of June the *jirga* of the Pass Afridis came into Kohat, but, after much useless discussion, they refused to give in or to allow the passage of salt which had paid the enhanced duty through the pass. They were accordingly informed that their allowances would cease from the 1st of July, and the pass would be closed so far as Government was concerned, but that traders and travellers could continue to use the road at their own risk. The *jirga* then took leave, after protesting that they did not wish for a cessation of friendly relations. On the 7th of September, seeing the uselessness of resistance, and fearing to lose their allowances altogether, the representatives of the Pass Afridis, with the exception of the Misri Khels, an unimportant sub-section of the Bosti Khels, again came into Kohat, and said that they had agreed no longer to oppose the passage of salt. On the 10th the Misri Khels also came in, and the same day a proclamation was issued in Kohat notifying that the pass was open to salt traders as before.

Since then the Kohat pass has remained open, and the Afridis continue to enjoy their allowances.

With regard to the behaviour of the other sections of the Adam Khel Afridis up to the present time, few important offences have been committed, though numerous thefts and burglaries have been recorded against them.

In spite of many endeavours made by the other clans to induce them to join in the rising of 1897, the Adam Khel remained quiet, and troops constantly marched from Peshawar through the Kohat pass without molestation.

In 1901, a metalled cart-road was made through the pass, and tongas now run regularly between Kohat and Peshawar.

Lee-Metford and Martini-Henry rifles of good quality are still made in the pass, which continues to be the chief manufactory of these weapons on the North-West Frontier.

APPENDIX A.

Proclamation issued by the Commissioner of Peshawar on the 1st of December 1877.

1. The Jawaki Afridis, a section of the Adam Khel Afridis, inhabit a small strip of independent territory, which runs south from the Jawaki pass into the Kohat district, nearly touching the main military road half-way between Khushalgarh and Kohat.

2. Within the last few months this section has assumed an attitude of hostility, defied the authority of the British Government, and perpetrated numerous unprovoked outrages and treacherous murders within British territory.

3. On the night of the 15th of July they cut the telegraph wire between Kohat and Khushalgarh in several places; and, when reparation according to tribal usage was required, they sent an insolent reply. On the 24th of July a party of Jawakis rescued two of their section from a guard of British police, and carried of three of the latter into the Jawaki hills. On the 27th of July the guard was released, but on the next night the telegraph wire was cut again. On the 13th of July the Jawakis submitted, came into Kohat, and gave satisfaction for its offences. Scarcely, however, had this quarrel been settled, when, without any assignable cause, they again exhibited hostile designs, and began to remove their property and grain from the villages on the plains to their fastnesses in the hills. This movement was accompanied with the most insolent demands for remission of the fines recently imposed on them; for an indemnity on account of cattle seized during the Kohat pass difficulties; for the restoration of their pass allowances; and for exemption from responsibility both for the good behaviour of their clansmen and for the safety of the telegraph wire skirting their hills, which they had engaged to protect.

4. The answer of the local authorities to these demands was still under consideration of the section when, in defiance of Pathan usage, and with a treachery unexampled among the tribes of the frontier, the Jawakis recommenced hostilities. On the 17th of August they carried off thirty-six commissariat mules from the Khushalgarh road, and killed one of the muleteers. The same night a small party of sepoys of the 3rd Sikh Infantry, proceeding on leave, was attacked on the Khushalgarh road. Three were killed, and a traveller with them; and the telegraph wire was cut again. On the 19th of August

a portion of Gandiali, a village in British territory, was burnt, and one man wounded. On the 20th of August a convoy of mules escorted by troops was attacked by 500 Jawakis. The following night the telegraph wire was again cut. A bridge on the Khushalgarh road was burnt on the 27th of August, and two days later an unsuccessful attempt was made to burn a second bridge.

5. The British Government was still unwilling to proceed to extremities with this petty people. On the 30th, a small force of British troops entered the Jawaki country for the purpose only of intercepting the persons concerned in the perpetration of the above-mentioned outrages.

6. Meanwhile, aggressions on British territory did not cease. On the 9th of September a number of camels were carried off from the Saramela plain. On the 11th the telegraph wire was cut again. A fews day later the British police station at Shadipur on the Indus was fired upon. On the 17th of September a large band of Jawakis attacked the village of Koteri. They killed and wounded some of the villagers, and carried off much plunder. The same day another band made a successful raid upon the village of Kheri Shekh Khan. On the 24th the Deputy Commissioner and Major Lance, commanding the 2nd Punjab Cavalry, were fired upon while inspecting sites near the Gandiali ravine. The latter officer was badly wounded. The same day an outlying picquet near Gumbat was attacked, and four Khattaks killed. On the 11th of October an attempt to carry off cattle was frustrated; but on the 20th of October the Jawakis attacked in force the Khattak village of Ghorizai. Three villagers were killed, two were severely wounded, and much plunder was carried off. The village of Kamar on the Indus, nine miles north of Khushalgarh, was attacked on the night of the 23rd. Five men were killed, five were wounded, and some cattle were carried off. On the night of the 25th a havildar's party of the 22nd Punjab Native Infantry was surprised at the Shahkot encamping-ground near the foot of the Cherat hill. The havildar, five sepoys, and one policeman were killed, seven sepoys were wounded, and eight rifles carried off. Shahkot was again attacked on the night of the 27th of October, but no casualties occurred. These last raids were perpetrated by the Bori Jawakis in violation of the treaty of 1854. Besides the above, many other outrages have been perpetrated by the Jawakis, to detail which would be tedious.

7. The forbearance of the British Government having thus been misunderstood, and every effort to bring this petty border section to reason by peaceful means having failed, the Governor-General in Council finds himself reluctantly compelled to have recourse to severe measures in order to exact reparation for past misdeeds, to render the Jawakis powerless to commit such outrages in the future, and to maintain peace and security of life and property on this portion of the Punjab frontier.

8. His Excellency in Council has, therefore, resolved to occupy the villages of Turki and Paia, and a portion of Jawaki country, maintaining a tight blockade upon the rest. The two villages named will be held, and the blockade maintained, until such time as the Jawakis shall tender their absolute submission.

9. The Governor-General in Council desires that the object of these measures—*viz.*, the righteous punishment of a series of unprovoked outrages committed by the Jawakis on British territory—should be explained to the neighbouring sections. Those sections will be expected not to afford shelter or evasion to the Jawakis. It is a matter of satisfaction to His Excellency in Council that the Jawakis at present stand alone in the hostile attitude they have assumed, and that the elders of the Adam Khel clan of the Afridi tribe, as yet unimplicated in the misconduct of their neighbours, have furnished hostages as pledges for their neutrality, and have engaged to allow the Jawakis no passage through their hills, and to afford them no shelter when retreating before the British troops. The neighbouring sections may be assured that no harm will be done to them as long as they hold aloof, and that the chastisement of the Jawakis is a measure of a purely local and domestic character.

By order of the Governor-General in Council,

SIMLA: *The 5th November* 1877.

(*Signed*) C. U. AITCHISON,

Secretary to the Government of India.

APPENDIX B.

Genealogy of the Adam Khel Afridis.

Clans.	Divisions.	Sub-divisions.	Sections.
ADAM KHEL ..	GALAI (1,000) ..	Tor-Sapar or Yagi Khel	Nekzam Khel. Feroz Khel. Aba Bakar or Kui Khel.
		Zargun Khel ..	Muhammad Khel. Mulla Khel. Talim Khel. Sunni Khel. Shpalkai Khel.
		Sharaki	Bash Khel. Mubarak Khel.
		Bosti Khel	Misri Khel. Yunas Khel. Tashi Khel.
	JAWAKIS	Haibat Khel ..	Mawal Khel. Ghulam Khel. Shahi Khel. Sultan Khel.
		Kimat Khel ..	Kasim Khel. Ismail Khel. Ibrahim Khel. Bashi Khel.
		Bazid Khel	Sarbur Khel. Saadat Khel. Lakkar Khel.
	HASAN KHEL ..	Tatar Khel or Akhorwal	Bolaki Khel (Tatar Khel). Gaddia Khel (Mashakkai). Pirwal Khel (Nur Malik).
		Janakhwari	Zakho Khel. Tutkai Khel. Barkai Khel. Mian Khel.
	ASHU KHEL	Ali Khel	Siffat Kor. Battu Kor. Miru Kor. Alamsher Kor. Kalla Khel.
		Muhammadai ..	Pakhai. Pridai. Rukhan Khel. Muhabat Khel. Sambhi or Hasan Beg Khel.

CHAPTER IV.

THE ORAKZAI TRIBE.

THE Orakzais are a branch of the Karlarni tribe of Pathans, and are connected with the Afridis, Wazirs, and Khattaks. Their original ancestry is carried back to Wurak, a descendant of Kais, or Abdul Rashid, the Pathan.

The primary divisions of the Orakzai clans, which are seven in number, are given in the following table:—

Clans.	Sections.	Fighting strength.	Factions.	Sect.
Ismailzai	Rabia Khel	700	Samil	Sunni.
	Akhel	600	Gar	,,
	Mamazai	200	Samil	,,
	Khadizai	200	,,	,,
	Isa Khel	250	,,	,,
	Sada ,,	80	,,	,,
Massuzai [1]	Landaizai	2,800	½ Gar	,,
	Khwaja Khel	2,000	½ Samil	,,
	Alizai	200		
Lashkarzai	Alisherzai	3,000	Samil	,,
	Mamuzai	3,500	Gar	,,
Daulatzai	Firoz Khel	1,000	Samil	,,
	Bizoti	500	,,	,,
	Utman Khel	600	,,	,,
Muhammad Khel.	Bar Muhammad Khel	1,000	Gar	Shia.
	Abdul Aziz ,,	80	,,	,,
	Mani Khel	1,000	,,	,,
	Sipaya	400	,,	,,
Sturi Khel or Alizai.[1]	Bara Sturi Khel	700	,,	½ Shia and ½ Sunni.
	Tirah ,,			
"*Hamsaya*" clans.	Ali Khel	3,000		,,
	Mala ,,	800	Samil	Sunni.
	Mishti	3,000	,,	,,
	Sheikhan	3,000	,,	,,
	TOTAL	28,610	15,930 Samil. 12,680 Gar.	22,680 Sunni. 5,730 Shia.

[1] Some authorities are of opinion that the Massuzai are a division of the Lashkarzai clan, but this is not borne out by the above genealogical tree nor by private inquiries. Similarly it is customary to class the Sturi Khel with the Firoz Khel, Bizoti and Utman Khel as Daulatzais. It is undoubted that the Sturi Khel are a separate clan, though an unimportant one; they are closely allied to the main Daulatzai clan (which includes the Muhammad Khel), but the Shia portion of the clan are affiliated with the Muhammad Khel while the Sunnis go with the Firoz Khel, etc., it is therefore impossible to class them wholly with either portion of the Daulatzai clan.

The Orakzais are wiry looking mountaineers, but they are not such fine men as, nor are they so formidable as, the Afridis, though they are much more liable to fanaticism.

The tribe occupies the Khanki, and the greater part of the Khurmana valley and in addition the southern slopes of the Torghar range (Kurram) from the left bank of the Khurmana to the Murghan pass.

They engage a good deal in trade and give shelter to a number of Hindu *bannias* and artizans, who are principally located at Khanki Bazar, Star Killa (Upper Khanki), and Mishti Bazar.

They were formerly hand in glove with the Khans of Hangu, but this family has now lost its former great influence, and though the members of it are past masters in the art of intrigue, it may be considered extinct for all political purposes.

Ismailzai.

Of the various Orakzai clans the Ismailzai has at all times proved itself the most troublesome, but this is due more to the fact that they are the nearest to British territory than to any especial predilection on their part to marauding propensities. The clan is of the Sunni persuasion in religion, and Samil in politics, with the exception of the Akhels and a small section of the Isa Khel, who, being *hamsayas* of the former, are also Gar. They do not hold a very high reputation for courage and are badly armed. They muster about 2,030 fighting men.

The clan is very much disunited and distracted by feuds, and, except the Rabia Khel and Akhel, the other sections are rapidly becoming extinct. The Rabia Khel, though as much disunited as the rest of the clan, are perhaps tending to increase rather than to diminish, as they are overflowing into the lands held by their less fortunate kinsmen.

Both the Rabia Khel and the Akhel have settlements in the Miranzai valley (British territory) but they do not engage much in trade, and would be but slightly affected by a blockade.

Beginning from the east, but not inclusive of Abdul Khel, the settlements of the clan extend along the right bank of the Khanki river to within a short distance of Shahu Khel, and include all the northern slopes of the Samana. This tract belongs to the Akhel and Rabia Khel who, in addition, own a small strip along the left bank of the river, the boundary between the two divisions being a line drawn from the Samana Suk to Sadakada on the Khanki, the Rabia Khel living to the east and the Akhel to the west of the line. Sadakada, which is on the left bank of the river, belongs to the Akhel, and below this point, also on the left bank, lies a narrow strip held by the Rabia Khel, where are situated some of the villages leased by them from the Khadizais, notably Nakhshband, Jhandasam, Narai, and Katsa. The principal Rabia Khel villages are Gwada, Inzaur, and Ghauz Darra, and of the Akhel, Torkanrai, Sirki, Star Killa, and Kharappa; the latter, which is situated at the mouth of the junction of the Chagru with the Khanki, was in former days called Mad Sher Garhi and consisted of 200 houses, but it fell into decay owing to feuds and was ultimately destroyed by us during the Tirah Expedition. It has since been partially rebuilt. The Mamazais live in the Daradar glen which drains into the Khanki on the left bank; the most important village being Arkhi which is famous for the manufacture of arms. The other sections are scattered about in small settlements on the left bank of the river, the Khadizais at Sadarai and Tutgarhi, the Sada Khels at Ghundaki at the foot of the Sampagha pass, and the Isa Khel in hamlets on both sides of the pass.

Lashkarzai.

Of the two Lashkarzai sections, Alisherzai and Mamuzai, the former are reputed to be very warlike, though they have never shown their mettle to us. Tradition also states that at one time they were able to bring a number of well-mounted horsemen into the field. They are said to muster 3,000 fighting men.

In religion the Alisherzais are of the Sunni sect and in politics Samil, with the exception of the Kaisa Khel who are Gar. The section is one of the two among the Orakzais in which a hereditary Khanship is recognized. It is vested in a family residing at Tatang, the present head of which is Haji Khan, a very fanatical man, who was concerned in the risings on the Samana in 1897-98. Another member of the family is Muhammad Ali Khan who, for services rendered during the above disturbances, was rewarded with a grant of land at Sadda in Kurram, with an annual allowance of Rs. 300. The whole family is so distracted by feuds that the Khanship is merely nominal.

The Alisherzai country is divided into the Pitao and Sweri tracts. The former means literally "Sunny side" and is applied to the country which lies on the southern slopes of the Tor Ghar, towards the Kurram valley; the principal places in this quarter are the Tatang, Talpak, and Murghan glens. Sweri, which means "Shady side," is the name given to the lands which lie on the northern slopes of the Tor Ghar, and Zawa Ghar, at the head of the Khanki valley, and comprises chiefly the Minjan Darra.

The Mamuzais are Gar in politics, while in religion they are of the Sunni persuasion. There is perhaps no other tribe between the Kabul and Kurram rivers which is so much under the influence of the *mullas* and so fanatical as are these people. They are not renowned for their fighting qualities, but, owing to the fact that they are extremely prosperous and consequently far better armed than their neighbours, they, for the latter reason, are the leaders of the Gar faction and in addition have a good deal to say to the management of affairs affecting the Orakzai tribe as a whole. Considerable trade is carried on with the Kohat district; and at Khanki Bazar, which is the head-quarters of the section, there are a number of Khatri Sikh *bannias* and several artizans. It is supposed that the section can turn out 3,500 fighting men.

The Mamuzais reside at the head of the Khanki valley, to the north of the Minjan Darra. Here is Khanki Bazar, situated in a position commanding the entrance to a formidable defile, known as the Kahu Darra, in which is situated the Sipah village of Mopati, where the Mamuzai *jirgas* assemble. The Kahu Darra is formed of a number of deep narrow glens such as the Kama Darra, Tambu Darra, Chinghakh, and the Torsmats Darra. During the winter these glens are to a great extent deserted, but in the summer all the various sections migrate to them to escape the heat in the main valley.

Massuzais.

The Massuzais are descended from an ancestor called Masud, whose shrine is to be seen at Barezona in the Landai valley. In point of numbers the clan, which can muster about 5,000 fighting men, is the most powerful among the Orakazis, but it has a poor reputation for courage.

The clan is Sunni in religion, and is partly Gar and partly Samil in politics. These two factions are fairly equal in strength, but the Samil faction is the most powerful as it has strong allies among the Zaimukhts, Alisherzais, and Mamuzais. Several of the neighbouring tribes have settled in Massuzai country and thus become *hamsayas*. It is difficult to ascertain the relationship which exists between Massuzais and their Afridi *hamsayas*, but it does not appear that the latter admit any strong claims on the part of their overlords, and it is more than probable that they are the more masterful and that, in process of time, the Massuzais will be driven forward.

The Massuzais dwell in the Landai, Dargai, Shaonkanri, (including the Gandao and Lozaka) Laili Band, Gondal, Goadarri and Ghwaianghara glens of the Khurmana valley.

Daulatzais.

The three sections of the Daulatzai clan are of the Sunni persuasion as regards religion, and are Samil in politics, but the Firoz Khel hold themselves aloof from the Utman Khels and Bizotis, who together form a coalition against them. In many ways there is a marked difference between the two factions; the Firoz Khel are in no way dependent on trade with British territory, while the other two sections would feel a blockade to a very appreciable extent, as they trade largely with Kohat. Again, whereas the Bizotis and Utman Khel have been a constant source of trouble to us on the Kohat border, the Firoz Khel have been well behaved, though, in justice to other sections, it is right to state that the Firoz Khel, being situated at a greater distance from the border, have not the same temptations as their neighbours. The Firoz Khel and Utman Khel possess a considerable amount of rice cultivation in the upper Mastura valley, but the Bizotis are badly off in this respect, and their settlements are more scattered than those of the other two sections. Riches across the border go hand in hand with efficiency in armament, with the result that while the poor Bizoti is badly armed, his more wealthy brethren are far better so and, in proportion to their numbers, the Utman Khel are better armed than the Firoz Khel. The latter are essentially a warlike tribe, and the Bizotis proved themselves staunch fighters in the affair on the Ublan with Major Jones, on the 11th March 1868. The Utman Khels are said to be lacking in martial qualities.

The Firoz Khel live in the Firoz Khel Darra in the Upper Mastura valley, and, in addition, own all the north-eastern slopes of the Molai Ghar, south-east of a line drawn from the Kukakada pass to the mouth of the Sapri Nala. The Utman Khel inhabit a tract of country in the upper Mastura, between the river and the Tor Ghar range to the north, from Bizoti on the west to the mouth of the Khoa Darra on the east; in the Lower Mastura the section hold the western slopes of the Murgha China hills, from the Asman Darra to the junction of the Mastura and Bara rivers, and, at the same time, have winter settlements at the head of the Zia-ud-din Darra, which drains into the Kohat pass at Akhor. The Bizotis are intermixed with the Utman Khel in the Upper Mastura, having settlements at Bizoti and Karghan, but along the lower reaches of the river they lie between the Ublan pass and the Asman Darra along the right bank.

Muhammad Khel.

The Muhammad Khel are, without exception, of the Shia persuasion, and possess a tract of country which has considerable strategical advantages. It is, therefore, a matter of regret that they are not more united, for they are, taking them all round, a remarkably well behaved clan and well disposed towards Government, and, surrounded as they are by a cordon of Sunni foes, it is a simple matter to alienate them from the rest of the Orakzai clans and bring them bodily over to our side. Were it not for their disunion, the clan, which is reputed to be among the bravest of the Orakzais, could muster about 2,500 fighting men, all well armed.

The strategical value of the Muhammad Khel country lies in the fact that it is easy of access from Kohat, and, being centrally situated in the Mastura valley commands both the upper and lower portions of the valley, turns a great portion of the Khanki valley, and affords a convenient advanced base for operations towards the valleys of Maidan and Bara. The Mani Khel hold the right bank of the Mastura for a distance of three miles eastward of, and inclusive of, the Mani Khel Darra, their principal villages being Kalaia, Sabzi Khel, Kalat, and Ainposh. Beyond the Mani Khels, to the east, are the Abdul Aziz Khel, who extend up to and inclusive of Sultanzai, which with Darma is the head-quarters of the section. From Sultanzai to the Gudar Tangi there is a break in the continuity of the territory belonging to the clan, for here the Sturi Khel interpose, till Muhammad Khel country is again entered, where the Sipaya settlements commence at the Tangi and, from thence extend along both banks of the river up to, but not inclusive of, Bizoti. Their principal villages are Palosi, Kharpushta, and Toimela. The Muhammad Khel own a small glen in the Mastura valley between the Mani Khel and Sheikhans, which is known by their name. In it are the villages of Trangai and Sarobi; to the south of the Mizzio Ghar they own all the Nanaki and Kurez Darra valleys, and the western end of the Laghar Darra, beginning at, and inclusive of, Pitaomela; this and Kuriacha are their principal villages. The Thali caves, where a number of the clan reside during the winter, are situated at the extreme limit of the Laghar Darra, where British territory begins.

Sturi Khel.

The Sturi Khel are divided into the Tirah and Bara Sturi Khel, which division is not only a topographical one but is at the same time real, in that they are at mortal feud with each other, half being Shia and half Sunni in religion. The Tirah Sturi Khels are a poor people, possessing but little cultivation, and have practically no trade with British territory; the residents of Bara, on the other hand, are well off and possess a considerable amount of cultivation, while at the same time they engage in trade with the Peshawar district. The clan as a whole has a very poor reputation for courage and can only muster some 700 badly armed fighting men, of which the Bara Sturi Khel supply 300. They derive their importance from the fact that they command the Sapri route into Mastura and the Bara river route as far as Galli Khel. Generally speaking they are well behaved.

Roughly speaking, the clan possesses all the country from the left bank of the Mastura river to the right bank of the Bara which lies between a line drawn from the west of Sultanzai, on the Mastura, past the eastern boundary of the Khoa Darra to Galli Khel on the Bara, and a line drawn obliquely from the western entrance of the Gudar Tangi through the Jhandarak pass to Mamanai at the junction of the Bara and Mastura. In the Mastura valley the principal places are And Khel and Shiraz Garhi, and in the Bara, Barkai, Barwan, and Mamanai. The latter, though only a small cave village, is important in that it is situated at the junction of the Mastura and Bara rivers.

***Hamsaya* clans: Ali Khel.**

The Ali Khels are said to be descended from some Yusafzai emigrants who, detaching themselves from their tribe, became *hamsayas* of the Orakzais. They are Gar in politics but, at the same time, form a coalition with the Mishtis, who are Samil; the alliance is, however, explained by the fact that the latter are also of Yusafzai origin. In religion they are of the Sunni persuasion except the Brahmin, Baba, Sarwar, and a portion of the Khwaja Nmasi sections, who are Shias. The valleys in which the clan live are very confined, and they have but little arable land and practically no trade. Want of pasturage in their country during the winter forces them to emigrate annually to the Miranzai valley, and they are thus particularly dependent on British territory, and a blockade would be severely felt by them. They hold a very high reputation for courage, but are badly armed; they can muster 3,000 fighting men. They have constantly proved themselves troublesome, but at the same time, mettlesome neighbours, not only towards us, but also towards the Mamuzai and Rabia Khel and the Malikdin Khel Afridis. Their position in Orakzai country is in many ways analogous to that held by the Zakha Khel among the Afridis, for their territory extends without a break from the Khanki river northward to the crest of the Tor Ghar, overlooking Maidan, and they are thus able, like the Zakha Khel, to bar the passage of all the other clans moving to and from their winter quarters. Many is the time that the other clans have endeavoured to reduce them, but all attempts have failed, and the Ali Khel are free to permit or refuse the right of road, which can only be purchased by payment of blackmail. They are troublesome neighbours to all with whom they come into contact, and there is no Orakzai clan which has caused so much annoyance and trouble on our border as this.

Along the left bank of the Khanki they possess a small strip of land about two miles in length, near Ramadan, but from here their possessions increase in breadth and may be said to lie between a line drawn from the Chagru ravine through the Torsmats peak to within a short distance of the Chinghakh pass, and another line drawn from Turupe to the Arhanga pass; their principal villages are Isa Khel, Kot, and Ramadan, in the Khanki valley, Gandithal, Shinani, Baliana, Zakhtan and Targhu in the Mastura valley.

Malla Khel.

Second among the Orakzai *hamsaya* clans come the Malla Khel. There is some doubt as to the origin of this clan, there being two versions, one of which states that they are the descendants of a Sherazi *mulla* who married a Bizoti woman, while the other considers them to be an offshoot of the Ghilzai tribe. They are Sunni in religion and Samil in politics. They are a brave race and can muster about 800 well-armed men. Notwithstanding the fact that they cultivate largely in the Miranzai valley and are, in consequence, open to sharp reprisals, they are troublesome neighbours. This is, however, due to the fact that they are under the thumb of the Mishtis, who determine the policy of the Samil party, and through whose lands they must pass to and from their summer quarters in the Mastura valley. They are very well off, and their settlements, though limited, are fertile and densely populated.

In the Mastura valley they live to the north of the Sampagha pass, in a strip of territory about three miles long, along both banks of the river to the east of Mastura camp. Star Killa, Badaon, and Kharkhi are their principal villages. In about 1760 Wali Muhammad Khan, tenth Khan of Hangu, in order to strengthen himself against the Khan of Kohat, invited the tribe to aid him in his feud and, as a reward, made over to them the Darband village, on the southern slopes of the Samana in the Miranzai valley. The land inside the glen in which the village is situated was given them in perpetual gift while of that outside the glen a certain portion is held by them on perpetual fixed lease of the Bangashes of Kotgai, and the remainder on an annual lease, terminable at pleasure. The hamlet of Turki, also in British territory, is similarly held by them.

Mishtis.

The Mishtis, like the Ali Khel, are Yusafzai in origin but are Samil in politics, whereas the latter are Gar. The bond of kinship, however, induces these two *hamsaya* clans to form a coalition for their mutual advantage. Though not of the true Orakzai stock, the Mishtis are now more powerful and influential than their original protectors, the Orakzais, and take the lead in all matters relating to the Samil faction. They are very well off and engage to a considerable extent in trade, and are, therefore, closely connected with British territory. They muster 3,000 well-armed fighting men, but their reputation for courage stands below that of the Ali Khel and Malla Khel. In religion they are of the Sunni sect.

Their settlements are somewhat scattered. In the Mastura valley they possess a considerable glen which lies on the southern slopes of the Shirmast spur, where is Mishti Bazar, a flourishing village with over sixty shops kept by Hindu *bannias.* At the entrance to the Khanki valley their possessions run up both banks of the stream from beyond Shahu Khel to Khaori; in this quarter there are several good-sized villages, of which the largest is Kasha. In the Upper Khanki valley they live to the south of the Tsappar range, in the Kandi Mishti Darra, at the head of which lies the Sampagha pass; in this glen, giving it its name, there were three villages, which were destroyed in 1897. They also possess a small glen called Tsappar Mishti, close on the north-west corner of the Samilzai border.

Sheikhans.

The Sheikhans are believed to be of Wazir origin and the physical appearance of the men seems to favour this theory. They are of the Sunni sect in religion and of the Samil faction in politics. They can muster about 3,000 fighting men, but do not bear a very high reputation for courage and are badly armed; nevertheless they are an important tribe and one difficult to control. They are poor, and engage but little in trade, and the lack of sufficient pasturage in the Khanki and Mastura valleys forces them to come down annually into British territory, where they even hold a small tract of land near Shahu Khel. They are thus dependent on us to a considerable extent and would suffer from a blockade.

In the Mastura valley they live on both banks of the Khatang Darra, in which the principal villages are Rangin Khel and Laghunai. In the Khanki valley they hold the Thahtak Darra; here is Khangarbur destroyed by us in 1897. Crossing the Nakata pass, which lies on the eastern watershed of the Tahktak glen, the Laghar Darra glen is entered, which, as far as Pitao Mela (Muhammad Khel), also belongs to the Sheikhan. It will thus be seen that their possessions form one compact tract.

Expedition against the Rubia Khel Orakzais by a force under Brigadier N. B. Chamberlain, in September 1855.

Up to 1855 the Orakzais, though occasionally committing petty depredations on the border, and known to be capable of mischief if so inclined, gave no positive trouble to the British authorities, but in the spring of that year many of the tribe were concerned in the demonstrations and attacks on the Miranzai Field Force (*see* Chapter VI).

During the time the force was halted at the village of Kai, the Akhel section of the Orakzais attacked the British village of Baliamin, and drove off 156 head of cattle. On the force proceeding to Darsamand, the Orakzai tribe, with the Afridis and the Zaimukhts, collected from 1,500 to 2,000 men to attack the camp, but were driven off with loss on the 30th of April 1855.

On the return of the Miranzai Field Force in the following month, Major J. Coke reported that the conduct of the Orakzais bordering on Hangu and the Miranzai valley had been so hostile to the Government, and their aggressions had been so insulting and unprovoked, that some punishment was necessary to repress the spirit of hostility evinced by them since the force under the command of Brigadier N. B. Chamberlain entered the Miranzai valley.

After the return of the troops the Orakzais continued to commit depredations upon the Bangash people of the Kohat district, making no less than fifteen raids, in which several hundred head of cattle were carried off, and some British subjects killed. In these the Sheikan and the Mishti sections were concerned, but the Rabia Khels were conspicuous. A feud at this time commenced between the Orakzais and the Hangu people. The Chief of Hangu was murdered by one of his own relations, and the murderer fled to the Orakzais. On the 15th of July 1855, Major J. Coke, commanding the 1st Punjab Infantry, and also Deputy Commissioner of Kohat, reported that, on the night of the 12th, the Orakzais had carried off 660 head of cattle from the neighbourhood of Hangu, and that he had at once proceeded there with a troop of the 4th Punjab Cavalry. He added that a hostile movement was apparently going on among the tribe, and that as he felt apprehensions for the safety of the village of Hangu, 250 men of the 1st Punjab Infantry had been sent out to protect it.

The raids of the Rabia section of the tribe still continuing, Major Coke reinforced Hangu with the marginally named troops. With this force he reported that he proposed to attack the Rabia Khel village of Nasin, and with the aid of our Bangash subjects of Togh, and of Khwaja Muhammad Khan, the Khattak Chief, he hoped to be able to check the hostile movement of the

No. 3 Punjab Light Field Battery (2 guns).
2nd Punjab Infantry, 150 bayonets.
3rd Punjab Infantry, 150 bayonets.

Orakzai tribe in general, and the Rabia Khel section in particular, with whom the hostilities first arose.

The Chief Commissioner, however, directed that no hostile movement should be undertaken beyond the British boundary without his orders, but added, that if the tribe could be attacked to advantage within our territory, there would be no objection to it being done.

Brigadier Chamberlain, commanding the Punjab Irregular Force, was also averse to the employment of troops against the Orakzais at that time of the year (July), unless political reasons absolutely required it. His reasons for suggesting delay were that operations against the Orakzais would probably involve complications with other tribes; and at that season the difficulty of moving troops would be great, with the certainty that regiments would suffer much from sickness. Instructions were accordingly sent to Major Coke that defensive measures only were to be adopted. If the border villages could not be protected from Kohat, a small portion of the Kohat garrison was to be moved to Hangu.

On the 13th of August news was received that at a *jirga* of the Rabia Khel, Mamazai, and Ali Khel sections, it was agreed that if the Ali Khel and Akhel would join, the combined sections should make an attack on British territory, either before or after the *Eed* (the 25th of August).

By the 20th of the month matters had progressed considerably, and Major Coke reported to Brigadier Chamberlain that an attack would probably be made by the united clans of the Orakzais after the *Eed*, on some point between Baliamin and Samilzai, a distance of twenty miles; that the rest of the hill tribes were in the most excited state, and that they were all trying to foment a *jehad*. Major Coke asked that at least two more regiments might be sent into the district.

Brigadier Chamberlain had by this time arrived at Kohat, and the following arrangements were made. Reinforcements were called for from Peshawar, consisting of 800 infantry and 6 mountain guns; the detachments garrisoning the outposts of Nari, Latamar, and Bahadur Khel were recalled, and their duties taken up by similar detachments from Bannu, from which station a troop of the 3rd Punjab Cavalry was moved up to Kohat. An engineer officer was ordered to put the border villages threatened in a state of defence, and to open out the roads most likely to be used for the protection of the frontier. The different chiefs, amongst whom were Khwaja Muhammad Khan, the chief of the Khattaks, and Bahadur Sher Khan, Bangash, were directed to collect armed retainers, horse and foot. Every endeavour was at the same time made to collect commissariat supplies and carriage.

Peshawar Mountain Train Battery (4 guns).
No. 3 Punjab Light Field Battery (5 guns).
4th Punjab Cavalry.
1st Punjab Infantry.
2nd Punjab Infantry.
3rd Punjab Infantry.

On the 25th of August the force, as per margin, was assembled at Hangu, under the command of Brigadier N. B. Chamberlain. The cantonment of Kohat was occupied by one troop, 3rd Punjab Cavalry, from Bannu, and the 1st Native Infantry from Peshawar.

On the 29th of the month the Deputy Commissioner wrote to the Brigadier recommending the destruction of the villages of Nasin[1] and Sangar, in the Samana range, both belonging to the Rabia Khel Orakzais. He represented that the conduct of that tribe had been so atrocious and insulting, and the injuries they had inflicted on the Government so great, that the necessity for inflicting on them some punishment was apparent. He also proposed that the village of Katsah, on the banks of the Khanki stream, should be destroyed, with its rice cultivation.

In reporting his determination to carry out these punitive measures, Brigadier Chamberlain, in writing to the Chief Commissioner, after stating that he was not unmindful of the great responsibility he was taking on himself in adopting such a course, went on to say: "As the officer in command of the troops on the frontier, and more especially of the field force in this camp, I conceive that occasion may arise when it becomes my bounden duty to exercise a very great discretionary power; and I trust in the present instance it will not be deemed that I have exceeded or abused the authority I suppose to be vested in my office, and for the judicious exercise of which I hold myself to be just as much accountable to Government as for the discipline and efficiency of the troops." He added that he quite concurred with the Deputy Commissioner in the necessity of adopting aggressive measures, that he looked upon an attack

[1] This village no longer exists.

on the Rabia Khel Orakzais as unavoidable, and that the urgency of the case rendered immediate steps compulsory.

On the 1st of September, therefore, arrangements were made to attack early on the following morning the villages of Nasin, Sangar, and Katsah.

The plan of operations was to make simultaneous attacks on the different points, the main object being the destruction of the villages and defences of Nasin and Sangar; for the *maliks* of those villages were notorious freebooters, and the inhabitants were those who had been most active in making raids, into British territory.

The village of Sangar was situated on the very crest of the Samana range. It was well built, the dead walls of the houses being faced outwards for strength, and the whole was perfectly commanded by a high loopholed tower of two storeys. Water was not procurable on the top of the hill, the inhabitants of the place supplying themselves either from the spring just below Nasin or from the Khanki stream, which flows at the northern base of the range.

Nasin was situated in the centre of a sloping plateau about three-quarters of a mile below Sangar, and from this amphitheatre two spurs ran down from the Samana range parallel to, and close to each other, terminating in the Miranzai valley below.

The cliffs, which the inward faces of these spurs presented to one another, formed the gorge up which led one of the only two paths to Nasin. The other path was along the ridge of the eastern spur, and, though difficult and precipitous at the bottom, was practicable for mules. The two villages were connected with each other by a winding path, and the ascent was everywhere practicable for infantry.

The village of Nasin was defended by a square fort, with walls about nine feet high. Its position was such as to completely command and close the paths leading up the gorge, while just below it, and within range of its fire, was the spring which supplied its defenders with water. The houses of the village were scattered in rows of five and six, the ground being terraced for the sake of cultivation.

The difficulties the troops had to contend with were thus great, and the loss of life, if the ascent had been undertaken by daylight and the tribe prepared to meet our troops, would probably have been large. Success depended almost entirely upon both villages being surprised, and, as any forward movement of the camp would have tended to create suspicion, it was absolutely necessary to make Hangu the starting-point.

This involved a march of fourteen miles before the commencement of the ascent; or, if the range were ascended opposite camp, there was still about the same distance to be accomplished along its ridge before Sangar could be reached. It was determined, therefore, that these villages should be attacked both from above and below, and the following dispositions were accordingly ordered.

The force was divided into three columns of attack. The first was under the command of Major J. Coke, and consisted of the 1st Punjab Infantry and three companies of the 2nd Punjab Infantry. To this force was entrusted the attack on the village of Sangar. The column was provided with small shells, to be used as hand grenades, bags of powder, crowbars, etc., and was accompanied by Lieutenant J. H. Bryce, Bengal Artillery, as engineer officer. It was to leave camp at 10 P.M. (the night was moonlight), and to ascend the Samana range near the camp, which was pitched about a mile to the south-west of Hangu, and move along the ridge until the village was reached, which, it was hoped, would be before daybreak. The village was then to be immediately attacked and destroyed. If, on arrival at Sangar, Major Coke found that the second column had not established itself at Nasin, or was hard pressed, he was to detach a party to its assistance; this party, acting from above, had everything in its favour, and as soon as the village of Sangar had been taken and destroyed, the remainder of the first column was to move down to aid in the attack on Nasin.

The second column, which was under the command of Captain B. Henderson, 3rd Punjab Infantry, consisted of three companies of that regiment, and was to move at 9 P.M. on the village of Nasin. On reaching a hill on the right of the gorge, Captain Henderson was to take up such a position above and near the village as would give him the command of it, as well as of the path by which the mountain guns were to ascend; his subsequent action was to be guided generally by the movement of the first column and main body.

The third column was composed of levies under Khwaja Muhammad Khan, and to it was allotted the destruction of the village of

Katsah, with its rice crops and mills. This village was situated on the northern side of the Samana range, on the banks of the Khanki stream, and was reported almost undefended. All prisoners taken were to be spared and brought into camp, and the levies were on no account to attack any other tribe except in self-defence, nor to go down the stream. This column was to follow Major Coke's, and was to leave a body of footmen on the top of the range when the column descended, to cover its return.

The main body, consisting of the troops noted in the margin, under the immediate command of the Brigadier, was to leave camp shortly after the march of the first column, and, ascending the same spur as the second column, was to move on Nasin, ready to support either of the other parties. A reserve with the field guns was to follow this column, so as to reach the foot of the spur by dawn, ready to cover the retirement.

Peshawar Mountain Train Battery (4 guns).
No. 3 Punjab Light Field Battery (2 guns).
2nd P. I., 3 companies.
3rd P. I., 4 "

The guard for the camp, under Captain G. O. Jacob, 4th Punjab Cavalry, consisted of that regiment and one company from each of the infantry regiments.

The troops were only to be warned an hour before starting, and great care was to be taken that no sickly men accompanied the columns. Plundering was to be strictly prohibited.

The first column gained the crest of the Samana range by three o'clock on the following morning, when the troops, having rested an hour, continued their march. As they reached the foot of the last crest, having traversed some most difficult ground, they descried the second column below them at Nasin. Major Coke then pushed on, as fast as the nature of the ground would admit, against Sangar, which he came in sight of at break of day. A rush was made on the village, and, before ten shots had been fired, many of the sepoys had got beyond it, thus enabling the troops to capture nearly the whole of the cattle, which had by this time got half a mile away under the main range. The villagers did not attempt to make a stand, but fled, leaving a number of women and children in the village; none of whom, however, were in any way injured. Sangar was found to contain about sixty houses, which, with the tower and the *jowar* crops on the plateau below, were entirely destroyed. The first column then joined the main body.

The second column, after marching fourteen miles, and carefully avoiding the only village met with *en route*, began the ascent of the crest at 2-30 A.M., and, getting as quickly and silently as possible over the ridge, gained its position over Nasin at 4 A.M. Shortly before it reached this point the enemy began beating their war drums, but the column continued its movement in perfect silence and unseen. As soon as the position was gained, the men were collected and ordered to lie down under cover, waiting for dawn. The drums continued sounding, and the enemy endeavoured to ascertain the exact position of the column by firing a few random shots from the ridge and tower, which did no harm, and which were not returned. As dawn broke, the second column made a rush on the village, and the enemy, taking instantly to flight, were driven along and over the highest crest (the one commanding the village of Sangar) without any loss to us. The leading men of the column, led by Subadar Faiz Muhammad Khan, pushing on over the crest, captured some hundreds of cattle, which the enemy were driving off.

The main column having left camp at 11 P.M., came in sight of Captain Henderson's troops at daylight; but before the guns could be got into position, the enemy, finding themselves threatened from above by the 1st column, and from below by the other two, were in full flight up the Samana range.

The troops were now actively employed, covered by picquets, till 10 A.M., blowing up the towers and destroying the villages and crops.

The signal for our retirement had been anxiously looked for by the mountaineers, and no sooner had it been given, than they began following up, beating their drums, and shouting their war cry. As the skirmishers of the 2nd Punjab Infantry, under Captain G. W. G. Green, were abandoning one of the commanding points, they were attacked and driven back by a sudden rush of the enemy, but Captain Green, of whose conduct the Brigadier spoke very highly, rallied his men under cover of the fire of two mountain guns, and retook the position.

The retirement was then continued in good order. Before the troops had reached the foot of the hill the enemy had ceased to follow up, and the whole force reached camp by sunset.

In the meantime, Khwaja Muhammad Khan, with 300 footmen and 60 horse, had moved down into the Khanki valley, and destroyed the village of Katsah and several of the neighbouring hamlets. As this column had been ordered not to descend into the valley until firing was heard from Major Coke's troops, many of the villagers had moved off to assist Sangar before Khwaja Muhammad Khan arrived, and the cattle had almost all been driven off; what remained, however, were captured.

The men of Togh and Kai also aided in the operations against the Rabia Khels; and the former had four men killed, but reported the loss of the enemy to have been more than their own. Brigadier Chamberlain stated that, in consenting to the employment of our Miranzai subjects against the Rabia Khels, he was guided by the consideration that, for the subjugation of both parties, the feuds between the independent hill tribes and our Bangash subjects of Miranzai could not be made too wide; for in that part of the country a blood-feud well established was a difficulty almost beyond the bounds of amicable settlement.

The casualties on our side were eleven killed and four wounded, while the loss of the Rabia Khel tribe was estimated at twenty-four killed and wounded, amongst the former being four *maliks.*

A few days after this punishment the Mishti section came to terms, and gave hostages; this was shortly followed by the submission of the Rabia Khels, who brought back a great number of the plundered cattle, agreeing to pay for the remainder, which they had eaten. The tribe was also willing to pay a grazing tax for the pasturage ground near our frontier, but Government declined to receive any revenue from them. The Sheikhan section also came to terms, and the force returned to Kohat on the 7th of October, when it was broken up.

Affair with the Bizoti Orakzais at the Ublan pass in March 1868.

After 1855 the Orakzais did not trouble our border again until 1868, when complications arose with a portion of the Daulatzai clan, and more especially the Bizoti section. The Bizotis have little or no trade to lose by misbehaviour, and their main strength lies in their insignificance; and as their chief settlements were in Tirah, they had, previous to 1868, escaped punishment for their misdeeds.

In the early days of British rule trans-Indus, the Bizotis were constantly cattle-lifting on our border, and they attacked and plundered travellers and grasscutters whenever they could lay hands on them. In 1853, in consequence of the misbehaviour of the Afridis, they were admitted, amongst others, to a share of the allowances paid for the peace of the Kohat pass. Besides the Bizotis, who touch our border, the other two sections of the Daulatzai clan, namely, the Firoz Khel and the Utman Khel, are generally one with them in all their political moves, and the allowance given to the Bizotis on this occasion was shared by them also.

The Sipaya section of the Muhammad Khels adjoins the winter settlements of the Daulatzais, and are associated with them in the protection of the Kohat *kotal*. Though a small section, they are notorious as plucky men and great thieves. They have not more than four hundred fighting men, but they are well armed, and they have the character of being the best marksmen with the rifle amongst the tribes. They do not migrate in summer to Tirah, as do the Bizotis.

In 1865 a Sipaya and two Bizotis were convicted of robbery in British territory and sentenced to imprisonment; the Bizotis, Utman Khels, and Sipayas interceded for the release of the robbers, and, on their petition not being granted by the Deputy Commissioner, took to making raids in British territory; they killed two of our subjects, and captured some of our cattle. Colonel J. R. Becher, C.B., then Commissioner of Peshawar, settled the case by releasing the prisoners, and exacting a small fine as compensation for the loss of the cattle, and the lives of our subjects who had been killed.

At the beginning of 1867, one Fateh Khan, a British subject of the village of Alizai, in the Kohat district, bordering on the Sipaya hills, petitioned the Deputy Commissioner of Kohat that a civil suit which had been decided against him in 1854 by Captain J. Coke, then Deputy Commissioner of Kohat, (whose decision had been confirmed on appeal in 1855) should be reopened. The Deputy Commissioner declined to reopen a case which had been finally decided twelve years before; but, as Fateh Khan appeared in difficulties, he was promised a situation as a mounted orderly when a vacancy should occur.

At the close of 1867 Fateh Khan went over to his independent neighbours, the Daulatzais, and induced them to take up his cause. On learning this, the Deputy Commissioner notified to the adjoining tribes that any intercession for Fateh Khan could not be attended to, as the matter was one which exclusively concerned British subjects. Notwithstanding this warning, on the 23rd of December 1867 a deputation from the Daulatzais, including representatives of the Bizoti, Utman Khel, and Firoz Khel sections, and also from the Sipaya section of the Muhammad Khel clan, came into Kohat (without, as usual, asking permission to enter British territory) to make intercession for Fateh Khan. They were received in durbar by the Deputy Commissioner, and informed that their request could not be granted; and they were at the same time reminded that they had been duly warned of this.

After this interview, all the tribe, except a section of the Bizoti under the leadership of one Saiyid Raza, intimated their intention of abandoning the cause of Fateh Khan.

On the 15th of January news was received that Saiyid Raza was collecting his followers for a raid into British territory, and preparations were made accordingly, the Bizotis being warned that if they did not prevent the raid they must take the consequences. On the morning of the 16th a demonstration was made against the police posts located in the towers at the foot of the Ublan pass, a defile through which ran the direct road from Kohat to the Bizoti villages; but the Bizotis dispersed on the neighbouring villagers turning out.

Meanwhile the representatives of the recusant sections had been summoned to Kohat, and, after some delay, the *jirgas* of the Bizotis, the Utman Khels, and the Sipayas appeared. A proclamation was then read out to them, pointing out the various acts of hostility which had been committed, and calling upon them to exact from the actual perpetrators compensation for injury done and restoration of the plundered cattle, and (according to tribal usage) the destruction by fire of two houses in each of the implicated sections, in token of submission. The *jirgas* expressed their inability to coerce the ill-disposed members of their respective sections, and the sections were then debarred from trade with British territory, and the Bizotis further deprived of the office of guarding the Kohat *kotal*, and of their allowances on that account.

On the 10th of March a party of men, chiefly Sipayas, made a demonstration against the towers at the Ublan pass, and did everything they could to bring on an engagement; but, acting on the orders of the Deputy Commissioner, the police remained on the defensive. Failing in this attempt, it was reported that the following morning the Bizotis, some four hundred in number, would attack the towers or the village of Muhammadzai, and during the night Lieutenant P. L. N. Cavagnari, the Deputy Commissioner, went out with 60 police and 180 levies.

After the affair of the 16th of January, Major L. B. Jones, Commandant, 3rd Punjab Cavalry, who was commanding at Kohat, had, in company with the Deputy Commissioner and the officer commanding the artillery, examined the ground at the Ublan pass. The pass itself, which is about six miles from Kohat, was found to be open, its width in some places being half a mile, and its length to the beginning of the ascent about a mile. Major Jones considered that if the Bizotis occupied a small hill in advance of the towers, as they had previously done, they could be easily driven off by the troops, when considerable punishment could be inflicted on them in their retreat, without the necessity for our advancing on to the main range. This hill was not under fire from the crest of the high ridge in rear, which, although British territory, was such difficult ground that it was determined no advance on it should be made.

Lieutenant Cavagnari, accordingly, on the morning of the 11th of March occupied the hills on the left of the gorge, leaving the right open for the raiders to occupy if they came down.

About 9 A.M. the news received showed that a raid was intended, and, on the call from the Deputy Commissioner, 100 bayonets, 3rd Punjab Infantry, under Captain P. C. Rynd, were sent out from Kohat to the Muhammadzai post to reinforce the levies at the towers, and there to await further instructions from the Deputy Commissioner, but on no account to move against the enemy until support arrived from cantonments.

Shortly after this, some men came down from the direction of the Sipaya hills, and occupied a position in front of the levies on the left side of the pass.

About 11-30 A.M., the enemy, who had collected on the Ublan *kotal*, began to descend and occupy the hills on the right, some thirty or forty men occupying the small hill already mentioned. There were probably about two hundred in various other positions.

No. 2 Punjab Light Field Battery (2 guns).	
3rd Punjab Cavalry,	80 men.
3rd „ Infantry,	280 „
6th „ „	200 „

On this, Lieutenant Cavagnari again reported to Major Jones, and that officer moved out from cantonments with the troops as per margin, and rode on ahead to consult with the Deputy Commissioner.

Major Jones found Lieutenant Cavagnari with his levies holding the Bizotis in check. The enemy had, as already mentioned, taken up the position it was expected they would on the low hill to the east of the pass, which was erroneously supposed to be detached from the main range by some two or three hundred yards of open ground, and from which it was expected that their retreat to the *kotal* could be cut off either by the cavalry or infantry.

Major Jones immediately ordered the detachment of the 3rd Punjab Infantry, under Captain Rynd, which had remained at the towers, to advance towards the *kotal*, halt out of fire, and cut off the retreat of the Bizotis, should they make for the *kotal* after having been driven off the low hill. A small body of police was posted in support. Major W. D. Hoste, commanding the 6th Punjab Infantry, was posted with his men on the *kotal* side of the small hill, with directions to take a knoll about half-way up, from which a few of the enemy were firing, and to halt there until further orders. The 3rd Punjab Infantry, under Captain A. U. F. Ruxton, were posted to the right of the hill, with orders to advance to the summit, take the position, and halt until further orders. The Artillery, under Captain R. J. Abbott, supported by a body of cavalry, were placed in such a position as to cover the advance of the two columns. The gorge to the right was watched by forty sabres, 3rd Punjab Cavalry.

These arrangements were completed by about 1-30 P.M., and the troops advanced to take the small hill on the guns opening fire. The hill was gained without any loss on our side, and two of the enemy were believed to have been killed by the column under Major Hoste.

The enemy retired up the spur, which was now found to connect the small hill with the Ublan ridge, to a higher peak, where they had erected a breastwork. This peak was exceedingly steep to the south. Through a misunderstanding of orders, or ignorance of the ground, Captain Ruxton considered that he was to take this hill also, and he accordingly advanced against it. This he did in the most gallant style, but at the foot of the breastwork he fell, and soon after Lieutenant C. K. Mackinnon, his adjutant, was wounded, while his best native officer, Ram Singh, was killed; many casualties having occurred, the regiment retreated to the hill they had first taken.

On seeing this unexpected movement of the 3rd Punjab Infantry, Major Jones ordered the guns to change ground and shell the position on which they were advancing. The 6th Punjab Infantry were at the same time brought down from the low hill, to support the 3rd Punjab Infantry in case of necessity, and they were subsequently ordered to move up the gorge to the left. They advanced to the support, and the two regiments attempted a rush on the position; but it was found impossible to enter it, though a heavy fire was kept up by the guns to support the advance. Finding the position was not likely to be taken, both regiments, placed themselves under cover to rally.

No. 2 Punjab Light Field Battery (2 guns).
1st Sikh Infantry.
Wing, 6th Punjab Infantry.

Major Jones now ordered out the reinforcements, as per margin, under Major J. P. W. Campbell, from Kohat. The enemy, encouraged by their success, and by the reinforcements they were receiving from all sides, again moved forward. Consequent on this, a further advance of the British troops was ordered under fire of the guns, and reinforced by the detachment under Captain P. C. Rynd. The bugle was sounded, and a third attempt was made to take the position, but this also failed.

It was now 4-30 P.M., and darkness was approaching. As it was reported that the position was impregnable, the troops were ordered to retire under cover of the artillery fire, and reached the plain without further loss. Soon after, Major Campbell arrived with reinforcements, but as the sun was setting, it was deemed unadvisable to attempt any further operations, and the troops returned to cantonments. The total loss in the day's operations, was eleven killed and forty-four wounded. It was afterwards ascertained that Captain Ruxton had not been killed at the time of his fall, but was eventually cut up by the enemy, and his head carried off. The enemy were believed to have suffered considerably, to which Major Jones attributed the fact that the retirement was in no way pressed by them.

Expedition against the Bizoti Orakzais by a force under Lieut.-Colonel C. P. Keyes, C.B., in February 1869.

After the affair at the Ublan pass above narrated, the blockade against the offending sections was made more stringent, but, although it was worked as strictly as was possible, its good effects were considerably lessened owing to the insignificance of the sections and their independence of British territory for their actual wants.

An attempt was then made to induce the other sections of the Orakzais to coerce or punish the Bizotis for a pecuniary consideration of Rs. 600; but the scheme fell to the ground, and the Bizotis and Utman Khels went off to their summer quarters.

As the time approached for them to return to their winter settlements, it was determined, as the blockade in its then limited extent had proved ineffectual, and as the Orakzais had failed to coerce the offending sections, that, after due warning, the blockade should be extended so as to affect not only the offending sections of the Daulatzais, but the Orakzais clans collectively. There was every hope of this measure soon causing the other sections to bring such pressure on the Daulatzais as would induce them to tender their submission, and give full satisfaction for their misconduct. Meanwhile, on the night of the 13th of February, a fresh outrage was committed, a small party of the Utman Khel section surprising our police post at the foot of the Koh... *kotal*, killing one policeman, who resisted and carrying off three others.

Although a large part of the Orakzai tribe desired to remain at peace and cultivate friendly relations with us, it was now evident that owing to the feelings of Afghan pride, and the complicated relations existing among the different divisions of the tribe, it was hopeless to expect the well-disposed sections to coerce the offending clans, unless aided in their endeavour by an exhibition of the power of the British Government. There was also every probability that delay in noticing this outrage would cause matters to assume a still more serious aspect; and, on the strong recommendation of Lieutenant Cavagnari, and Lieut.-Colonel C. P. Keyes, C.B., sanction was accorded by the Lieutenant-Governor for a sudden raid to be made into the territory of the offending sections, as it was hoped that chastisement inflicted on them at their homes (hitherto vaunted as inaccessible) would show such a determination on our part not to be trifled with, that the prestige of the offending section would be destroyed, and the action of the friendly clans in coercing their fellow tribesmen to come to terms would be greatly stimulated.

The plan of operations was to cross the Ublan pass, and, if not opposed at the village of Gara, to pass on to that of Danakhula, the head-quarters of Saiyid Raza, which was to be destroyed, as well as the settlements of the Utman Khels; but if any opposition was met with at Gara, no attempt to surprise Dana Khula and the Utman Khels was to be made, as the delay would afford ample time to the enemy to make preparations.

A demonstration was made on the Peshawar side, with the view of checking the Aka Khel Afridis, especially the Basi Khel section, and also to attract the attention of the Utman Khels.

The Deputy Commissioner had no fear about the Kohat Pass Afridis joining, as they had no sympathy with the Daulatzais; but, as a precautionary measure, their representatives, who were at Kohat, were to be detained there whilst the force was out; and as the troops moved out of cantonments, Rustam Khan, son of Bahadur Sher Khan (who had the management of the pass arrangements), was to proceed to the village of Bosti Khel.

Information regarding the nature of the country beyond the Ublan showed that it was impracticable to carry out the proposed plan of operations except by seizing the *kotal* by a sudden surprise. Everything therefore depended on secrecy regarding our movements; so much so, that it was determined that, if the *kotal* could not be seized without any alarm to the enemy in the valley below, it would be useless to push on with any reasonable hope of success, in which case the troops were to be withdrawn, and the expedition abandoned.

At midnight on the 24th of February, a complete cordon was formed by the 4th Punjab Cavalry round the town of Kohat, to stop anyone attempting to enter or leave it, and police picquets were placed at all the likely places by which a man might attempt to enter the hills.

No. 1 Punjab Light Field Battery (2 mountain guns).
1st Punjab Infantry.
4th " "

At 1 A.M. on the 25th, the force, as per margin, moved from Kohat under the command of Lieut.-Colonel C. P. Keyes, C.B. This force was followed by a reserve, consisting of the 2nd Punjab Infantry and two 24-pounder howitzers, under Captain H. Tyndall.

On reaching the foot of the Ublan pass, Lieut.-Colonel Keyes and Lieutenant Cavagnari, with a few picked men from the police, headed by four *maliks* of the friendly portion of the village of Gara, ascended the pass as quickly as possible, leaving the column to follow slowly after them. A small picquet of the enemy had generally been posted at the top of the pass, and arrangements were made to seize this by stratagem. When challenged, the four *maliks* were to reply, assuring their people that, provided they kept quiet and did not raise the alarm, no harm would come to them; the police were at the same time to rush forward and seize them. This was the point that was to decide whether the enterprise was to be carried out or not; for, had the enemy been found on the alert, the troops would have at once been ordered to retire, and the expedition abandoned. Fortunately, however, the enemy, never dreaming that such an attempt would be made, and confident in the boasted strength of their position, had on this night neglected their usual precautions; no watch had been set, and quiet possession of the *kotal* was taken.

The four *maliks* of the Bizoti and Firoz Khel sections who were with Lieutenant Cavagnari, and who had, since the opening of hostilities with the Daulatzais, professed friendship, were now sent on to assure the friendly portion of the village of Gara that we only intended destroying Saiyid Raza's quarter of the village, and that, if unopposed, the troops would pass on to Danakhula and the Utman Khel country; but that, if any resistance was offered, Gara would be destroyed. The Firoz Khel *maliks* were to warn their tribe of the penalties which would be incurred by their hostages if they assisted the Utman Khels. The 4th Punjab Infantry, and a wing of the 1st Punjab Infantry then moved quietly down the pass with Lieut.-Colonel Keyes.

The *maliks*, when permitted to start, lost no time on the road; and, on arrival at the village, passed the word that the troops were coming, and proceeded at once to remove their families and property to a place of safety—their example being immediately followed by the rest of the village, the men and women setting to work at once to drive their flocks and herds up to the higher ranges. Consequently, when the troops arrived in front of Gara, not a quarter of an hour after the *maliks*, all, except a portion of the fighting men, had cleared out of the village, and a fire was opened on the column from the so-called friendly quarter. The design of saving Gara in the hope of surprising Danakhula was thus frustrated.

The troops immediately opened out, and took the village with a rush, the left assault being made by the 4th Punjab Infantry, and the right by the wing of the 1st Punjab Infantry, led respectively by Lieut.-Colonel J. Cockburn-Hood and Lieutenant H. W. Pitcher, V.C. In carrying the village our loss had been—in the 1st Punjab Infantry one man killed and eight wounded, and in the 4th Punjab Infantry eleven wounded.

The surprise of Danakhula was now no longer practicable, for the troops would have had to fight their way for two miles, and everything would have been cleared out of the village long before it could be reached. The troops would also have had to fight their way back against increasing numbers, and no advantage that could have been gained by the destruction of the empty village would have warranted the risk that would have attended the operations, and the heavy loss of life that must have occurred. The mountain guns were, therefore, brought into action on the crest of the *kotal*, and made some admirable practice on the advancing bodies of the enemy, thus materially assisting the retirement.

On reaching the top of the *kotal*, the 4th Punjab Infantry and the wing of the 1st Punjab Infantry were sent down, while the crest was held by the left wing of the 1st Punjab Infantry, under Captain T. Higginson, supported by picquets of the 4th Punjab Infantry on the right and left spurs, under Lieutenants A. Gaselee and A. McC. Bruce respectively. These picquets were necessary, as the crest of the pass was bare of cover, and without them the ground held by the 1st Punjab Infantry would have been altogether untenable; but when the crest had to be evacuated, their withdrawal was a matter of some difficulty. The descent from the spurs to the *kotal* was steep and difficult, and the retirement was necessarily slow—much slower than the movements of the enemy. The latter had pressed the retirement closely to gain these points, and were not long in seizing the vantage ground, and opening a smart fire on the retiring picquets, which the 1st Punjab Infantry had to keep down in the best way it could from the crest.

Covered, however, by the fire of the mountain guns, and by that of the howitzers in reserve, which opened on the enemy as soon as they occupied the *kotal*, the men were withdrawn with great steadiness; and the whole force reached Kohat at 1 A.M., having been twelve hours absent. Our loss was three killed and thirty-three wounded.

Royal Horse Artillery, 2 guns.
2 companies, 36th Foot.
3 troops, 19th Bengal Cavalry.
1 company, Sappers and Miners.
5 companies, 3rd Native Infantry.
19th Punjab Native Infantry.

Whilst these operations were being carried on from the Kohat side, a column, consisting of the troops as per margin, had moved out from Peshawar, under Brig.-General D. M. Stewart, C.B., for the purpose of distracting the attention of the Utman Khel Orakzais and Basi Khel Afridis. Early on the morning of the day that Lieut.-Colonel Keyes crossed the Ublan, an official was sent to the village of Akhor, in the Kohat pass, to say that the troops were close behind, and must be allowed temporarily to hold the village. At the same time, detachments of cavalry and infantry were placed in front of Jana Garhi and Fort Bara, to keep the Basi Khels at home. They began making off on seeing the troops, but on being reassured, they waited on the officer commanding the detachments.

The main body of the troops, accompanied by the Commissioner, moved into the Kohat pass about daybreak, and advanced about two miles beyond Akhor, whence a party was sent on to reconnoitre.

The force halted until 1 P.M., and then fell back upon Fort Mackeson, returning to Peshawar the following day.

These movements excited much attention, and they probably proved indirectly beneficial to the Kohat column.

After the destruction of the village of Gara, the Bizotis began to evince signs of submission, and on the 4th of April following, the *jirgas* of the Bizoti, Utman Khel, and Sipaya sections came into Kohat, and tendered their submission to the Deputy Commissioner. They agreed to pay a fine of Rs. 1,200, and to give nine of their principal headmen as hostages for their future good behaviour. After an appropriate warning, their submission was accepted, and the blockade was removed.

In the following year a large caravan of the Alisherzai section of the Orakzais was seized near Kohat. This section, on account of various acts of petty theft, had been excluded from British territory, but they now sent in their *jirga*, begging for a settlement. On the 23rd of March 1870 the representatives of both Pitao and Sweri Alisherzais arrived at Kohat, and agreed to pay Rs. 1,100 for past offences, and to behave well in future, the headmen of Torawari being their sureties.

In 1873 reprisals were made on the Sipaya section for petty offences committed on the Kohat border; but in January 1874 they submitted, paid full indemnity for losses incurred by British subjects, and gave security for future good behaviour.

In April 1874 an attack was made on a hamlet belonging to the Akhels, situated on the Miranzai border, by a party of six or eight men of that section, in pursuance of a blood-feud, and the individual against whom the attack was made was murdered, and his property plundered. The Akhels were called upon to deliver up the murderers, or to pay a fine of Rs. 1.000, and they chose the latter alternative.

In August of the same year, the Muhammad Khel clan of the Orakzais, who are Shias, and are followers of the Tirah *Saiyids*, were attacked by a large coalition of the Sunni tribes of Tirah, and some of their principal villages were destroyed, and the *saiyids*, as already stated, were driven to seek refuge in British territory. Great excitement was created along the Miranzai and Hangu borders, and it was with difficulty that British subjects were restrained from taking part in the affair.

In 1878 the Alisherzai and the Massuzai began to assume a hostile attitude toward us. This found vent in petty offences on the upper Miranzai border, as well as in Kurram.

On the outbreak of the Afghan war in November 1878, there was much agitation amongst all the Sunni Orakzai clans, caused by emissaries from the Amir of Kabul, and the preachings of the *mullas*; but on the first of January 1879 a settlement was effected with them by the Deputy Commissioner.

On the 3rd of March the Alisherzai aided the Zaimukhts in an attack on the Gandiawar *sarai*, a commissariat station a few miles east of Thal, in which our loss was six killed and five wounded. In this outrage, however, the Alisherzais played a subordinate part, only five out of the twenty-five raiders belonging to their section. The party, moreover, passed through the Zaimukht limits on their way to British territory.

The conduct of the Mamuzais was also hostile, and they were guilty of several offences on the British border. The most important of these was the murder of two *munshis* and a servant, between Kai and Nariab, on the 27th of June 1879, and the robbery of property valued at Rs. 200. In this outrage they were joined by the Akhels. Again, on the 19th of July, a party of Mamuzais, about 150 in number, made a raid on the cattle belonging to the village of Kai, and carried off animals to the value of Rs. 2,750, one man being killed on each side. They were aided in their retreat by the Akhel section.

On account of these repeated outrages, the Government of India sanctioned the adoption of punitive measures against the Alisherzai and Mamuzai sections of the Lashkarzai Orakzais, to be undertaken, if possible, in conjunction with the expedition against the Zaimukhts (to be described in Chapter V). The rapid success, however, of the British force employed against the last-named tribe so alarmed the Alisherzais, that their *jirga* attended and accepted the terms proposed, *viz.*, payment of Rs. 4,000 fine and the surrender of twenty-eight hostages. The Mamuzais also agreed to pay a fine of the same amount and to furnish hostages; but subsequently a claim was raised by one party in the section that the fine agreed to should include all payments on account of a raid by the entirely distinct section—the Ali Khel—on a *serai* at Mazam Talao on the night of the 14th of November 1879. This claim could not, of course, be entertained, and the Mamuzais were accordingly blockaded.

The raid above mentioned upon Mazam Talao, between Togh and Sarozai on the Kohat-Thal road, was of a very serious nature. The raiders, belonging chiefly to the Ali Khel Orakzais, were under the leadership of one Malik Hawas of that section. The party consisted of thirty-seven men, and, owing to the gross cowardice of the guard of road police stationed in the *serai*, no resistance was offered. The casualties were thirteen killed and sixteen wounded, chiefly unarmed coolies and travellers. The garrison of the road post was subsequently severely punished. Four of the neighbouring British villages, which enjoyed a remission of revenue in consideration of the duties of frontier watch and ward, had failed either to oppose or to follow up the retreating raiders, and their revenue demands were accordingly raised to the full amount for a term of five years. For this raid a fine of Rs. 4,500 was imposed on the Ali Khels.

On the night of the 5th of August 1880 another serious raid was committed on the Bagatukh *serai*, three miles west of Hangu. The marauders, who were about forty in number, and were chiefly men of the Mamuzai and Ali Khel sections, having found the sentry asleep, entered the enclosure by scaling the walls. There were at that time in the *serai* twenty-two coolies, protected by a garrison of nine road police, recruited from the neighbouring villages. Of the former, two were killed and three wounded, and of the police six were killed and one wounded. The raiders then set fire to one side of the *serai* and carried off four rifles, some matchlocks, some pickaxes, and about Rs. 150 in cash. The party approached Bagatukh through the lands of the Rabia Khel and Malla Khel Orakzais, and retired unmolested with their plunder into the territory of the Akhels. As a punishment to the villagers of Bagatukh for their apathy in not turning out to repel this raid, the assessment of the village was raised from Rs. 300 to Rs. 500 for a period of three years. To punish the sections who had given a passage to the raiders, a fine of Rs. 1,000 was imposed on the Akhels, of Rs. 750 on the Rabia Khels, and Rs. 750 on the Malla Khels; and, in addition to these, Rs. 1,000 was to be added to the amount already due from the Mamuzais, the sum previously standing against the Ali Khels being held to be sufficient.

The fines now imposed upon the Orakzai tribe amounted to no less than Rs. 15,200, and proposals were made for the payment of this amount being enforced by a military expedition; but punitive measures had to be deferred in consequence of the operations against the Mahsud Wazirs. (*See* Chapter VIII.) The necessity of reducing this larger and more important tribe to submission was regarded as being more urgent, and the opportunity of utilizing the force on the spot against the Orakzai clans was lost.

After this, the attitude of the Orakzais gradually became so openly defiant and contumacious that they eventually exhausted the patience of Government, and brought upon themselves the long-deferred punishment inflicted by the two Miranzai Expeditions of 1891. Before proceeding to an account of these punitive measures, however, it is necessary to relate in some detail the events which made them necessary.

In 1884, the Sturi Khels still owed the Rs. 1,500 imposed upon them; the Rabia Khels and Akhels behaved badly, though the latter paid up Rs. 661, leaving Rs. 2,200 still owing for old and new offences. The Mishtis, by cattle-lifting, etc., added another Rs. 600 to the Rs. 1,894 previously due.

During 1885 the Akhels and Mishtis gave further trouble; the Rabia Khels and Malla Khels were allowed to compound for their offences on easy terms.

In 1886 the Sturi Khels, who had paid no part of the Rs. 1,500 against them, made two fresh cattle raids. The Mishtis continued to give trouble, many of their cattle thefts being traced to Chapar Mishti, a village only a mile or two beyond our border in fairly open country. The Rabia Khel and Akhel also committed further depredations; the latter, the worst behaved section on the border, added 33 fresh offences during the year, claims for Rs. 5,153 still remaining due from them from 1885.

The Deputy Commissioner, in his annual report, made suggestions for an expedition to include the Akhels and other offenders, and considered that it would be impossible ever to check these incessant outrages until this was done.

During 1887 the Sturi Khels avoided all settlement of cases against them, besides committing fresh offences. This being a section which does not visit British territory, reprisals, other than by a punitive expedition, were not feasible. The Mishtis and Rabia Khels behaved worse than ever; while the Akhels committed 48 fresh offences; and the Deputy Commissioner again urged the necessity for strong measures.

During 1888 matters went on much as before, the Rabia Khel, Mishtis, and Akhels committing a number of serious outrages, and no clan (except the Sipayas, who paid up for some misconduct of the preceding years, but committed new offences as well), attempted to settle the amount due from it. The Sheikhan, Ali

Khel, and Mamuzai also added some offences to their lists. Trouble of a new kind, however, due to the intrigues of Mozuffer Khan, arose with the Malla Khel and Rabıa Khel.

At the beginning of 1888 the Malla Khel suddenly made a claim that Darband and their other settlements in the Miranzai plain south of the Samana should be treated as independent territory. In 1855 the Rabia Khel had formally acknowledged that the crest of the Samana was the boundary of British territory; and though the strip of territory in question was not marked on our survey map as British, yet it had been assessed as such, and always acknowledged by the tribes as within our borders. On the claim being rejected by the district officer, the Malla Khel at once evacuated these settlements and went off to the hills. The Rabia Khel then broke out into open hostility, and, passing through the evacuated territory, committed eight outrages, besides threatening various British villages. To stop these raids a new frontier post was built at Shinawari. This post, garrisoned by forty men of the Border Militia, was attacked on the night of the 3rd–4th March by a mixed band of Malla Khel and Rabia Khel. They were beaten off with a loss of two killed, upon which they plundered the British hamlet of Torwatti. For this and previous offences a fine of Rs. 1,400 was imposed on the Malla Khel. In March and April they returned to Darband and the vicinity, and pending the orders of Government no action was taken against them.

In 1889 another attempt was made to effect a settlement with the Rabia Khel and Mishtis. By April 1889 there were 90 offences charged against the former, for which the compensation due was Rs. 6,100, besides Rs. 2,000 fine; while against the Mishtis the total claim was Rs. 8,500. At this time the Akhels were giving more trouble than any other of the Orakzai sections. A large amount of compensation was due from them, and, on the 8th May 1889, a large party of them attacked a police guard taking prisoners from Kai to Hangu, rescued the prisoners, wounded a constable, and carried off some arms. On the 13th May, Mr. Davis, the police officer sent to investigate this outrage, came upon a raiding party of Akhels near Togh, and found the bodies of two men who had been shot. Mr. Davis and his escort pursued the raiders, who fired upon him and escaped.

Captain Leigh, the Deputy Commissioner, expressed his opinion that this state of lawlessness could not be ended without strong measures; in which view he was supported by the Lieutenant-Governor of the Punjab, who urged upon the Government of India the necessity of action.

The conclusions arrived at by Sir James Lyall were briefly as follows:—

(1) That the country up to the foot of the Samana Range, should be declared to be British territory, and dealt with accordingly.

(2) That the *Khan Tehsildar* should be told to collect from the Malla Khel, Rabia Khel, Mishti and Sheikhan sections under his political charge, the fines and compensation due from them, under penalty of loss of office, *jagirs* and allowances.

(3) That the Deputy Commissioner be authorised to call in the Akhel *jirga*, and, if a proper *jirga* came in, to take their reply, and, if necessary, to threaten an expedition against them. If no proper *jirga* attended, the section to be at once formally blockaded.

(4) That a small military detachment of rifles and sabres be posted at Hangu to protect this part of the border.

The Government of India agreed to the above, and steps were at once taken to carry them into effect.

At the beginning of 1890 the *Khan* had done nothing to realize the fines: Makhmaddin and his party were openly defiant: and there was reason to believe that Mozuffer Khan and his son Sarwar Khan were encouraging the tribes not to pay.

The Punjab Government accordingly proposed that if, by the beginning of March, Mozuffer Khan had not coerced Makhmaddin and recovered the sums due, he should be removed from office and an expedition despatched: the scope of the expedition to also include the Zaimukht, Chikkai of Chinarak, who had been mixed up in these troubles.

Genuinely alarmed, the Khan now paid up Rs.19,000 (out of Rs. 24,385 demanded), and Chikkai, Makhmaddin, the Malla Khels and the Akhels made submission and promise of payment. The *Khan* resigned his political appointment and took two years' furlough from his tehsildarship.

In June the Rabia Khels broke out again, raiding a British village close to Hangu, and firing upon the police sent after them. The Deputy Commissioner summoned the tribal *jirgas*, but none appeared; and the police messengers sent to call them in were deprived of their arms and threatened with death. This misconduct being due to the intrigues of the Khan of Hangu, he was deported to Abbottabad. As he still continued intriguing and stirring up trouble from that place, he was removed to the Central Jail at Lahore, and the tribes were informed of the fact. The tribes were further informed that a punitive expedition would be sent against them.

Upon this Chikkai and the Akhels paid up their fines, and the Samil clans also sent in a *jirga* and promised to pay all outstanding amounts, giving hostages for payment. No money, however, was forthcoming by the date agreed upon; outrages began again as before, and two British officers were fired upon without provocation. It was quite clear that the tribes had come to the conclusion that, when an expedition was imminent, they had only to send in a *jirga* and promise compensation and amendment, in order once more to delude the authorities into a belief that they really intended to behave better in future. As both the Deputy Commissioner and the Commissioner were still of opinion that there was no chance of a permanent settlement of this border without an expedition, the Lieutenant-Governor, on the 2nd December, recommended this course to be taken. In his letter he drew particular attention to the attitude of the Payavi Nmasi and Ayaz Khel sections of the Rabia Khel, who had not paid a penny of the heavy fines due from them, and to the conduct of their leader Makhmaddin, who had just sent a message to Captain Leigh, the Deputy Commissioner, to say that he had no intention of paying; an example promptly followed by the Sturi Khel.

First Miranzai Expedition, 1891.

On the 2nd January 1891 the Government of India, concurring with the Lieutenant-Governor, decided that an expedition should be despatched, with the special object of punishing and enforcing the submission of the four Samil sections, *viz.*, the Rabia Khel, Sheikhan, Mishti, and Mamuzai, as well as the Sturi Khel, should the latter fail to submit when the Khanki valley was occupied. The sections were to be informed that, whatever overtures they might make, the troops would start and would occupy the Khanki valley; and that, if submission were not then offered, they would be severely dealt with. The following were to be the terms exacted from the refractory tribesmen on their submission :—

(i) Full and immediate payment of all outstanding fines.

(ii) An agreement to the location of posts on the Samana range at any points which might be chosen, and an agreement to the Kohat Border Police patrolling the Samana range whenever it was necessary or desirable to do so.

(iii) An agreement to pay revenue to Government, and *malikana* to the Bangash owners, for all holdings and grazing on the south of the Samana Range.

(iv) An agreement accepting the tribal responsibility of the clans for offences committed by members of them, and accepting the principle of the settlement of all claims against them or of claims by them against British subjects by tribal *jirgas* before the Deputy Commissioner.

The command of the expedition was entrusted to Brig.-General Sir William Lockhart K.C.B., C.S.I., then commanding the Punjab Frontier Force, with chief political as well as military authority. Major Leigh, Deputy Commissioner of Kohat, was appointed Political Officer. The composition of the force, which was styled the "Miranzai Field Force," was as shown in the margin. The detail of the staff will be found in the Appendix. Each infantry regiment was 600 strong; and the following orders with regard to equipment, etc., were amongst those issued :—

Head-quarters and two squadrons, 5th Punjab Cavalry.
No. 3 (Peshawar) Mountain Battery.
No. 4 (Hazara) " "
No. 5 Company, Bengal Sappers and Miners.
3rd Sikh Infantry.
1st Punjab Infantry.
2nd " "
4th " "
5th " "
23 d Bengal " (Pioneers).
29th " "

Winter scale of clothing for troops and followers; 200 rounds rifle ammunition per man in regimental charge; heavy entrenching tools only to be taken; ten days' supplies to be collected at advanced base; 15 days' supplies in reserve at Kohat; two and a half Native Field Hospitals allotted to the force, with mule transport for half that number; riding mules or ponies to be substituted for ambulance tongas; five days' rations (1 day's in haversacks) to accompany troops across the border; tents for troops to be provided as transport became available.

It was not considered likely that other Orakzai clans or the Afridis would offer any assistance to those against whom action was being taken, both on account of the heavy snow on the high ranges to the north of the valley, and also because the Afridis did not appear to interest themselves in the Samil clans of the Khanki valley. The Khaibar Rifles, indeed, even volunteered for service on the Miranzai border.

Hangu was the advanced base. The Field Force (numbering something over 5,000 fighting men) was concentrated at Kohat by the 12th January, its advance across the border being arranged for the 19th. On the 12th proclamations were issued to the four Samil clans, warning them not to resist, and to the other Orakzai clans informing them that they would not be interfered with if they did not in any way oppose us.

The force was divided into three columns as per margin, and Shahu Khel, Togh and Hangu were fixed upon as the starting points of these columns respectively. One troop of the 5th Punjab Cavalry was detailed for keeping up communication between Darband, Hangu, and Kohat, the last-named place being garrisoned by the 22nd Bengal Infantry and detachments of other regiments. Heavy rain and snow prevented the columns moving as arranged: but by the 21st of January they were in position at their starting points. Nos. 2 and 3 columns had meantime pushed reconnaissances to the crest of the Samana, now nearly a foot deep in snow. The roads from Darband and Pat Darband had been found capable of being made into good mule roads; the road from Hangu to Lakka proved to be unfit for animals.

No. 1 Column.

Colonel A. McC. Bruce.

5th Punjab Cavalry, Head-quarters and three troops.
No. 4 (Hazara) Mountain Battery.
Half Company, Bengal Sappers and Miners.
1st Punjab Infantry.
4th ,, ,,
23rd Bengal ,, (Pioneers), Head-quarters and Wing.
29th Bengal Infantry.

No. 2 Column.

Lieut.-Colonel A. H. Turner.

No. 3 (Peshawar) Mountain Battery.
Half Company, Bengal Sappers and Miners.
2nd Punjab Infantry.
5th ,, ,,

No. 3 Column.

Lieut.-Colonel C. C. Brownlow.

3rd Sikh Infantry.
23rd Bengal Infantry (Pioneers), Wing.

On the 23rd a reconnaissance was made from No. 1 column up the Khanki valley to the Mishti Khel village of Khaori. The route was found practicable for laden camels, and the Mishtis in the villages were quite peaceable. On the 24th Colonel Bruce again reconnoitred up the Khanki valley, this time to Gwada. The reconnaissance when returning was fired upon from Gwada, Jandasam, and Katsa. On this day the Mishti *jirga* submitted at Hangu; the Mamuzais had already submitted at Kohat on the 6th. The Sheikhans, and Makhmaddin's faction of the Rabia Khel, were thus the only sections still recalcitrant.

On the 25th orders were issued directing the various columns, marching by different routes, to concentrate at Gwada on the 27th. In accordance with this scheme, Nos. 1 and 2 columns concentrated as arranged, but No. 3 column, which on the 26th had reached Darband, was prevented by snow and rain from reaching Gwada till the 29th. No opposition had been encountered by any column, nor by a reconnaissance from Gwada to Ghuzghor on the 28th. The following villages were destroyed by the columns when passing:—Katsa, Saifaldarra, Nadirmela and Sarmela—belonging to the Makhmaddin faction—and Tor Pokho, near Tsalai.

On the 28th the Sheikhan *jirga* came into camp, also the Payavi Nmasi section. The latter were, however, informed that until Makhmaddin came in their submission could not be accepted; he being now the only Rabia Khel headman who had not submitted.

On the 29th a reconnaissance was pushed up the Daradar valley, through Starkili to the Kharai Kotal, leading from the Daradar valley into the Sheikhan country. The reconnaissance reported that the road from Gwada to the *kotal* was quite practicable for mules, and that the road down the Laghardarra, through Dran, and round through Mir Asghar back to Shahu Khel, appeared also practicable.

Makhmaddin being still obdurate, the destruction of the towers of the Payavi Nmasi commenced at Inzaur, a couple of miles west of Gwada, on the 31st, Makhmaddin's own tower at Jandasam being blown up on the following day, and three more at Ghuzghor on the 2nd February. On the 3rd the villages of Darwazamela and Fakirmela, belonging to Makhmaddin's section, and on the 4th the Ayaz Khel portion of Ghuzghor, were destroyed.

The Kharai Kotal being found impassable from recent heavy snow, orders were now issued for the force to return to Shahu Khel and enter the Laghardarra valley from the east instead of from the west as originally intended.

On the 4th, the 2nd column, reconstituted as per margin, under Lieut.-Colonel Turner and accompanied by Sir William Lockhart, marched for the Sheikhan country, pushing out reconnoitring and survey parties in various directions *en route*. No. 3 column was temporarily broken up, and the 5th Punjab Cavalry and 5th Punjab Infantry were sent back to Kohat, the 22nd Bengal Infantry being moved to Shahu Khel. Two guns, No. 4 (Hazara) Mountain Battery, Royal Artillery, and the 1st Punjab Infantry remained at Gwada, where two more towers were blown up on the 4th. No. 1 column, marching on the 5th *viâ* Shahu Khel and Hangu, proceeded to Darband to furnish escorts for working-parties on the roads to the Samana crest. They destroyed Shakartangi, the last remaining village of the Makhmaddin section, *en route*.

No. 3 (Peshawar) Mountain Battery, Royal Artillery.
No. 5 Company, Bengal Sappers and Miners.
3rd Sikhs.
2nd Punjab Infantry.
23rd Pioneers.

On the 6th, No. 2 column, which had marched *viâ* Khaori and Mir Asghar, arrived at Dran. Makhmaddin's cattle, which had been harboured in Laghardarra, escaped; but the Sheikhans were fined Rs. 500 for allowing them to be there, security for payment being immediately enforced under threat of destroying towers. Proclamations were sent to the Sturi Khel to say that a force would visit their country, and the Zera pass, leading into Sturi Khel country, was reconnoitred. On the 8th the column was back again at Shahu Khel, having completed its survey work.

At Shahu Khel Nos. 2 and 3 columns were again reconstituted as per margin: on the 9th No. 2 column marched for Hangu, where it remained until the force was broken up. On the same day No. 3 column, taking with it five days' supplies, reached Bar Marai; and on the 10th marched for Zera. From early morning the Sappers and Pioneers were at work on the Zera pass, but it was 3 P.M. before the force could advance; and the difficulties of the road, enhanced by a fresh fall of snow and a hard frost, made the progress of the baggage very slow. Before the column left Bar Marai the Sturi Khel *jirga* had come in and given security for the payment of

No. 2 Column.

No. 3 (Peshawar) Mountain Battery (4 guns).
2nd Punjab Infantry.

No. 3 Column.

No. 3 (Peshawar) Mountain Battery (2 guns).
No. 5 Company, Bengal Sappers and Miners.
3rd Sikh Infantry.
22nd Bengal Infantry.
23rd Bengal Infantry (Pioneers).

their fine (Rs. 1,000); Malik Mastan, Mani Khel, did the same, giving security for Rs. 3,000, and returning a boy whom he had kidnapped. On the 11th the force remained halted at Zera, reconnaissances proceeding through the Gudar Tangi defile to Sultanzai and Shiraz Garhi. On the 12th the Zera pass was recrossed without difficulty, the road having been much improved, and on the 14th the column arrived at Hangu.

Meanwhile the 1st column from Darband, and the troops left to garrison Gwada, had destroyed the village of Bazai and the towers of Tangi China, belonging to the still obstinate sections of the Rabia Khel.

On the 16th, after a careful examination of the Samana range, Sir William Lockhart had an interview at Kohat with the Lieutenant-Governor of the Punjab, regarding the protection of the Miranzai border.

As a result of this interview the following proposals were submitted by Sir William Lockhart:—

(a) The establishment of three posts on the Samana ridge: the western one at Gulistan, the central one on a site west of Sangar, and the eastern one at Lakka. All three posts to be connected with each other by a mule road near the crest and by similar roads with Baliamin, Darband, and Hangu respectively. The work to be put in hand at once, the money required for the purpose being advanced from provincial funds.

(b) The garrisons of these posts to be as under:—

Western post.—One company of native infantry under a native officer with a few Border Police and tribal levies attached.

Central post.—Thirty Border Police and tribal levies.

Eastern post.—Thirty Border Police and tribal levies.

(c) The retention of the garrison at Gwada until revenue and other civil matters should be finally arranged, this force being withdrawn probably about the first week in March.

(d) The retention in the country of a native infantry regiment for some time longer, for the protection of the coolies working on the Samana roads.

These proposals were approved by the Government of India, it being understood that the retention of troops at the western post would be a temporary measure, the border police and tribal levies eventually taking it over altogether.

On the 17th Malik Makhmaddin with two of his relatives, Hazrat Shah and Khawas, both bad characters, surrendered themselves at Gwada, on condition that their lives were spared, and that they would not be transported.

The troops were now withdrawn to Kohat, with the exception of the 29th Punjab Infantry, left to protect the working-parties on the Samana, and the field force was broken up on the 1st March.

Although, in this expedition, the opposition encountered was almost negligible, the hardships undergone by the troops were exceedingly severe. Thirty-three severe cases of frost-bite were dealt with in hospital, the temperature at night being at times as low as 20° below freezing.

The political results of the expedition were in the opinion of the Punjab Government, satisfactory. All the sections had made full submission, had agreed to the terms imposed, and had also agreed to eject undesirables and outlaws. The Sheikhan, Mishti, Mamuzai, and Sturi Khels had paid up in full. The Rabia Khel, though they had submitted, still owed Rs. 6,748,—all, except a little over Rs. 900, due from Makhmaddin's faction. The destruction of some twenty of their towers was, however, estimated as the equivalent of Rs. 15,000 damage, and Makhmaddin and Khawas were in custody pending the payment of arrears. The tribes had only agreed to the construction of forts on the Samana with reluctance; but their submission had been so complete that further trouble in the immediate future was not anticipated.

Second Miranzai Expedition, 1891.

Only a few days after the Miranzai field force had been broken up, Major Leigh telegraphed that he had heard from several reliable sources that the Samil clans were being so taunted with cowardice by *mullas* and others, that they were contemplating a combination to oppose the construction of the posts, and that the Rabia Khel were especially sore at the idea of the posts, the revenue, and the *malikana*. A battery and a regiment were consequently ordered to be held in readiness at Kohat to reinforce the Samana; but the danger was held to be remote. On the 25th March Major Leigh again telegraphed that the Rabia Khel were in a sulky and dangerous humour, and that they were endeavouring to stir up a general combination of the tribes against us.

On the 4th April, the distribution of the British troops on the Samana was as follows:—

Two hundred and fifty rifles, 29th Begnal Infantry, at Baliaman, under Lieut.-Colonel Reid.

Two hundred and fifty rifles, 29th Bengal Infantry, at Tangai, under Captain Maisey.

Two hundred and thirty rifles, 3rd Sikhs, at Darband, under Captain Fasken.

Twenty rifles, 3rd Sikhs, and twenty Border Military Police, at Tsalai.

On that morning the guards for the working-parties went out as usual. About 10-30 A.M., without any previous warning, the 29th Bengal Infantry guards on the Sangar section of the road were attacked and driven in with a loss of twelve killed and two wounded; three of those killed were reported to have been made prisoners at the time, and subsequently butchered in cold blood in the mosque at Sangar. The two wounded and four others escaped to Tsalai. On hearing the firing, Lieut.-Colonel Reid immediately communicated with Kohat, and then, taking with him every available man—only seventy-two rifles—started for the Dhar spur. Pushing forward as rapidly as possible, he met the enemy at the foot of the spur near Pat Darband, and drove them steadily up the hill into Dhar village. Between this and Sangar over 1,000 men were collected; and it being impossible to advance further, the party retired, followed by the enemy, to Baliamin, which they reached at 8 P.M., with a loss of two men wounded. Captain Fasken, meantime, had got into Tsalai with a reinforcement of fifty men, where he remained the night, the enemy surrounding him but afraid to attack the post. The Gulistan section was attacked at 2-30 P.M., but Captain Maisey succeeded in bringing in all his men to Baliamin, losing only one killed and one wounded in the retirement.

The attack had been made with characteristic Pathan treachery. Some men of the Rabia Khel got taken on as labourers on the road, and then suddenly turned on the guards, who, unsuspicious of any danger, were protecting them. The enemy, who were waiting in large numbers on the north side of the Samana, immediately poured over the crest, and fighting became general. The picquet at Tangi (eight men of the 29th) was taken by surprise in a similar way. The villagers, with arms concealed, drove their cattle past, and, suddenly throwing off their blankets, they fell on the picquet, killing one and wounding two, and securing six rifles. Two of the picquet subsequently received the Order of Merit for their gallantry on this occasion.

On the morning of the 5th Lieut.-Colonel Reid, with a couple of companies, proceeded to Tsalai, but finding that the enemy on the Samana were in constantly increasing numbers, and that they held the Tsalai water-supply, he evacuated that post, and heliographed to Kohat—"Rising general, strong reinforcement required at once, evacuating Tsalai, nothing gained by holding it."

Our total losses, during the attack on the guards and subsequent fighting, were fourteen killed and seven wounded: the enemy's loss was unknown, but included three men of influence. Subsequent reports proved that the Rabia Khel, Mamuzai, Sheikhan, and Mishti sections were the originators of the outbreak. The inevitable temporary abandonment of the crest of the Samana naturally encouraged the enemy, who were now estimated at thousands—including not only all the Khanki Valley Orakzais, but a certain number of Afridis under the notorious Mir Bashar, (Malikdin), who assumed the title of "King of Tirah" for a time during the Afghan war, and had been pensioned by the Amir. He was reported to be supported by the Afghan Commander-in-Chief, and was preaching a *jehad*, aided by Aka Khel and Mamuzai *mullas* and others.

In the opinion of the Lieutenant-Governor, the tame submission of the Samil clans, in the first expedition, had been due, firstly to climatic reasons, rendering coalition and the active support of neighbouring tribes difficult; and secondly to a feeling that the clans affected had brought on their own punishment. But the establishment of posts on the Samana overlooking the Khanki valley had, His Honour considered, not only made the Rabia Khel fancy that their old complete independence was gone, but had aroused the suspicions and apprehensions of other Orakzais and had enlisted the sympathies of the more fanatical amongst the Afridis on the side of the Samil clans.

On the 5th, Major Leigh issued a proclamation to the Orakzais and Tirah Afridis. He pointed out that the establishment of posts on the Samana was a defensive measure which had been forced on Government for the protection of its subjects against the Rabia Khel, and assured them that we had not, and never had, any designs against their independence. The Political Officer in the

Khaibar also took action in disabusing the tribes of ideas of this kind.

Brig.-General Sir William Lockhart, then commanding the Reserve Brigade of the Hazara Field Force, was ordered to proceed to Kohat with his brigade at once, and arrived there on the 7th. Reinforcements began to reach Darband on the 6th; and on that date the disposition of troops in the Miranzai valley was as per margin, while additional troops were being pushed up from the plains. On the 8th a small party of the 1st Punjab Infantry was attacked near Hangu; on the 10th the camp, which had moved to Darband from Baliamin, was attacked by about 1,000 tribesmen, who were beaten off without loss to us. On this date a definite answer came from the tribes to Major Leigh's proclamation of the 5th, in which they demanded the abandonment of the Samana, and the release of Makhmaddin and others.

Hangu.

5th Punjab Cavalry	..	25 sabres.
1st Punjab Infantry	..	50 rifles.
Khattak levies	..	250 „

Darband.

No. 3 (Peshawar) Mountain Battery (2 guns).

3rd Sikh Infantry	..	250 rifles.
1st Punjab Infantry	..	125 „
2nd Punjab Infantry	..	250 „

Baliamin.

No. 3 (Peshawar) Mountain Battery (2 guns)

1st Punjab Infantry	..	125 rifles.
29th Bengal Infantry	..	475 „

The troops designated to form the second Miranzai Field Force were divided into three columns as shown in the margin, exclusive of the divisional troops, which consisted of the 5th Punjab Cavalry (two squadrons), 19th Bengal Lancers, Punjab Garrison Battery (three guns), and No. 5 Company, Bengal Sappers and Miners. A detail of the staff is given in Appendix B. The force numbered approximately 7,400 men, and was subsequently joined by a half battalion, Manchester Regiment (304 rifles) and the 1-4th Gurkhas (717 rifles), the latter forming the garrison of Kohat.

1st Column at Hangu.

Colonel J. M. Sym, C.B.
No. 3 Mountain Battery, Royal Artillery.
1st Battalion, King's Royal Rifles.
Half No. 5 Coy., Bengal S. and M.
1st Punjab Infantry.
27th Bengal „
1-5th Gurkha Regiment.

2nd Column at Darband.

(Lieut. Colonel A. H. Turner.)
No. 3 (Peshawar) Mountain Battery.
Half No. 5 Coy., Bengal S. and M.
3rd Sikh Infantry.
2nd Punjab „
15th Bengal „

3rd Column at Darband.

(Lieut.-Colonel C. C. Brownlow.)
No. 2 Mountain Battery (3 guns).
6th Punjab Infantry.
19th Bengal „
29th „ „

Sir William Lockhart was again Chief Political as well as Chief Military Officer, with Major Leigh as Political Officer on his staff.

On the 16th the General Officer Commanding proceeded from Kohat to Hangu, and the column commanders here received their final instructions previous to the beginning of operations on the following day. Three days' supplies for men (one in haversacks), and three days' grain for animals were to be carried, and the scale of carriage was reduced to what was known as the "Black Mountain scale," namely, 135 mules per British, and 119 per Native, regiment, in addition to carriage for greatcoats.

It was reported that about 1,000 men—Mishtis (Tirah), Sheikhans, Mamuzais (Daradar) and Rabia Khels—were on the Samana, with several thousands, Gar and Samil, in support in the Khanki valley.

On the 17th the advance from Hangu took place, the General Officer Commanding accompanying No. 1 column. This column having reached Lakka unopposed, the General heliographed to No. 2 column to advance from Darband to the Darband Kotal, and to No. 3 column to move from Darband *viâ* Pat Darband to Sangar. No. 1 column then continued its advance along the crest, meeting No. 2 column at the Darband Kotal. The latter column, plus the 27th Bengal Infantry, was then ordered *viâ* Saifaldarra to Gwada, which it reached after some opposition, losing one killed and four wounded.

Meanwhile No. 1 column advanced on Tsalai, which was assaulted and carried, the King's Royal Rifles, covered by the fire of No. 3 Mountain Battery, leading the attack. Their Commanding Officer (Colonel C. P. Cramer) and three men were wounded; also Major C. C. Egerton, Assistant Adjutant-General, and his orderly. Gogra and Sangar were next carried by the 1st column without further casualties; and at the latter place the 3rd column was met. Both columns bivouacked at Sangar, within sight of the 2nd column at Gwada.

The following day (the 18th) the advance was continued by the 1st and 3rd columns. Sartop was attacked, and cleared of the enemy, the 3rd column attacking in front and the 1st column advancing against it in flank from our left.

Our losses here were Lieutenant F. R. Patch and six men wounded. Before midday the whole Mastan plateau (which is between Sartop and Gulistan) was in our hands without further loss; and the 1st column then returned to its bivouac, the 3rd column being left to hold the plateau. The Akhels on this day sent in a letter to say they had been forced by circumstances to join the opposition against us. They were informed in reply that their country would be visited and a fine inflicted, and that any further resistance would be severely dealt with.

On the 19th, Nos. 1 and 3 columns remained halted, No. 2 column moving up to Sangar in order to simplify the question of supplies. The enemy, who had collected in large numbers near the Mastan plateau, began an attack on the 3rd column in the morning, from the west, gradually enveloping it until it was surrounded on three sides. To keep them in check, Lieut.-Colonel Brownlow extended his force from the extreme right, across the plateau to a point opposite Saragarhi, keeping six companies in reserve in camp. A desultory fire was kept up all day long; and at 7 P.M., when the picquets were withdrawn, the enemy followed up and fired into camp, some advancing up to within fifteen yards of the picquets. Our losses at Mastan during the day were three killed, and four wounded.

On the 20th the picquet positions of the previous day were re-occupied, and were subjected to a continuous fire from the direction of Saragarhi and Ghuztang. Considering that he had not enough men at his disposal to attack both these places simultaneously, Lieut.-Colonel Brownlow heliographed for reinforcements. At 1-15 P.M. the marginally named troops reached him, and he then advanced against Saragarhi, covered by the fire of No. 3 Peshawar Battery. The 5th Gurkhas, led by Captain Martin, formed the first line, and attacked with great spirit and dash, supported by the King's Royal Rifles. Ghuztang was attacked simultaneously, and the enemy retired precipitately towards the Khanki.

1st Battalion, King's Royal Rifles (4 companies).
No. (Peshawar) Mountain Battery.
2nd Punjab Infantry.
1-5th Gurkha Battalion (4 companies).

Our casualties during the day were one man of the King's Royal Rifles killed and Captain Macleod, 29th Bengal Infantry, and six men of various native corps wounded. The enemy's losses were subsequently ascertained to have been about 300 killed and wounded, 25 of the Akhels being amongst the killed. All sections of the Orakzais were represented in this engagement; also numbers of bad characters from our own side of the border. After destroying the towers and hamlets of Saragarhi, and the tower and village of Ghuztang, the troops retired to Mastan and Sangar.

On the following morning it was evident that the enemy were disheartened by their losses, no opposition being offered to the two columns which left camp. One of these columns, under Lieut.-Colonel Turner, marched to Gulistan from Sangar and camped there; while the other, under Lieut.-Colonel Brownlow, destroyed the Ibrahim Khel hamlets with their three towers and then returned to camp.

No. 3 (Peshawar) Mountain Battery.
No. 5 Company, Bengal Sappers and Miners.
15th Bengal Infantry.
3rd Sikh "
1st Punjab "
2nd " "
27th Bengal "

On the morning of the 22nd, the General Officer Commanding, with the whole of Lieut.-Colonel Turner's column, as per margin (except fifty men per regiment left as camp guard), left Gulistan, and advanced along the crest towards the Akhel country. After marching about a mile a high point was reached, overlooking the Chagru valley, the Chagru Kotal being about a mile distant and 1,200 feet below. Down in the valley, on open ground adjoining one of the villages, a large number of men, estimated at about 1,500, were assembled.

As Major Leigh informed Sir William Lockhart that the Akhels were preparing to send in a *jirga*, the troops were halted, and a message was sent to the nearest village to say that if they offered resistance or attempted to leave their villages they would be fired on.

Maddu Khan, the most turbulent of the Akhels, then came in, and explained that the men below were Alisherzais, Mamuzais, and Massuzais, who had come to punish the Akhels for not joining the combination against Government. As this was an obvious invention to try and escape punishment, and as the *lashkar* below now began advancing in a threatening manner towards the Chagru Kotal, orders were immediately given to the troops to advance.

The 15th and 27th Bengal Infantry being left with the guns on the crest, the 1st Punjab Infantry advanced along the ridge towards the Chagru Kotal, with orders to work from there down the Akhel (or Chagru) valley. The 2nd Punjab Infantry and 3rd Sikhs meanwhile descended directly to the Chagru valley to cut off the enemy's retreat towards the Khanki, with orders to work up the valley and meet the 1st Punjab Infantry. Fire was opened on the latter as they advanced; but, aided by the guns on the crest, they soon cleared out the villages to their front; and the enemy, in retiring towards the Khanki, were caught by the fire of the 2nd Punjab Infantry, and suffered heavily. The 2nd Punjab Infantry then moved up the valley destroying the villages and towers.

In the meantime another strong *lashkar* estimated at some 1,500 men, was seen coming up the bed of the Chagru from the direction of the Khanki. At the junction of the Narik and Chagru this force divided, part ascending the Narik valley and gaining the heights to the west of the Chagru, whence they continued to annoy our troops in the valley below: the remainder moving up the spur below the village of Margharu, nearly due east of Dargai. The 27th Bengal Infantry and two guns, moving along this spur, destroyed the village and effectually checked the enemy's further advance. The force then retired to camp; and an attempt to press towards our advanced picquets, later in the evening, was repulsed without difficulty.

Our losses during the day had been one killed and thirteen wounded, while the enemy, who were said to consist of Mamuzais, Alisherzais, Massuzais, Ali Khels and Akhels, lost between fifty and sixty killed.

On the same day another column, about 1,000 strong, under Lieut.-Colonel Reid, marched from Mastan and destroyed the Rabia Khel villages of Bazai, Ghokai, and Pamdapatta, on the Ghuztang spur, east of Ghuzghor. Very slight opposition was met with, and the retirement was unmolested.

The following day, large numbers of the enemy having collected on the spur north of Margharu, Lieut.-Colonel Turner moved out to attack them with his whole available force, a wing of the 19th Bengal Infantry from Mastan guarding Camp Gulistan in his absence. The enemy had erected *sangars* on the hill just beyond Margharu, which were held by Malikdin and Kambar Khel Afridis. From these fire was opened on the troops, but within half an hour the enemy were in full flight towards the Khanki. A part of the force then moved down and destroyed Talai, out of which the *lashkar* had come on the previous day. The subsequent retirement to camp was unmolested. It was reported that some 400 or

500 Afridis had taken part against us on this day, and that another 500 of them had been in the Khanki valley, awaiting developments. Our casualties had been one man killed and six wounded.

On the 24th no movement of troops took place. The enemy had completely cleared off from the vicinity, a large gathering being reported at Kharappa in the Khanki valley. An Afridi *jirga*, of Malikdin, Kambar, Kamar, and Zakha Khels was interviewed on this day by Major Leigh, at their own request. They denied having taken any part in the recent fighting, but this we knew to be untrue. The objects of the expedition, and the policy of Government in the whole matter, were nevertheless carefully explained to them; and they were then told that any further communications they might have to make should be addressed to the Political Officer in charge of the Khaibar. They were quite respectful in their demeanour, and professed themselves satisfied, saying they had only come to plead for their neighbours the Orakzais, and that they would now return home at once. They were provided with rations and allowed to stay the night in a village near Gulistan; and in the morning they started off for Tirah. Subsequent to this the Afridis do not appear to have come into Orakzai territory.

The Akhel and Ali Khel *jirgas* were interviewed by Major Leigh on the following day. He informed them that, so long as their territory was used as a battle-ground either by themselves or by other tribes, he could not guarantee the safety of their property. He reiterated our claim to the south slopes of the Samana, and our right to make posts on the crest, and to impose revenue; but informed them that, if they behaved well, we had no wish to eject those already there. To all this the Akhel and Ali Khel unconditionally agreed.

The heat had now become so great that the following day orders were given to provide tents for all troops on the Samana. As reports had been received that the gathering at Kharappa was dispersing and that the Alisherzai and Mamuzai *jirgas* were desirous of coming in, Sir William Lockhart determined to take advantage of this mood, and to advance at once into their country *viâ* Shahu Khel and the Laghardarra valley, postponing his visit to the upper Khanki valley until this should have been done. As the garrison of Kohat was considered dangerously weak, consisting of only four companies, 1-4th Gurkhas, and some details, orders were issued on the 26th for it to be at once strengthened by the other half of the 1-4th Gurkhas and a half battalion of the Manchester Regiment.

Leaving the whole of the 2nd column under Lieut.-Colonel Turner at Gulistan, and a garrison at Sangar of two guns, No. 3 Mountain Battery, a half battalion of the King's Royal Rifles, and the 19th Bengal Infantry, Sir William Lockhart marched on the 27th to Hangu. He took with him No. 5 Company, Bengal Sappers and Miners, the 1st Punjab Infantry, and the 27th Bengal Infantry.

On the 28th he remained halted at Hangu. Orders were now issued to break up the camp at Darband, the troops there being transferred to Baliamin; the Darband Kotal route was then abandoned and all convoys were sent by the Pat Darband road.

On the 29th, the General Officer Commanding with the column as per margin, under Colonel J. M. Sym, C.B., marched to Mir Asghar. On the 30th Dran was reached, after slight opposition, and the towers at that place and at Leghardarra were blown up.

No. 3 Mountain Battery.
Half bn., King's Royal Rifles.
No. 5 Coy., Bengal S. and M.
1st Punjab Infantry.
27th Bengal ,,
1-5th Gurkha Regiment.

Meanwhile Major Leigh had received the Gar Mamuzai and Alisherzai *jirgas* at Gulistan on the 28th. They were reminded that they had already lost heavily in the fighting, and warned that they would be further punished if they did not submit. They were advised to go home, and agreed to do so; but added in the most open manner that if they had had the power to turn us off the Samana they would have done so: finding they could not, all they could do was to submit.

On the 29th the Samil *jirgas*—Sheikhan, Mamuzai, Rabia Khel and Mishti—also applied for permission to come in. Major Leigh told them that before negotiations could be opened they must first return all Government property in their hands, and that, if they really meant to submit, they had better collect this property and go to meet Sir William Lockhart in the Sheikhan and Mamuzai (Daradar) countries, whither he had gone to blow up their towers and inflict a fine.

On the 1st May Sir William Lockhart marched to Kharai Kotal. The Samil *jirgas* met him, and were informed that their submission could not be accepted until the whole of the Government property in their possession had been restored; that in any case certain of their towers would be destroyed as a permanent punishment; and that a fine of Rs. 2,000 would be exacted from the Sheikhan and Mamuzai (Daradar). If the troops were not opposed the villages were to be spared.

After a night of heavy rain in open bivouac on the Kharai Kotal, the column marched on the 2nd to Starkili in the Daradar valley. From Starkili a small column under Colonel Sym went on up the valley to Torsmats and thence to the Nakatu Kotal. Whilst halted there some men on the further side of the pass shouted to the advanced picquets that if they dared to move beyond the *kotal* they would be fired on. In consequence of this, Colonel Sym continued the advance to the Sheikhan villages of Takhtak, where he destroyed one tower and then returned to camp.

Of the twenty-one rifles belonging to the 29th Bengal Infantry, due from the tribes, fourteen were brought back this day, and promises were given for the restoration of the remainder. The Samil *jirgas* remained in camp, and accompanied Sir W. Lockhart to Sangar.

On the 3rd the column marched to Gwada. As two villages belonging to the Sheikhan and Mamuzai had been destroyed, contrary to orders and to the promise given to the *jirgas*, Sir William Lockhart remitted the fines imposed on those sections.

Sir William Lockhart arrived at Sangar on the 3rd. He then dismissed the *jirgas*, with instructions to bring in the remainder of the Government property, their submission not being accepted until this had been done.

On the 5th, Mr. Udny, Commissioner of Peshawar, arrived at Mastan to discuss future proceedings with Sir William Lockhart. It was reported that the enemy contemplated fresh hostilities on the *Eed* festival (May 10th); and a large hostile gathering at Khangarbur, said to number 2,000 men, was plainly visible from Mastan. It was now decided to allow the clans until the 7th May to restore the remainder of the Government property; if, by that date, the *lashkar* had not dispersed, it was to be attacked.

On the 6th an Afridi native officer who had been sent to find out what was going on in Tirah, returned with information that, in spite of our repeated assurances, there was considerable suspicion amongst the Afridis as to our designs against their country. A reassuring letter, explaining exactly the situation and our intentions, was accordingly sent them by the same native officer.

On the 9th work was commenced on the Gulistan post. The *jirgas* had returned to the camp, but had not yet brought back everything. They, however, gave security for what still remained undelivered, so there was now no reason against accepting the submission of the Samil clans.

With the Rabia Khel, Sheikhan, Akhel, and Mishti clans our account was now declared closed, except for the fine due from the Rabia Khel before the outbreak. All these clans had suffered heavily in men, and in towers and villages destroyed. The Malla Khel and Mishtis, however, had not lost nearly so heavily in the field, nor had we damaged their villages; to deal with them adequately, therefore, a different procedure had to be followed. Both these sections had their principal settlements in the Mastura valley, which lay outside of the proposed operations. The Malla Khel, whose share in the disturbances was small, were punished by having their villages in British territory placed under a regular assessment. The Mishtis had taken a prominent part against us, and it was felt necessary to mark the displeasure of Government by as exemplary a punishment as had been meted out to other clans in the Khanki. They had no property in British territory upon which we could distrain, and a money fine, even if recoverable, would have been an inadequate penalty. They had, it is true, Kasha and a few small hamlets near the mouth of the Khanki valley; but these villages, knowing how easily they could be reached, had been careful to give no offence, and their destruction would have been no punishment to the mass of the section. The large villages of Kandi Mishti, however, lay in the Khanki valley, and were consequently within the sphere of the present operations. These villages, which relied for impunity on their distance from our frontier, had always borne a bad character for lawlessness, and many outrages had been traced to them. It was therefore decided that the Kandi Mishti towers should be blown up in presence of the Mishti *jirga*, the Samil *jirgas* being also required to accompany the column to witness the infliction of this punishment. The Mishti *jirga* was warned that if a shot were fired, not only the towers, but the villages and crops as well would be destroyed.

All the *jirgas* were then brought before Sir William Lockhart, their submission formally accepted, and an agreement drawn up, and signed by them, accepting out terms regarding the Samana.

On the 10th, Sir William Lockhart, with the column as per margin under Lieut.-Colonel Turner, marched from Gulistan to Kharappa. Six days' supplies for men and two days' for animals were taken. The main body marched down the Margharu-Talai spur, while Sir William Lockhart, with the 3rd Sikhs, 6th Punjab Infantry, some sappers, and the whole of the baggage, followed the longer route by the Chagru Kotal. The Akhel villages had been re-occupied; and no trace was seen of the recent gathering at Khangarbur. Camp was pitched a mile from Kharappa, at the junction of the Khanki and Kandi valleys.

Half battalion, King's Royal Rifles.
Half battalion, Manchester Regiment.
No. 3 (Peshawar) Mountain Battery (4 guns).
No. 5 Company, Bengal Sappers and Miners.
3rd Sikhs Infantry.
2nd Punjab ,,
6th ,,
29th Bengal ,,

Taking with him a portion of the force, Sir William Lockhart pushed on *viâ* Gundaki to the Kandi Mishti villages. The towers (three in number) were blown up, without opposition, in presence of all the *jirgas*, and the troops then returned to Kharappa camp.

On the 11th the force remained halted at Kharappa, whilst Sir William Lockhart interviewed the Ali Khel, Alisherzai, and Mamuzai *jirgas*. As they had lost many men in the fighting of the 20th–23rd April, and had also sent in delegates on the 28th, since when they had refrained from all hostility, they were informed that no damage would be done to their villages, provided they continued to act in a friendly manner. But Sir William Lockhart insisted that the force should march through their country, as a public token of their submission; and he warned them that, in case of any opposition, their towers, villages, and crops would pay the penalty.

To the Mamuzai, who are the most powerful section in the Khanki, the acceptance of this condition was a bitter humiliation. They had always fancied that their position at the head of the valley placed them beyond our reach; and had we turned back without visiting their country, they would have been able to continue to boast that, whatever might happen to other clans of the Khanki, they had themselves nothing to fear from us. They had, however, no alternative, and, in common with the Ali Khels, and Alisherzais, accepted the conditions laid down. Their *jirgas* were then sent on ahead to arrange that the march was unmolested; the jirgas of the Samil clans being kept to accompany the column.

On the 12th the column marched to Sadarai a large Khadizai village on the left bank of the Khanki, the 2nd Punjab Infantry, 29th Bengal Infantry, and the sappers being left at Kharappa; on the 13th Mamuzai Bazar, the head-quarters of the Mamuzai, was reached; and Sir William Lockhart, with a strong escort, proceeded to the Alisherzai Kotal, overlooking the Kharmana valley, which is inhabited by the Massuzai clan. This had the effect of bringing into camp a Massuzai *jirga*, who asked to be allowed to settle up all outstanding questions, and were informed that they would be summoned to the Samana for that purpose later. A great deal of valuable survey work was accomplished on this occasion. The Ali Khels and Akhels on this day signed an agreement to accept the occupation of the Samana.

On the following day (14th) the column returned to Kharappa, and on the 15th to Gulistan. The field force was now gradually broken up, and ceased to exist officially on the 8th June.

On the 23rd May the Daulatzai and Sturi Khel *jirgas* arrived on the Samana, having been summoned to answer for two letters they had sent to the Political Officer. They explained that they had done nothing hostile, though they had sent a contingent to the Khangarbur gathering; and that the letters in question were intended as warnings, not as threats. Their explanations were accepted.

Sites were now chosen for certain posts which were afterwards built on Samana: the position of these will be described more in detail when dealing with the attack on them by the Orakzais in 1897. A written compact was also concluded with the Rabia Khel, in which they agreed to our placing a cantonment or hill station, if we wished, on the north slope of the Samana. At the conclusion of operations, the garrison left on that range consisted of two squadrons, a battery, and four battalions, with two squadrons, three guns, and three battalions in reserve at Kohat.

On the 5th June the Payavi Nmasi brought in the bulk of what was still due from them.

The general results of the expedition were eminently satisfactory. The Samana had been retaken, with heavy loss to the enemy, who were subsequently defeated and dispersed wherever they opposed us; adequate punishment had been inflicted upon all offending sections; and they had all made formal submission and restored all Government property. The Rabia Khel, who were primarily responsible, had been, in particular, very heavily punished by losses in action, destruction of towers and villages, and fines; and Rustam Khan, Rabia Khel, had been expressly excluded from the settlement, for having murdered the three captured sepoys of the 29th Bengal Infantry in the mosque at Sangar. Moreover, the Rabia Khel, at the conclusion of the second expedition, agreed to protect the border with posts garrisoned by their own people, which they had refused to do after the first expedition. The Alisherzais and Mamuzais had had their country traversed and mapped for the first time; while the Massuzai had been overawed into sending in a submissive *jirga*. On the Afridis the moral effect of our march through the Khanki valley up to their own borders was useful, showing them that we possessed the power to reach them, but had no desire to molest them unprovoked.

Results of the expedition.

The total British casualties between the 4th April and the 15th May amounted to twenty-eight killed and seventy-three wounded.

The Indian Medal, with a clasp for "Samana 1891" was subsequently granted to the troops who took part in the above operations against the Orakzai tribe.

Operations against the Orakzais and Chamkannis[1] in 1897.

From the conclusion of the second Miranzai Expedition to the warfare in which almost the whole North-West Frontier was plunged by the risings of 1897-98, the Orakzais, as a whole, gave little trouble, though cases of misbehaviour by individuals of course occurred.

In spite, however, of the fact that during these six years, the conduct of the Orakzai tribe was almost all that we could hope for, there were not wanting signs of smouldering discontent at

[1] The Chamkannis are included in this chapter as they occupy a part of the country dealt with in these operations. They are, however, quite a distinct tribe from the Orakzais. They number about 4,000 fighting men.

our occupation of the Samana posts. At the beginning of 1892 Orakzai deputations interviewed the Amir, and invoked his assistance to procure the abandonment of the Samana by our troops. His Majesty, however, whilst assuring them of his sympathy with their grievance, would not commit himself to any action on their behalf; and the *jirgas* returned disappointed.

In May 1897 reliable reports came to hand of Afridi and Orakzai deputations having again approached the Amir with requests for his intervention; and although the news was regarded as disquieting by the Government of India, yet it was at first considered very unlikely that the Orakzais would commit themselves to any overt acts of hostility, and it was hoped that this excitement might die out without leading to any serious breach of the peace on the border.

That the situation was serious was, however, fully realized by Government. The gradual development of the situation, and the various measures of precaution taken to prepare for eventualities, have been followed in detail in the chapter dealing with the Afridi rising, to which the reader may be referred. It was not until the 15th of August 1897, on which night some shots were fired into Fort Lockhart, that the situation on the Kohat border was looked upon as sufficiently alarming to warrant the despatch of strong reinforcements to the Miranzai valley, and previous to their arrival the distribution of troops on this border was as shown in the margin.

Kohat.
4 guns, No. 2 (Derajat) M.B., R.A.
2 squadrons, 3rd Punjab Cavy.
2nd Punjab Infantry.
5th " "
Parachinar.
2 guns, No. 2 (Derajat) M.B., R.A.
2 squadrons, 3rd Punjab Cavy.
4 companies, 5th Gurkhas.
250 rifles, 36th Sikhs.
The Samana.
36th Sikhs.

By the 20th August the following additional forces had arrived at Kohat:—9th Field Battery, R.A., 18th Bengal Lancers and the 15th Sikhs.

Owing to urgent information received from the Political Officer in Kurram on this day, a flying column, strength as shown in the margin, was immediately formed from the troops under his orders by Colonel G. Richardson, C.I.E., 18th Bengal Lancers, commanding the forces at Kohat, for prompt action in the Kurram valley.

4 guns, No. 2 (Derajat) M.B., R.A.
18th Bengal Lancers.
2 squadrons, 3rd Punjab Cavalry.
5th Punjab Infantry.

On the 21st Major-General Yeatman-Biggs arrived and took over command of the forces on the Kohat–Kurram border; Colonel Richardson, with the flying column, proceeded the same day to Hangu. Information was now received that the rising was becoming general, and that at a *jirga* held the previous day it was arranged that the Massuzais and Chamkannis should move against the Kurram, the Daulatzais against Kohat, the Orakzais generally against the Samana forts, and the Afridis against the Khaibar.

On the 22nd the 3rd Gurkhas and four companies of the Royal Scots Fusiliers joined at Kohat; and 500 Enfield rifles were distributed amongst the villagers in the vicinity of the Border Police posts at Kachai and Marai. On the 24th the 15th Sikhs reached Hangu.

Orders were now issued to Major-General Yeatman-Biggs directing him to put more ammunition and supplies into the Samana forts, to relieve Sadda and Parachinar, and to disperse all hostile gathering along the Kohat–Kurram line; but on no account to involve himself in the hills, even to follow up a defeated enemy.

On the 25th in accordance with these orders, Colonel Richardson with a portion of his force visited Fort Lockhart on the Samana, taking with him sufficient ammunition to bring up the supply in the Samana posts to 400 rounds per rifle. News had been received this day that a *lashkar* of 12,000 Ali Khels, Alisherzais, Mamuzais, and Malla Khels was concentrating at Kharappa in the Khanki; but that the Mishtis and Akhels had not, so far, joined the hostile gathering. Nothing was seen of the enemy by Colonel Richardson's force, nor did it meet with any opposition.

On this day a deputation from the Mishtis reached the Political Officer at Fort Lockhart (Mr. D. Donald), to say that great pressure was being brought to bear on them to join, and that in the end they would have to do so; and an ultimatum was received by the Deputy Commissioner of Kohat from the tribesmen upon the Ublan pass, to the effect that they would disperse if the Kohat salt duty were reduced and the Swat valley evacuated by our troops. This gathering had collected on the Ublan pass with the object of attacking the Muhammadzai Police Post, four miles from Kohat, and was said to consist of Daulatzais, Bizotis, Utman Khels, and Firoz Khels. The action of the Akhels, however, was friendly up to this time: and the Ali Khel tribesmen, who would have attacked Shinawari post, were dissuaded from doing so by that section.

It was considered inadvisable to attack the Orakzais until they had committed some overtly hostile act, as it was most important to have them neutral, if possible, when the time should come for moving against the Afridis. The aspect of affairs in Orakzai country, however, had now become very serious, and an attack in force in any direction was daily expected. Disquieting news was being received daily from the Kurram, and much anxiety was felt regarding the safety of Sadda and Parachinar; but the moveable column at Hangu could not move forward until the hostile gathering in Orakzai country had been dispersed. Great difficulty, moreover, was being experienced in feeding the troops and animals at Hangu, as all supplies had to be sent from Kohat and the district had already been almost entirley denuded of transport by the earlier urgent requirements in other parts of the frontier.

On the evening of the 26th, the enemy on the Ublan pass, being reinforced by 600 Firoz Khels and Bizotis, descended from the hills, with the evident intention of attacking Muhammadzai post. Accordingly at 8 P.M. a company of the 2nd Punjab Infantry under Captain L. E. Cooper started to reinforce the post. At about 9 P.M., the old police post, held by twenty-five Border Police and a few armed villagers, was attacked and taken, the enemy losing one killed and one wounded. The garrison, who had lost one policeman killed, took refuge with the 2nd Punjab Infantry in the new post, upon which no attack was made.

The following day, hoping to cut off the tribesmen who had attacked the Muhammadzai post before they could regain the hills, Major-General Yeatman-Biggs left Kohat at 4 A.M., with the force as per margin, so as to be at the entrance of the Ublan pass at dawn. The enemy, however, had already gained the hills, and were found in a position overlooking the pass, about three miles from Muhammadzai post. Covered by the Artillery fire, the infantry at once advanced to attack them in this position; two companies, 2nd Punjab Infantry, crowning the heights on the right (east) of the pass, the remainder of that regiment making the direct attack,

No. 9 Field Battery, Royal Arty.
1 squadron, 3rd Punjab Cavy.
180 rifles, Royal Scots Fusiliers.
487 rifles, 2nd Punjab Infantry.

with the two companies, Royal Scots Fusiliers, in reserve. The heights on the left (west) were inaccessible, and were held throughout by the enemy's marksman, to whose fire most of our casualties were due. The *kotal* was reached without much opposition, the enemy, 700 or 800 in number, retiring north towards the Bara valley. Our retirement from the *kotal* began about 10-30 A.M. under cover of the fire of the Royal Scots Fusiliers. The enemy at once followed up; and Captain Baird Smith and Lieutenant North were wounded. The heat was intense and the troops were without water; with the result that by the time the foot of the hills was reached, the force was quite exhausted. Twenty of the Royal Scots Fusiliers were prostrated with sunstroke, of whom one died; and eighty-six of this regiment had to be carried back to Kohat in ambulance tongas. Our total casualties were: one private and one sepoy killed; two officers and seven sepoys wounded.

The following reinforcements had arrived at Kohat on this date :—

3rd Field Battery, Royal Artillery.
2nd Royal Irish Regiment.
12th Bengal Infantry.
No. 4 Company, Bombay Sappers and Miners.

Whilst this action was being fought on the Ublan pass, matters had assumed a far more serious aspect on the Samana, and the Orakzais were active all along the range. Early in the morning the Lakka post, held by local levies, was surrounded by the enemy, whose numbers rapidly increased. At 8 A.M. the garrison signalled for assistance, and Colonel Richardson immediately sent Lieut.-Colonel Abbott from Hangu to its relief, with the force as per margin. After considerable opposition, the ridge was finally crowned at 3 P.M., and the garrison relieved. At Lakka news was received that the small levy post at Saifaldarra, west of Lakka,[1] was also hard pressed, and Lieut.-Colonel Abbott proceeded immediately to its relief, although the enemy were in force on a strong position between him and that post.

2 guns, Derajat M.B., R.A.
½ squadron, 3rd Punjab Cavy.
15th Sikhs.
A Wing, 5th Punjab Infantry.

[1] This post was not near the village of Saifaldarra, which is in the Khank valley.

Colonel Richardson, meanwhile, seeing that the enemy were now in great numbers on the Samana, became apprehensive that Lieut.-Colonel Abbott's force might experience some trouble in retiring. He accordingly moved out with the remaining wing of the 5th Punjab Infantry, and moved along the base of the ridge parallel to Lieut.-Colonel Abbott's column. After having relieved Saifaldarra and brought away the garrison, the force under Colonel Abbott retired on Hangu. They were followed up and harassed by the enemy; but their retirement was covered by the troops under Colonel Richardson, who had been placed in an excellent position for that purpose. Camp was reached at 11 P.M.

In despatches relating to this day's action Colonel Richardson wrote that he could not speak too highly of the manner in which Colonel Abbott had handled his small force; and that the trifling losses sustained (two killed, and two wounded), in relieving the Samana on an August day, testified to the skill which he had shown.

Lakka and Saifaldarra were both burnt by the enemy that night.

The extensive nature of the rising was now proved beyond a doubt by the wide area covered by hostilities. In addition to the attacks upon Muhammadzai and Lakka just related, the eastern end of the Samana had been threatened by large gathering on the same day; the hills around Gulistan being crowded with tribesmen, and a small party of the 36th Sikhs sent out from that post being obliged to retire. The Border Police post at Shinawari, which had been attacked the preceding night, was again attacked on the night of the 27th, and the enemy again repulsed; and news was also received of large gatherings to attack Sadda in the Kurram.

On the 28th the Shinawari post was again attacked; and at about 4 P.M. the garrison, although they had sufficient ammunition and had had no casualties, abandoned the post, which was immediately destroyed by the tribesmen. The garrison withdrew to Nariab, with their arms, ammunition, and treasure chest, losing one man killed in retiring.

On the night of the 29th the enemy, emboldened by their successes in destroying Lakka, Saifaldarra, and Shinawari, raided down into the plain country south of the last named place, and plundered the large villages of Nariab and Kai, besides firing into Hangu camp.

By this time Colonel Richardson's force at Hangu had been strengthened by the arrival of the 1-3rd Gurkhas, the 3rd Field Battery, Royal Artillery, six companies of the Royal Irish Regiment, and a company of Bombay Sappers and Miners; and Kohat had also been reinforced with the 6th Bengal Cavalry, the 1-2nd Gurkhas and the 30th Punjab Infantry who had marched from Peshawar through the Kohat pass without encountering any opposition.

Colonel Richardson now made arrangements to detach another column for the protection of the frontier further to the west; and on the 30th he despatched Lieut.-Colonel Abbott, with the force as per margin, to Doaba, twenty-two miles to the west of Hangu. The Mishtis had at length decided to join the rising; and sent a letter to Mr. Donald informing him that they had joined with reluctance but would now pursue hostilities to the bitter end and burn every village to the foot of the Safed Koh, unless the demands of the Afridis were complied with.

2 guns, No. 2 M.B., R.A.
1 squadron, 18th B. L.
15th Sikhs.
½ company, Bombay S. and M.

Although the forces now at Hangu and Kohat were amply sufficient to occupy the Samana position, in addition to holding those places, the water-supply on the crest was totally inadequate for the permanent location there of a force any size. There was accordingly no alternative to the course now adopted, *viz.*, to hold the crest with the garrisons of the small posts upon it, troops being held in readiness in rear of the range, at Hangu and Kohat, to advance at once to the relief of these posts if they should be threatened by an attack in force.

On the 31st Major-General Yeatman-Biggs left Kohat for Hangu, and formed the troops at that place into two brigades as shown in the margin.

No. 1 Brigade.
4 guns, No. 2 (Derajat) Mountain Battery.
18th Bengal Lancers.
15th Sikhs.
5th Punjab Infantry.
1-3rd Gurkhas.
½ No. 4 Coy., Bo. Sappers and Miners.

No. 2 Brigade.
9th Field Battery, R. A.
3rd Bengal Cavalry.
2 squadrons, 3rd Punjab Cavalry.
2 Royal Irish Regiment.
2nd Punjab Infantry.
1-2nd Gurkhas.
½ No. 4 Coy., Bo. Sappers and Miners.

On the 1st September, information having reached the general that an attack in force upon Sadda and Parachinar was expected on the 3rd September, he immediately directed Colonel Richardson, Commanding the 1st Brigade, to proceed to their relief as rapidly as possible. Sadda being seventy, and Parachinar ninety-two, miles distant, no time was to be lost. Colonel Richardson at once sent off orders to Lieut.-Colonel Abbott at Doaba, to push on to Sadda with all possible expedition; he himself, with the rest of the 1st Brigade—now formed into a flying column—marched at midday for Doaba, which was reached at 10-30 P.M. Lieut.-Colonel Abbott, meanwhile, was already at Thal; hearing from the Political Officer of the gravity of the situation, he had anticipated Colonel Richardson's orders, and marched at once.

On the 2nd September, leaving the 3rd Gurkhas and a squadron of 3rd Punjab Cavalry at Doaba to keep the line of communications open, Colonel Richardson reached Thal by midday. The advance so far had been practically unopposed; an unsuccessful attempt had been made to ambuscade Lieut.-Colonel Abbott's cavalry near Doaba, and his camp had been heavily fired into; but there had been no casualties, except to the enemy. At Thal, however, the 18th Bengal Lancers were fired upon while watering their horses in the Kurram river, and one sowar was killed. They immediately pursued their assailants, killed five, wounded one, and took fourteen prisoners.

Relief of Sadda.

As Lieut.-Colonel Abbott's force had had a night's rest, he was ordered to push on to Sadda, leaving his cavalry at Thal; the valley between Thal and Sadda being narrow and unsuited to cavalry action. Starting at 6-45 P.M., and marching all night, Colonel Abbott reached Sadda next afternoon at 6-30,—a march of 34 miles within 24 hours, in intense heat. Colonel Richardson with the 18th Bengal Lancers, reached Sadda, on the same evening, the rest of his force halting for the night at Manduri, 13 miles from Thal.

This rapid advance had an immediate effect upon the tribesmen, who, seeing Sadda so strongly reinforced, now declined to attack it for the present. The force had, however, only arrived just in time. On the 30th, the Border Police post at Thal, held by sixty-two rifles of the 36th Sikhs, had been fired into; and the Torawari post on the Zaimukht frontier had been burnt. On the 1st September, the Massuzais of the Khurmana valley had joined the rising and attacked Balish Khel, a post on the border about three miles from Sadda, held by twenty Kurram militia men under an Afridi havildar. The attack began towards evening, and continued for five hours. The little garrison behaved with the greatest gallantry: their ammunition was nearly expended, and the door of the post had been beaten in with axes, when help came. A contingent of some fifty armed Turi villagers from Sadda were the first to arrive, and pluckily threw themselves into the fray—the darkness of the night preventing the smallness of their numbers being perceived by the enemy, who then drew off, leaving two of their dead actually in the gateway of the post. Almost simultaneously with the Sadda contingent, a detachment arrived from the 200 militia at Hasan Ali, seven miles west of Sadda. The eagerness of the Turis to get at their neighbours was most remarkable,—the former being Shias and the latter nearly all Sunnis. They everywhere hurried out to protect all threatened points; and with the assistance of the moveable column, which had been formed at Parachinar, would have been able to deal with anything short of an attack in force—and from that the timely arrival of the troops had saved them.

So far, although sorely tried, the Chamkannis had not joined the rising.

There being now no necessity for haste, Colonel Richardson's force at Manduri made two marches to Sadda, arriving there on the 5th. Camp was pitched on a plateau north-east of Sadda, about a mile south-west of the Khurmana defile. Nothing happened until the 16th September, on which date, at about 10-30 P.M., about 2,000 Massuzais, who had collected in the defile, suddenly attacked the camp. A picquet of the 5th Punjab Infantry, in a *sangar* about 100 yards to the south-east was driven in; and for an hour and a half the attack continued, the fire being hottest on the east face. It was 1 A.M. before the last of the enemy had been driven off. Our losses were one killed, and ten wounded, while a number of horses and mules were also hit. The losses of the tribesmen were considerable; and up to the 1st October, when Colonel Richardson's force was broken up and merged into the Tirah Expeditionary Force, no further attack was made on the camp.

Attack on Sadda camp.

Whilst these operations were in progress in the upper part of the Kurram valley, the Samana had been the theatre of the most desperate fighting. The Orakzais had thrown the whole weight of their attacks against these little posts: in one case, only too successfully.

Operations on the Samana.

The whole of our long history of frontier fighting furnishes us with no more dramatic incidents than the defence of Gulistan, and the fall of Saraghari after prolonged and heroic resistance.

On the eastern end of the Samana, the posts at Lakka and Saifaldarra had been abandoned and destroyed, as already related. The other two small police posts of Gogra and Tsalai had also been evacuated and burnt. There remained the two large posts of Mastan (Fort Lockhart) on the centre of the range, and Gulistan (Fort Cavagnari) at the western extremity. These two forts had been erected on the conclusion of the Miranzai Expedition of 1891. Both were small rectangular works, consisting of dry stone walls fourteen feet high, and had flanking bastions with machicolated loopholes at opposite diagonal corners. Both were capable of holding the same number of men in garrison; but whereas, in the case of Fort Lockhart, all the men of the two companies could be accommodated within the walls, in the case of Gulistan one company only could be accommodated inside, the other being placed in a small hornwork to the west, which consisted of an enclosure surrounded by a low stone wall. In addition to these two larger forts, there were small picquet posts, similar in construction, at Saraghari, the Crag picquet, the Sangar picquet, Sartop, and Dhar, each of which was capable of holding outlying picquets of from twenty-five to fifty men. Saraghari was the most important of these smaller posts as it was situated on the highest point of the range between Fort Lockhart and Gulistan, and signalling communication was maintained through it along the Samana.

The loyalty of the police in the post of Dhar being considered somewhat doubtful, and it being now liable to the severest test at any time, Colonel Haughton reinforced it with thirty-seven men of his regiment (36th Sikhs).

From the 28th August to the 3rd September, the enemy remained inactive, though known to be in great force in the immediate neighbourhood. On the latter date, in the afternoon, a message was received at Fort Lockhart, from Gulistan that the enemy were advancing in force from the Samana Sukh. Taking with him fifty men—all that could prudently be spared from his small garrison—Colonel Haughton immediately proceeded along the ridge towards Gulistan. Leaving fifteen of these men in

Saraghari, he pushed on with the remainder, under a heavy fire, to the fort. The enemy were in force quite close up, their standards being planted within 150 yards of the south face, while others had crept up and set fire to the thorn hedge which was outside the hornwork, as an obstacle to a rush. Twice this hedge had been set on fire; but volunteers from the garrison, rushing out under a hot fire from only 150 yards away, had each time extinguished it in the most gallant manner.

By 8 P.M. the enemy were evidently collecting rapidly outside the hornwork; a bonfire, which had been prepared beforehand outside it, was then lighted by two sepoys[1] who volunteered for this most dangerous feat. Both of these brave men were among those who volunteered for the sortie of the 13th September, about to be related, and both were dangerously wounded, one dying of his wounds.

A heavy fire was kept up by the enemy till midnight; but their losses were severe, and by the following morning they had retired to a safe distance. Later in the day they disappeared entirely; and Lieut.-Colonel Haughton then returned with his fifty men to Fort Lockhart.

Thinking that the fort, without this reinforcement, would be undermanned, a considerable number of tribesmen returned the same evening (September 4th) and renewed the attack,—but with no better success than before. For the next few days they withdrew entirely from the Samana. Their losses had been so great, and so little success had attended their efforts, that they determined to leave the Samana posts alone in future, unless assisted by the Afridis, and to concentrate their efforts on Hangu and the villages on the Kohat border. The Mishtis and Sheikhans were so disgusted with the way things were going that they sent in a message to the Deputy Commissioner of Kohat to say that they "had eaten filth and were going home."

Raids and outrages, however, in which our own subjects frequently took part, occurred all along the border, and the troops at Hangu, under Major-General Yeatman-Biggs, were kept very busy in attempting to cut off the raiders. The Major-General, considering he was strong enough to take the offensive

[1] Wariam Singh and Ghula Singh.

had now asked to be allowed to advance against the Orakzais in the Khanki valley, but the requisite permission had not been accorded to him, this action being reserved for the Tirah Expeditionary Force, on the assembly of which Government had already decided. The Mishtis of the Lower Khanki, however, were within easy reach of Hangu, and, were punished by the destruction of their fortified villages of Nawamela, Ajmir, and Turi, by a small column sent out under Lieut.-Colonel Sturt, 2nd Punjab Infantry. A message was then sent to the enemy informing them that all their villages would be similarly treated if raiding continued.

The question of commissariat had hitherto been a difficult one, and the troops on the Samana were on half rations. As a fresh supply had now arrived in Hangu, Major-General Yeatman-Biggs determined to throw a month's rations into the Samana forts; and since definite information had been received that the Afridis had decided to join the Orakzais in a combined attack on them on the 10th September no time was to be lost.

4 guns, 9th Field Battery.
2 squadrons, 3rd Bengal Cavalry.
1 squadron, 3rd Punjab Cavalry.
300 rifles, Royal Irish Regiment.
500 ,, 1-2nd Gurkhas.
500 ,, 1-3rd Gurkhas.
500 ,, 2nd Punjab Infantry.
½ company, No. 4 Bombay S. & M.

At 10 P.M. on the 7th September, therefore, with a force of over 2,000 men, detailed in the margin, the General Officer Commanding started from Hangu, and reached Fort Lockhart at midday on the 8th without coming across any signs of the enemy. The guns were unable to proceed beyond Pat Darband, owing to the bad state of the roads, and had consequently been sent back to Hangu from that place, escorted by the cavalry. On the 9th September a reconnaissance was made to the Samana Sukh, from whence a large force of Afridis and Orakzais, with twenty-nine standards, was seen collected at Khangarbur.

During this day troops from Hangu and Kohat were ordered out for the protection of Marai, at the instance of the Deputy Commissioner, who had received information that 5,000 Afridis and Daulatzais had started to attack it. The Mani Khels and Sipahs, however, refused either to join them or to give them passage through their territories, and the attack never came off.

On the 10th of September the defences of Fort Gulistan were improved by the Sappers and Miners; and the first part of the main Afridi *lashkar* joined the Orakzais. This contingent consisted of the Kambar, Malikdin, and Kuki Khels with fifteen standards; the rest of the *lashkar* arrived on the 11th. At about 10 A.M. on the 10th, the enemy, estimated at 10,000 men, were seen moving down the Khanki valley with twenty-two standards. A few shots were exchanged between them and one of our advanced picquets, which were now drawn in. As the advance continued, and it really appeared probable that the enemy intended to attack Hangu, or Shahu Khel, Major-General Yeatman-Biggs began moving eastward along the Samana, parallel to them. At the Pat Darband Kotal he met a convoy of fifty-one camels, which had been ordered out from Hangu with two days' supplies, and which now joined the column. About sunset the enemy's *lashkar* split in two, one part hurrying back up the valley. Yeatman-Biggs, however, continued his march eastwards, and at 9 P.M. the force bivouacked in a strong position between the Darband Kotal and Lakka. Meanwhile the rear-guard—four companies, 3rd Gurkhas, and two companies, 2nd Gurkhas—had been assailed by some 4,000 of the enemy, and harassed throughout their retirement on camp, which they did not reach until 2 A.M. They had lost some six killed, and Captain Robinson, 1-2nd Gurkhas, and eight men wounded. The enemy, however, acknowledged having lost 100 killed and wounded.

The most serious loss which we suffered was that of most of the fifty-one supply camels with their loads. As soon as the first shots were fired the camel drivers bolted; the camels stampeded and threw their loads, and in the darkness and confusion could not be recovered. A couple of companies of the 2nd Punjab Infantry, sent out at midnight to assist in bringing in the convoy, succeeded in recovering a few camels; but some forty were still missing. A force of two companies of the Royal Irish and five companies from each of the Native Regiments, the whole under Colonel Lawrence, was consequently sent back at daybreak to try to recover the animals and their loads. The enemy retired on their approach, and thirteen camels and two intact loads were found; but of the other loads, such as had not been carried away, were found ripped open and their contents scattered.

On the return of Colonel Lawrence, the General decided to push on to Lakka, from which place he was best able to assist either Hangu or Shahu Khel. On arrival at Lakka, however, it was found that the water-supply there was very deficient, and as the column was also now without food, owing to the loss of the convoy, the only course open was to proceed at once to Hangu. This was accordingly done, and, in spite of the fact that the road had been destroyed by the enemy in several places, Hangu was reached by nightfall.

Meanwhile, the whole strength of the enemy, exulting in General Yeatman-Biggs' retirement, had been thrown against the little post of Saraghari, held by twenty-one men of the 36th Sikhs. At 3-30 a message came through that Saraghari was hard pressed: by 4 o'clock it had fallen.

Gulistan, already surrounded, was now assailed by thousands of the tribesmen fresh from their capture of Saraghari; and at about 3-30 P.M. on the next day a letter from Major Des Vœux, commanding at Gulistan, was received at Hangu, asking urgently for help. Major Middleton, 3rd Bengal Cavalry, with that regiment and two guns of the 9th Field Battery was immediately sent off at a gallop to the nearest point they could reach under the hills south of Gulistan, to signal to the garrison that relief would reach them by midday the following day. This message was successfully signalled just before sunset, and a few rounds were fired by the guns at the enemy crowding round the fort.

The same night, at midnight, the marginally noted force, under Major-General Yeatman-Biggs, marched out of Hangu for the relief of the Samana posts. Moving *viâ* Lakka, the advanced guard first came under fire at about 7 A.M., from a force estimated at about 4,000 men with eleven standards, on Gogra hill and near the ruins of Tsalai post. The column at once attacked, the two Gurkha battalions leading; and the enemy fled in confusion down the Sarmela spur into the Khanki valley; the garrisons of Sangar and Fort Lockhart, as the relieving column approached, turning out to pour volleys into the fugitives. Passing Fort Lockhart—which had not been seriously attacked—the column again came into action against a second force, numbering several thousands, who were holding the Saraghari ridge, where *sangars* had been erected. Without

4 guns, No. 2 (Derajat) M.B., R.A.
300 rifles, Royal Irish Regt.
500 " 1-2nd Gurkhas.
500 " 1-3rd Gurkhas.
500 " 2nd Punjab Infantry.
1 company, No. 4 Bombay S. and M.
1 section, No. 23 British Field Hospital.
1 section, No. 62 Native Field Hospital.

waiting for the infantry to close with them, the enemy hastily retired down the Khanki valley. The Saraghari post was found almost levelled to the ground, the bodies of the gallant Sikh garrison, stripped and horribly mutilated, lying among the ruins. Gulistan was seen to be still surrounded by swarms of tribesmen, the number investing it being estimated at about 6,000. The column hurried forward, eager to exact retribution for the slaughter of the Saraghari garrison: but the enemy, refusing to await their attack, disappeared with all speed into the Khanki valley.

The garrison of Gulistan, which was reached about 1 P.M., was found to be in excellent spirits, and had captured three of the enemy's standards during the investment. Their losses had amounted to 2 killed and 39 wounded out of a total of 175. The relieving column had lost one killed and six wounded, and had marched twenty-seven miles under the most arduous conditions. They bivouacked on the crest of the Samana, where a telegram reached them from His Excellency the Commander-in-Chief, congratulating them on their fine performance.

We will now turn to the events which took place upon the Samana between the retirement of the column to Hangu on the 12th September and the relief of the forts on the 14th.

On the 12th the force left on the Samana consisted of the 36th Sikhs, distributed as shown to the margin.

Fort Lockhart	168
Crag Picquet	22
Sartop	21
Sangar	44
Dhar	28
Saraghari	21
Gulistan	175
TOTAL ..	489

In addition to the above native ranks of the regiment, there were two British officers (Lieut.-Colonel Haughton, commanding, and his Adjutant, Lieutenant Munn) in Fort Lockhart, and four (Major Des Vœux, Lieutenant A. K. Blair, 2nd-Lieutenant H. R. E. Pratt, and Surgeon-Captain C. B. Prall) in Gulistan.

The first post to be seriously attacked was Sangar, during the night of the 11th–12th September. This post was better situated for defence than most of the others, being on rising ground with little cover near it. The enemy were repulsed, losing a standard; nor were they more successful in any subsequent attempts against this post. Nothing daunted, however, they began a vigorous attack upon Saraghari on the following morning. This little post was not capable, from its weakness of construction and situation, of prolonged defence against the overwhelming forces by which it was soon surrounded. Although every phase in the attack, and its eventual fall, could be clearly seen from Forts Lockhart and Gulistan, those posts were powerless to avert the disaster; the garrisons of both being very small. Moreover, Gulistan was itself being vigorously attacked, and the villages between Fort Lockhart and Saraghari were full of the enemy. The first determined rush on Saraghari was driven back with a loss of sixty killed and wounded. Two of the tribesmen, however, had remained close under the north-west corner of the post, where there was a dead angle. Here, covered from view and fire, they commenced to hammer at the stones and gradually pick a hole in them. From Gulistan, Major Des Vœux could clearly see what was going on, and tried, but in vain, to signal to the garrison and warn them. An effort to cause a diversion was made from Fort Lockhart about noon, by sending out a small party under Lieutenant Munn, but without effect. The enemy, covered by the fire of thousands of fire-arms, were now within a few yards of the walls.

Defence of Saraghari.

About 3 P.M. the Saraghari signaller heliographed that ammunition was running out. Seeing the desperate situation of the garrison, Lieut.-Colonel Haughton made a final effort, with every available rifle that could be spared from Fort Lockhart, to create a diversion in their favour. He himself, with Lieutenant Munn and ninety-three men, started off for the relief of the post. He could only fight his way very slowly: and when he had got about three-quarters of a mile from Fort Lockhart, the end came. At about 3-40 the enemy simultaneously rushed the breach—the corner being now battered down sufficiently to admit them—forced the door, and swarmed over every point of the walls. The garrison, who were killed to a man, fought on heroically to the very last. The tribesmen's casualties were very heavy and they admitted to have lost 180 killed. The last survivor of the Sikhs, taking refuge in the guard room, accounted for no less than twenty of the enemy, by their own subsequent admission, before he was overpowered.

Having wreaked a barbarous vengeance upon the bodies of the gallant defenders and destroyed the post as far as possible, the tribesmen, flushed with success, now turned their attention to Gulistan. That post had also been closely invested since noon; but it was not until after the fall of Saraghari that the enemy was enabled to put forth their whole strength against it.

The post at Gulistan had the same fatal defect as that at Saraghari: there was dead ground at the point of each bastion, which could consequently be reached by the enemy, under cover of a hot fire from outside. Foreseeing that they would probably attempt to breach the walls in the same manner as they had already done at Saraghari, Major Des Vœux had the lower corner rooms of the bastions cleared out, and with bags of rations, etc., had breastworks built across the corners to form a second line of defence if the wall should be breached. Men were also told off to listen for sounds of tapping or hammering, and the garrison was apportioned to every point. All night long a hot fire was maintained from close quarters upon the post; and when morning came the enemy were found entrenched in *sangars* in great force within twenty yards of the walls. Major Des Vœux came to the conclusion that it was absolutely necessary to strike a blow that would dishearten the enemy; and that for this purpose a sortie must be attempted. A standard had been planted within twenty paces of the south-west end of the hornwork: this he decided should be captured.

Defence of Gulistan.

Colour Havildar Kala Singh and his section of sixteen men at once volunteered for this enterprise. Under cover of a heavy fire kept up by the whole garrison upon the *sangars* to be assaulted, they left the hornwork by the southern gate, and, having crept along the south face until opposite the *sangars*, assaulted it. The enemy were in great force at this place and now displayed three standards. At six paces from the *sangars* the fire was so heavy that the assailants were stopped by it and had to lie down. Seeing this, Havildar Sundar Singh and eleven others, of their own accord, sprang over the hornwork wall and, joining Kala Singh's section, the combined parties carried the *sangar* and captured all three standards. On their return it was found that two wounded men had been left behind; on which three sepoys at once sprang over the wall and brought them in. Of the twenty-nine men who took part in these dashing sorties, thirteen had been wounded, two mortally and several others dangerously; but the moral effect had been enormous, both in raising the spirits of the defenders and in disheartening the enemy. The latter had, moreover, lost very heavily, especially the three sections of the Mamuzai represented by the three captured standards. Although for the next thirty hours the struggle continued without intermission or rest for the defenders, Gulistan was never really in danger. The spirit shown by the garrison was magnificent; every wounded man, who could stand, returning to his post the moment his wounds had been bound up. Throughout the rest of the day and the ensuing night the attack continued; but there was no attempt to press it home as in the case of Saraghari.

On the morning of the 14th, Major Des Vœux felt so confident in his power to repel all assaults, that he sent a letter to Major-General Yeatman-Biggs to tell him so, in order that the latter might not be hampered in his operations by the supposed necessity of immediately relieving Gulistan. The letter unfortunately miscarried. About noon the relieving column was in sight; and there being no longer any necessity to husband ammunition, a hot fire was opened from every available rifle in Gulistan as long as any of the enemy were within range.

The total losses of the enemy on the Samana were ascertained later to amount to about 400 killed and 600 seriously wounded. The tribesmen, thoroughly dispirited, now dispersed to their homes; nor can there be much doubt that the half-hearted nature of the resistance subsequently offered by the Orakzais, and their rapid and complete submission, was due to the moral effect of the stubborn defence of Gulistan and their own heavy losses at that place.

The preparations now going forward convinced the Orakzais that the invasion of their country and immediate punishment were close at hand: and on the 19th the Akhel *jirga* came in to discuss terms with Major-General Yeatman-Biggs, who, with his column, was still on the Samana. Although the other Orakzai clans would not permit the Akhels to make special terms independently of the rest, they showed, in the frequent *jirgas* held with the Afridis at Bagh, how thoroughly alarmed they were at the prospect before them; and as an outcome of their united deliberations, a large deputation of Afridis and Gar Orakzais left for Kabul to ask assistance from the Amir. In this deputation, however, the Samil Orakzais declined

Submission of the Orakzais.

to join; and on the 22nd September they sent in to the Deputy Commissioner of Kohat to say that they had been driven into hostilities against their will and now desired peace. This they followed up, on the 25th, by asking Major-General Yeatman-Biggs to receive their submission. Their submission was not, however, finally accepted until all the Orakzai clans, Gar as well as Samil, submitted unconditionally to the terms imposed by Government at Maidan on the 12th November, as has been related in the chapter on the Afridis. The terms then imposed upon the Orakzais were—

Surrender of 500 breech-loaders.

Payment of a fine of Rs. 30,000.

Forfeiture of all allowances.

Restoration of all Government property in the possession of the tribe.

By the 20th December every rifle and every rupee of the above had been paid; and, in addition, every rifle captured at Saraghari or elsewhere had been handed in.

On the 3rd October the column on the Samana under Major-General Yeatman-Biggs was incorporated in the Tirah Field Force, and subsequent operations against the combined Afridi and Orakzai tribes have already been described in the chapter dealing with the Tirah expedition (Chapter II).

There remains, however, one set of operations in this campaign still to be described under the heading "Orakzais." When the bulk of the Orakzais finally submitted at Bagh on the 12th November, as detailed above, certain clans of that tribe, living to the west of what had hitherto been the theatre of active operations, still remained defiant. These people embraced roughly the population of the area drained by the Khurmana river, which falls into the Kurram at Sadda, and included Massuzais, and certain sections of the Alisherzais and also the Chamkanni tribe.[1] Their attitude was undoubtedly the outcome of an idea that their country lay outside the proposed scheme of our operations, and that, with our hands full elsewhere, we would be unlikely to attempt the invasion of such rugged and difficult territory.

Operations of the Kurram Moveable Column under Colonel W. Hill.

[1] See footnote on the Chamkannis, page 247.

It will be remembered that a *lashkar* of the above clans was only deterred from attacking Sadda by the forced march which brought the advanced guard of Colonel Richardson's column to that place on the 3rd September; and that these clans were concerned in the attacks upon Balish Khel, Torwari, and other small posts. These outrages, it will also be remembered, culminated in the determined and audacious attack made on Colonel Richardson's column at Sadda on the night of the 16th–17th September. Although, subsequent to this last attack, the above-mentioned clans had remained quiet and had taken no active part in hostilities, beyond occasional firing on patrols, it was nevertheless absolutely necessary to call them to account for what they had done.

Sir William Lockhart's proclamation of the 6th October, warning the tribes that they must make immediate submission to Government, if they wished to avoid punishment, was replied to on the 17th October by insolent and defiant replies from these clans, who further offered Government peace upon certain terms of their own dictation. On the 26th October a large *lashkar* built a barrier right across the Khurmana Darra; and although a reconnoitring party from the Kurram Moveable Column, who visited the locality some three or four days later, saw no signs of the *lashkar*, the tribesmen assembled to the number of between 3,000 and 4,000 in the same locality on the 4th November.

Up to that time no forward movement had been undertaken against these clans, the operations of the Kurram Moveable Column—the command of which had been taken over by Colonel W. Hill on the 10th October—being confined to a purely defensive *rôle*.

Reconnaissance of the Khurmana defile

Central India Horse, 100 lances, mounted.
Central India Horse, 100 lances, dismounted.
12th Bengal Infantry, 100 rifles.
1-5th Gurkhas, 260 rifles.
Kapurthala Infantry, 100 rifles.
Kurram Militia, 400 rifles.
Maxim Gun Detachment of the Royal Scots Fusiliers.

To remove the standing menace which the presence of this *lashkar* constituted to Sadda, a reconnaissance in force, as per margin, moved out into the Khurmana defile on the morning of the 7th November. The defile was found to be about seven miles long, the hills on either side of it being very steep, and covered with scrub jungle. Some slight opposition was encountered at Hissar, at 11 A.M.; but the enemy were taken by surprise; and were not able to collect in sufficient force to attack until 1 P.M., when the retirement began. As soon as the rear-guard, composed of the 5th Gurkhas, had proceeded about a mile down the defile, a delay of nearly an hour occurred, on account of the slow retirement of a picquet of Kapurthala Infantry. During this interval the enemy attacked in force, but were beaten off with heavy loss, our casualties being one killed and three wounded. At Janikot the Kapurthala picquets were reported "all present," and camp was reached without any further casualties being reported, the enemy not attempting to follow up the retirement.

Late that night the Officer Commanding the Kapurthala Infantry discovered that a non-commissioned officer and thirty-five men were missing. No report of this circumstance was, however, made to the Officer Commanding the main column until 9-30 A.M., on the following morning. This party had formed part of a picquet on a hill overlooking the defile; and when the retirement began, they were recalled by signal. The signal was duly acknowledged, and the picquet started to rejoin the column; it was, however, quickly hidden from the view of the troops waiting for it at Janikot, owing to the intervening ravines, and to the smoke of a jungle fire, which the enemy had lighted. When finally the picquets were reported "all present," at Janikot, the retirement was continued. By this time the enemy had completely disappeared, and no firing had been heard for an hour.

As soon as Colonel Hill heard that the party was still missing, he ordered out a column and some friendly tribesmen to search for them, but no news of them was obtained until night. At 9 P.M., after the return of the search party, friendly villagers brought in information that the whole party had been overpowered and killed. It would appear, from subsequent information, that the party attempted to take a short cut to rejoin the rear-guard, and descended into the ravine in which a jungle fire was burning. The enemy immediately appeared on spurs above them, and hurled down rocks upon the party. The latter, in addition to the disadvantage of ground, were hampered by the jungle fire; and the enemy, closing in upon them, destroyed them to a man. The Sikhs, however, fought on to the last: and the enemy acknowledged to losing fourteen killed.

After this, nothing of importance occurred until the advance of Colonel Hill's troops into the Chamkanni country to co-operate with the column from Sir William Lockhart's forces at Bagh, at the end of the month.

On the 25th November, the Massuzais, who had meanwhile been watching the progress of events in Tirah before making any signs of submission, sent in to Sadda to say that they desired peace; that they had collected the money and rifle fines against them; and that they requested permission to bring the same in to Sadda.

Operations against the Chamkannis.

The Chamkannis, however, whose settlements are more remote than those of the Massuzai, remained defiant, and finally declined to accept the terms of Government. Orders were therefore immediately sent to Colonel Hill, directing him to advance to Hissar on the 29th, to co-operate with a force to advance into the same country from Bagh, to compel the submission of the Chamkannis.

In accordance with this plan, on the 26th November a force under Brig.-General Gaselee, strength as per margin, left Bagh *en route* for the Khurmana valley. The column met with considerable opposition during its first march. The Kambar Khel and Malikdin Khel Afridis, whose representatives were then in camp, discussing terms, opened fire almost as soon as the column had left camp, and a constant running fight ensued. One company of the Queens, under Lieutenant H. A. Engledue, in storming a *sangar*, inflicted considerable loss upon the enemy. Our total casualties for the day were one private of the Queens killed, and eight native rank and file wounded. Camp was eventually pitched at Kahu, at the junction of the Durbi Khel and Khwajal Khel valleys, about 4½ miles from Bagh, where the ground was fairly open.

Gurkha Scouts of both Divisions.
2-4th Gurkhas.
The Queen's (Royal West Surrey) Regt.
3rd Sikhs.
28th Bombay Pioneers.
No. 1 (Kohat) Mountain Battery, R. A.
No. 3 company, Bombay S. and M.
No. 4 company, Bombay S. and M.

The following day (27th) the advance was continued over the Durbi Khel Kotal, very little opposition being encountered. The road over the pass was rough and difficult, and required a good deal of attention from the Sappers before it was practicable for transport. Part of the force was able to get to Tambu, about a mile down the further side of the pass; while the remainder with the General Officer Commanding and staff, remained on the summit for the night. The greater part of the baggage had to stay at the foot of the pass under escort. During the day, a force as per margin, under Lieut.-Colonel J. H. Spurgin, marched from Bagh to camp Kahu, accompanied by Sir William Lockhart. The advance was continuously opposed, and the Yorkshires had one killed and one wounded. Twenty-five fortified villages of the Kambar Khel were destroyed in retaliation for their continued opposition.

No. 2 (Derajat) M. B., R. A.
2nd Yorkshire Regiment.
4 companies, Royal Scots Fusiliers.
1-2nd Gurkhas.

On the 28th Brig.-General Gaselee's force reached Dargai, about five miles from the summit of the Durbi Khel Kotal. The track lay through a most difficult and dangerous defile, with precipitous cliffs, but no opposition was offered. The Massuzai *jirga* met the column *en route*, and offered to do all they could in the way of obtaining supplies and giving information about the country. Sir William Lockhart arrived at Tambu on this day; but the difficulties of the ascent again prevented the whole force from crossing the *kotal*, part reaching Tambu, part bivouacking on the summit, and part on the eastern slopes. The advance was not opposed, but the rear-guard was persistently harassed by the Kambar Khel; in retaliation for which seventy-five more of their fortified houses were demolished.

On the 29th, Brig.-General Gaselee remained halted at Dargai, where he was joined by the rest of his baggage, and by Sir William Lockhart, who, escorted by the 2-4th Gurkhas, pushed on to join him. A Samil Massuzai *jirga* met Sir William Lockhart on his arrival. Their attitude was submissive, and they promised compliance with the terms, as far as their own section was concerned, by the evening. Heliographic communication was opened with the Kurram Moveable Column, which, with a strength as per margin, was debouching from the Khurmana Darra; and arrangements were made for the junction of the two forces on the following day.

Maxim Gun Detachment, Royal Scots Fusiliers.
200 sabres, 6th Bengal Cavalry.
220 sabres, Central India Horse.
(50 sabres of each regiment mounted.)
400 rifles, 12th Bengal Infantry.
220 rifles, 1-5th Gurkhas.
220 rifles, Kapurthala Infantry.

Meanwhile the force under Lieut.-Colonel Spurgin had had to fight a most difficult rear-guard action in crossing the Durbi

Khel Kotal; the enemy's tactics being much favoured by the wooded nature of the country on that side. Most of the troops did not reach Dargai until very late at night; the rear-guard not arriving until 2 A.M. on the 30th. Fortunately the enemy did not follow up beyond the summit of the *kotal*, or our losses would probably have been heavier: as it was, they numbered two men killed; Maharaja Sir Partab Singh (extra orderly officer to Sir William Lockhart), Lieutenant B. C. W. Williams, Yorkshires, Lieutenant F. O. Wyate, R.E., and 14 men wounded. The enemy's losses, during the 28th and 29th, were reported to be 100 men.

On the 30th, the advanced column with Sir William Lockhart, and Colonel Hill's column from Sadda, concentrated unopposed at Lwara Mela, six miles from Dargai, along a track comparatively easy from that place. The column under Lieut.-Colonel Spurgin meanwhile remained halted at Dargai, with orders to improve the track leading south-east towards Khanki Bazar.

Seeing that the bulk of the British force had begun to move away from their immediate vicinity, and hoping to be able to procrastinate until the immediate danger had passed, the Samil Massuzais now sent a deputation to Dargai with various plausible excuses to evade their promised compliance with the terms. As ample time had been given them in which to comply and to collect the fine, a couple of their fortified houses were immediately destroyed by order of Sir William Lockhart. Rifles and money were at once forthcoming; and after some unavailing attempts to palm off native-made weapons, the whole fine (33 rifles and 2,727 Kabuli rupees) due from this section had been paid in full by the following morning. Their request for a cessation of the blockade and other favours was refused until such time as the whole Massuzai tribe should have complied with the terms.

There now remained to be dealt with the Gar Massuzais—who had only complied in part with the terms—and the Khani Khel Chamkannis, who were still absolutely defiant. To bring the former to submission a column under Brig.-General Gaselee, strength as per margin, proceeded up the Lozaka defile, as far as the junction of the Shaonkanrai and Lozaka streams, along a narrow ravine with

No. 2 (Derajat) M. B., R. A.
1-2nd Gurkhas.
4 companies, the Queens.
4 companies, 3rd Sikhs.

precipitous hills on either side. The inhabitants offered no opposition, but handed in nine rifles and three *jezails* to Sir R. Udny (Political Officer with the column) as an instalment.

On the same day another force under Colonel Hill, strength as per margin, also left Lwara Mela with orders to advance into the Khani Khel Chamkanni country, and to destroy their principal village, Thabai, distant about seven miles from camp. The right column, under Lieut.-Colonel G. Money, Central India Horse, advanced through Gar Massuzai country, past the villages of Mobin and Tsappar. The Massuzais watched the operations from a *kotal* to the east of the line of advance, but offered no resistance. To guard against eventualities, a dismounted squadron of the Central India Horse was dropped in the deserted village of Mobin. At 10 A.M., the right column had arrived at a *kotal* to the left of Tsappar which commanded the Thabai valley. From this place the battery shelled the Khani Khel Chamkannis at Thabai while the majority of the column descended towards the Thabai stream. Meanwhile the left column under Lieut.-Colonel C. Gordon, 6th Bengal Cavalry, advancing by an exceedingly difficult track, had not been able to make the same rapid progress, and a junction between the two columns was not effected till noon. A company of the 4th Gurkhas was now sent up to occupy a hill to the left of Thabai : but it was impossible, in the time available, to dislodge the enemy from all the rugged and precipitous cliffs surrounding the valley.

Right Column.

Gurkha Scouts.
½ company, Bombay S. and M.
Kohat Mountain Battery.
150 sabres, Central India Horse (dismounted).
2-4th Gurkhas.

Left Column.

Maxim gun, Royal Scots Fusiliers.
300 rifles, 12th Bengal Infantry.
150 rifles, 1-5th Gurkhas.
150 sabres, 6th Bengal Cavalry (dismounted).
100 rifles, Kapurthala Infantry.

The retirement began at 4 P.M. The enemy, as usual, followed up, and attempted to get possession of some hills commanding the line of retreat of both columns ; but the Gurkha Scouts were too quick for them, and got there first. Our losses for the day had been :—killed, Lieutenants R. M. Battye, 6th Bengal Cavalry, and five men ; wounded, Lieutenants W. H. Pennington, 12th Bengal Cavalry, and W. D. Villiers-Stuart, 1-5th Gurkhas, one native officer, and fifteen men. The enemy lost heavily both from Artillery and Infantry fire.

On the following day (December 2nd) the operations against Thabai, and against the Gar Massuzais, were resumed. Colonel Hill, with the force as per margin, followed the route taken by the right column on the previous day. The enemy again occupied the position to the left of Thabai; and the advanced guard, while clearing them out from this place, met with the most determined opposition from some 300 tribesmen posted in a succession of *sangars*. These *sangars* were stormed by the Gurkha Scouts led by Captain F. G. Lucas; and the enemy left no less than thirty dead bodies on the ground. The troops, picqueting the heights as they advanced up the valley, then thoroughly destroyed the fortified villages, mills, etc., and burnt immense quantities of forage: the guns meanwhile shelling the enemy as opportunities occurred. No attempt was made on this day to follow up the retirement. The hills covering the line of retreat were held throughout the afternoon, until the rear-guard had passed, by a company of the 12th Bengal Infantry from Lwara Mela. Our casualties amounted to two men killed, Major E. Vansittart, 1-5th Gurkhas, and three men wounded. The Chamkannis, as already indicated, had lost very heavily.

Advanced Guard.
5th Gurkha Scouts.
200 rifles, 5th Gurkhas.

Main Body.
½ battalion, "The Queen's" Regt.
No. 1 (Kohat) M.B., R.A.
½ battalion, 3rd Sikhs.

Rear-guard.
2-4th Gurkhas.

The force under Brig.-General Gaselee, which again visited the Lozaka valley this day, met with no opposition. The fine against the Massuzais not having been paid in full, fifteen of their fortified villages were destroyed.

On the 3rd December the two columns parted, Colonel Hill marching unopposed to Sadda, and the column under Brig.-General Gaselee camping about a mile east of Dargai, *en route* to Khanki Bazar. Sir William Lockhart and staff pushed on ahead to Miran Khel, an Alisherzai village about five miles from Dargai, to which Lieut.-Colonel Spurgin's force had already marched. At Miran Khel the Alisherzai *jirga* came in, with promises to pay in full the fine demanded from them (Rs. 3,750 and 62 rifles), half of which was assessed on the Sweri section and half on the Pitao. The fine was paid in full by the 20th December.

On the 4th December, the whole of Brig.-General Gaselee's force concentrated at Khanki Bazar, no opposition whatever being offered. On arrival at that place, the Mamuzai *jirga* was warned to produce the balance of their fine (Rs. 50 and 17 rifles) by 5 P.M., and as this demand was not complied with, a tower, belonging to one of the head *maliks*, was blown up. As a result of this action, six rifles were immediately produced, and the balance of the fine was paid in the following morning.

On the 5th, the force crossed the Chingakh pass; and Bagh was reached, without opposition, on the 6th. The further movements of Brig.-General Gaselee's column will be found detailed in the chapter assigned to the Afridis (Chapter II), against whom all subsequent operations were directed; these operations just described being the last that were undertaken against the Orakzai and Chamkanni tribes in this campaign. The Gar Massuzais finally submitted later on; and the Chamkannis, though they had not made formal submission, had been very severely punished for their contumacy.

From the conclusion of the war in 1898 the behaviour of the tribes in this area has been generally as satisfactory as could be hoped for. The only military expedition found necessary since that date was undertaken in 1899, against the Chamkannis, who, as we have seen above, were the only tribe mentioned in this chapter who had not eventually been compelled to make formal submission to Sir William Lockhart. The operations in question, which consisted of a raid in force, and had the most complete success, may be briefly related.

Captain Roos-Keppel's Raid 1899.

Early in 1899 the tribe again began to give serious trouble. On the 27th January they raided the villages of Ibrahimzai and Jalandar, killed four villagers, wounded and captured eight others, and drove off a large number of cattle. Captain Roos-Keppel, the Officer on special duty in the Kurram, obtained permission to make a counter-raid on the nearest Chamkanni villages, and made all his preparations without arousing the suspicions of the tribe. On the evening of the 1st March, with 200 rifles, 22nd Punjab Infantry, 300 rifles, Kurram Militia, and tribal *lashkars* amounting to 700 men drawn from the raided district, he attacked the villages of the Haji Khel and Mirza Khel Chamkannis in the

Kirman Darra, and by 11 A.M. on the following morning, the whole force was back in Kurram. They had burnt 9 large villages, captured 113 prisoners, about 3,000 cattle, sheep, and goats, and between 150 and 200 fire-arms. The Chamkannis lost some six or eight men killed in this attack, while our only casualty was one man of the Jalandar *lashkar* wounded.

With so large a number of prisoners, cattle, and fire-arms as security for payment in our hands, the Chamkannis had no option but to pay the fine demanded from them, consisting of 50 rifles and 306 matchlocks; and since this episode they have given no great trouble.

APPENDIX A.

Detail of Staff, Miranzai Field Force, January 1891.

Brig.-General Sir W. S. A. Lockhart, K.C.B., C.S.I.	Bengal Infantry	..	Commanding the force.
Lieutenant H. G. Maxwell ..	.. 16th Bengal Cavalry		Orderly Officer.
Major C. C. Egerton ..	.. 3rd Punjab Cavalry	..	A. A. G.
Captain R. F. Gartside-Tipping	.. 1st Bengal Cavalry	..	D. A. A. G.
Captain A. H. Mason ..	.. Royal Engineers	..	D. A. Q. M. G. I.
Captain T. W. G. Bryan ..	.. Royal Artillery	..	Field Intelligence Officers.
Lieutenant P. G. Shewell ..	.. 1st Punjab Infantry.		Field Intelligence Officers.
Major W. T. Shone, D.S.O. ..	.. Royal Engineers	..	Commanding Engineer.
Captain E. C. C. Sandys ..	.. Bengal Staff Corps	..	Chief Commissariat Officer.
Captain H. Wharry ..	.. Madras Staff Corps	..	Divisional Transport Officer.
Brigade-Surgeon R. Harvey, M.D.	Indian Medical Service		P. M. O.
Captain R. A. Wahab ..	.. Royal Engineers	..	Survey Officer.
Major H. P. P. Leigh ..	.. Bengal Staff Corps	..	Political Officer.

2 M 2

APPENDIX B.

Detail of Staff, Miranzai Field Force, April 1891.

Brig.-General Sir W. S. A. Lochkart, K.C.B., C.S.I.	Bengal Infantry	Commanding the force
Lieutenant the Hon'ble C. G. Bruce	5th Gurkha Regiment.	Orderly Officer up to the 28th April.
Lieutenant G. P. Brazier Creagh	9th Bengal Lancers	Orderly Officer from the 29th April.
Major C. C. Egerton	3rd Punjab Cavalry	A. A. G.
Captain D. W. Hickman	34th B. I.	D. A. A. G.
Captain A. H. Mason	Royal Engineers	D. A. Q. M. G. I.
Lieut.-Colonel E. J. de Lautour	Royal Artillery	C. R. A.
Major W. T. Shone, D.S.O.	Royal Engineers	C. R. E.
Captain E. C. C. Sandys	Indian Staff Corps	Chief Commissariat Officer.
Captain H. Wharry	Indian Staff Corps	Divisional Transport Officer.
Brigade-Surgeon R. Harvey, M.D.	Indian Medical Service.	P. M. O.
Captain R. J. H. L. Mackenzie	Royal Engineers	Survey Officer.
Major H. P. P. Leigh	Indian Staff Corps	Political Officer.

APPENDIX C.

Genealogy of the Massuzai Orakzais.

CLANS.	Divisions.	Sub-divisions.	Sections.
MASSUZAI	LANDAIZAI	Abdul Mirzi (Gar)	Khuni Khel.
MASSUZAI	LANDAIZAI	Abdul Mirzi (Gar)	Jani Khel.
MASSUZAI	LANDAIZAI	Abdul Mirzi (Gar)	Rab Khel.
MASSUZAI	LANDAIZAI	Abdul Mirzi (Gar)	Ibrahim Khel.
MASSUZAI	LANDAIZAI	Mastu Khel (Gar)	Abdal Khel.
MASSUZAI	LANDAIZAI	Mastu Khel (Gar)	Ulus Khel.
MASSUZAI	LANDAIZAI	Ash Khel (Samil)	Shahi Kor.
MASSUZAI	LANDAIZAI	Ash Khel (Samil)	Ikhtyar Kor.
MASSUZAI	LANDAIZAI	Ash Khel (Samil)	Wali Khel.
MASSUZAI	LANDAIZAI	Ash Khel (Samil)	Aimat Khel.
MASSUZAI	KHWAJA KHEL	Maudu Khel	Mir Said Khel.
MASSUZAI	KHWAJA KHEL	Maudu Khel	Alladad Khel.
MASSUZAI	KHWAJA KHEL	Nasarzai.	
MASSUZAI	KHWAJA KHEL	Miran Khel.	
MASSUZAI	KHWAJA KHEL	Shahabdin Khel.	
MASSUZAI	ALIZAI	Umar Khel.	
MASSUZAI	ALIZAI	Mahmaddi Kor.	
MASSUZAI	ALIZAI	Jan Muhammad Kor.	
MASSUZAI	ALIZAI	Farig Shah Kor.	
MASSUZAI	ALIZAI	Baki Kor.	

APPENDIX D.

Genealogy of the Lashkarzai Orakzais.

Clans.	Divisions.	Sub-divisions.	Sections.
LASHKARZAI	ALISHERZAI (Samil)	Umar Khan Khel	Saifo Khel. Isa Khel. Daulat Khel. Aziz Khan Kor. Nazar Khan Khel. Sahib Khel. Aimal Khan Kor. Ghulam Ali Kor. Gaju Kor. Adu Khan Kor. Misri Khel.
		Bain Khel.	
		Mir Ahmad Khel	Umla Kor. Taji Khel. Shaib Khel. Ghalib Khan Khel.
		Kaisa Khel	Mirza Nmasi. Isalor Nmasi. Tor Kor. Kambar Ali Kor.
		Masar Khel.	
	MAMUZAI (Gar)	Adu Khel	Umar Khan Khel. Haidar Khel, Said Khan Khel. Ali Khan Khel.
		Sipah	Sultan Khel. Khalal Khel. Raza Kor. Pukhtano. Adam Nmasi. Yusaf Nmasi. Talab Nmasi. Khawas Khel. Ambara Khan.
		Abdur Rahman Khel	Jani Khel. Mardu Khel. Karimdad Khel. Kaisar Nmasi. Rasul Khel. Shabra Khel. Ali Muhammad Nmasi. Mushki. Jamsheri.
		Abdur Rahim Khel	Shekh Mali Nmasi. Mir Ali Khel. Lashkari Khel. Askari Khel.
		Mir Kalan Khel	Takhta Beg. Mirza Ali Khel. Abdur Rahman Khel. Haibat Khel. Bela Khel. Shadu Nmasi. Nazar Khel.
		Mir Kalan Khel	Bai Nmasi. Shahi Nmasi. Khadi Nmasi. Mian Nmasi.

APPENDIX E.

Genealogy of the Alizai or Sturi Khel and Muhammad Khel Orakzais.

Clans.	Divisions.	Sub-divisions.	Sections.
ALIZAI OR STURI KHEL.	BARAWAL..	Afzal Khel	Ismail Khel.
		Lalbi Khel	Barid Khel.
	TIRAHWAL	Saidan.	
		Chamkanni.	
		And Khel .. (Shias).	
		Tazi Khel .. (Shias).	
		Anjanni .. .. (Shias).	
		Skundai .. .. (Shias).	
MUHAMMAD KHEL	BAR MUHAMMAD KHEL (1,000).	Baba Kmasi.	
		Mir Aziz Khel.	
		Khwaidad.	
		Allahdad Khel	Ali Khurdza Khel.
			Durga Khel.
			Sheikh Mali Khe'
		Tirahi *Hamsayas*.	
	ABDUL AZIZ KHEL ..	Kamal Khel.	
		Kadam Khel.	
		Azar Khel.	
	MANI KHEL	Badda Khel.	
		Mast Ali Khel.	
		Saburai Khel.	
		Mirwaz Khel.	
		Zikria Khel.	
		Sabzi Khel.	
		Isa Khel.	
		Ahmad Khel.	
	SIPAH	Mitah Khan Khel.	
		Sultan Khel.	
		Ambara Khel.	
		Lakhkari Khel.	

APPENDIX F.

Genealogy of the Daulatzai Orakzais.

Clans.	Divisions.	Sub-divisions.	Sections.
DAULATZAIS	FIROZ KHEL (Samil) ..	Jaisal Khel	Mir Hussen Khel. Tajak Khel. Shekh Mali Nmasi. Muwali Khel.
		Sarang Khel	Zaina Khel. Dost Nmasi. Adam Khan Nmasi. Dadar Khel. Miranzai Khel. Kimat Khan. Haidar Khel. Ghairat Khel. Ismail Khel. Mir Ahmad Khel. Kasim Khel.
	BIZOTI (Samil) ..	Kambar Khel ..	Shahbad Khel. Aba Khel. Betani. Mir Beg Khel. Gadai Khel.
		Yarkulli Khel	Yaru Khel. Said Ali Kor. Zamur Khel. Salim Kor. Aidu Khel. Zafran Kor. Khesri Khel.
		Chawar Khel	Amir Khan Kor. Khwaidad Khel. Pula Kor. Sharif Khel. Muhammad Amir Shah Kor. Paiao Khel.
		Mir Kulli Khel ..	Shabi Khel. Bahadur Khel. Timar Khel. Khwaja Khidar Khel. Batar Khel. Tor Khel. Tuti Khel. Maram Khel. Raji Khel.
		Mir Ali Khel.	
	UTMAN KHEL	Baranka Khel	Dost Mali Khel. Rajmir Khel. Kadu Khel. Buzar Khel. Hashmi Khel.
		Fateh Khad Khel ..	Haider Ali Khel. Shahi Khel. Yar Ali Khel. Aba Khel.

APPENDIX G.

Genealogy of the Ismailzai Orakzais.

CLANS.	Divisions.	Sub-divisions.	Sections.
SMAILZAIS (Part Gar, part Samil).	RABIA KHEL (Samil) ..	Babi Khel	Dalak Beg. Haidar Beg. Waz Beg. Khan Beg.
		Afzal Khel	Bazid Nmasi. Sikandar Nmasi. Shamsho Nmasi.
		Paiavi Khel	Mirza Ali Nmasi. Dur Nmasi. Alahdad Nmasi. Khwaja Ali Nmasi.
		Farigh Shan	Miadad Nmasi. Tarkhan Nmasi. Tarakki Nmasi.
		Ayaz Khel	Nani Nmasi. Nuri Nmasi. Kajir Nmasi. Matta Khel.
	BAHRIM KHEL	Zari Nmasi .. .. Tul Nmasi	Baria Khel *Hamsayas*.
		Maddu Khel .. .. Shah Mansur Khel ..	Ali Khel *Hamsayas*.
	AKHEL (Ibrahim Khel) (Gar).	Masan Khel	Mahlam Kor. Sheikh Kor. Mahwali Kor.
		Mandrak Khel	Shahmali Nmasi. Dallak Nmasi. Humai Nmasi. Painda Khel. Said Khel. Hindki Khel.
		Sarki Khel	Rain Khel. Daulat Nmasi. Jabbaro Nmasi.
	MAMAZAI (Daradar) (Samil).	Machi Khel	Allah Khan Nmasi. Bura Khan Nmasi. Imam Din Nmasi.
		Khadi Khel	Kamal Nmasi. Ashraf Nmasi. Said Ali Nmasi. Sardar Nmasi.
		Miro Khel	Bada Khan Nmasi. Daria Khan Nmasi. Said Khan Nmasi.
	KHADIZAI (Samil) ..	Sikandar Khel. Khawas Khel. Malam Kor. Nur Sher Kor. Miru Khel. Ramdad Khel. Bahadur Khan Nmasi. Tar Khan Nmasi.	

APPENDIX G—*contd.*

Clans.	Divisions.	Sub-divisions.	Sections.
ISMAILZAI (Part Gar, part Samil).	Isa Khel (Samil) ..	Gowaro Nmasi. San Khel. Kali Khel. Miru Khel.	
	Sada Khel	Nakshband Kor. Kabir Khel. Suliman Khel. Farid Khel. Muhammad Khel.	

APPENDIX H.

Genealogy of Orakzai Hamsaya Clans.

Clans.	Divisions.	Sub-divisions.	Sections.
MISHTI (Samil) ..	MAMIZAI	Bazid Khel. Miru Khel. Khoidad Khel. Sakki Khel. Aziz Khel. Ayaz Khel. Saddo Khel. Char Khan Khel.	
	DREWANDI OR WANDGRAI.	Mamazai. Dad Khel. Bahlolzai.	
	HASSANZAI	Shirak Khel. Masti Khel.	
	UTMANI	Moza Khel. Husain Khel.	
	DARWI KHEL	Mand Akhel. Shaib Khel.	
	HAIDAR KHEL OR KHUMARAI.	Ali Khan Khel. Gujar Khel. Mama Khel. Ghulam Ali Khel.	
MALLA KHEL (Samil)	AZIZ KHEL	Fakir Khel. Sabro Nmasi. Langar Khel. Shinko Khel.	
	KUTAB KHEL	Abdul Khel. Khiddar Khel. Daris Khel. Darwez Khel.	
	CHAR KHEL	Khadi Khel. Nazar Ali Khel. Lakri Khel. Barak Adam Khel.	
SHEIKHAN (Samil) ..	BAZID KHEL	Rangin Khel. Abdul Rahman Khel. Muhammad Khan Nmasi.	
	UMARZAI	Kambar Khel. Musa Khel. Tirahi.	
	SAMOZAI	Suliman Khel. Ali Khan Khel.	
ALI KHEL (Gar ½ Shia)	KHWAJA HAWAS KHEL	Churi Khel. Sahib Khel or Mirwas Khel. Baland Khel. Sarmarst Khel or Shahwas Khel. Niamat Khel. Alaf Khel or Sher Khel.	

APPENDIX H—*contd.*

Clans.	Divisions.	Sub-divisions.	Sections.
ALI KHEL (Gar ½ Shia).	JASRAT KHEL	Alam Khan Nmasi. Fattu Nmasi. Nazu Khel. Naku Khel. Bari Khel. Isaf Khel.	
	AIMAL KHAN KHEL ..	Yarki Khel. Masti Khel. Shah Ali Khel or Zaru Khel. Tuti Nmasi. Tamash Khel. Darbush Khel or Aka Khel.	
	ZANKA KHEL	Kucha Khel. Marus Khel.	
	MATANNI	Ismail Khan Khel. Hasham Khel.	
	TSAKARAI..	Malik Nmasi. Shahu Nmasi. Paiavi Nmasi.	
	BABA NMASI SAIDAN ..	Mir Niamat Khel. Mir Shahwali. Mir Karim.	

CHAPTER V.

THE ZAIMUKHT TRIBE.

THE Zaimukhts are a tribe of Pathans inhabiting the hills to the south of the Orakzais, between the Miranzai and Kurram valleys.

They are divided into two main branches—(I) Mamuzai, or Western Zaimukhts; and (II) Khoidad Khel, or Eastern Zaimukhts; and their total fighting strength is about 3,500 men. The Zaimukhts are Sunnis in religion and Samil in politics. They are physically a fine-looking, powerful race, forming in this respect a striking contrast to their Turi neighbours. They do not move about so much as other tribes, but remain in their villages all the year round. The Khoidad Khel branch of the tribe are brought more into contact with our officers than the Mamuzai, and have the reputation of being more enterprising and daring than their fellow-tribesmen to the west.

The tribe live on the southern slopes of the Zawa Ghar range, and their country is thus described by Brig.-General Tytler, who commanded the expedition against the tribe in the winter of 1879-80:—

The valley generally presents many difficulties for the movement of troops in the face of an enemy. The country throughout is more or less a close country. The roads, as they are at present, are nothing more than cattle tracks, and would require much labour and time before being rendered good. At this particular season of the year very little water was found anywhere, except at the different camping-grounds, although the numerous ravines intersecting the country in every direction show that at some seasons water must be superabundant, so much so that traffic of any sort would be found difficult. From Balish Khel to Torawari, by the route followed by the column, is about thirty-two miles, more or less, and throughout its entire length it is open to easy attack, not only by the Zaimukhts, but by neighbouring tribes from whose countries passes lead into the valley; so that to ensure safe communication being kept open, a very considerable force would have to be kept along the line. The fertility of the country is unquestionable, indian corn, wheat, barley, and other cereals being grown in large quantities. There are also large numbers of cattle, sheep, goats, and poultry, sufficient for the requirements of the inhabitants; but I saw that, had a force of merely the strength of that under my command been quartered for any time in any particular place, the supplies would very soon have failed. I consider that I visited the country under exceptionally favourable circumstances. The weather was dry and cold, the crops off the fields, and the fields themselves dry, affording excellent camping-grounds.

The Zaimukhts also own certain villages within British limits in the Kurram valley, such as Arawali, Mandori, Durani Kila, Kuchi, Jalamai, Pustawani, Mom Darra, and Sara Gurgai. In the limits of Miranzai, (British territory) they own Torawari and Dolragha.

The Zaimukhts only depend upon us for salt, but they would feel a blockade very much. They can generally reckon on aid from the Alisherzai in their external quarrels, and they are sometimes joined by the Mamuzai and the Massuzai Orakzais.

There is a bitter blood-feud between the eastern and western divisions of the Zaimukhts. The quarrel arose sixty years ago from their joining opposite sides in a dispute between the Kabul Khel Wazirs and the Turis. Another cause of contention has been the possession of the village of Thana, which, from its position on an eminence, not only commands the Sangroba stream, but also one of the principal passages into Kurram. For many years this village was constantly changing hands, for being entirely dependent for water on the Sangroba stream, which flows some 200 or 300 feet below the village, a besieging party encamping in the low hills on the banks of the river could easily prevent the villagers from going down to draw water. In 1867 this difficulty was provided for by the Khoidad Khels, who, having regained possession of the village by the aid of the neighbouring Wazirs, constructed a subterraneous passage from the village to the bed of the stream. Thana has since then remained in the undisturbed possession of the Khoidad Khel branch, for without guns it would be very difficult to oust the defenders by assault. On account of this feud, owing to both parties having supporters in Miranzai, it has occasionally been a matter of some difficulty to prevent British subjects mixing themselves up in the quarrel.

In the early years of the annexation the Zaimukhts gave little trouble, but in 1855 they assumed a hostile attitude, and, among other acts of hostility, they took part in the affair near Darsamand on the 30th of April (to be described in the next chapter). After the expedition to the Miranzai valley in 1856, however, their behaviour became good.

During that expedition Brigadier Chamberlain examined the ground in the neighbourhood of the villages of Dolragha and Admela, and rode through the gorge leading to the villages of Thana and Sangroba, which he found to be more accessible than reports had made out. On the march from Ibrahimzai to Hazar Pir Ziarat the western entrance to the Zaimukht country was also explored. Sketches were taken, and the fact established that the Zaimukht country was more accessible than had been supposed. From 1856 to 1878 the Zaimukhts gave little trouble on our border.

Expedition against the Zaimukhts by a force under Brig.-General J. A. Tytler, V.C., C.B., in December 1879.

Soon after the outbreak of the Afghan war in November 1878, the Zaimukhts began to give trouble on the line of communications of the Kurram Valley Field Force, both on the Kohat-Thal road in British territory and also in Kurram. On the 27th of December 1878 twenty-four camels were carried off while grazing at some distance from the military camp at Thal by Zaimukhts of the Babakar section. Eighteen of the camels were recovered, and a fine of Rs. 500 was imposed on the Khoidad Khels for this offence. On the night of the 2nd-3rd of March 1879 a much more serious raid was committed on the *serai* at Gandiaor, in Miranzai. The raiders were twenty-five in number, twenty being Khoidad Khel Zaimukhts and five Alisherzai Orakzais. They moreover came into British territory through the Khoidad Khel limits. The raiders entered the *serai* about 11 P.M., and succeeded in killing five mule drivers and wounding three, besides killing one sepoy of the road police and wounding two others. They then escaped, carrying off with them twenty-eight mules, of which seventeen were subsequently recovered through the men of Torawari. On the 9th of March two Hindu postal carriers were murdered in Wattizai limits, between Chapri and Mandori. The raiding party consisted of eighteen Zaimukhts and three Alisherzai Orakzais.

On the 6th of May a havildar and three sepoys of the Patiala Contingent were attacked by Khadu Khel Zaimukhts of Zawo, on the road between Thal and Chapri. The havildar and one sepoy, after a short resistance, were killed, but the other two sepoys, one of whom was wounded, succeeded in making their escape. On the 25th of June Surgeon W. B. Smyth was murdered at Chapri, seven miles from Thal; the murderers belonged to the Wattizai section. On the 7th of the following month the mails were robbed on the Mandori road by Zaimukhts of the Daudzai section.

On the night of the 27th of July an attack was made near Gandiaor on a party of seventy-two armed sepoys of the 5th Punjab Infantry, who were proceeding on furlough. These men were travelling at night, in disregard of orders forbidding them to do so, and were attacked by marauders numbering sixty-nine, sixty of whom were Zaimukhts and nine Alisherzais. The raiders were eventually driven off by two volleys, leaving two men killed on the ground, carrying off two others killed and several wounded. Of the furlough men three were killed and ten wounded, including the subadar; also two cartmen and seven bullocks.

On the 29th of September the Zaimukhts crowned their long list of evil deeds by the cruel and dastardly murder of Lieutenant F. B. Kinloch, 5th Bengal Cavalry, between Chapri and Mandori. This officer, accompanied by one sowar, was riding along, when some forty men, lying in ambush near the road, fired a volley at him. He fell, and the men then rushed on him and murdered him. The sowar who was with him escaped to Chapri, and, having procured assistance, brought the body back to Thal. The murder was committed within Wattizai limits, but the marauders belonged to the Khoidad Khel division of the Zaimukhts. In the above list of offences committed by this tribe, minor offences, such as petty thefts, cutting the telegraph wire, etc., of which several occurred, have been omitted.

The hostile attitude which the Zaimukht tribe had assumed was generally attributed to the residence of Mulla Wali Khan for some months in their village of Sperkhwait, and to their having been guided by his ill advice. The total claim against the Zaimukht on account of these outrages and raids amounted to no less than Rs. 25,000.

The cup of their iniquities being full, sanction was given by the Government of India for punishment to be inflicted on the tribe, and orders were accordingly issued for the assembling of a force to enter the Zaimukht country in the middle of October 1879. The command of the expedition was entrusted to Brig. General J. A. Tytler, V.C., C.B.

The main objects of the expedition were four in number. Firstly, to punish the Zaimukht tribe for their raids and outrages on the Kurram road and the Miranzai border; secondly, to extend the operations, should it be found convenient and desirable to do so, to the Mamuzai and Alisherzai sections of the Orakzais, in consequence of their recent misbehaviour, or in the event of their joining the Zaimukhts in attacking or withstanding the British forces; thirdly, it was required by the Adjutant-General of the Army that a right of way should be admitted by the Zaimukhts through their territory between Torawari, in British territory, and Balish Khel, in Kurram, and that they should give hostages for the security, and undertake the responsibility, of this road; and, fourthly, it was intended generally to secure the safety of communications on the Thal-Kurram road.

Previous to active operations being commenced, a proclamation (*see* Appendix A) was issued to the independent tribes on the Kohat border, in which the causes and the objects of the proposed expedition were set forth, and in which they were warned against affording aid to the offending tribes.

Owing to renewed active operations in Afganistan, consequent on the murder of the British envoy at Kabul, the expedition against the Zaimukhts had to be postponed for a time, chiefly on account of want of transport. At the end of October some 3,000 Lashkarzais had assembled in the neighbourhood of Balish Khel, and on the 29th of that month Lieut.-Colonel R. G. Rogers, 20th Punjab Native Infantry, with a flying column, consisting of detachments of the 85th Foot and the 20th Punjab Native Infantry, with two mountain guns, made a demonstration against this gathering, and dispersed the enemy with a few shells at long ranges. There were no casualties on our side.

On the 21st of November a raid was made on the independent Zaimukht hamlet of Dand, about five miles from Torawari. The object was to capture some relatives of Malik Hawas, Ali Khel, the leader of the attack on Mazam Talao on the night of the 14th of November, in which a large number of coolies had been killed and wounded. These men were known then to be living at Dand. The party consisted of eighty sabres of the 18th Bengal Cavalry, under Major T. R. Davidson of that regiment, and was accompanied by Major E. R. Conolly, Assistant Commissioner of Kohat. The distance turned out to be greater, and the road rougher than had been expected, but the surprise was successful, and it was not until the party arrived within a quarter of a mile of the hamlet that any move was observed among the villagers. They then attempted to fly, but were stopped, and, seeing resistance to be hopeless, they stated their readiness to give in. The party then returned to Torawari, taking with them twelve prisoners, six of whom were Ali Khels, and related to Malik Hawas, and five were Zaimukhts, the remaining man being an Alisherzai.

On the 22nd of November about one thousand Zaimukhts, Mamuzais, and Alisherzais had assembled one mile and a half from the Chapri Post, in the Kurram valley, but they were driven off by the little garrison of the 18th Bengal Cavalry (thirty-six sabres), under Ressaldar Nadir Ali Khan. The enemy lost thirteen killed and many wounded, and we had three sowars wounded.

Preparations were, in the meanwhile, rapidly pushed on for the expedition into the Zaimukht country, and on the 28th of November Brig.-General Tytler reached Balish Khel, from which place the expedition was to start.

On the 1st of December two reconnaissances were made into Zaimukht territory, in a northerly direction; one party, consisting of 500 infantry and two mountain guns, under Colonel J. J. H. Gordon, C.B., 29th Punjab Native Infantry, accompanied by Major T. J. C. Plowden as Political Officer, ascended the Drabzai mountain, 7,300 feet high, seven miles from Balish Khel, which commands the whole southern Alisherzai valley, with the passes leading to the Northern Alisherzai and Massuzai country. A second force of 400 infantry, 100 cavalry, and 2 mountain guns, under Lieut.-Colonel R. C. Low, 13th Bengal Lancers, accompanied by Captain A. Conolly as Political Officer, passed round the foot of the Drabzai mountain, through Tindoh, as far as the entrance to the Krumb defile. Both columns returned to camp that evening without having met with any opposition.

On the 3rd of December a reconnoitring party, under Lieut.-Colonel R. C. Rogers, C.B., 20th Punjab Native Infantry, consisting of 400 infantry, 50 cavalry, and 2 mountain guns, explored the Tatang defile and the Abasikor pass, the latter distant about 13 miles from camp, and 7,700 feet in height. Passing by the village of Tindoh the force halted at the village of Tatang. Here the inhabitants appeared anxious to show their friendly intentions, and readily offered their services as guides. After passing this village, the road entered the Tatang defile, a very narrow path about forty or fifty yards long, and with precipitous rocky sides overhanging the roadway. After this the pass widened considerably till within about a mile from the crest, when the ground rose abruptly to the summit. The road throughout was rough, and the latter part especially would have been found difficult for any but lightly-laden baggage animals. From here a good view was obtained of the Massuzai valley; a few shots were fired at the troops, but these were not returned, and the force reached camp the same evening without any casualties.

On the same day a small body of the 13th Bengal Lancers, under Major C. R. Pennington, reconnoitred the country in the direction of the old *kafila* road from Durani to Gowakhi. The road was found to be fairly good, and it was determined to follow this route.

On the 8th of December Brig.-General Tytler moved into the Zaimukht country, with the force noted in the margin. Major T. J. C. Plowden, Captain A. Conolly, and Mr. G. C. Walker, B.C.S., were attached to the column as Political officers; and Mr. G. B. Scott, of the Survey Department, also accompanied the force.

	All ranks.
1 8th Royal Artillery, 4 guns (screw)	195
No. 1 (Kohat) Mountain Battery, 2 guns.	78
2-8th Foot	41
85th „	733
1st Bengal Cavalry	57
13th Bengal Lancers	155
18th Bengal Cavalry	55
8th Company, Sappers and Miners	57
13th Native Infantry	323
4th Punjab Infantry	557
20th Punjab Native Infantry ..	398
29th „ „	568

Eleven days' supplies were taken with the troops, and provisions for ten days were collected at Doaba, from which place a convoy was to meet the troops at Tarai. The force reached Gowakhi on the 8th. The main body marched by Durani, while the cavalry, with the exception of one troop, which preceded the column, was sent by the direct route, in order to diminish the length of the column as much as possible, and also to intercept any fugitives in case of the enemy showing fight. No opposition was made, although, on the reconnaisance of the 3rd, *sangars* commanding the road from the right and left were observed to be occupied. The village was found deserted, the inhabitants having fled on the approach of our troops, taking with them their property and cattle.

On the following day the march was continued to Manatu, nineteen miles from Balish Khel; several portions of the road had to be improved by the Sappers, the baggage animals experiencing much difficulty. This village was not deserted (although it was afterwards discovered that large quantities of their grain had been sent into the Wattizai valley), and the inhabitants were apparently anxious to come to a friendly understanding. The Manatuwal section, to which the village belonged, had accepted the terms offered to them before the force started.

Right Column, under Colonel J. J. H. Gordon, C.B.
2 guns, No. 1 (Kohat) Moun. Battery.
600 Infantry.

Centre Column, under Colonel R. G. Rogers, C.B.
600 Infantry.

Left Column, under Lieut.-Colonel R. C. Low.
2 guns, 1-8th Royal Artillery.
200 Cavalry.
150 Infantry.

On the 10th, three columns, as per margin, were detached to burn certain villages of the Wattizai section, the inhabitants of which had been implicated in several offences on the Thal-Kurram road, and more especially in the murder of Surgeon Smyth at Chapri. The first two columns, under Colonels J. J. H. Gordon and R. G. Rogers, met with no opposition; the last, however, under Lieut.-Colonel R. C. Low, was checked at the villages of Kandolai and Katakomela, about five miles from camp. The enemy was soon dislodged by the fire of the screw guns, upon which the infantry advanced, and carried the villages, together with others in the neighbourhood. These villages were found stored with large quantities of grain, the whole of which, together with the houses, was destroyed by fire on the morning of the 11th. Over four hundred and fifty head of cattle were taken, together with thirty prisoners. No casualties occurred among the troops.

The Wattizai valley was found to be about six miles long, well cultivated and watered. The inhabitants were evidently taken by surprise, as few cattle or little property had been removed.

The damage inflicted by the burning of the villages must consequently have been considerable, and was estimated by the Political Officer at Rs. 60,000.

Simultaneous with the advance of the troops into the Wattizai valley, the villages of Sereverge, Pustawani, and Imamdarra, also belonging to this section, were attacked from Kurram by a body of Turi levies (horse and foot) under their chief, Muhammad Nur Khan, and were completely destroyed.

On the 11th the troops returned to camp, and the force, after destroying one tower at Manatu, pushed on to Zaitunak, a village about five miles and a half distant, and situated on the southern slopes of the main watershed, on the summit of which was the village of Manatu. At Zaitunak the representatives of the Mandani section came in and made their submission and accepted the terms offered to them.

On the 12th the column marched five miles to Chinarak, distant about eight miles from the stronghold of Zawo, the objective point of the expedition. Chinarak was situated on a fairly open and level plateau, surrounded by terraced fields, through which ran numerous water channels, and was almost at the foot of the defile leading to Zawo. In the afternoon the Brig.-General reconnoitred the fastness, which was deemed impregnable by the enemy. On Chinarak the three main routes into the Zamukht country converge, *viz.*, from Balish Khel, from Torawari, and from Thal by the Sangroba defile, and it may, therefore, be looked upon as the most important strategical point of the whole valley. The inhabitants had not deserted the village, and appeared willing to be friendly, readily furnishing supplies of food and fodder. A sepoy of the 29th Punjab Native Infantry was, however, shot dead on picquet duty during the night. From the hills above Chinarak, as previously arranged, heliographic communications was opened with a station on the lower slopes of the Dandoghar hill, and thence to Thal.

On the following morning (the 13th) the camp was left in charge of Colonel R. C. Rogers, C.B., with a small force, and the remainder of the troops, as shown in the margin, moved out to attack Zawo.

1-8th Royal Artillery, 2 guns.
No. 1 (Kohat) Moun. Battery, 2 guns.
85th Regiment, 400 bayonets.
13th Bengal Lancers, 50 sabres.
Half 8th Company, S. and M.

		Bayonets.
13th Native Infantry	..	100
4th Punjab Infantry	..	350
20th Punjab Native Infantry	..	200
29th " " "	..	300

There are three approaches to this fastness—one by a difficult ravine about seven miles long and ten feet wide; one to the left, over a steep spur on the west of the ravine; one to the right, over high hills west of the valley of Surmai.

The plan decided on was that the commanding ground on the right should be held, while the main advance should be by the ravine.

No. 1 (Kohat) Moun. Battery, 2 guns.
Four companies, 85th Regiment.
Four companies, 29th Punjab N. I.

The advanced guard, consisting of the troops as per margin, under Colonel J. J. H. Gordon, C.B., reached the village of Ragha at 8 A.M., and occupied a plateau close under the ridge on the eastern side of the entrance to the defile leading to Zawo. Meanwhile, the Brig.-General with the main body (which had now become the left column, Colonel Gordon's detachment forming the right column) followed the same route as far as the plateau of Ragha, from whence the enemy could be seen occupying the ridge in front. The tribesmen were soon dislodged by the fire of the screw guns, while the right column carried the lower spurs without opposition.

It was now 10-30 A.M., and the Brig.-General, entering the defile to the west of the ridge, pushed on to the village of Bagh, his left being secured by a flanking party of three companies of the 4th Punjab Infantry, under Lieut.-Colonel H. P. Close, which occupied the high ground on the west of the ravine. The bed of the defile was excessively difficult, and on arrival at 2-30 P.M. at Bagh, distant about three miles and a half from Chinarak and four and a half from Zawo, it was decided to postpone any further advance till the following day, and to bivouac at Bagh for the night.

Colonel Gordon, meanwhile, with the right column, having cleared the ridge on the east of Ragha, had opened fire on the village of Bagh lying on the opposite side of the valley (which is here about 1,000 yards wide), while the enemy took up a very strong position on a rocky hill and ridge from which all attempts by the 85th Foot to dislodge him by a direct attack failed. A flanking movement by two companies of the 29th Punjab Native Infantry, under Lieutenant R. W. Macleod, followed by the two remaining companies of the same regiment in support, under Major C. E. D. Branson, resulted, by 2-30 P.M., in the capture of a point from which the enemy's line could be enfiladed. The enemy advanced in great force from the low ground north of the ridge, and a hand-to-hand fight ensued on the crest, in which they were repulsed, and the four companies firmly established themselves in their new position.

About this time the two guns of the Kohat Mountain Battery had worked round by Bagh, and were brought up from the westward to within 700 yards of the enemy's main position, on which they opened fire soon after three o'clock, while it was attacked simultaneously by the 85th in two columns from the south and south-east, and by the 29th from the west, aided by a small detachment from the left column. At 4 P.M., Colonel Gordon was in possession of the whole ridge, and there bivouacked for the night, the enemy retreating to a fresh position behind a rocky and well-wooded ridge some 1,500 yards further north. The 85th occupied the ground won, the 29th holding the rear ridge and protecting the communications, while the two guns were posted on the crest of the Bagh-Surmai pass.

At 7-30 A.M. on the 14th Colonel Gordon, leaving one company of the 85th at the bivouac, sent three companies of that regiment to drive the enemy out of the position he had taken up on the previous night, and to occupy the high ground to the north, flanking the approach to Zawo from Bagh, while the two guns, with three companies of the 29th Punjab Native Infantry, reached the same ridge at 10 A.M., by a detour round the head of the Surmai valley. A little later two companies of the 85th were sent down to burn the three villages of Surmai.

At 11 A.M. the enemy endeavoured to reinforce Zawo from the eastward, but dispersed on being fired on by the mountain guns. The right column now completely commanded the approaches to Zawo from the east, while two companies of the 85th on the left of Colonel Gordon's position were pushed forward to aid the left column while debouching from the Bagh defile. Colonel Gordon remained in the position he then occupied during the rest of the operations against Zawo.

Meanwhile, leaving Bagh in charge of Major C. R. Pennington, 13th Bengal Lancers (the road in front being impracticable for cavalry), Brig.-General Tytler, with the left column, continued his advance up the gorge, when large bodies of the enemy appeared on the hills on both sides. The screw guns were brought into action, and, under their cover, the infantry were pushed on, the hills on the left being crowned by parties of the 4th Punjab Infantry and of the 20th Punjab Native Infantry; and at the same time the guns of No. 1 (Kohat) Mountain Battery opened fire on the right. The columns now pushed on to the foot of the pass leading to Zawo itself, the men moving in single file under a heavy fire and shower of rocks from the heights. Here Lieutenant T. J. O'D. Renny, the Adjutant of the 4th Punjab Infantry, fell mortally wounded, and a havildar of the same regiment was dangerously wounded. Upon gaining the summit of the pass, the villages of Zawo appeared below in a horse-shoe shaped valley.

After a short rest on the summit of the pass, covering parties of the 4th Punjab Infantry were detached to the heights on the right, and detachments were sent down to burn the villages and to destroy the forage, etc., in and near them. This having been done the column began to retire, and arrived at Bagh at 5 P.M., entirely unmolested, several hamlets having been burnt on the way, and two towers in the village of Bagh having been blown up.

The troops bivouacked that night at Bagh, and on the 15th returned to Chinarak, being joined *en route* by the right column which, after the Brig.-General had returned through the Zawo pass on the 14th, had withdrawn to the hills above Bagh.

The enemy had four standards with him, and his losses were estimated at over forty killed and one hundred wounded. The British casualties were one officer and one sepoy killed, one native officer and one non-commissioned officer wounded.

The result of the operations against Zawo was the complete destruction of the settlements of the Khadu Khel section. The Zaimukhts were aided by a strong force of from 2,000 to 3,000 men from the Alisherzai and Mamuzai Orakzais. So confident were they of the natural strength of Zawo that they hardly began to desert the village until the ridge above Zawo had been taken by our troops. In the flight of the enemy from the village the greater part of their losses occurred, and it is probable that it was owing to the severe loss then sustained that no attempt was made to molest the troops when they retired.

On the 16th of December the column marched from Chinarak to Nawakila (nine miles), passing the village of Warmegi about half way.

On the following day the force arrived at Sperkhwait (seven miles), and found it half deserted and all the grain removed, but fodder and grass in abundance. On the same day all available carriage was sent to Torawari to bring up supplies, and returned to camp on the following day.

On the 18th a detachment of four mountain guns, 50 cavalry, 30 sappers, and 700 infantry was moved out to burn the village of Yasta, about seven miles from camp. This village belonged to the Babakar Khel section, which had been mainly implicated in the raid on Gandiaor on the 2nd of March, in the attack on the 5th Punjab Infantry furlough men on the 27th of July, and in the murder of Lieutenant Kinloch on the 29th of September. No real opposition was met with, although the enemy showed themselves on the neighbouring heights, and fired a few shots, but without effect. The force returned to camp the same day, having destroyed the village, demolished two towers, and seized a large quantity of forage. On their return information was received that a large number of the enemy, consisting of Alisherzai and Mamuzai Orakzais, with sixteen standards, were assembled in the higher range in front of the camp to dispute our passage of the Mandatti pass.

On the 19th, orders were received from Brig.-General J. Watson, V.C., C.B., commanding the force in the Kurram valley, at once to conclude operations against the Zaimukhts, with a view to releasing the column for a demonstration in the direction of the Shutargardan, so as to assist Lieut.-General Sir F. S. Roberts, who was repoted to be hard pressed at Kabul. Accordingly, on that day, the 13th Native Infantry, accompanied by the head-quarters and one squadron of the 13th Bengal Lancers, marched for Thal *viâ* Torawari. The rest of the force, however, remained halted at Sperkhwait.

To have retired hastily without attacking the enemy or bringing him to terms would have nullified the good effect which our late operations had had upon the Zaimukhts and their neighbours. Advantage was, therefore, taken of this effect, and of the fact that no Kabul news had as yet reached the enemy, to consent to listen to the overtures that the Alisherzai and Mamuzai Orakzais had that day made with a view to saving their country from attack and their villages from destruction.

Accordingly, the next day, the 20th, the force halted at Sperkhwait, and negotiations were entered into with these sections, which resulted in their agreeing to pay a fine of Rs. 4,000 each, and to furnish hostages—the Mamuzai twenty and the Alisherzai twenty-eight. The *jirgas* came into camp in the afternoon, and on these terms their submission was accepted.

On the same day the Hasan Khel section of the Zaimukhts in whose limits the force was then encamped, also surrendered in full to the terms offered them.

Their villages of Sperkhwait and Mandzakai were very strongly fortified with towers and walls, and their *jirga* was informed that two of these towers would be blown up, so as to mark the passage of a British force through their valley, and that the remainder were spared solely with a view to enable them effectually to bar in future the passage of Alisherzai and other Orakzai raiders through the Mandatti pass (of which they held the mouth) to British territory. Failure to do so would, they were further informed, inevitably lead to the complete destruction of both villages.

On the 21st the column marched to Chinarak through Tarai, Chingai, and Warmegi; several houses in the first village were burnt; and a tower at Warmegi was destroyed. The Tapai *jirga* came into camp, and accepted the terms imposed on them. The Daudzai *jirga* also this day paid their fine in full, and surrendered the arms demanded of them.

On the 22nd of December the column marched to the village of Sangroba, through the difficult and narrow defile of the same name. This village is situated at the head of the Sangroba valley in which are also the villages of Thana, Admela, and Dolragha. These four villages, together with Mandori on the Thal-Kurram road, had been subsidised for the protection of that road; but for their breach of faith in not acting up to their engagements and responsibilities a fine of Rs. 7,000 had been imposed upon them. To realize this fine, the advanced guard, under Colonel J. J. H. Gordon, C.B, moved down the valley, and surrounded the villages of Admela and Dolragha, and made them pay their share of the fine, whilst similar proceedings were taken by the main body at Sangroba and Thana. In Dolragha two men implicated in the murder of a syce of the 1st Bengal Cavalry, on the high road near Gandiaor on the 9th August 1879, were captured, and in

Sangroba one Gul Nur, who was implicated in Lieutenant Kinloch's murder (being the guide to the raiders, who came from the northern Zaimukht country), was seized.

Of the total sum of Rs. 7,000, Rs. 3,100 were at once recovered in cash, and hostages taken for the punctual payment of the balance in five days' time.

On the 23rd the expeditionary force marched to Thal, where it was broken up. Just before the column moved off from Sangroba, Gul Nur, the man above mentioned, was shot in the presence of the whole force, and the other two men were shot at Dolragha (their native village), where the usual half-way halt was made.

The results of the expedition may be considered satisfactory. The four objects, for which punitive measures against this tribe had been undertaken, had been fulfilled. The Zaimukhts had been severely punished, their country had been traversed from end to end, the villages of the notorious Wattizai section had been visited and destroyed, and several important and difficult places such as Zawo and Yasta, which had been considered impregnable, were taken. The total claim against the Zaimukht tribe, as already stated, amounted to Rs. 25,000, but to this was added a further sum of Rs. 1,100, subsequently due from the subsidised villages of the Sangroba valley, making the total fine demanded Rs. 26,100. This amount the tribe agreed to pay, and Rs. 21,100 was realised from the different sections in addition to the sum of Rs. 5,000 demanded from the tribe as a whole. They had also agreed to the surrender of 500 matchlocks and 500 swords, and had given forty-eight hostages for the fulfilment of these terms.

With regard to the second object, the Alisherzai and Mamuzai Orakzais had made their submission, and had agreed to pay a fine of Rs. 4,000 each, and to give hostages for the payment of the amount.[1] With reference to the proposed road from Torawari to Balish Khel, which was the third object of the expedition, it was found that the country over which the road would lie was extremely difficult, and that while the distance saved by following this line, as compared with the road by Thal, was no more than seven miles, it would be even more exposed to raiders than the

1 The Alisherzai fulfilled these terms, but the Mamuzai, as stated in the last chapter, subsequently refused to do so, and were accordingly placed under blockade.

latter route. Hostages had been, however, taken for its construction, if it should be considered necessary. The fourth and last object of the expedition had been fully obtained, and the Thal-Kurram road, subsequent to these operations, enjoyed an immunity from outrages which had not previously known since the beginning of the operations in Afghanistan.

Since these operations the Zaimukht tribe have given no trouble on our border.

APPENDIX A.

***Proclamation issued to the independent tribes—Afridi, Orakzai, and Wazir—on the Kohat Border, previous to the expeditionary force entering the Zaimukht country in* 1879.**

At the commencement of hostilities with His Highness the Amir of Kabul, in November 1878, the causes which had led to such hostilities, and the policy which the Government of Her Imperial Majesty the Queen-Empress of India had decided to pursue towards the people of Afghanistan and the independent tribes, were publicly announced to all the tribes on the Kohat border, agreeably to instructions received from His Excellency the Viceroy and Governor-General of India.

In this announcement they were distinctly warned that Her Majesty's Government particularly desired to maintain friendly dealings with them, to avail itself of and reciprocate their good offices, and abstain from all interference with their internal affairs or their possessions; also that, so long as they continued friendly, and in good faith held aloof from any collusion with those opposed to the British Government, they need be under no sort of apprehension regarding the advance of British troops into Afghanistan.

The warning was also added that grave consequences would speedily follow any act or attitude on the part of any tribe or tribes that might denote opposition to the movements of such troops or imply a breach of neutrality.

The various tribes—Afridi, Orakzai, and Wazir—on the Kohat border have, for the most part, wisely, hitherto appreciated the above warning, and maintained a strictly neutral attitude during the present war.

The only exception has been in the case of the Lashkarzai section of the Orakzais, and the Zaimukhts, who have committed repeated and very serious outrages for some months past, both in the Kohat and Kurram valleys, and recently aggravated their misdeeds and exhausted the patience of the Government on the 29th of September 1879, by cruelly murdering, near Chapri, Lieutenant Kinloch, of the 5th Bengal Cavalry.

Certain sections of the Zaimukhts have, moreover, broken the engagements into which they had voluntarily entered with the British Government, and to which they had pledged themselves in writing. Although they were in the receipt of allowances for the protection of the tract of territory which they inhabit, they have nevertheless themselves treacherously raided, or permitted raids to be made, upon the very parts which they were subsidised to guard.

Under these circumstances His Excellency the Viceroy and Governor-General has determined to despatch an expeditionary force against the offending tribes to punish them for their misconduct; but at the same time an assurance is hereby publicly conveyed to all the neighbouring tribes—Wazirs, Orakzais, and Afridis—that so long as they adhere to their present attitude of neutrality, and abstain from affording aid to, or otherwise co-operating with, the offending sections, they need be under no apprehension for themselves or their possession.

They are, moreover, in conclusion, specially exhorted in their own interests to pay no heed whatsoever to any report or rumour to a contrary effect which designing and malevolent persons may strive to disseminate and spread abroad.

APPENDIX B.

Genealogy of the Zaimukhts.

Clans.	Divisions.	Sub-divisions.	Sections.
MAMUZAIS or MUHAMMADZAIS or WESTERN ZAIMUKHTS.	MANATWAL ..	Sadu Khel ..	Mir Khan Khel. Karamdad Khel. Abbas Khel. Khoji Khel.
		Musa Khel ..	Talab Khel. Gohar Khel. Kadal Khel. Bash Khel. Shamshahi Khel.
		Bagzai ..	Bazu Khel. Sarwar Khel. Indu Khel. Balli Khel. Thaktai. Alambeg Khel.
	MANDANI ..	Mamad Nmasi	....
		Khurma Khel ..	....
		Razbai ..	....
		Muhsam Nmasi	....
	WATTIZAI ..	Char Khel ..	Bazid Nmasi. Hasan Khel. Tor Khel.
		Mitha Khan Khel	Muhabat Khan Nmasi. Mastu Nmasi. Mir Khan Nmasi. Shahi Khel.
	DAUDZAI ..	Isaf Khel ..	....
		Daulat Khel ..	....
		Isa Khel ..	....
		Ballu Khel ..	....
		Bostan Khel ..	....
		Bosai Khel ..	....
KHOIDAD KHELS or BAYUKS or EASTERN ZAIMUKHTS.	HASAN KHEL	Yasin Khel ..	Umar Khel. Ismail Khel. Mirak Khel.
		Khwaidad Khel	Kamal Khel. Piral Khel.
	BABAKAR KHEL	Barat Khel ..	Mamad Khel. Ali Khan Khel. Mughal Khel. Khwajawas Khel. Par Khel. Sangu Khel. Mitha Khan Khel. Kara Khan Khel.
		Ibrahim Khel	Piyas Khel. Shah Alam Khel. Madshah Khel. Bahadur Khel. Wald Khel.

CLANS.	Divisions.	Sub-divisions.	Sections.
KHOIDAD KHELS or BAYUKS or EASTERN ZAIMUKHTS.	TAPAI ..	Nazu Khel	....
		Mir Khel	....
		Ba Khel	....
	KHADU KHEL ..	Ali Khel	Umar Khel.
		Kaddam Khel ..	Kamal Khel.

CHAPTER VI.

THE TURI AND BANGASH TRIBES.

The Turis.

LITTLE is known as to the origin of the Turis, but nearly all authorities are agreed that they are not Afghans of pure descent, if Afghans at all. Lumsden says that they are of Mogul descent, whilst Edwardes and others say that they are a Hindki race, some sixty or seventy families of whom, about four or five hundred years ago, migrated from their native country in the Punjab (opposite Nilab on the Indus in the Kohat district) to the Kurram valley. The Turis themselves have two stories as to their origin, one of which is that they were formerly settled in Persia, but, troubles breaking out, Toghani Turk, the common ancestor of the Turis and Jajis, fled eastward and eventually settled at Nilab; while the other story states that they came originally from Samarkand to Nilab. Both of these stories, though differing as to the original habitat of the tribe, are agreed that the tribe claims descent from a Turk, named Toghani. The Awans of the Jhelum District, who claim descent from one Kutab Shah, a former ruler of Herat, state that the Jajis and Turis are also descended from him but by a Turki wife. Whatever may be the origin of the tribe, there is little doubt that, at some period or other, they were settled at Nilab, but probably only as nomads, migrating annually from thence to the Kurram valley. During one of their annual migrations, about five generations ago, a quarrel broke out between the tribe and the Bangash owners of Kurram. At this time the Jajis and Turis were united, and the first assault made on the Bangash took place in the Hariab valley, which the Jajis seized. From Hariab the tribe descended into the Kurram valley, the Jajis taking Jaji Maidan and the Turis the main Kurram valley below Karlachi. The first place taken by the Turis was Burkhi, then Paiwar, after which Shalozan was besieged, but the Bangash, who withstood all attacks, compromised and became Turi *hamsayas.*

Thus, by degrees, the Turis made themselves masters of the whole valley. From all accounts the Turi conquest of the valley must have occurred somewhere about the year 1700 A.D. The Emperor Babar, writing so far back as 1506 A.D., mentions the Buri (undoubtedly a misprint for Turi) inhabitants of the valley, but this probably only refers to their presence in the district as nomads, for he mentions the valley as belonging to the Bangash.

The Turis are of the Shia sect in religion and so are the Bangashes of Upper Kurram, who are so thoroughly identified with the Turis in religion and common interests that the latter have foregone all their rights and claims over them as *naiks*, and the Shia Bangash take their place with the Turis, in all matters affecting Kurram, as their equals. In the lower portion of Upper Kurram, and in Lower Kurram itself, there are a number of villages owned by the Sunni Bangashes. These have been parcelled out among the Turis, who exact from the Sunni Bangashes, not rent for land, but feudal dues, in return for which they are expected to, and till lately did, protect their Sunni Bangash clients or *hamsayas* from oppression and violence. Whatever feeling there may have been between the Turis and Shia Bangashes, arising out of the ancient conquest of Kurram by the former, has long ago completely died out, and the two bodies are thoroughly amalgamated. It is not so as regards the Turis and the Sunni Bangashes, and the hatred of the conqueror and the conquered is much accentuated by religious differences; and when, as will be seen, troubles fell upon the Turis, the Sunni Bangash treacherously assisted the surrounding Sunni tribes in their attempt to wrest Kurram from them.

It is not very clear when the Turis were, in their turn, conquered by the Afghans, but, until 1850, there was no attempt at actual occupation, the Afghans satisfying themselves with periodical expeditions every five or six years to collect the revenue, the soldiery living meanwhile on the people. In about 1850, however, both Khost and Kurram were occupied and an Afghan Governor appointed, who built a fort at Ahmadzai and maintained a strong garrison in the valley. Until the outbreak of the Afghan War, 1878-79, Kurram was ruled by a succession of Afghan Governors, and the Turis were so heavily oppressed at times that they rose in rebellion and, on one occasion, assaulted the Durani camp and slew 500 men.

Like all Eastern Pathans the Turis are intensely democratic, no man can bear to see another in authority over him, and they are eaten up by private, family, village, or clan feuds and factions. A further disturbing element, utterly destructive of tribal combination, is introduced by the peculiar institution of *pir muridi* which is rampant in Kurram. Every Turi conceives himself bound to be the spiritual disciple of some *saiyid* or other, and, in the course of time, four great families of *saiyids* have practically monopolized all the Turis and Shia Bangashes as their disciples. A *murid* (disciple) is supposed to, and generally does, follow the dictates of a *pir* (spiritual guide).

The four great families of *saiyids* are :—

(*a*) of Tirah
(*b*) of Ahmadzai }
(*c*) of Kirman } in Kurram.
(*d*) of Maora }

The lay followers of the Tirah *Saiyids*, (*a*), compose the Mian Murid faction in Kurram. The other three great families (*b*), (*c*), and (*d*) compose the Drewandi faction and are all of them opposed to (*a*), but are ever caballing and quarrelling among themselves, each to increase its own personal following of disciples. The consequence is that the Mian Murid faction, though numerically weaker, is more united and, therefore, stronger than the Drewandi faction, which, though stronger in numbers, unites only for common action under considerable pressure. Lastly, the heads of the Mian Murid faction, being really residents of Tirah, do not care much who governs Kurram, so long as their personal following flourishes and increases. The Drewandi leaders, on the other hand, may be said to be slightly more national and Turi, as it were, in their attitude. All this mass of Pathan and spiritual faction feeling was thoroughly, for their own purposes, exploited by the Afghan Governors, who played off man against man, family against family, clan against clan, and *saiyid* against *saiyid*, till the whole valley was a seething hotbed of intrigue, and the Túris were corroded to the core with party spirit. This ended in a universal detestation of Afghan rule. On the outbreak of the Second Afghan War the advance of the British forces in the Kurram valley was hailed with delight by the Turis, and throughout the campaign their attitude towards us remained consistently friendly. Prior to the withdrawal of our troops from the valley in 1880 they made a formal petition to Government in which they asked that they should be regarded as totally independent of Kabul, and prayed for the recognition by Government of two men, Muhammad Nur Khan, head of the Mian Murid faction, and Saiyid Badshah Gul, head of the Drewandi faction, whom they had chosen as their leaders and under whom they proposed certain arrangements for the future administration of the valley, including the raising and maintenance of a tribal corps, 600 strong, for the protection of their country. In reply Government consented to recognise their independence of Kabul, and further stated that the Turis would be left free to make their own arrangements for the management of the valley, and would not be interfered with by us.

For a short time all went well under the tribal administration thus inaugurated. It was not long, however, before faction fighting amongst the Turis themselves broke out on an extensive scale, and a long period of total anarchy ensued in Kurram. The Sunni tribes, by whom the Turis are completely surrounded, and the Afghans also, sought to take advantage of this state of things and to oust them from their rich lands in the Kurram valley.

It was during this period that the notorions Zaimukht free-booter, Sarwar Khan, nick-named Chikai, made for himself the great name as a leader which he maintained till his death in 1903. Originally of obscure birth this man had already raised himself to the position of a local "Rob Roy" on this part of the frontier. He was summoned to Kabul, and, on his return, organized the campaign of the Sunnis against the Turi Shias. In this he was clever enough to take full advantage of the hatred existing between the two great factions into which, as already described, the Turis are divided. With the treacherous aid of their Sunni Bangash *hamsayas* the Drewandi Turis were ousted from Lower Kurram in 1891, the Mian Murid Turis looking on. The Sunnis then suddenly turned on the Mian Murids and ousted them also, thus making themselves masters of all Kurram between Sadda and Thal.

Happily for the Turis we decided to go to their assistance, and Mr. Merk was deputed to bring about a settlement, and thus it occurred that the Kurram valley was occupied by us in October

1892. Immediately before our advance the Sunni conquerors of Lower Kurram were ordered to leave the valley, and this they did without it being necessary to exert any pressure. We then appeared on the scene as impartial and irresistible peace-makers, restoring to each man his ancestral possessions and status, which he enjoyed before the struggle began. On account, however, of their undoubted treachery, it was decided that the Bangashes should make public submission to the Turis, which they did.

The Mian Murid and Drewandi are sometimes called the Ting Gundi (of firm faction) and the Sust Gundi (or lax faction), respectively; and in addition to these two religious factions there are two other political parties called the Thor Gundi and Spin Gundi.

The Turis are a bold, reckless, and vigorous race, still conscious of their conquest of Kurram from the Bangashes, proud of the fact, and inspired thereby to hold their heads high. It is true that they nearly lost Kurram at one time, but the combination against them was too strong, and it is an accepted fact that against any single tribe in the neighbourhood of Kurram they can fully hold their own and have always done so.

The tribe is now controlled by a political officer; the valley is to all intents and purposes British territory; and in the Turis we possess a true and loyal race with a country which has great strategical advantages.

The Turis helped us against the Zaimukhts in 1879, stood to us in the 1897 disturbances, and were foremost in Captain Roos-Keppel's raid against the Chamkannis in 1899.

The Bangash.

The Bangash are a tribe of Pathans, who inhabit the Miranzai valley, the valley of Kohat in British territory, and also the valley of Kurram. The name is said to be derived from 'ban' a root, and 'kashtan,' to tear up, meaning that the Bangash were such thorough-going radicals that they exterminated, or tore up by the roots, all who interfered with their interests or possessed what they coveted.

The Bangash are said to have come originally from Gardez, in the Ghilzai country, from which they were driven out by the Ghilzais about five hundred years ago. They then settled in Kurram, where they remained for another hundred years, when a feud with the Orakzais broke out. With the aid of the Khattaks the Orakzais were dispossessed of Kohat; and though there was much fighting afterwards, they were never able to regain their territory; and it was settled that the boundary of the Bangash should be limited by the foot of the Orakzai hills.

Another story is that they came from Seistan, and are of the same race as the Jats; but this is improbable.

The Bangash formerly owned the whole of Kurram. The Emperor Babar (1504) enumerates this tribe as inhabiting one of the fourteen provinces then dependent on Kabul, so that their settlement is of very ancient date. The valley was then known as the Darra-i-Bangesh.

Their country was formerly divided into Bangash Ulia or Bala, and Bangash Siflia or Pain. The former, which is now more the property of the Turis than the Bangash, extends from the Paiwar pass to Biland Khel, and the latter extends from Biland Khel to Gandiali, east of Kohat.

About four hundred years ago the Turis first began to take root in Bangash-i-Bala. Little by little they gradually dispossessed the Bangash, until these said they had only Shalozan and Ziran under the hills and Aza Khel in the plains that were free; the rest belonged to the Turis, by whom they were at first reduced to the condition of dependents. Latterly, however, the Bangash of Upper Kurram have become entirely identified with the Turis and are regarded as in all respects the equals of the latter.

It is said that in Mazandaran, in Persia, there are some families of Bangash, and it is well known that the descendants of this tribe exist to this day in various parts of Hindustan, especially Farakhabad, the old Nawab of which was descended from one. His conduct during the mutiny of 1857 was most atrocious, and he expiated his treachery on the scaffold.

The three main recognised divisions of the tribe now are—(*i*) Miranzai; (*ii*) Baizai; (*iii*) Samalzai.

The Miranzai section are divided into—(1) the *Bada Khel*, who at the first distribution of land had 500 shares, took up their quarters in Nariab, Upper Miranzai, and split into two sections, Yusaf Khel and Kha Khel, who gradually occupied the villages of Kai, Sarozai, Doaba, Torawari, Thal, Chapri, and Shinawari beyond the border; (2) the *Hasazai*, who had 500 shares, and resided in Raisan, Ibrahimzai, Bazar, Jabar, and Bakar Mela.

The *Umar Khel*, who are now reckoned in the Miranzai section, received 1,000 shares, and were sub-divided into (*i*) *Mir Ahmad Khel*, with 500 shares, inhabiting Baliamin, Togh Bar, and Kotkai; and (*ii*) *Alisherzai*, who live in Hangu and Aza Khel (in Kurram) Shahu Khel, and Lohi Khel.

(*ii*) The Baizai section inhabit the Kohat valley proper, and inhabit Kohat, Chikar Kot, Tapi Miroz, Mia, Kaloch, and Gidar Kot; Togh, Gandiali, Siah Kot, Siagal, and Kamardand; Kamal Khel, Mandu Khel, Daud Khel, Shadi Khel, Dhoda and Oada Khel. Besides these, the Jamshedi section occupy Darsamand and Daland.

(*iii*) The Samalzai live in the wild jungle district of the same name, and are divided into (1) Ilam Khel, who live in Shalozan (in Kurram), Yusafi, Chardeh, Ziran (in Kurram), Agra, Sultan, Haji Kirman; (2) Hasan Khel; (3) Landi Khel; (4) Maiwai, who have the hamlets of Ustarzai, Alizai, Khadizai, Sherkot; (5) Kaghazi, residing in the village of the same name.

The Bangash are nearly all of the Shia persuasion of the Muhammadan faith, and are Gar in politics. Aga Abbas, a Persian, mentions that he had often met Bangashes performing the pilgrimage to Meshed. Their great saint is one Madat Shah, whom they appear to hold in extraordinary reverence.

Muhammad Hyat says they are a brave and warlike race, but this opinion differs from that of most English officers, who have but little opinion of their courage. They are said to be very hospitable. They wear white clothes with a Hangu lungi, and sandals on their feet. As far as physique is concerned, they are quite as fine men as the Pathans round them, excepting perhaps the Afridis. The western Bangash are known from the eastern by their long beards, the latter clipping them short.

During the Kohat pass difficulties of 1853 the Bangash came forward and asserted their right to the crest of the *kotal* as a part of their ancient boundaries.[1] They stated that in olden times they had received an allowance from the Muhammadan emperors, and had viewed the usurpation of Rahmat Khan, Orakzai (he being the chief of a distant clan), as an injury and loss, and they, therefore, asked to be allowed to undertake the responsibility of that portion of the pass from the Kohat side to the top of the *kotal* on the same

[1] See Chapter III.

emoluments as were enjoyed by Rahmat Khan. Their offer was accepted, and they occupied the *kotal* in strength, and commenced building breastworks and towers of loose stones. On the second day the Afridis, who had been attentively observing the arrangements, suddenly made an attack with 700 or 800 men from their own side, where the ridge is not very precipitous. They completely surprised the Bangash, and drove them off the crest. In this affair several *maliks* of the Bangash were killed, and Captain Coke, who was present with four orderlies, was slightly wounded. After this the Bangash, by Captain Coke's consent, entered into a confederation with the Jawaki Afridis, the Sipahs, and Bizotis, the consequence of which was that the Afridi opposition died out, and an arrangement was come to, by which the Bangash share of the pass emoluments was settled at Rs. 3,200; and this they have retained ever since.

The Bangash have suffered a good deal at different times from the raids of their neighbours—the Orakzais, Turis, and Wazirs. Generally speaking, they have behaved well towards the British Government; but without wishing to disparage them, it cannot be said that we owe them much gratitude for this, as surrounded by enemies their only chance has been to keep in with us, their villages being quite open to attack. Yet they have failed us sometimes, as, for instance, when they deserted Coke on the Kohat *kotal*, and when Bahadur Sher, urged by consciousness of evil intentions, retreated over the border in 1851.

Expedition to Miranzai, by a force under Captain J. Coke in 1851.

During the time of the Sikh rule, Miranzai remained under the Governor of Kohat, but much interference was not attempted.

On the annexation of the Punjab, being an outlying territory, it was overlooked when the rest of Kohat was taken possession of. The Kabul Government accordingly made arrangements to occupy Miranzai, and in 1851 the Amir's son, Sirdar Muhammad Azim, who was then Governor of Kurram, sent some cavalry to occupy the villages of Biland Khel, Thal, and Torawari. The people of Miranzai thereupon appealed to the British Government, and made a petition that their country might be included in

British territory, offering to pay Rs. 7,500 to the Government as revenue.

Their request was acceded to, and in August 1851 a proclamation was issued declaring Miranzai to be a portion of the Kohat district, and at the same time orders were sent to each village that, in case of attack, they were to aid each other with all their disposable men, as they were quite able to protect themselves from any Wazir or Orakzai inroads, the village of Kai having, in 1848, successfully resisted for three months the attacks of 8,000 Wazirs.

The proclamation also stated that anyone exercising authority, except by order of the Deputy Commissioner of Kohat, would be punished, and that all foreign troops must at once be withdrawn, or they would be ejected.

At the same time Captain Coke, commanding the 1st Punjab Infantry and also Deputy Commissioner of Kohat, addressed a letter to Sirdar Muhammad Azim, requesting him to withdraw his troopers from the Miranzai villages. The *Sirdar* replied with scant courtesy and scarcely veiled threats, advising Captain Coke that the occupation of Miranzai was not worth the while of his Government; the revenue was small, and the difficulties great; that complications with the hill people would arise, and that they would make a religious war on us, which he would not be able to stop. At the same time there is no doubt that Muhammad Azim did all in his power to bring about the very complications against which he warned the Government. On receipt of this communication, Captain Coke earnestly begged for permission to move a force into Upper Miranzai before the *Sirdar's* intrigues had brought down the Wazirs and Zaimukhts on the Bangash villages. This was all the more necessary, as the Wazirs were reported at the end of September to have collected near Biland Khel for the purpose of attacking Darsamand; and although their advance had been checked by Khwaja Muhammad Khan, the Khattak chief, who had assembled his people for the purpose, it became advisable to move troops into the valley, not only for the dispersion of the Wazirs, but to enable the Deputy Commissioner to make a circuit of this part of his district, to settle the revenue, and to arrange a system of defence amongst the villagers, who were, many of them, at feud with each other.

Permission having been granted, Captain J. Coke, with the force as per margin, marched from Kohat to Hangu on the 14th of October 1851. The 1st Punjab Cavalry was commanded by Lieutenant H. Daly; the Artillery was under Lieutenant J. R. Sladen; and Captain Coke himself commanded the 1st Punjab Infantry.

No. 1 Punjab Light Field Battery (3 guns).
1st Punjab Cavalry.
Half company, Sappers and Miners.
1st Punjab Infantry.

From Hangu the force proceeded to Kai, Nariab, Torawari, and Darsamand, having been joined by a body of levies (145 horse and 510 foot) under Khwaja Muhammad Khan. Up to the last place the troops had been well received, and not a shot had been fired. From there the column proceeded to Thal. On arriving at this place there was some firing at the picquets; and at Biland Khel, where the column was halted from the 26th to the 30th, this increased considerably, and was continued nightly. On the night of the 30th intelligence was brought in of the Wazirs being assembled in force, and during that night there was a sharp attack on the picquets, especially on that held by Khwaja Muhammad Khan's Khattaks; but as the picquets were placed at a great distance from camp, and were protected by a breastwork, the attacks were repulsed without loss. In these night attacks there was no doubt the villagers of Biland Khel took part with the enemy, but Captain Coke did not attach much importance to this, as he considered the village to be entirely in the hands of the Wazirs, who from time to time, during a space of fifty years, by purchase or mortgage, had possessed themselves of a greater portion of their lands.

On the return of the column to Thal on the 31st, attacks were again made on the picquets at night, but with more spirit than before.

There was no doubt that the villagers here also were implicated in these attacks, and Captain Coke, therefore, told the headmen, and especially Hazrat Nur, a *saiyid* of much influence in this village, that if they were repeated, he would burn the village; after which intimation the attacks ceased.

On the 2nd of November the force returned to Darsamand. Captain Coke then assembled all the headmen of Miranzai, and explained to them the Government intentions, and called on the three most powerful villages to give two hostages each for their good behaviour. He also had a paper drawn up and signed by the whole of the villages, with the exception of Thal and Biland Khel, which he did not think it desirable to include in this arrangement, because, till something definite was settled about Biland Khel, it would have been useless to call on them to attempt to throw off the Wazir yoke, and Thal was able, with the aid of the Turis, to defend itself against any attack of the Wazirs. Two hostages were, therefore, taken from Nariab, Darsamand, and Torawari.

The force returned to Kohat on the 11th of November, after much hard work and unpleasant night duty. The casualties during these operations were one sepoy killed and one sepoy severely wounded, both belonging to the 1st Punjab Infantry.

Expedition to Miranzai, by a force under Brigadier N. B. Chamberlain, in 1855.

Although the people of Miranzai had petitioned to be included in the Kohat district, they were, in their hearts, hostile to the British Government, as, indeed, they were to any Government whatever. Thus, after the return of the force under Captain Coke in 1851, Miranzai was as unsettled as ever, no revenue was paid, and the frontier continued in a most unsatisfactory state.

Darsamand was constantly being threatened by Wazirs, and the Turis committed several serious raids against the Khattak villages on the Miranzai border. This state of affairs induced Captain Coke to recommend that he should be permitted, in the cold weather of 1852, to proceed with a force to Miranzai, and erect a post in some suitable position, so as to check these raids; but the Commissioner, for various reasons, was averse to the measure, and matters were allowed to continue in the same state.

During March 1855 it was arranged that the village of Biland Khel should be made over to the Kabul Government, and the Kurram river should in future be the British boundary. Major J. Coke was much opposed to this transfer, and protested against it, on the ground that it would not fall to the Kurram authorities but to the Kabul Khel Wazirs, who would thus gain for themselves a secure base for carrying on further depredations amongst the Miranzai and Khattak villages.

Meanwhile, it was reported that no revenue had been paid by certain villages for three years; that two of the largest of the Hangu villages on the Miranzai border had betaken themselves to arms for the settlement of a dispute arising out of some ordinary judicial proceedings of the criminal court at Kohat; and that the *maliks*, when summoned to answer for the affray, had refused to obey the order of the Deputy Commissioner, going off instead to Miranzai and Kurram. The Deputy Commissioner said that the valley was fast becoming the asylum of all the robbers and murderers of the Kohat and adjoining districts, who looked upon it as a place the Government were either afraid or unable to control; that the Wazir, Turi, Zaimukht, and Orakzai tribes, joined with the villages of Miranzai, had made that valley a rendezvous, from which they could assemble to plunder all the well-disposed villages on the Hangu and Khattak frontier; and that, owing to the distance of Kohat from the Turis and others, pursuit was unavailing. At the same time, the moment the people of Miranzai were threatened from without, they were loud in their call for aid, urging absurd reasons for their past misconduct. It was, therefore, decided by the Government of India that an expedition should be sent to enforce the submission of the Miranzai villages.

To subjugate such a people two courses were open—either to march in and punish them by force of arms, without asking any questions, or first to offer them the alternative of giving full and reasonable satisfaction. The Commissioner, Major H. B. Edwardes, C.B., did not think the former would be just, because these people had been less accustomed to the requisitions of a regular Government than almost any other tribe on the frontier. It had never been their habit to pay tribute annually. They used to be left entirely alone for several years, and then a Barakzai *Sirdar* would come from Kohat with a force, and exact all he could by violence and plunder. It therefore seemed unreasonable to expect them all at once to pay regularly and behave well; and as a matter of policy, it was unwise to weaken our own subjects. The rich plain of Upper Miranzai had already been encroached on by hungry mountain tribes; and to level a village, or decimate its fighting men, would be only to let in a new stream of enemies from the hills. We desired to interfere in Miranzai as little as possible, and to keep it as a barrier on our frontier. Our policy, therefore, was not to weaken it, but to keep it strong. For these reasons it was determined to give the people every opportunity of satisfying the demands of Government without using force.

The marginally named force, under the command of Brigadier N. B. Chamberlain, and accompanied by Major H. B. Edwardes, C.B., marched from Kohat on the 4th, and arrived at Togh on the 7th, of April 1855. The headmen of all the villages were formally summoned to come in to Togh, which is a few miles only from the border of Upper Miranzai. In the course of two days they all presented themselves, except the *maliks* of Torawari, which was supposed to indicate that the Zaimukht interlopers, who had settled in that village, were the least inclined to be dictated to. On the 11th the troops moved to Kai, where a halt of five days was made. Immediately on arrival at Kai the Brigadier reconnoitred the village.

No. 1 Punjab Light Field Battery (3 guns).
No. 3 Punjab Light Field Battery (6 guns).
4th Punjab Cavalry.
Detachment, Sappers and Miners.
Wing, 66th Gurkhas.
1st Punjab Infantry.
3rd Punjab Infantry.
Sind Rifle Corps.[1]

The men turned out and stood on their houses during the reconnaissance, and conversed in a very independent tone when spoken to; but no collision took place. In the evening the missing *maliks* of Torawari also came in, and in full durbar all the chiefs of the valley were informed of the respective quotas of revenue which every village would have to pay, that the arrears of the last three years would be rigidly exacted, and that fines would also be levied for every criminal offence that stood against them.

The revenue of Upper Miranzai was fixed at Rs. 6,300, of which Rs. 4,860 was to be expended in maintaining a body of horse, consisting of one jemadar and fifteen sowars, and in good service money to the leading men of the valley. These terms were submitted to with the air of men who would have resisted if they could, and they then dispersed to their several villages to make arrangements.

It appeared that the Torawari men had sent emissaries to the camp at Togh to see the strength of the force, and that the report being "just a little too much," the *maliks* had come in. One of the *maliks* of Kai, in a friendly chat with Brigadier Chamberlain, went further, and said to him—"We could manage this force, but we don't know what is behind."

The strictest discipline was enforced in camp, and no plundering of any kind was allowed. Everything required was fairly bought

1 Now the 59th Sind Rifles (Frontier Force)

and paid for, and the people, seeing themselves protected, instead of robbed (as they had always been by the Barakzais), soon took confidence, and old men, women, and children might be seen bringing wood into camp to sell, and fearlessly bargaining with the soldiers. On two successive nights a few shots were fired at the advanced cavalry picquets; the villagers were suspected, and on being warned by the Deputy Commissioner that the village would be fired if the practice was continued, it at once ceased.

Arriving at Nariab on the 17th the troops were halted there till the 27th. The picquets were fired on nightly, but with a worse result to the enemy than to the troops, as the latter were protected by breastworks, while of the former, the son of a Zaimukht *malik* was mortally wounded, besides other losses.

On the 28th the troops marched to Darsamand, *viâ* Torawari, that the defences of that place might be examined. The camp was pitched as far from the hills and broken ground as possible; and, being well protected by picquets in *sangars*, it was not annoyed at night.

On the evening of the 29th April some 4,000 *ghazis*, belonging chiefly to the Zaimukht, Orakzai, and Afridi tribes, assembled on the hills in rear of Darsamand and to the front of the camp. At 10 A.M. on the 30th they descended from the main range, and, to the number of about 1,500, occupied a small ridge of hills which rose immediately behind Darsamand, and which was only separated from the high range in its rear by a very narrow glen; there they remained for some time, firing their guns, and beating drums. Finding that the troops remained inactive, they became bolder, and some few of them began to descend into the more open ground, and advance towards the cavalry picquet. This being seen, Captain G. O. Jacob was instructed to have a party of cavalry in readiness to cut them off whenever they should advance sufficiently far from the hill; and between one and two o'clock the opportunity was afforded.

A portion of the enemy were seen approaching the front cavalry picquet through the jungle, and Captain C. R. Fraser, 4th Punjab Cavalry, advanced with thirty-five sabres to cut them off. As the enemy opened fire on the picquet, Captain Fraser, whose detachment was reinforced by the fifteen sabres of which the picquet consisted, charged them in a very gallant manner, under a heavy fire from the hills. He was immediately joined by a few Pathan horse, belonging to the Khattak chief, led by Major J. Coke, these being shortly followed by thirty sabres, 4th Punjab Cavalry, under Captain G. O. Jacob.

The enemy attempted to regain the hill, whilst their brethren, who were in large numbers on the hillside, opened fire to protect their retreat.

In the meanwhile, Lieutenant E. J. Travers, of the 1st Punjab Infantry, who was on picquet duty with a company of his regiment, advanced to the support of the cavalry, and immediately attacked the enemy on the hill. During this time a body of 50 dismounted men of the 4th Punjab Cavalry, from a breastwork, and 250 of the 1st Punjab Infantry from the camp, were advancing to the assistance of the other parties, and, on their being united, they soon drove the enemy from every point, with the loss of twelve or fifteen left on the ground, in addition to any killed or wounded who were carried away. Our loss was small, consisting of fourteen wounded.

The enemy were so completely routed and panic-stricken that at dark not a flag, or man, or watch-fire was visible.

Up to this time it had been the boast of these hill tribes that, were it not for our guns, we could never oppose them; and, therefore, not the least advantage of this engagement was their having been made to experience the falsity of this assertion. Other hill tribes were assembling and sending their quotas, but the ignominious defeat of the first body at once put a stop to any further exhibitions of fanaticism.

On the 6th of May the troops were moved to Thal, where a halt was made till the 17th, to enable a settlement to be made with the Turis and the Wazirs.

The settlement with these tribes having been satisfactorily accomplished, on the 17th the force started on its return to Kohat, where it arrived on the 21st, and was then broken up.

The Indian Medal, with a clasp for the "North-West Frontier" was granted in 1869 to all survivors of the troops engaged in the above operations.

Expedition to Miranzai and Kurram, by a force under Brigadier N. B. Chamberlain, in 1856.

The expedition into the Miranzai valley in 1855 had been attended by the best effects; but, subsequently, Darsamand, one of the largest of the villages, withheld the land revenue due from it. Numerous raids were also committed on our Khattak, Bangash, and Wazir subjects, resident in the valley, by the Turis, whom the Kabul Government were unable to control; and these incursions were abetted by the Zaimukht tribe.

The Turis, on the first annexation of the Kohat district, had given much trouble. They had repeatedly leagued with other tribes to harass the Miranzai valley, harbouring fugitives, encouraging all to resist, and frequently attacking Bangash and Khattak villages in the Kohat district.

In August 1853 Captain J. Coke moved from Bahadur Khel with 100 bayonets, 1st Punjab Infantry, and 45 sabres, 1st Punjab Cavalry, to seize a large armed Turi caravan. Pushing on with the cavalry, after a march of forty miles, the convoy was sighted, and after some resistance, in which one of them was killed and one wounded, thirty-seven Turis with all their property were captured, their goods being taken as security for the repayment of the value of the plundered property, and the men as hostages for their tribe. This measure was soon followed by an embassy from the tribe, petitioning the restoration of the caravan, and promising to abstain from further raids on British territory. An agreement was then concluded with the tribe, dating from the beginning of 1854. The value of plundered property was made good, the prisoners were released, and five Turis were made over to the British as hostages.

Within one month, however, the tribe again gave way to evil counsels, and in the following March (1854) a serious attack was made by the Turis with 2,000 men (horse and foot) on a Miranzai village; lives were lost on both sides, and the Turi hostages were then incarcerated in the Lahore jail.

This instance of misconduct was followed by other raids. In the autumn of 1854, when the expedition against the refractory British villages of Miranzai was proposed, it was under consideration whether the opportunity should not be taken of punishing the Turis; but as they were subjects of Kabul, and negotiations with the Amir were shortly expected, the Government decided on first arranging with the latter on the subject.

During the negotiations for the treaty at Peshawar in March 1854, it was explained to the Afghan representative that either the

Kabul Government must restrain the Turis from incursions into British territory, or else the British Government itself would undertake to chastise them. As a result it was resolved that another trial should be given to the tribe before further measures were taken, as the Kabul Government promised to control them. During the expedition to Miranzai in 1855, the Turis, having seen that display of force, desired to make peace with us, and, as already stated, a settlement was effected with them at Thal, and their men were then released from confinement. These measures, however, had not the desired effect, and the Turis continued their raids.

With regard to the Zaimukhts, their object had long been to encroach on the valley of Miranzai, in which they had already acquired the village of Torawari. It was, therefore, determined tc send a force to punish the Turis, to compel an understanding with the Zaimukhts, and to make an example of the refractory village of Darsamand. Previous to the advance of the force, however, the recusant village paid up its revenue, together with the fine of Rs. 1,000 imposed.

As regards the time of year for the operations, the Deputy Commissioner, Captain B. Henderson, remarked that it would then (in the autumn) be fine and settled weather; that forage would be abundant, water plentiful, and the Kurram river at its lowest; and that, moreover, it was very advisable that the Miranzai valley should be visited at as early a date as possible.

Accordingly, the marginally noted force, under the command of Brigadier N. B. Chamberlain, consisting of 4,896 men of all ranks, with fourteen guns, was ordered to assemble at Kohat. The Deputy Commissioner of Kohat was to be informed of the daily requirements of each regiment or corps, and he was directed to collect supplies for the force, and to arrange for forage, etc., along the line of route; and if firewood was scarce in any parts of the country, to have supplies of it stacked at the nearest possible places.

Detachment, Peshawar Mountain Train Battery.
Detachment, No. 1 Punjab Light Field Battery.
No. 3 Punjab Light Field Battery.
Detachment, 1st Punjab Cavalry.
4th Punjab Cavalry.
2nd Company, Sappers and Miners.
66th Gurkha Regiment.
1st Punjab Infantry.
2nd " "
3rd " "
5th " "
6th " "
Khattak levies.

On the 21st of October 1856 the force marched from Kohat towards Hangu, where it arrived on the following day. On the

23rd the march was continued to Togh, and on the 24th the column arrived at Kai, the border village of Upper and Lower Miranzai.

A great difference was perceptible in the feeling of the people. In 1855 the walls and houses had been covered with armed men; now all was quiet, no notice was taken of the arrival of the troops, and the men and women of the villages pursued their usual avocations. They had already paid their revenue, and, having defied no orders, seemed perfectly to understand that they were safe, though 5,000 soldiers were encamped under their walls. Nothing had tended more to create this confidence than the strict discipline maintained by Brigadier Chamberlain.

At Kai the Deputy Commissioner had received intelligence that a large number of Miranzai criminals had taken refuge in Torawari, which was inhabited by Zaimukht settlers from the hills north-west of Miranzai. In the expedition of 1855 greater consideration had been shown to Torawari than to any of the other villages, through the good offices of Khwaja Muhammad Khan, the chief of the Khattaks, who to gain the friendship of the Zaimukht clan, went so far as to himself pay most of the Torawari revenue. In consequence of this prompt payment, the force had then no occasion to encamp at Torawari, even for a single day. But, as usual, mild treatment was attributed to weakness, and not only the Zaimukhts, but their Bangash neighbours, came to regard Torawari as an impregnable fortress; hence, every run-away scoundrel in the valley, as our force again approached, sought and received asylum in this redoubtable Zaimukht village.

It was, therefore, decided to surprise the village, and, with this purpose, orders were issued for the usual march to Nariab on the following morning.

The Nariab road was reconnoitred by the engineer officers, and improved by the sappers, and the ground at Nariab was selected for the camp. An hour before the appointed time the morning bugle sounded. From Kai to Torawari is about nine miles, and for half the distance the road is the same as that to Nariab. Up to this point the whole force proceeded leisurely, and none but commanding officers knew what was going to happen. At length, however, the troops broke into two columns, one keeping the road to Nariab, and the other striking off to Torawari. When within four miles of the place, and as day was breaking, the cavalry pushed on in two bodies; the broken nature of the ground prevented any rapid movements, but, by keeping a tolerably wide circle, they succeeded in surrounding the place before the inhabitants had any warning, and the Zaimukhts and their guests awoke to find themselves caught in a net.

So entirely helpless were these boasters now, that not a sign of resistance was made. The headmen were summoned from the village to hear the terms dictated to them, but, after two hours' negotiations, nothing could be settled, and they were sent back with the intimation that they must either surrender the criminals known to be harboured by them, pay a fine for previous misconduct, and give security for future good behaviour, or stand the consequences.

Meanwhile the Peshawar Mountain Train Battery and the 6th Punjab Infantry came up, shortly followed by the mountain guns of No. 1 Punjab Light Field Battery, and the 1st and 2nd Punjab Infantry; these were all placed in position, ready to act if required.

Half an hour had been allowed to the *maliks* for the surrender of the criminals, but this time expired without any sign of compliance on their part. A further quarter of an hour was granted, to enable them to send out their women and children; and during this period every endeavour was made to induce them to place their families in security, but with no effect. The time having expired, the guns were opened with blank cartridge, in the hope of intimidating the inhabitants, but without success.

At length shells were thrown into the village, and, after about thirty rounds, the women were seen running towards our position, waving clothes and holding up the *Koran*.

The fire of the guns was instantly stopped, and the women were sent back to tell the men that they must now come out and surrender, or the batteries would reopen. Slowly and angrily they came out and threw down their arms, but only by twos and threes; and still there was no sign of giving up the criminals. The 1st and 2nd Punjab Infantry were therefore ordered into the village to search for refugees. At length the stacks of winter fodder for the cattle were fired, and, the wind carrying the flames from house to house, the criminals were eventually brought out. The troops were then recalled from the village, and the inhabitants allowed to extinguish the flames, which had destroyed about one-third of their houses.

The arms that had been surrendered, and the thirteen criminals who had been captured, were all sent off to our camp at Nariab; and 100 hostages, with 200 or 300 head of cattle, were also carried away as security till a fine of Rs. 2,000 should be paid for the long-standing scores of Torawari.

Two or three lives only had been lost on the side of the villagers, and on our side two sepoys had been wounded in the village. The troops reached camp about two o'clock, no one attempting to molest them during their retirement. The force halted at Nariab from the 25th of October to the 4th of November, when it marched to Darsamand, and on the 5th to Thal.

As Ghulam Jan, the Deputy Governor of Kurram, had, notwithstanding orders received from Kabul, failed in securing the attendance of the headmen of the Turis, orders were issued for the force to advance from Thal.

On the 6th and 7th the troops were employed in entrenching a position on the left bank of the Kurram, and about 600 men were left to hold this and to protect the sick and all baggage which was not absolutely necessary to the force on its onward march.

On the 8th of November the force crossed the Kurram, and marched up its banks for ten miles, where it encamped for the night; neither a village nor a man was seen throughout the march; and for the whole distance the hills bounded the river on both sides.

The following day the march was continued to Hazar Pir Ziarat, fifteen miles, a rather difficult and tedious one for the guns and baggage, and it was nearly sunset before the rear-guard reached camp. The road was either on the banks or along the bed of the river. The Kurram valley and the Turi lands were entered immediately on leaving the encamping ground, when the valley increased in breadth, villages were numerous, and the whole country bore signs of careful cultivation. No resistance had been offered to the advance of the force, and the column was met by a representative of the Kabul authorities, and also by the principal Turi and Bangash *maliks*.

As it was desirable that the settlement with the Turis should take place near the fort (occupied by the Kabul *Sirdar* when in the valley, and at that time by his deputy), and as the opportunity for seeing and surveying the country was a favourable one, it was decided that the advance should be continued.

From Hazar Pir to the *Sirdar's* fort there are two roads, one being up the bed of the river and past numerous villages, the other by the Darwazagai pass ; the latter was said to be the more practicable, and was adopted. The troops, therefore, continued their march on the 10th, passing through narrow valleys, covered with high grass, but destitute of any signs of man ; although later in the year these lands are occupied by migratory tribes, who return to their hills on the approach of summer. The camp was pitched at the mouth of the Darwazagai defile, about eleven miles from Hazar Pir Ziarat.

The following day the column proceeded through the Darwazagai, and the camp was pitched, after a march of twelve miles, on the right bank of the Kurram, about one mile and a quarter from the fort, on the opposite side of the river. The defile was about eight miles in length, and, although large working-parties were employed to improve the road, and a regiment of infantry was detailed to assist the guns of No. 3 Punjab Light Field Battery, the axles of two of the four pieces gave way, and it was sunset before the battery was in camp.

For the first six miles the pass was so narrow that it was commanded by hills at matchlock range from both sides. The chief difficulties of the road were found in the first three miles. The *nala* draining the pass had frequently to be crossed, the ascents and descents being occasionally steep and rocky. In one place the path had been cut away by torrents, and there was a perpendicular drop of twenty feet into the *nala*. The hill above was very difficult to work in—rocky, covered with stunted palm bushes, and of a steep slope, and a road had to be made for the passage of the artillery.

The Kurram fort was found to be situated in the widest part of the valley, which was there about twelve miles broad ; the cultivated portion extending for about a mile on either side of the river. The villages were thickly clustered, and situated on these cultivated strips of land, with the exception of a few built at the gorges in the hills where there were springs.

Up to this time not a single shot had been fired into the camp. At Hazar Pir the headmen had been warned by the Brigadier that he would not submit to the indignity of being annoyed at night, and that if his picquets were fired into, every village in the neighbourhood of the camp would be destroyed.

The force was halted near the fort from the 11th to the 23rd of November. There was some difficulty about grazing for the camels, the nearest ground being in the Darwazagai, six or seven miles from the camp. As supplies were running short, little having been brought in by the people of the country, foraging parties had to be sent out with cattle and money, and a compulsory sale enforced in the neighbouring villages; but, although the operation was a tedious one, going from house to house to fill up the bags, no difficulty was experienced by the troops employed, and after a day or two the people of the country began to bring grain into the camp. A strong detachment of Khwaja Muhammad's horsemen was also sent back to Thal to bring up supplies, this detachment taking only two marches in reaching the camp from Thal.

The Turis, who at first intended to refuse compliance with our demands, hoping they would induce the surrounding tribes to unite against us, very soon changed their language and policy; and our claims against them having been amicably arranged, the 21st was spent by the Brigadier and the Commissioner, and other officers, in visiting the Paiwar pass. On the first arrival of the force in the valley, the Commissioner had mentioned to the Deputy Governor and headmen his intention of doing this; but as further notice might have led to difficulties, the determination was only made known to the Paiwar *maliks*, who were in camp, late on the night of the 20th, when they were warned to accompany the party. The escort consisted of 200 cavalry. The party left camp shortly after 3 A.M. on the morning of the 21st, and reached the village of Paiwar about 7-30 A.M. To the foot of the pass took another hour and twenty minutes, and its actual ascent a quarter of an hour more; the party then descended on the Kabul side, and after a ride of half an hour a halt was made, to enable Lieutenants A. W. Garnett and P. S. Lumsden to make a sketch of the country.

On regaining the summit of the pass, some time was spent in making additional observations, and it was sunset before the party reached the camp, the distance from the crest of the pass being twenty-four miles. The people were civil, ready to afford any information, and appeared quite to have made up their minds that they were shortly to expect a British occupation.

In camp the cold was now very trying at night, the thermometer falling 10° Fahr. below freezing-point; and the sick list was again on the increase.

On the 23rd the force began its return march to Thal, and it was determined, instead of returning by the Darwazagai pass, to follow the river route to where it joins the other at Hazar Pir Ziarat. Thal was reached without incident on the 28th.

On the afternoon of the 28th four grasscutters were killed and one mortally wounded whilst out cutting grass. Their ponies, carried off by the murderers, were recovered by the cavalry guard with them; but, from the nature of the ground, the cavalry could not succeed in coming up with the murderers.

The troops remained at Thal till the 5th of December, when, the murder of the grasscutters having been clearly brought home to the Miamai branch of the Kabul Khel Wazirs, and their *maliks* having declined either to wait upon the Deputy Commissioner or to afford any reparation, no alternative was left but to obtain redress by force of arms.

Although their conduct did not call for any consideration at our hands, both the Deputy Commissioner and the Brigadier were of opinion that the future peace of the frontier and the interest of Government would best be secured could punishment be inflicted upon the guilty only; and as the names of those actually implicated in the murder, and their precise location, had been made known to Captain Henderson, the operations were to be restricted, as far as possible, to their apprehension.

But to have required the surrender of criminals without being in a position to enforce the demand would have been considered by the Wazirs as an idle menace, and would have been treated with contempt; and, therefore, before any call of the kind could be made it was necessary to bring the whole section of the tribe under our control. It was only possible to effect this by a surprise, and arrangements were made accordingly.

After the murder of the grasscutters, such of the Miamais as had previously been encamped on the right bank of the Kurram crossed the river, and the whole of the section pitched their tents at the foot of a range of mountains which they had been accustomed to consider inaccessible, and where they supposed themselves secure from any attack except in front.

For the surprise to be successful two conditions were indispensable, *viz.*, the possession of the mountains in rear of their encampments, and the cutting off of their retreat down the left bank of the river.

To the force, as per margin, under Major J. Coke, was assigned the first of these operations. At midnight these troops fell in without noise, and, led by guides provided by the Deputy Commissioner, they started for the summit of the mountains by a circuitous and difficult path.

No. 1 Punjab Light Field Battery (2 guns).
1st Punjab Infantry.
6th " "

Two hours after the departure of Major Coke's column the remainder of the troops fell in, crossed the Kurram opposite camp, and marched down its right bank, under Brigadier Chamberlain.

On their reaching the village of Biland Khel the day began to dawn, so, leaving the infantry and guns to follow, the Brigadier pushed on with the cavalry; the Deputy Commissioner accompanied Khwaja Muhammad Khan's horsemen, for the double purpose of cutting off the retreat by the river bank, and of reconnoitring the river down-stream for a place practicable for infantry. On crossing the river and entering the broken ground, the cavalry came suddenly on an encampment of the Miamais, who, warned of their approach, were carrying their families and cattle up the steep mountain path in their rear. Here a few shots were exchanged, we having one sowar wounded and two horses killed, the Wazirs losing one man.

About this time intimation was brought that Major Coke's column had been seen on the summit of the mountain, so there was no longer any doubt as to his success. The Gurkhas and the Peshawar Mountain Train Battery, having meanwhile come up with the cavalry, turned the southernmost point of the Miamai encampments, and ascended the mountains, thereby completing the chain. Major Coke's column was above them, and entirely closed the few paths which led up the mountain. The 3rd Punjab Infantry and the guns of No. 3 Punjab Light Field Battery threatened their front from below; and lower down again the Gurkhas and mountain guns had the command of the hills; while the cavalry cut off all retreat by the plain.

As soon as all the troops were in position, the precise object of the visit was explained to the enemy, and they were assured that they would not be injured unless they resisted. Seeing that any attempt at escape or opposition would be useless, they at once gave up all who were present and called for. The troops then retired, and several hundred head of cattle and sheep were brought away, to be restored when terms were definitely settled with the tribe. The troops reached camp at 4 P.M., after a very hard day's work, and after being for nearly twenty-four hours without food. There were no other casualties besides those already mentioned.

As it was found that it would be impossible to convict the suspected men if tried in a criminal court, a fine of Rs. 1,200 was levied on the tribe.

Before the operations, the precaution had been taken of sending messages to the other branches of the Kabul Khel Wazirs not to interfere in support of the Miamais, and no aid was given them.

After two days spent in a settlement with the Miamais, the force moved to Gandiaor, where it was encamped till the 21st of December, pending the adjustment of certain difficulties with the Zaimukhts, as a party of that tribe, having no quarrel with the people of Darsamand, and solely with the object of outraging the British Government, had on the 14th of December seized three men belonging to that village, one of whom afterwards died of his wounds.

The Zaimukhts in the plains were not participators in this crime, and were powerless to procure the surrender of the culprits; but the demands of the Deputy Commissioner, backed as they were by the presence of such a large body of troops, had the desired effect, and a deputation was sent in and a fine of Rs. 1,000 paid.

The payment of the fine imposed on the Zaimukhts leaving nothing further to be done, the force, after marching to Torawari on the 22nd of December, where it halted for four days, was, on arrival at Kohat, broken up.

The conduct of the troops had been most exemplary; not one single act of violence had been committed, either against property or person, during the whole period. No stronger indications of the increase of our power and influence in these valleys could have been afforded than the fact that not a single shot had been fired at the camp at night; that with the exception of the murder of the grasscutters by the Kabul Khel Wazirs no camp follower had been injured, nor had a single animal been carried off.

At the end of 1859, Brig.-General N. B. Chamberlain, C.B., again passed through the Miranzai valley at the head of a force, with which he was about to punish the Kabul Khel Wazirs (to be related in the next chapter), and Captain James, Commissioner of Peshawar, who accompanied the force as Political Officer then took the opportunity of inspecting the valley, and spoke in the highest terms of the good fruits which the expeditions in 1855 and 1856, and the wise policy at that time inaugurated, had brought forth.

Since the expedition of 1856 the Turis, who had formerly been so turbulent, have given little trouble, and our relations with them and with the Bangash up to the present time have already been sufficiently alluded to at the beginning of the chapter.

CHAPTER VII.

DARWESH KHEL WAZIRS.

WAZIRISTAN, which for political and administrative purposes is divided into Northern and Southern Waziristan, lies on the western border of the Indian Empire, and forms the connecting link on the Afghan frontier between the districts of Kurram and Zhob.

On the west and north-west lie the Afghan districts of Birmal and Khost, while on the north-east and east Waziristan is coterminous with the districts of Kurram, Kohat, Bannu, and Dera Ismail Khan. On the south lies the Zhob district of Baluchistan.

In shape, Waziristan resembles a rough parallelogram, with an average length of 110 miles from north to south and an average breadth of 60 miles from east to west. At the north-east corner of the parallelogram a wedge of hilly country juts into the Kohat and Bannu districts.

Geography of Waziristan.

From north to south, and from east to west, situated as the country is in the Suliman range, it is intersected by chains of mountains, ridges, and ravines running now in one direction and now in another. The rugged and mountainous nature of the country becomes more and more accentuated the further an advance is made from the eastern boundary. The general trend of the main watercourses of this tangled network of hills runs from east to west, and the country rises to the watershed which divides the basin of the Indus from that of the Helmand. This watershed is situated in the western Suleiman range, which lies some distance to the west of the Afghan frontier. The ravines are generally flanked throughout their course by high hills, which occasionally recede enough to give the spaces enclosed the appearance of small valleys. The width of these ravines is very variable ; in some places being as much as a thousand yards, whilst at others they narrow to a hundred yards or less. The narrowest parts are where the water has had to pierce its way through a range crossing its course at right angles: these gorges, called by the native *tangis*, are the points usually occupied to oppose an enemy.

These ravines and watercourses form the only natural means of communication in so difficult a country, and are dignified by the name of "roads" by the inhabitants. The beds of the ravines are thickly strewn with boulders and stones. In fine weather a stream of water usually trickles down them, requiring to be crossed every few hundred yards; but after rain the beds suddenly fill, and often become dangerous torrents.

The land is essentially a barren one, and the poorness of the soil has hitherto proved an insuperable barrier to a large increase of the resident population. For generations the Wazir has been in the habit of supplementing the resources of his country by imports, forced or otherwise, from the plain country at his feet, although the natural products, aided perchance by smuggling, have been sufficient to enable him to endure successfully more than one prolonged blockade. The Tochi valley and the Spin plain alone furnish large tracts suitable for cultivation. In the rest of Waziristan agriculture is confined to the plateaux at the base of high mountains, and to the small valleys and stretches of alluvial land bordering the main ravines. These last are termed by the natives *kaches*, and are a feature in all the principal defiles of the Suleiman range. In the valleys and *kaches* the land is generally terraced and irrigated, and in many instances the water is led on to the fields by means of channels cut out of the hillside, exhibiting considerable engineering skill and great labour.[1] The borders of the fields are commonly planted with mulberry and willow which give to these spots a pleasing appearance compared with the rugged hills which encircle them.

In some parts, as at Maidani, south-west of Thal, Razmak, and Shawal, the hills lose their steep character and assume the appearance of downs.

In the south of Waziristan the tributaries of the Gumal river, the Dhana or Wana Toi and the Urghar, both flow through wide open plains, which present to the distant spectator the appearance of rolling grassy *pampas*, but a nearer view discloses the fact that

1 Here and there these irrigation channels are bored through a hillside, and occasionally, in plain districts, rising ground is pierced with a tunnel until water is struck. These irrigation channels are called *karez*.

they are covered almost entirely with stones and boulders, and scored through in all directions with watercourses usually dry. These plains are known as Wana, Spin, and Zarmelan, the second of these being the least stony.

The valley of the Gumal is distinguished by its excessive barrenness; there is hardly a blade of cultivation to be seen between Murtaza and Khajuri Kach, and no villages along the river itself.

The principal rivers in Waziristan are the Kurram, Kaitu, Tochi, and Gumal. None of these form serious military obstacles except when in flood, as there are many fords across them. The remaining rivers are but mountain streams insignificant as a rule, though dangerous and impassable during a spate. So suddenly do these spates occur that they are apt to prove costly to a force, caught in one of the numerous *tangis,* where the sides are so precipitous that escape is sometimes impossible. For the same reason camp should never be pitched in a dry river-bed, even though it may appear to have been in disuse for some time. Several instances have occurred of camps being washed away through neglect of this precaution.

The people of Waziristan.

The chief inhabitants of Waziristan are the Darwesh Khels who form the subject of this chapter, the Mahsuds, the Dawaris, and the Bhittanis. All these tribes have little in common with each other, and for generations past have been in a state of perpetual mutual strife. The Darwesh Khels and the Mahsuds are the only Wazirs proper, and strangely enough the name has been practically appropriated by the former, who are always known in the hill country as Wazirs; the Mahsuds are only described by that title by strangers to their country. They pronounce their own name "Mahsid."

The Darwesh Khel and the Mahsuds have a common origin, being descended according to tradition from Wazir, who had a son Khizri,[1] and several grandsons, two of whom were Musa, commonly called Darwesh, and Mahmud. Musa (Darwesh) had two sons, Utman and Ahmad. Mahmud again had a son Mahsud. The

1 Wazir had a second son, Lali, who fled, to escape vengeance for murder, to the northern slopes of the Safed Koh, where his descendants are still located. His third grandson was Mubarak who again had a son Gurbaz from whom are descended the Gurbaz Wazirs of Khost.

brothers Utman and Ahmad and their cousin Mahsud were the founders of the Wazir race.

The original home of the tribe was probably in Birmal[1]; and they began to move eastwards at the close of the fourteenth century, occupying Shamal and the Kohat border north of the Tochi, when they then migrated, crossing that river, and took possession of the mountainous region about Shuidar,[2] moving gradually south until they seized the whole country as far as the Gumal. It is probable that at the beginning of the last century they had not advanced into the valley of the Zam and Shahur, as Powindah caravans in those days used to move unopposed across the Zaterai range to Marghaband and Jandola.[3]

Relying on the inaccessibility of their country the Wazirs have defied for centuries the power of the rulers of India and Afghanistan, and on more than one occasion they engaged and defeated the invading armies of the Moguls. Their character as a people, and their organization have, therefore, been naturally independent and strongly democratic, so much so that even their own elders have little real control over the unruly spirits of their various clans. True sons of Esau, they always carry their lives in their hands, and finding that the natural resources of their country do not favour them enough, they eke out their existence by plundering their more peaceful neighbours. This mode of life has imbued in their men a free and independent manner and a fine active physique, and in their women a power of resisting fatigue and nurturing their children under most adverse circumstances.

Their legitimate occupations are chiefly pastoral, and it is the search for sustenance for their flocks and herds, constituting, as these do, their only property, that leads them to wander up and down their country, and in the case of the Darwesh Khel to move as far as British territory.

Strangely enough the Darwesh Khel and Mahsuds, although of the same stock, have long been at enmity with one another, and the feud has been aggravated by the Ahmadzai Darwesh Khels giving information and advice to the British Government in their expeditions against the Mahsuds. They differ, too, so much

[1] The tomb of Musa, the ancestor of the Darwesh Khel, still exists as a place of pilgrimage at the Ziarat named after him in the Zindawar valley above Shakin.

[2] The second highest mountain in Waziristan—11,000 feet.

[3] By the Karwan (Karavan) pass, hence its name.

in habits and characteristics that they may almost be regarded as a separate tribe. Notwithstanding this fact the villages of the Darwesh Khel and Mahsuds are much mixed up, and the leading men are also often connected by marriage.

The chief characteristic of the Darwesh Khel is their migratory habit; many of them migrate annually from their native hills in the autumn to the Bannu district in British territory, and return to their homes only after the severe winter of their inhospitable upland country, softening into spring, enables them to find pasture for their flocks and herds. Some of them are permanently settled in British territory, and have become revenue-paying cultivators.

The Darwesh Khel are divided into two main clans, the Utmanzai and Ahmadzai, descended from Utman and Ahmad, sons of Darwesh. The Utmanzais live in the Tochi, and the hills adjoining it on both sides, in Shawal, on the Khaisora, Kaitu, and Kurram, while the bulk of the Ahmadzais live round Wana, in Shakai, and on the western part of the Bannu district along the border.

Utman had three sons, Ibrahim, Wali, and Mohmit, who in their turn founded separate divisions. Of these the Ibrahim Khels have three main sections:—the Madda Khel, 1,600—2,000[1] strong, inhabiting the Kazah, Maizar, and Sheranni; the Manzar Khel, 400 strong, in the country between Kanirogha in the Tochi valley and Manirogha at the head of the Khaisora; and the Tori Khel, 3,000 strong, in a stretch of country reaching from near Karkanwam at the mouth of the Shaktu to Spinwam on the Kaitu.

The Wali Khel form three main sections:—the Bakka Khel, 1,000 strong, holding a few villages in the upper part of the Mana valley, and large possessions on the border of the Bannu district, and the mouths of the Tochi and Khaisora passes; the Jani Khel, 1,000 strong, holding land chiefly in the Bannu district near the fort of Jani Khel at the mouth of the Khaisora, and grazing grounds at the lower end of the Mana; and the Kabul Khel, including the Malikshahi, 3,000 strong, living during the winter on the Kurram between Thal and Zarwam, and migrating in summer to Birmal in Afghanistan, and to the western outskirts of Waziristan and Shawal.

[1] All numbers are approximate, and indicate fighting-men only. The localities given must only be considered to comprise the main settlements of each section.

The Mohmit Khel are divided into:—the Bora Khel, 1,000 strong, residing in the Sheratala plain, the Palosin plain, and on Kaitu, with summer quarters at Razmak and Dandi; the Wuzi Khel, 1,200 to 1,500, in the Khaisora, Dandi, and Kaitu, with summer quarters about Razmak and Sham in the Khaisora; the Khaddar Khel, 800, residing on the banks of the Tochi, between Datta Khel and Sheranni; and the Hassan Khel, 400, in the Kaitu valley, and migrating in summer to Laram.

The Ahmadzai clan has two main divisions: Kalu Khel and Sani Khel. The first of these is divided into two sections:—Isperka, 1,300, inhabiting the Bannu district with summer settlements in Razmak, Shuidar, and Shakai; and Nasradin, 7,210, dwelling at Wana, with settlements in British territory and Gumatti.

The Sani Khel is divided into three sections:—Hathi Khel, 2,000, who own lands in Bannu and the "Thal," extending back to the Kafir range between Barganatu and Spin Tangi; the Sirki Khel, 800, holding lands in Bannu and Wana; and the Umarzai, 600, who possess lands in Bannu district, near Mandawam, and on the Shaktu, near Chapri and Garang, and who take their flocks to graze at Razmak in summer.

Expedition against the Umarzai Wazirs, by a force under Major J. Nicholson, in 1852

At the time of the annexation of the Punjab in 1849, the Umarzai section of the Ahmadzai Wazirs, who cultivated land in British territory, which had been wrested from the neighbouring Bannuchis, gave much trouble on our border. Most of these Umarzais paid their revenue to a Bannuchi chief, named Bazid Khan, who was responsible for the collection, but some of them after reaping the harvest, would go off into the hills, leaving Bazid Khan to pay instead of them. Bazid Khan would then pay the revenue and occupy the lands of the defaulters. These defaults being repeated, some of the Umarzais were seized, as a last resource; and shortly afterwards two of the hostages were sent to ask their section to come into Bannu to settle accounts.

The day they came in (3rd December), there happened to be no British Officer in Bannu; and a dispute arising in their conversation with Bazid Khan, they attacked his villages that night, and after killing several people, and doing Rs. 12,000 worth of damage, escaped, without loss, by the Gumatti pass.

Soon after, on the 2nd of January 1850, another party, 1,500 strong, consisting of the Umarzai, Muhammad Khel, and Hathi Khel sections, and some Bara Khels, Kabul Khels, and Mahsuds, attacked the post of Gumatti, but were gallantly repulsed by a party of 350 footmen, under Mr. MacMahon, Extra Assistant Commissioner, with a loss of four killed and twelve wounded.

In November 1850 the Umarzais, having induced the Mahsud Wazirs to join them, made a formidable demonstration with several thousand men. They intended to attack the town of Bannu itself, had they not found a strong force ready for them. They, therefore, assailed some border villages, but were repulsed. In December of the same year they carried off a convoy of supplies on its way to Latammar.

From 1851 to 1852 the outposts of Bannu were constantly engaged in skirmishes with the Wazirs, who came down almost daily, and occupied the low hills in front of the Gumatti post, firing long shots at the men holding it; but the enemy never could be drawn into close quarters in the plain, and following them even into the low range of hills was strictly forbidden.

Efforts had been made to settle some terms with the Umarzais, but they continued not only to threaten overt attacks, but also to rob and murder by stealth. Thus, ever since the Umarzais had left their lands, they had been in open rebellion against us, and, at the end of 1852, permission was accorded to Major John Nicholson, the Deputy Commissioner, to arrange for their chastisement. At the time this permission was received, it was believed that a portion of the tribe would make submission, and operations were deferred while the result of their councils was at all doubtful.

Very shortly afterwards, the southern Umarzais, who were thinly scattered in the low hill between the Tochi river and Gabar mountain, incited by a holy man, suddenly marched down towards the Kurram, in the hope of surprising one of our villages. In this they were frustrated by the arrangements made by Major Nicholson; and the time had now arrived for showing them that it was not fear which had induced us to offer to listen to any offers of submission, and that we were not to be annoyed any longer with impunity.

As the greatest secrecy was necessary, the 4th Punjab Infantry was ordered to march from Bahadur Khel, as if in course of relief, and two companies of the 1st Punjab Infantry were ordered from Kohat, with the same reason assigned, while the 6th Punjab Police Battalion were ordered up from Dera Ismail Khan.

The plan of operations was as follows:—One column was to march from Bannu at 10 P.M. on the 20th December, through the Gumatti pass on Derabina and Garang, the former distant about fourteen, and the latter about seventeen miles, so that, if possible, a simultaneous attack might be made on both places at daybreak. The latter village was at the foot of a narrow, precipitous chasm in the Kafirkot range, through which ran the road to Sappari, which is not far from the summit of the ridge. If the surprise proved complete, and this pass was undefended, the force was to advance by it to Sappari, otherwise it was to await until Sappari had been taken by the second column in reverse.

The second column, consisting of the troops from Bahadur Khel and Kohat, was to move from Latammar at 9 P.M. on Sappari by the Barganatu pass (distance about twenty miles).

Both these columns were to bivouac the next night in the neighbourhood of Garang or Derabina.

A third column was to move from Bannu at 11 P.M. on the Umarzai encampments, thinly scattered among the low hills near the mouth of the Khaisora and Sein passes; it was to be accompanied by the *maliks* of the Jani Khel and Bakka Khel sections, who would be useful as guides, as well as to prevent any members of their sections from making common cause with the Umarzais. The *kiris* were so few and thinly scattered that it was not expected this column would be able to effect much, but it was considered its operations would show the Umarzais that they were no longer secure in that part of the country, and that they would have to seek other and inferior pasturage.

Major Nicholson added that the Umarzais were so weak that he would not have thought of taking so large a force against them were it not that the presence of a small force might, and probably would, induce the neighbouring sections to coalesce against us.

Mounted videttes from the levies were to be posted early on the night of the 20th of December at the mouth of the passes between the Kurram and the Latammar posts, to prevent any spies from Bannu preceding the columns with intelligence. The heights on each side of the Gumatti pass were also to be occupied by parties of foot levies as soon as the force had entered the hills.

On the night of the 20th December 1852 the three columns, as per margin, under the command of Captain J. C. Johnston, Captain T. P. Walsh, and Lieutenant J. W. Younghusband, respectively, moved off accordingly to the plans already detailed, Major Nicholson accompanying the second column.

1st Column.
2nd Punjab Infantry.

2nd Column.
Two companies, 1st Punjab Infantry.
4th Punjab Infantry—350 men.

3rd Column.

	Men.
2nd Punjab Cavalry	40
Mounted Police	50
6th Punjab Police Battalion ..	400

The first column entered the Gumatti pass at midnight, and, after a very difficult and fatiguing march of six hours, reached the friendly village of Gumatti. After crossing the valley in which Gumatti is situated, and a low range of hills, the village of Derabina was reached by the column, when all the flocks were captured and the village was destroyed. Captain Johnston then advanced, and with two companies crowned the hill above the Garang ravine, the remainder of his regiment holding the hills which commanded the entrance to it; and so correctly had the combination been arranged and executed, that, as this column arrived on the top of the hills, the head of the second column, under Captain Walsh, which had marched from Latammar, was seen emerging from the village of Garang.

The second column entered the Barganatu pass (nine miles from Latammar) at midnight, and following the course of the *nala* for about twelve miles, the crest of the Kafirkot range was reached a little before daybreak. After a short halt the troops descended into a *nala* leading towards the Kurram river; and after about a mile some Wazir encampments were seen. The first village, Sappari, was taken completely by surprise and destroyed, as were three other encampments in the very formidable Garang pass. The troops then proceeded to the village of Gumatti, in company with No. 1 column, where they bivouacked for the night.

The surprise to the enemy had been so complete that they were able to make only slight resistance, and our casualties in action only amounted to two men wounded; but twenty-one of our men, who had straggled on the road, were afterwards found to have been killed by the Wazirs in detail after the corps had descended from the heights.

The troops were not molested at their bivouac, nor on their return to Bannu by the Kurram pass the following morning. Before the column marched for Bannu, a wing of the 2nd Punjab Infantry, under Major Nicholson, destroyed some more encampments, without any resistance on the part of the enemy.

The 3rd column, after passing through low hills, reached open ground at daybreak, when the cavalry were pushed on against the nearest village, the cattle of which were captured and the village burnt. Two other villages were then destroyed by the infantry; but as the highest range had now been reached, and as the troops were within three miles of Dawar, no further advance, according to instructions, was made.

In the month of September 1853 Major Nicholson reported that the tribe were thoroughly humbled, and had several times sent in suing for peace; but he recommended that terms should not be accorded to them for a time. Their request was, however, subsequently granted, and they were re-admitted to their lands in Bannu.

Expedition against the Kabul Khel Wazirs, by a force under Brig.-General N. B. Chamberlain, C.B., in 1859-60.

Next to the Umarzai, the section of the Darwesh Khel Wazirs, which gave most trouble on our border after the annexation, was the Kabul Khel section of the Utmanzai branch.

In the autumn of 1850 they signalised themselves by an audacious attack on Bahadur Khel and its salt mines. For this purpose they assembled in considerable force, and induced many Khattak villages round Bahadur Khel to league with them.

Troops were, however, promptly brought up from Nari to the scene of action, and the Wazirs dispersed without effecting much mischief.

This attempt does not appear to have been prompted by any particular motive. There was no grievance with regard to salt; for any doubts which the Wazirs might have felt as to the intentions of the British Government had been long since removed, when the salt mines were opened at the beginning of 1850. Being, like the Afridis, largely engaged in the salt-carrying trade, they doubtless had perceived the political importance of the mines, and the great influence which accrued to the British Government from the possession of them. For the same reasons the Khattaks envied their masters the command of these valuable resources, and would have been glad if, in co-operation with the Wazirs, they could have secured their possession. It is probable, however, that no fixed idea existed in the minds of the tribesmen on this occasion, and there certainly had been no provocation whatever given.

After this attack it was determined to hold Bahadur Khel in force, and to construct a fort. During the constructions of this work, on which the 4th Punjab Infantry and the men of the Police Battalion were employed, the Wazirs gave all the opposition in their power, and constantly harassed the working-parties.

In 1851 they joined, as already shown, with the Umarzais in their misconduct, and on the 11th of March, in conjunction with them and others, they assembled and threatened the post of Gumatti, but were driven back by the 2nd Punjab Infantry with some loss. On the following days they also threatened the Kurram post, and on the 17th attacked it in force; but it being garrisoned by twenty sabres of the 2nd Punjab Cavalry and fifty bayonets of the 2nd Punjab Infantry they were driven back with considerable loss.

During Captain J. Coke's expedition to Miranzai in October 1851, already narrated, they annoyed the picquets while the column was halted at Thal, and also at Biland Khel. From 1852 to April 1854 no less than nineteen raids were committed by them, in which many cattle were carried off. As the practice was on the increase, Captain J. Coke took decisive steps, and the Kabul Khels were interdicted from trading at the salt mines. Two parties of these people, together with their cattle, were seized; and by the medium of one of their men a message was sent to the head-quarters of the section, to the effect that unless satisfaction was given the cattle would be sold, the proceeds being applied to the reimbursement of the sufferers by the raids, and the men would be detained as hostages. The tribe then lost no time in making terms; the value of the stolen property was realized, and the chief of another section of the tribe came forward as security for the future good conduct of the Kabul Khels. Their prisoners were then released; and for a time the tribe became more careful in their behaviour.

In 1855, as mentioned in the previous chapter, the Miranzai Field Force, under Brigadier N. B. Chamberlain, moved to Thal, to effect a settlement with the Kabul Khels on account of sundry questions and differences with the *maliks* of that place. The force arrived at Thal on the 6th of May, and was halted there until the 17th, and the mere exhibition of our strength was sufficient to bring them to terms, without resort to punitive measures.

The agreement between the Kabul Khel and the village of Thal, which was dated the 15th of May, was in the name of the whole Kabul Khel section, and they also undertook to be responsible for the Malik Shahi section, and not to allow a passage through their territory to other sections who were hostile.

In the following year (1856), when the force under Brigadier N. B. Chamberlain was returning from the Kurram valley, five of the cavalry grasscutters were murdered at Thal by a party of the Miamai section of the Kabul Khels; the Miamai settlements were accordingly surprised, as already narrated, and, as there was not sufficient evidence to prove the murder against any individuals, a fine of Rs. 1,200 was taken from the section.

The Kabul Khels did not again misbehave until 1859. On the night of the 5th of November of that year, Captain R. Mecham, commanding No. 3 Punjab Light Field Battery, was proceeding from Bannu towards Kohat, when about two miles from the outpost and village of Latammar he was set upon and murdered by a gang of marauders. Captain Mecham was at the time very ill, and was travelling in a *doolie*; his escort consisted of two sowars of the Bannu mounted police, he having sent on two men of his battery to Latammar to increase his escort from there. It does not appear that the murderers had any previous knowledge of an officer being likely to pass that way; they were simply prowling about on a marauding expedition, and seeing the approaching light of the torches, they had hidden themselves in some bushes to waylay the travellers. The moment the attack was made, the mounted police basely deserted Captain Mecham, and the *doolie*-bearers took to flight. Captain Mecham attempted to keep off his assailants with his revolver, but he was overpowered and cut down. The party consisted chiefly of Hathi Khel Ahmadzais, who fled for refuge to the Kabul Khels.

The Deputy Commissioner of Kohat at once proceeded to our frontier village of Thal, and summoned the chiefs of the different Wazir sections; but although it was known the act was greatly disapproved by other portions of the tribe, the Kabul Khels refused to render any satisfaction for the murder, or to give up the men implicated, from the strong prejudice amongst the border tribes against the surrender of any person seeking an asylum with them. Our sole object was then explained to the other Wazir sections; and they were warned of the penalties they would incur by siding with the Kabul Khels, from whom it now became necessary to exact retribution by force of arms.

Although the Kabul Khel section numbered only 3,000 men it remained to be seen whether the rapid advance of the troops would give sufficient weight to our warnings and threats to deter others from openly siding with them. The proverbial unity of the Wazirs was against such a supposition; nevertheless, Captain H. R. James, the Commissioner, did not anticipate opposition on the part of the other branches, as we had a great hold on many of them from the fact of their bringing their cattle to graze within our territory, and much could be done in the way of reducing opposition, and in preventing other tribes joining the Kabul Khels, by timely warning and advice. It was calculated that 6,000 men might be brought against us, but probably not more than half that number would be collected.

In the winter months the Utmanzais are mainly located on the right bank of the Kurram river, and at this time the several subdivisions of the Kabul Khels were thus located, below the Afghan frontier village of Biland Khel, cultivating for their spring crops.

Regarding the best time for operations, the Commissioner said that there were two seasons when the tribe would be peculiarly open to punishment, *viz.*, at the beginning of winter and in the spring; more real injury could be inflicted in the winter, more apparent in the spring. A force proceeding against them at the former season could carry off their winter stores, and compel them to retreat to their higher hills. In the spring the crops could be destroyed upon which the tribe is dependent in the summer. He, therefore, advocated immediate action, not only for the above reasons, but because a blow delivered at the time strikes greater terror into the mountain tribes than at a subsequent period.

With regard to the punishment of the Hathi Khel section the Commissioner considered no advance of troops would be required, but it would be necessary to bring strong pressure on the members of the tribe within our border, and to imprison such of their leaders as would not act vigorously in the matter.

The line of operations led through a portion of the territories of the Amir of Kabul, and communications had, therefore, to be addressed to His Highness on the subject.

As the refusal of the Kabul Khels to make restitution had all along been anticipated, orders had been early given for a force to be assembled at Kohat. It was impossible, as already stated, to say what numbers would be opposed to us, or what was the nature of the difficulties to be overcome, the country being then totally unknown. It was, therefore, necessary to employ a force large enough to meet all contingencies.

- Detachment, No. 1 Punjab Light Field Battery, 2 guns.
- Detachment, No. 2 Punjab Light Field Battery, 4 guns.
- Detachment, Peshawar Mountain Train Battery, 4 guns.
- Detachment, Hazara Mountain Train Battery, 3 guns.
- Detachment, Guide Cavalry.
- 2nd Punjab Cavalry.
- Detachment, Sappers and Miners.
- Detachment, Guide Infantry.
- 4th Sikh Infantry.
- 1st Punjab Infantry.
- 3rd " "
- 4th " "
- 6th " "
- 24th " " (Pioneers).[1]

The force consisted of the marginally named troops, numbering 3,916 of all ranks, and was under the command of Brig.-General N. B. Chamberlain, C.B. On the 15th of December 1859 it marched from Kohat, and reached Thal on the 19th. Here the column was joined by a body of Bangash and Khattak levies and police, numbering 240 horse and 1,216 foot, raising the total of the force to 5,372 men.

On the 20th of December the force crossed the Kurram river, encamping at the village of Biland Khel, in the territory of the Amir of Kabul; instructions had been sent by His Highness to render every assistance to the expedition, but the troops were only in Kabul territory whilst encamped there, as all the country to the south of that village formed the possessions of the independent Wazirs.

The main body of the Kabul Khels had determined to make their stand on a high range of hills called Maidani, and to this place

[1] Now the 32nd Pioneers.

they had, previous to crossing the Kurram, removed all their encampments, and had prepared for its defence by storing grain and raising breastworks.

Maidani was about eight miles south-west of Biland Khel, near Zakha Narai, and its general features might be described as two parallel ranges contiguous to each other, terminating at either end in a gorge, and enclosing a long, narrow valley ; the inward slopes of both mountains were tolerably easy, and covered with grass and bushes, but the outward sides or faces were rugged and precipitous.

The two gorges, which were the water channels, were the means of entrance to the valley,—the one facing the east being termed Gandiob, and the other to the south Zakha.

The enemy were variously stated at from 2,000 to 3,000 men, and it was known that no other clan had yet joined them ; some offers of arms and ammunition had been made, but proudly rejected in their self-confidence, and it was reported on all sides that they considered their position too strong to be attacked. On the 21st, however, there were rumours that the Wazirs were planning to remove as soon as the force should break ground, and it was arranged that night that an attack should be made as soon as possible.

Although it had been reported that the easiest and nearest approach was from the Gandiob side, for many reasons it was desirable that the Zakha entrance should be seen before the plan of attack was decided on, and on the 21st a reconnaissance was made by the Brig.-General with a strong body of cavalry. The distance to the Zakha entrance was found to be about sixteen miles from camp, and the gorge a difficult one. The Gandiob ravine was also examined, and the advantage of that route over the Zakha one verified.

At six o'clock the following morning the troops noted in the margin (the cavalry and field guns being ordered to follow at daybreak) marched upon Gandiob, to which place the camp was to be moved.

Peshawar Mountain Train Battery, 4 guns.
Hazara Mountain Train Battery, 3 guns.
Guide Infantry.
4th Sikh Infantry.
1st Punjab Infantry.
3rd „ „
4th „ „

Each corps of the main column was to carry fifty rounds of ammunition per man, and to be accompanied by two mule loads of ammunition. The horses of native officers of infantry were to be left at the camp. All men were to carry cooked food with them.

As Maidani was approached parties of the enemy were observed on the hill-tops, and the Guide Infantry, supported by the Peshawar Mountain Train Battery and the 4th Sikh Infantry, at once ascended the range of hills to the left, whilst the 1st Punjab Infantry supported by the Hazara Mountain Train Battery and the 3rd Punjab Infantry, crowned the range to the right.

The left column was under the immediate orders of the Brig.-General, while the command of the right column devolved upon Major F. W. Lambert. The orders for both columns were for each to advance along the ridge, and to drive off the enemy.

The 4th Punjab Infantry, in reserve, moved up the bed of the ravine (which runs between and separates the two ranges), so as to close that passage and be ready to assist either column.

It afterwards appeared that the enemy expected an attack by the Zakha gorge, and the main body of the Kabul Khels had, therefore, posted themselves at that entrance. Breastworks on the right side of the gorge had not been thrown up, and little or no resistance was offered to the column. This enabled Major Lambert from his side to outflank with the mountain guns the breastwork held on the opposite range, and to this circumstance was attributed the little loss sustained by the left column.

On the left range breastworks had been raised at several points, and at first they were bravely defended by the enemy, who numbered about 1,500 men. But it soon became apparent that the enemy were deficient in fire-arms; their defences were quickly carried, and after two hours' rough climbing, our men were in possession of the heights above the Wazir encampments.

As it was now past noon, and as there was no knowledge of the hills in advance, or of the enemy's line of retreat, and as moreover the troops had still to return some miles to camp, possibly followed the whole way, the halt was sounded, and the reserve ordered to destroy the three large encampments. In this work they were assisted by bodies of Turi foot levies, who had followed in rear, and in the course of two hours everything was either destroyed or carried off.

No attempt was made to molest the column during its retirement. The casualties were small, being only one killed and sixteen wounded, besides two of the levies wounded.

The enemy left some twenty bodies on the ground, three of their principal leaders being amongst this number; and they must have had about fifty casualties in all.

On the 23rd it was decided to follow up the advantage of the previous day. All the infantry (except the Guides) and the two Mountain Batteries returned to Maidani; whilst the camp, escorted by the Guide Infantry, field guns, and cavalry, under Lieut.-Colonel H. B. Lumsden, C.B., changed ground to Shiwa on the Kurram, ten miles below Biland Khel.

Lieut.-Colonel Lumsden was instructed to detach all his cavalry and two companies of infantry towards the Zakha gorge as soon as they could be spared from the protection of the baggage. If they reached that point before General Chamberlain's column arrived there, they were to harass the enemy without committing themselves to serious loss, and the two companies were to be posted on the hills commanding the gorge leading into the Zakha water-course, to keep a retreat open for the cavalry, should they be pressed.

The main body, after leaving Gandiob, passed the smouldering remains of the enemy's encampments, and were approaching the Zakha exit from the valley, when the Commissioner obtained information which made it appear probable that, by crossing over the range to the right and descending into a small valley named Durnani (which was occupied by the Hasan Khel Wazirs, who had declined to assist the Kabul Khels), the troops might be able to come up with some of the flocks and herds which had been driven off by that route. As the Hasan Khels had hitherto held aloof, warning was sent to them that they would not be injured, but that they must give up any property of the fugitives which might be with them.

Captain B. Henderson, the Deputy Commissioner, then pushed on with some of his levies, followed by the Brig.-General with a body of infantry, and the Hazara Mountain Train Battery in support. The remainder of the infantry and the other battery moved straight to the camp through the Zakha gorge, destroying *en route* one of the Kabul Khel encampments, which had escaped destruction the previous day, but which the Kabul Khels had not had time to remove.

Captain Henderson's foray proved most successful, and, although none of the Kabul Khels could be come up with, many flocks and herds fell into our hands.

The levies rejoined the troops about dusk at Durnani, and as the camp at Shiwa was some eighteen miles off, the column bivouacked in the dry bed of the *nala* for the night. The Hasan Khels were required to post picquets on the hills around, and not a shot was fired during the night. It was a strange duty for the Wazirs to find themselves called on to perform, and their readiness to comply with all our requisitions indicated how powerless they felt themselves.

At daylight the next morning the column began its march towards the camp, and some more flocks and herds fell into our hands. Owing to some high ranges which intervened between Durnani and Shiwa, a long detour had to be made *viâ* the Kaitu stream, and it was three o'clock in the afternoon before the troops reached their tents.

Representatives from the Kabul Khel, Tori Khel, and Hasan Khel section having come in, the force halted four days at Shiwa, when strong escorts were placed at the disposal of the engineer officers to enable them to map the country in the neighbourhood of the camp.

With the Kabul Khels it was determined to hold no immediate communications, but the other two sections were informed that if the Utmanzais would unite and deliver up Zangi, or two of the murderers, we would be satisfied. To this they agreed, giving hostages, and, in token of their sincerity, sent in the next day one Ghulam, a notorious robber, suspected of murder. But as, in case of laxity in carrying out the agreement, coercive measures might be necessary, it was determined to move a force into their country, and as their lands lay to the south of the Kaitu river, the village of Spinwam on that stream was selected for the camp.

Early on the morning of the 29th the main body moved to Spinwam, while the remainder of the force, under Lieut.-Colonel Lumsden, moved up the river towards Biland Khel, partly for the purpose of securing our communications with the rear and for the sake of supplies, etc., and partly because there was little grass or forage on the Kaitu.

It was known that the murderers of Captain Mecham had on their way back been hospitably entertained by one Umber Shah, at whose house they had been seen displaying that officer's property. The camp at Spinwam was in the neighbourhood of the settlements of the section to which this man belonged, and the headmen were therefore summoned; they arrived on the 31st in a great state of alarm, and were called on to give up Umber Shah, or to take the consequences. They were then allowed to leave the camp on the promise that they would give him up, hostages being taken from them for the fulfilment of this promise. The following day they kept their word, and Umber Shah was brought a prisoner, to stand his trial. This was a great triumph over Wazir prejudice, and gave promise of success in regard to the murderers.

On the 2nd January the troops moved back to the Kurram, to a spot called Karera, a little below Shiwa.

Brig.-General Chamberlain had now settled with the Wazirs located on the right bank of the Kurram, but there remained the Gangi Khel and the Umarzai and Hathi Khel sections inhabiting the rugged spurs of the Kafirkot range on the left bank of that river.

Early on the 4th of January the troops, as per margin, under the Brig.-General marched for Sappari leaving the Peshawar Mountain Train Battery and the 1st and 4th Punjab Infantry, under Major F. W. Lambert, encamped on the right bank of the Kurram, to keep open the communications.

Hazara Mountain Train Battery.
Detachment, Sappers and Miners.
3rd Punjab Infantry.
6th " "
One company, 24th Punjab Infantry (Pioneers).

Lieut.-Colonel R. G. Taylor had informed the tribes of our intention of visiting their country, and had called upon the chiefs to meet him at Sappari, promising that life and property would be respected if no opposition was offered. With the example of the Kabul Khels before them, resistance was considered by them as hopeless, and fully trusting to our word, their encampments remained as usual, and the chiefs arrived in camp in due course.

On the afternoon of the 6th the Ahmadzai *maliks* were assembled, and they were told that they must assist in the capture of the actual murderers of Captain Mecham, as some of these belonged to their branch of the tribe; they were reminded of the immunity and comfort they enjoyed in Government territory, and they were further warned that if they did not help, they must take the consequences. Several claims against the clan were then satisfactorily disposed of.

The object for which the expedition had been undertaken was now, as far as possible, accomplished, and the troops were free to return to cantonments. On the 7th of January, the 3rd and 6th Punjab Infantry, which were under orders for Dera Ghazi Khan and Dera Ismail Khan, marched by the Barganatu ravine towards Bannu; whilst the remainder of the force retraced its steps towards Kohat by the same route as that by which it had advanced, being joined by the detachments under Major Lambert and Lieut.-Colonel Lumsden, respectively, which had preceded them to Thal.

On the return march a halt of one day was made at Gandiaor, in Upper Miranzai, to enable the Deputy Commissioner to settle some outstanding cases with the Zaimukht tribe, and Kohat was reached on the 14th of January, a month from the date of starting, when the force was immediately broken up.

The Indian Medal, with a clasp for the "North-West Frontier," was granted in 1869 to all survivors of the troops engaged in the above operations.

After the termination of the expedition it was no easy task to get the Ahmadzais to take any steps towards the capture of the murderers. Nevertheless, Lieut.-Colonel R. G. Taylor, the Commissioner, made them assemble a regular little army and enter the hills, and, at length, having seized one of the murderers, by name Mohabat, at a place far in the interior, beyond Dawar, they brought him gagged and bound to the Deputy Commissioner of Bannu. On the very spot where the murder had been committed a gallows was erected and this miscreant was hanged.

There are no records of what ultimately became of the others of the gang; but some of them found shelter with Adam Khan, chief Madda Khel *malik*, in the Tochi valley; and Zangi, the leader of the gang, found refuge with the Mahsuds. The pressure on the Ahmadzais was apparently subsequently relaxed; time, the general results of the expedition, and the execution of the principal murderer, may all have operated as causes for this relaxation. In

June 1862, when an agreement was entered into with the Mahsud Wazirs, one of the stipulations was that those of the party which assassinated Captain Mecham, and who were still at large in independent territory, should receive no shelter from the contracting Mahsuds. But from what we know of Pathan character generally, and that of the ruder hill tribes in particular, it would be too much to expect that such a stipulation would be strictly acted up to, except under the certainty of immediate pressure in the event of its infringement.

The next occasion on which we came into contact with the Darwesh Khel Wazirs was in 1869. On the 5th of March of that year, the Tojiya Khels were preparing to return to their summer quarters, when they were drawn into an ambuscade by their enemies, the Turis, near the village of Thal. The Wazirs were overpowered and lost twelve killed and six wounded; and after stripping the bodies, the Turis retreated to their own country. The Wazirs believed that the inhabitants of Thal who are Gar in politics, and friends of the Turis, brought down the latter on them. Accordingly, on the 2nd of April 1869, a body of Wazirs, principally of the Kabul Khel and Tojiya Khel sections, retaliated by attacking the village of Thal, and succeeded in carrying off about 7,000 head of cattle.

Lieutenant P. L. N. Cavagnari, the Deputy Commissioner, at once demanded restitution of the stolen property; this the Wazirs flatly refused; and Lieut.-Colonel C. P. Keyes, commanding the troops of the Kohat district, was called upon to move such a body of troops into Miranzai as would enable him to destroy the crops of the Kabul Khels in the vicinity of the border, if the demand on them for reparation was not complied with.

Accordingly, a force as per margin, under Lieut.-Colonel C. P. Keyes, C.B., accompanied by 1,000 Khattak and 1,500 Bangash levies, and 120 police, marched from Kohat on the 17th, and reached Thal on the 22nd of April.

No. 1 Punjab Light Field Battery, 2 guns.	
Peshawar Mountain Battery, 2 guns.	
4th Punjab Cavalry	.. 250 sabres.
1st Punjab Infantry	.. 390 bayonets.
2nd " "	.. 390 "
4th " "	.. 380 "

On the day the force arrived at Thal, the chief men of the Kabul Khel section, with two exceptions, tendered their submission. The two other headmen came in two days afterwards; their absence had been caused by the Thal men having led them to believe that a surprise was intended, and that their crops would be destroyed without further parley, and they had consequently retired with their followers to a considerable distance. The *maliks* acknowledged they could not justify themselves for committing such an outrage in British territory, but pleaded it was only a just reprisal for the wanton attack which they said the men of Thal had committed; at the same time they declared themselves ready to comply with the Deputy Commissioner's demands, and paid up the fines imposed.

In the following year, 1870, the Muhammad Khel section began to give considerable trouble on the Bannu border. They had for many years been settled in the Bannu district, where they held the lands on either bank of the Kurram river where it issues from the hills.

They had, previous to this, been looked on as a well-behaved section, and with the exception of a slight *émeute* in 1848, at the beginning of the British connection with Bannu, had given little trouble.

At the beginning of 1870 a *bannia* was carried off in the Kurram pass, for which pass the Muhammad Khels were responsible, and they were, therefore, heavily, but according to their ideas unjustly, fined. Shortly afterwards the water in the Kurram fell very low, when they were ordered by the *Tehsildar* to repair a *band*, which diverted the little water that remained on to the Bannuchi lands. They did this grumblingly, because their own lands were dry, but they shortly afterwards cut the *band* and seized the water for themselves for which they were again heavily fined; and they now made up their minds to commit some outrage against the Government. They sold their property, abandoned their lands in our territory, and retired into the hills without attracting in any special manner the attention of the local authorities, who considered the matter to be unimportant, and failed to impress on the military authorities the necessity for any exceptional precautions.

At daylight on the morning of the 13th of June 1870, as a detachment of ten bayonets of the 4th Sikh Infantry, marching from Bannu for the relief of the Kurram outpost, was passing through the old Kurram post, it was fired on by a party of the Muhammad Khels, who lay concealed behind the walls and in the neighbouring *nala*, when six of the detachment were killed and one wounded.

About half-a-mile behind the infantry were eleven sabres of the 1st Punjab Cavalry, also proceeding as a relief to the Kurram post; this detachment, on hearing the shots, immediately galloped up, and were joined by a similar detachment from the post. The Muhammad Khels, who numbered about 140 men, then retreated, leaving two men dead on the ground. The casualties in the 1st Punjab Cavalry were two non-commissioned officers and one sowar wounded, and two horses killed.

The Muhammad Khels were at once proclaimed outlaws; all members of the tribe found in British territory were arrested, and their lands were sequestered till such time as the whole tribe should submit unconditionally, and should give up to justice the men who had joined in the attack on the British detachment.

To those terms the Muhammad Khels refused to submit. From June 1870 to September 1871 they wandered among the hills bordering British territory, supported by the charity of other tribes, who sympathized with them and aided them as much as they dared. They constantly threatened raids in force, and committed numerous petty robberies.

On the 12th of Febuary 1871 a party of 80 or 100 raiders made a night attack on the village of Sukhi, situated only 800 or 900 yards from the Gumatti post. Although the picquet on duty, on hearing the alarm, instantly galloped towards the place, and soon afterwards actually came upon the Wazirs, yet the ground was so unsuited for cavalry that they were not able to inflict any loss on the enemy, who escaped in the darkness, leaving their booty behind them.

After this, the Muhammad Khels made two attempts to prevent the erection of the new tower on the Kurram *band* but without success. At length, weary of being hunted from place to place, dependent for the means of subsistence on the charity of others, they were anxious to come to terms, and would gladly have accepted any punishment short of surrendering the original offenders. This was the one condition to which their Afghan pride would not submit, and which long delayed the settlement of the case. But the Lieutenant-Governor was convinced that nothing less than unconditional surrender should be accepted, and pressure was put on the neighbouring clans to expel the offenders from their limits.

They were at last driven to extremities, and on the 20th of September 1871 they surrendered unconditionally to the Commissioner of the Derajat.

Complete pardon for offences of such enormity it was impossible to accord; but, on the other hand, the Government desired that the punishment inflicted should bear in the eyes of border tribes no appearance of revenge. The humiliation of the Muhammad Khels had been so unprecedented, and the assertion of the authority of the British Government so complete, that there was no fear of mercy being mistaken for weakness. The six headmen of the section were accordingly sentenced to varying terms of imprisonment in the Lahore jail, and heavy fines were imposed on the section, on payment of which they were permitted to return to their lands in British territory.

To render this lesson more impressive, it was determined to call to account the several sections which, during the outlawry of the Muhammad Khels, had afforded them assistance or shelter. First were the Umarzais. They had not only passively, but actively, assisted them. Some were engaged in the attack on the village of Sukhi on the 12th of February, others were present at the skirmish in the Kurram pass on the 24th of April, and others were guilty of separate acts of hostility. They were accordingly ordered to produce all the men concerned in these outrages. These, with three exceptions, were given up, when fines proportionate to their offences were levied.

The Bizen Khels were next called to account, and paid without demur the fine imposed on them.

Lastly, the village of Gumatti, inhabited by Sudan Khel Wazirs, who had harboured the Muhammad Khels, and covered their retreat from the plains with stolen property, was destroyed. The order for the burning of the village was carried into effect by the inhabitants themselves, in presence of Man Khan, Chief of the Sudan Khel Wazirs, and Muhammad Hyat Khan, Extra Assistant Commissioner, Bannu.

The villages of Lower Dawar, however, who had also given shelter to the Muhammad Khels, did not submit, and refused to pay the fine imposed, and in consequence, Brig.-General Keyes, commanding the Punjab Frontier Force, visited that valley with a force, the operations of which are described in Chapter X.

At the end of 1872 Lord Northbrook saw the Muhammad Khel prisoners in the Lahore jail, and, considering that they had been sufficiently punished, he directed their release.

In January 1874 reprisals were made on the Miamai section of the Kabul Khel Wazirs for plundering a caravan of Ghilzai traders proceeding from British territory to Kurram, and in the following March troops were moved to Thal for the purpose of settling claims against the different Wazir clans on the Kohat border.

A satisfactory settlement was then effected with the Kabul Khel, Malik Shahi, Khojal Khel, and Tojiya Khel sections, and the force returned to Kohat on the 22nd of April.

During the next few years the Darwesh Khel Waziris gave but little trouble on our border. They were engaged in carrying on a tedious war in the independent hills, beyond the frontier, with the other great branch of the Wazirs—the Mahsuds. This feud had no injurious effect on our border administration, but rather the contrary; the occupation of these predatory tribes in internecine strife tending to withdraw their attention from plundering in British territory. In this feud, owing to the dissensions amongst the different sections of the Darwesh Khel branch, the Mahsuds had the advantage in almost every instance of hostile collision. In September 1878 a truce was agreed to by the two belligerents, and the feud which had lasted for so long was patched up.

At the beginning of the war in Afghanistan, the Wazirs, and more especially the Mahsud clan, as will be seen in the next chapter, were incited from Kabul to commit depredations on the British border. The Darwesh Khels as a body do not appear to have given way to this excitement, but one section of the Ahmadzai clan, the Zalli Khel, was guilty of an attack on the Jatta post.

For this outrage, all property belonging to the section found in British territory was seized, and in the following January Captain E. A. Money, commanding at Tank, in consultation with the Deputy Commissioner of Dera Ismail Khan, made a raid on a party of Zalli Khels and captured a large number of their cattle.

After this the Zalli Khels offered to make good the damage caused to property in the raid in January 1879, and also to pay any fine the Government might think fit to impose upon them.

This led to the recovery of the sum of Rs. 16,021, at which the fine and compensation had been fixed, and the section was again admitted to intercourse with British territory.

Returning now to the Kohat and Bannu borders. On the outbreak of the war in Afghanistan a convoy route was opened between Thal and Bannu. This route, which followed for the most part the line of the river Kurram, passed through the independent territory of the Utmanzai and Ahmadzai Wazirs, and had not been traversed by British troops since the Kabul Khel expedition of 1859, above related. During the winter of 1878-79 several detachments of British cavalry and infantry, and the whole of the Jind and Kapurthala Contingents, marched by this route, and it was very extensively used for convoys of supplies and transport animals for the Kurram Valley Field Force, Wazir camels being employed largely in carrying commissariat stores. In spite of the efforts of the well-known Mulla Adkar of Khost to interfere with the arrangements entered into with the Darwesh Khel Wazirs, the route remained open for troops and supplies until the 21st of March 1880.

Umarzai.
Sudan Khel.
Muhammad Khel.
Khojal Khel.
Sadda Khel.

For the protection of convoys on the Bannu side, escorts or *badragas* were enlisted from the Ahmadzai sections named in the margin, and small personal allowances were made to some of the more important chiefs. On the Kohat side similar arrangements were made with the Malik Shahi and Kabul Khel Utmanzai sections. The total allowances amounted to about Rs. 1,000 a month.

During the time the route was open one hundred and nineteen convoys passed through. In the first campaign only four offences of any importance were committed upon this road; in the second, parties of robbers from Dawar made two successful raids, on the 29th of September 1879 and 31st of January 1880. In March 1880, chiefly in consequence of the excitement among the surrounding clans produced by the preaching of the Mulla Adkar, it was deemed expedient to close this route.

This man, whose influence was felt throughout the whole of the Wazir hills, was a fanatical disciple of the late Akhund of Swat, and aspired to occupy his position; but, unfortunately, he was not such a respectable character. He had, for many years, established his head-quarters at Kadam, in Khost, but on the occupation of that valley by British troops in January 1879, he fled to Upper Dawar, and was untiring in his efforts to organise a general crusade among the hill tribes, and, when that failed, to incite and encourage smaller incursions for plunder and assassination.

Almost immediately after the closing of the Thal–Bannu route, a serious outrage was committed, in which a Turi caravan was attacked near Thal, and suffered considerable loss. The raiders were about sixty in number, and consisted of thirty Tori Khel Wazirs, twenty-four Dawaris, and a few Mahsuds. The party passed through the territory of the Mohmit Khels on their way to and from the scene of the outrage. The raid was the outcome of the evil influence and fanatical preaching of Mulla Adkar, and another outrage due to the same influence was committed a few days later in an attack by a party of raiders, composed of Mohmit Khels (Hassan Khel section), Mahsuds, Dawaris, and disciples (*talib-ul-ilms*) of Mulla Adkar, on a Khattak labour camp, three or four miles from Thal, on the Thal–Kurram road.

After this, on the night of the 1st–2nd of May, an attack was made on the military post of Chapri, which was garrisoned by fifty bayonets of the 5th Native Infantry and thirty sabres of the 1st Bengal Cavalry, under the command of Lieutenant W. H. Cazalet, of the latter regiment. The Chapri post consisted of a walled enclosure some sixty yards square, standing close to the Thal–Kurram road, at a distance of eight miles from Thal. It stood on ground sloping slightly down towards the road, and was roughly divided into two parts—the upper occupied by the troops garrisoning the post, and the lower by the transport convoys. In the lower half also stood the officers' tents, the tent for the guard at the gate, and those occupied by shopkeepers, *kahars*, and officers' servants. This lower half was not fortified, and was only enclosed by a wall eight or nine feet high. It was into this half that the raiders gained access, after having pulled down a foot or two of the west wall at a corner where there was no sentry.

The party did not probably number more than two hundred men, and of these only some forty or fifty gained access, and it is supposed that they must have been inside some minutes before any one in the post was aware of their presence. When, however, they were observed and challenged, they rushed in among the *kahars* and camelmen, slashing at and cutting down every one they met.

On hearing the noise the garrison turned out, but for a short time all was confusion. Eventually, however, the raiders, finding they were likely to get the worst of it, turned, and escaped from the enclosure over the north and west walls. The troops in the post kept up a fire, as they retreated, but no pursuit was attempted.

Our loss had been eleven men killed, including Lieutenant O. B. Wood, Transport Officer, and sixteen wounded.

From information subsequently received, it appears that the raiders started from the country of the Mohmit Khel Wazirs, and were made up of members of that section and of Dawaris, with a few Mahsuds. The Tori Khels and Hasan Khels gave a passage to the offenders through their limits, although they were quite able to have denied this if they had wished.

In forwarding the report of this affair, the Commissioner of Peshawar recommended that, when occasion should offer in the autumn, an expedition should be organised against the Mohmit Khel and Tori Khel Wazirs, to punish them for their repeated acts of hostility to the Government; but the day of reckoning never came.

Expedition against the Malik Shahi Wazir settlements, by a force under Brig.-General J. J. H. Gordon, C.B., in October 1880.

In October 1880 fines and penalties, aggregating Rs. 13,200, were due from the Kabul Khel and Malik Shahi Wazirs, chiefly for minor offences, such as thefts of cattle and property, committed by them on the Kurram river route, and in the neighbourhood of Thal during the war; and in order to bring pressure to bear on these sections for the recovery of this amount, a force consisting of two guns, 250 cavalry, and 500 infantry, under the command of Brig.-General J. J. H. Gordon, C.B.

1-8th Royal Artillery ..	2 guns.
85th King's Own Light Infantry ..	250 of all ranks.
18th Bengal Cavalry ..	250 " "
20th Punjab Native Infantry.	250 " "

and accompanied by Major T. J. C. Plowden as Political Officer, entered the Kabul Khel hills on the evening of the 27th of October 1880.

The object of the expedition was to seize men and cattle of the Malik Shahi section as security for their share of the fine. This section is almost entirely nomadic, spending the summer on the slopes of the Siah Koh mountains and the winter in their lands on both banks of the Kurram river, extending from the 9th to the 16th mile on the Thal-Bannu road. In order to reach them the whole Kabul Khel settlements had to be traversed, and they would thus have time to escape from the comparatively open country through which the Kurram river flows into the more intricate hill country to the west, in the direction of the Siah Koh. The Malik Shahis, conscious of the advantages of their position, and the facilities with which they could escape on our moving out against them, had been more reckless than the Kabul Khels in their conduct towards us. The difficulty, therefore, of the enterprise was for the column to move through the country of the latter without notice of its approach reaching the Malik Shahi section.

The force marched from Thal at 9-30 P.M., on the 27th of October, and, by making a detour, avoided the large Bangash village of Biland Khel, and reached the positions which had been previously assigned them before daybreak.

The advance party surrounded the Malik Shahi encampment at the south-west end of the valley; another party had been detached to the left to surround the Malik Shahi settlements on the Charkhanai plateau; and a third small party had proceeded to the right, to try and capture some noted Wazir thieves. The supports remained at Drozanda, the first encamping ground from Thal on the Thal-Bannu road. The surprise was complete, and two thousand head of cattle, and one hundred and nine prisoners were captured. The force returned to Thal on the 28th.

On the 30th the Kabul Khel *jirga* attended at Thal and made their submission, and by the 18th of December the whole fine of Rs. 13,200 was realized from the Kabul Khel and Malik Shahi sections; the prisoners were then released, and Rs. 6,000 taken as security for future good behaviour.

In spite, however, of the punishment that they had received, the conduct of the Kabul Khel Wazirs continued to be unsatisfactory. With the Hathi Khel and other sections residing on the Bannu border, and with the support of Khattak outlaws, they committed numerous raids during the following year (1881) into the heart of the Khattak country. In some of these they succeeded in carrying off large herds of *Powindah* camels; in the majority they were unsuccessful, the stolen cattle being recovered in pursuit. The head-quarters of the raiders was in Hathi Khel territory, but most of the stolen cattle found their way to the Saifali Kabul Khels. The *jirga* of the Kabul Khels was, therefore, summoned to Kohat by the the Deputy Commissioner in February 1882, and fines were imposed in cases brought home to them, and the conduct of the section was then more satisfactory.

Our further dealings with the Darwesh Khel Wazirs up to the present time will be narrated in Chapter IX.

APPENDIX A.

Genealogy of the Darwesh Khel Wazirs.

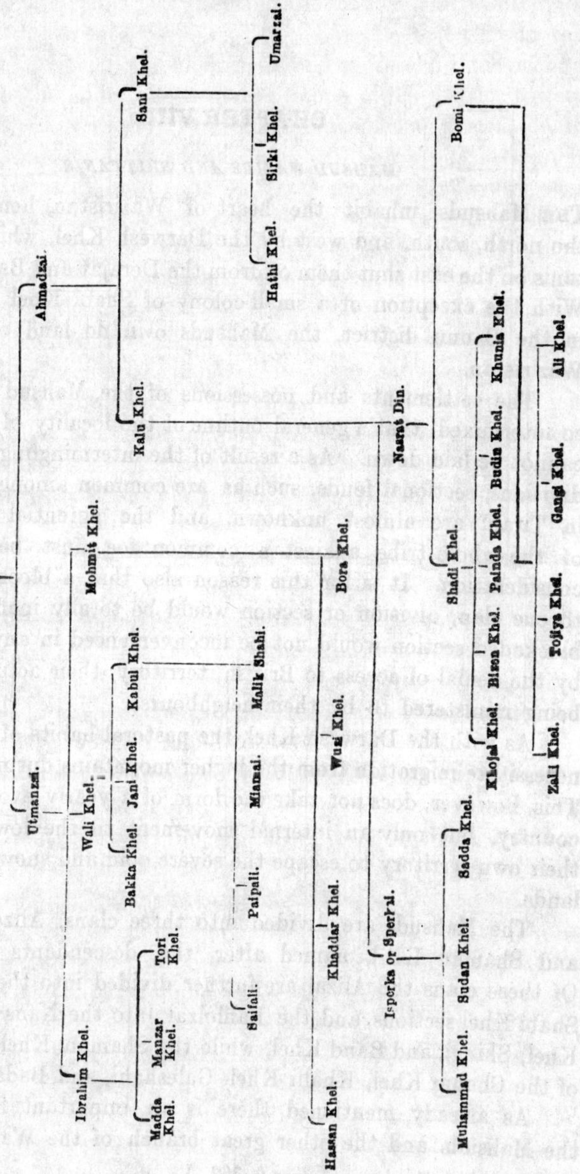

CHAPTER VIII.

MAHSUD WAZIRS AND BHITTANIS.

THE Mahsuds inhabit the heart of Waziristan, hemmed in on the north, south, and west by the Darwesh Khel, whilst the Bhittanis on the east shut them off from the Derajat and Bannu borders. With the exception of a small colony of Shabi Khel at Landidah in the Bannu district, the Mahsuds own no land outside south Waziristan.

The settlements and possessions of the Mahsud sections are so intermixed, that a general outline of the locality of each section cannot be laid down. As a result of the intermingling of the tribal divisions, sectional feuds, such as are common amongst the Afridis in Tirah, are almost unknown, and the potential combination of the whole tribe against a common foe must be taken into consideration. It is for this reason also that a blockade confined to one clan, division or section would be totally ineffectual. The blockaded section would not be inconvenienced in any way except by the denial of access to British territory, their actual necessities being ministered to by their neighbours.

As with the Darwesh Khel, the pastoral habits of the Mahsuds necessitate migration from the higher mountains during the winter. This, however, does not take the form of a yearly exodus from the country, but only an internal movement to the lower valleys of their own territory to escape the severe cold and snow of the highlands.

The Mahsuds are divided into three clans, Alizai, Bahlolzai, and Shaman Khel, named after the descendants of Mahsud. Of these clans the Alizai are further divided into the Manzai and Shabi Khel sections, and the Bahlolzai into the Nana Khel, Aimal Khel, Shingi, and Band Khel, while the Shaman Khel are made up of the Chahar Khel, Khalli Khel, Galeshahi, and Badanzai.

As already mentioned, there is an important feud between the Mahsuds and the other great branch of the Wazir tribe, the

Darwesh Khels. The Mahsuds attributed much of the success of Brig.-General Chamberlain's expedition in 1860 to the information given by the Ahmadzais to our officers. This feud, in which the Mahsuds generally have the best of it, was patched up in 1878.

Chamberlain says of the Mahsuds, that it was their boast that, while kingdoms and dynasties had passed away, they alone, of all the Afghan tribes, had remained free; that the armies of kings had never penetrated their strongholds; that in their intercourse with the rest of mankind they knew no law or will but their own; and lastly, that from generation to generation the *daman* (or the plain country), within a night's run to the hills, had been their hunting ground from which to enrich themselves.

Under the Sikh rule, this state of things was even worse; for, through misgovernment, the chief of Tank became a refugee in the Wazir mountains, and his country was farmed out to Multani or Tiwana mercenaries, according as either class was for the time being in favour at the Lahore court. The chief being expelled from his territory, his course was naturally to ally himself with the Mahsuds (which he did by marriage), and to keep the country in so distracted a state, that it became almost uninhabited; the town of Tank at last contained nothing but its garrison and a few *bannias.* On one occasion it was attacked and plundered by the Mahsuds, when they retained possession of it for three days.

After the first Sikh war the rightful owner was restored, and things returned to pretty much their usual state, the Mahsuds not causing uneasiness as a tribe, but raids being of constant occurrence.

Bhittanis.

The Bhittanis inhabit the hill country on the borders of Tank and Bannu from the Gabar mountain on the north to the Gumal valley on the south. They claim descent from Baitan, the third son of Kais, the founder of the Afghan race. Their fighting-men amount to 6,000, but of these the large proportion are revenue-paying British subjects.

The independent Bhittani are politically controlled by the Deputy Commissioner, Dera Ismail Khan. They are the hereditary enemies of the Mahsuds, although they have more than once foregone their time-honoured feud and either combined with or aided and abetted their more rapacious Mahsud neighbours in attacks and raids in British territory. Now, however, they have practically become identified as a tribe with British interests, and they furnish valuable material for one company of the cis-border half-battalion of the new Militia Corps.

In appearance the Bhittanis are not so rough as the Mahsuds, though in physique they closely resemble them; they have discarded the dress of their neighbours of the Waziristan highlands for the more civilized apparel of the *daman*, and present a much cleaner appearance. Their pronunciation is also not so provincial as the Mahsuds', and their speech consequently approximates to the usual Pushtu of more civilized tribes.

Their country beyond the administrative border consists of rough stony hills scored by deep valleys, along which there is a little cultivation here and there, where the inhabitants have been able to lead the rather intermittent water-supply of the *nalas* on to the culturable *kaches* by irrigation channels. The Bhittani hills are extremely rough and almost devoid of verdure, and the tribesmen have the reputation of being better mountaineers than their western neighbours.

Though insignificant, they have always been a troublesome tribe, but have generally been engaged as the spies and guides of their powerful neighbours rather than in any large plundering raids on their own account. In 1853, however, tired of their usual *rôle* of jackals, they undertook the part of the lion, and attacked and plundered two villages within British territory, in retaliation for the death of a brother of one of their chiefs, killed by the police in a plundering excursion. A party of the tribe in British territory was at once seized, and they then made terms. Had they not done so, it was proposed to despatch an expedition to chastise them. After this they behaved better, and in the expedition against the Mahsud Wazirs in 1860, about to be described, they gave the British force some little assistance by supplying information, and in other ways.

Expedition against the Mahsud Wazirs by a force under Brig.-General N. B. Chamberlain, C.B., in 1860.

The Mahsuds were formerly celebrated as the earliest, the most inveterate, and the most incorrigible of all the robbers of the border.

From the earliest days of our rule they were guilty of a long list of raids on British territory, and they were in the habit of attacking the *Powindah*[1] caravans, as their country commands the Gumal pass, the main avenue through which these traders enter British territory; but the merchants, themselves of the Pathan race, being invariably armed, were able to offer a stout resistance. As soon as they encamped in British territory, however, they often neglected the precautions which they adopted across the border, and the frontier was kept much disturbed, and the outposts were harassed, by the plundering attacks made on their *kiris* and herds by the Wazirs.

In the spring of 1855 the Chief Commissioner (Mr. John Lawrence), being impressed with the injuries committed by the Mahsuds, recommended that a force should be sent against them that autumn, but the proposal was not carried out. In February 1857 Sir John Lawrence again found occasion to recommend "that retributive measures be no longer delayed," and Government sanctioned their being undertaken; but again circumstances arose to prevent their being carried into execution.

[1] The tribes of warrior traders included under the term *Powindah* (probably from the same root as the Pushtu word for "to graze") belong chiefly to the great tribe of Ghilzai Pathans.

They are almost wholly engaged in the carrying trade between India and Afghanistan and Central Asia. They assemble every autumn in the plains east of Ghazni, with their families, flocks, herds, and long strings of camels laden with the goods of Bokhara and Kandahar; and forming enormous caravans, numbering many thousands, march in military order through the Kakar and Waziri countries by the Kurram, Tochi, and Gumal passes into British territory.

Entering the Dera Ismail Khan district, they leave their families, flocks, and some two-thirds of their fighting-men in the great grazing grounds which lie on either side of the Indus, and while some wander off in search of employment, others pass on with their laden camels and merchandise to Multan, Rajputana, Lahore, Amritsar, Delhi, Cawnpore, Benares, and Patna.

In the spring they again assemble, and return by the same routes to their homes in the hills about Ghazni and Kelat-i-Ghilzai. When the hot weather begins, the men, leaving their belongings behind them, move off to Kandahar, Herat, and Bokhara with the Indian and European merchandise which they have brought from Hindustan. In October they return, and prepare to start once more for India.

About 50,000 of these nomads enter the Dera Ismail Khan district every year by the Gumal pass between the 20th of October and the 15th of December, and return between the 20th of March and the 10th of May.

For generations the Wazirs carried on war to the knife with these merchant traders. To meet the opposition that awaited them at this part of the road, the *Powindahs*, who were heavily armed, moved in large bodies of from 5,000 to 10,000, and regular marches and encampments were observed, under an elected *Khan* or leader, exactly like an army moving through an enemy's country. They more than once attempted to come to a compromise with their enemies and arrange for an unmolested passage on payment of a fixed blackmail, but the Wazirs invariably refused to listen to any compromise. At the present time these nomads are annually escorted through the pass, stage by stage, by the Southern Waziristan Militia.

In 1859 Brigadier-General N. B. Chamberlain, C.B., then commanding the Punjab Irregular Force, thus wrote of the raids of the Mahsuds—

In the course of my annual tour I see much of all classes of the people, and nowhere now do I hear the cry for justice until I come within reach of the Wazirs. Then commences a train of injuries received and unredressed; and I know of no more pitiable sight than the tears and entreaties of a family who have lost their only means of enabling them to accompany the tribe (the *Powindahs*) on its return back to summer quarters. Supposing that our backwardness arises from fear, several times have the men, and even women, counselled courage, saying, "we will assist you; they cannot stand before guns and percussion fire-arms."

In the winter of 1860–61, Brig.-General Chamberlain intended to resign the command of the Punjab Irregular Force, preparatory to proceeding to England, and as he did not wish to leave the Wazir question in the state it then was, and as he felt that sooner or later an expedition would have to be sent against the tribe, he proposed that punitive measures should then be adopted, as it was utterly hopeless to expect them to mend their ways till punished.

The matter was submitted to Government, but Lord Canning eventually decided against an expedition, on the ground that it was a cumulative case, and not actually pressing at the time, as the border was then quiet. But before Lieut.-Colonel Taylor, the Commissioner, was half-way back to Dera Ismail Khan on his return from visiting the Viceroy, news of great importance reached him.

Emboldened by years of immunity, and believing that they could successfully oppose any attempt to penetrate their mountains, the Wazirs had, on the 13th of March 1860, without provocation or pretext of any kind, come out into the plains to the number of some 3,000, headed by their principal men, with the intention of sacking the town of Tank, which stands on the plains some five miles from the foot of the hills. The Nawab's agents having obtained previous notice of their gathering, on the 12th informed Saadat Khan, the native officer in command of the troop of the 5th Punjab Cavalry, then holding Tank. This officer at once summoned the sowars in the neighbouring regular outposts, besides collecting twenty of the Nawab's horsemen, and some other irregular horse;

so that the force at his disposal was 158 sabres, 5th Punjab Cavalry and 37 mounted levies.

On the morning of the 13th the whole party moved out towards the mouth of the Tank Zam, on arriving near the entrance of which they found the Wazirs drawn up about half a mile on the plain side of the pass. The Wazirs immediately opened fire upon the cavalry, on which Ressaldar Saadat Khan ordered his detachment to retire, with the intention of drawing the enemy further into the plains. The stratagem was successful, and the enemy followed with shouts of derision; but when they had come nearly a mile, the cavalry turned and, having first cut off their retreat to the hills, charged in the most dashing manner. The Wazirs, though personally brave, wanted the power of combination to resist effectually the charge of our cavalry. Cut down and ridden over, they fled in confusion, till all became a helpless rabble straining to regain the safety of the mountain pass.

The result was that about 300 Mahsuds were killed, including six leading *maliks*, and many more wounded. Among the former was Jangi Khan, the leading chief of the whole tribe. Our loss was one jemadar of levies killed, two non-commissioned officers and eleven sowars of the 5th Punjab Cavalry, and three of the levies wounded.

This outrage was considered as filling up the cup of their iniquities, and orders were accordingly issued to Brig.-General Chamberlain for the assembling of a force to enter their hills, and there exact satisfaction for the past and security for the future. General Chamberlain had the option of advancing from either Bannu or Tank, and he chose the latter—first, because he thought it more appropriate to commence from the Tank side, as that was the route used by the Wazirs when descending for the above raid; secondly, the most mischievous portion of the Mahsud tribe, with whom the quarrel especially was, inhabited the hills immediately above Tank, and it was more natural to attack them in the first instance; and thirdly, the line of road was better known, and, though it had difficulties, was known to be practicable, while nothing was known concerning the road from the Bannu side.

The Brig.-General hoped, in the event of the tribe not coming to terms after the force had entered the Tank–Zam pass, and if further ingress did not prove to be impracticable, to penetrate to Kaniguram and Makin, their two chief places, and then return to British territory by the Khaisora defile in front of Bannu.

Lieut.-Colonel R. G. Taylor, the Commissioner, anticipated the Wazirs adopting one of the three following courses:—

The first and most probable was that they would make their grand stand at Shingi Kot, their traditionary strong point, like the Khan Band of the Bozdars. This was a fairly strong place, protecting the head of the country, and was decidedly the most likely place for them to defend with all their available strength and means.

Secondly, that they would come further forward to the Hinis Tangi. This is a much stiffer place than the Shingi position, and their holding it would make the first action in all probability a more serious matter than if they waited at Shingi, as they might inflict a good deal of loss before being driven off the heights. On the other hand, the Hinis Tangi was rather an advanced position for the Wazirs to take up, as they would be further from support than at Shingi, and there they would not be sure of a safe retreat.

The third plan Lieut.-Colonel Taylor thought they might adopt was to avoid resisting the force in large bodies, and only harass it by day and night, attacking the baggage, etc.; this was in all probability their safest plan, but he thought, however, that they would most likely adopt one of the first two courses.

It was probable that, if once well defeated, they would break away, and not offer much further resistance; but no precedent could be counted on, as this was the first time these Wazirs had been assailed in their homes. After defeating the enemy, the force could advance *viâ* Kaniguram and Makin, either into the Bannu or Dawar valley, concluding matters which were still pending with the Kabul Khels and Tori Khels; or, if the country was found stiffer than was expected, after taking full satisfaction from the Mahsuds at Shingi Kot, which is well in the Wazir country, the force could return from there.

Arrangements had been made for a large body of levies to take part in the expedition. These levies were drawn from the frontier classes, and were under their *Khans* and *Tumandars.* It was considered that they might be employed in the attack of minor places on the flanks of the main column (thus distracting the enemy, and affording a hope of seizing cattle), in holding points to keep open the communications, and on other duties ; and it was thought that advantage would be derived from the force being thus accompanied by the frontier classes and chiefs, all hereditary enemies of the Wazirs, as the operations would thereby be more clearly shown to be in the cause of order, and in a great measure on behalf of our subjects.

The *Powindah* merchants were also ordered to assemble in front of the Gumal valley, to act, if required, against their declared and bitter enemies; but there were some difficulties in the way of their employment. The *Powindahs* had doubts how their joining in the expedition would be regarded by the authorites and tribes above the pass; and there was the likelihood that if, taking advantage of the advance of a Government force, the *Powindahs* took severe revenge for former injuries, it might be revisited on them and their caravans by the Wazirs as a body when our quarrel had been settled.

On the 16th of April 1860 the marginally named force, consisting of 5,196 of all ranks, was assembled at Tank. Lieut.-Colonel R. G. Taylor, the Commissioner, was to accompany the force as Political Officer.

No. 2 Punjab Light Field Battery	3	guns.
No. 3 " " " " ..	3	"
Peshawar Mountain Train Battery ..	4	"
Hazara " " " ..	3	"
Guide Cavalry	108	all ranks.
3rd Punjab Cavalry	131	" "
Multani Cavalry [1]	100	" "
1st Company, Sappers and Miners ..	60	" "
Guide Infantry	407	" "
4th Sikh Infantry	427	" "
1st Punjab Infantry	397	" "
2nd " "	684	" "
3rd " "	373	" "
4th " "	381	" "
6th " "	400	" "
14th " " [2]	207	" "
24th " " (Pioneers) [3] ..	418	" "
Hazara Gurkha Battalions [4]	464	" "
6th Police Battalion	394	" "

Before advancing, a proclamation was addressed to the Mahsud chiefs, to announce the object for which the Government forces were about to enter their hills; to tell them that, within a fixed period, they were free to attend the camp for the purpose of hearing the demands of the British Government;

[1] Now the 15th Cureton's Multanis. It was at this time (1860) attached to the Punjab Irregular Force.

[2] Subsequently disbanded.

[3] Now the 32nd Pioneers.

[4] The 25th Punjab Infantry, or Hazara Gurkha Battalion, became the 5th Gurkhas.

and that, on their failing to appear, or not complying with the demands, they and their tribe would be treated as enemies, and punished.

No reply having been received to this proclamation, and reports having reached the camp that the Wazirs were assembling within a few miles of the plains, further delay was considered inadvisable, and, on the morning of the 17th of April, Brig.-General Chamberlain, with the whole of his force, which had been augmented by 1,600 levies, horse and foot, crossed the border by the Tank Zam. This is a huge ravine, the bed of which is paved throughout with boulders and stones; in fine weather a clear stream from two to three feet deep winds down it, requiring to be crossed at every few hundred yards; after rain the whole bed suddenly fills, and is impassable.

After a march of eleven miles and a half, the camp was pitched on a stony plateau, the present site of the Kot Khirgi outpost. The pass as far as the Hinis Tangi was reconnoitred. It was reported that the enemy intended to make a stand at this point, and had barricaded the pass. The gorge, however, was found unoccupied, and the Pioneers were sent to remove the breastwork which had been thrown across it.

The next day the column marched to Palosin Kach, a detachment being sent off to destroy Shingi Kot on the way.

The village of Jandola, situated at the western mouth of the Hinis Tangi, belonged to the Bhittanis, and as the position commanded the passage to and from the plains, the greater portion of the levies were placed there for the convoy of supplies from Tank.

That every facility for making overtures might be given to the Mahsuds in case they were disposed to negotiate, the force was halted during the 19th of April. But as it was reported that, so far from being inclined to submit, the Wazirs were assembling for hostilities, the destruction of their houses and property was ordered.

Before advancing on Kaniguram, it was decided to penetrate up the Shahur Zam towards the Kundighar mountain, to examine the country, and to destroy the crops and property of the Shingi and Nana Khel sections, who had been always foremost in plundering attacks on the Tank border.

On the 20th, therefore, the head-quarters and the marginally named troops, as per margin, moved with eight days' supplies to Haidari Kach.

No. 3 Punjab Light Field Battery.
Peshawar Mountain Train Battery.
Hazara " "
Detachment, Guide Cavalry.
Detachment, 3rd Punjab Cavalry.
Detachment, Multani Cavalry.
1st Company, Sappers and Miners.
Guide Infantry.
1st Punjab Infantry.
2nd " "
3rd " "
4th " "
6th " "
Detachment, 24th Punjab Infantry (Pioneers).
6th Police Battalion.

It was necessary to keep possession of Jandola, that supplies might be collected there for an immediate advance on Kaniguram on the return of the troops from the Shahur valley; and as the strength of the force admitted of a division Lieut.-Colonel H. B. Lumsden, C.B., was left at Palosin, with discretionary orders to fall back on Jandola if any gathering of the Wazirs rendered it advisable.

The move upon the Shahur gorge was not expected by the enemy, and it was found unoccupied, save by a small party, who retired as the infantry ascended the heights.

The defile was found to be narrow and difficult, and about three miles in length, the hills on either side closing in, in a manner to preclude artillery being turned to much account. To command the sides, either a great circuit had to be made to reach the main range, or each spur had to be ascended in succession,—a most fatiguing operation, involving much exposure.

On the 21st, after sending back the guns of No. 3 Punjab Light Field Battery with their elephants and the Guide Infantry, the Brig.-General advanced to Turan China, only four miles, as the stream he had been following suddenly ceased to flow above ground, and as the distance to the next water was uncertain.

On the following day, the 22nd, the force marched to Barwand, at the foot of the Kundighar mountain. On this and the previous march the country was found to be more open than any that was either before or subsequently passed through, but beyond the camp the hills again closed in, and the bed of the ravine was the only practicable road.

On the 23rd the march was continued up the bed of the ravine for four miles, when Jangi Khan's fort was reached, and the camp pitched. Jangi Khan, who had been the principal chief of the whole Mahsud tribe, had been killed, with his son and nephew the previous month in the attack upon Tank. The fort was blown up, and the village, as well as the cultivation, of the Nana Khels destroyed.

By the defile by which the troops were moving, Kaniguram could be reached, and the Wazirs, supposing this to be the real object of the movement, determined to defend the passage at a gorge leading into the Khaisora valley, three miles beyond the camp.

As to reach Kaniguram by this route, however, was no part of the general plan, to have forced the gorge would have been an expenditure of life without any object; and having now seen and surveyed the best part of the north-west portion of the district, and consumed half the supplies, it was time for the force to return.

The absence of men on the distant hills, or even the usual look-out on the heights in the neighbourhood of the camp, had been remarked during the last two days, and this was now explained by their having collected all their numbers to close the passage to Kaniguram; and also, as will be shown, to attack Lieut.-Colonël Lumsden's camp; the news of which attack reached Brig.-General Chamberlain by a Bhittani spy as the troops were falling in at daybreak on the 24th, preparatory to moving back to Palosin.

No. 2 Punjab Light Field Battery.
No. 3 " " " "
3rd Punjab Cavalry.
Detachment, Guide Cavalry.
Guide Infantry.
4th Sikh Infantry.
14th Punjab Infantry.
Detachment, 24th Punjab Infantry.
Hazara Gurkha Battalion.

The force under the command of Lieut.-Colonel Lumsden consisted of the troops noted in the margin, with a body of levies, as well as the sick of those corps which had gone with Brig.-General Chamberlain, with the spare carriage and establishment, supplies, and war material. It occupied a position on the *kach* land on the left bank of the Tank Zam, its right resting on an old Wazir tower (distant some 800 yards) overlooking the stream; and the left protected by a picquet on the abrupt peak to the south-east, having the scarped bank of the stream in its front and the edge of the high tableland immediately in the rear.

On the night of the 22nd the outlying picquets were at their posts on the ridge behind the camp; a complete company occupied the tower, three other parties, each of one havildar and eight sepoys, were posted along the rear, and one of thirty men was on the high peak just mentioned,—each picquet had a support of equal strength behind it.

The little information which could be obtained from scouts tended to the assurance that no bodies of the enemy had yet assembled, and that they would not do so till the force proceeded further into their country ; but, owing to the unanimity among the Mahsud branch of the Wazirs, it was almost impossible to obtain anything like reliable information of the movements of the tribe.

During the night a few stray shots were fired by the sentries at intervals, but all appeared tranquil, till, just as the *reveille* sounded, the camp was alarmed by a volley fired by the rear picquet.

A body of 3,000 Wazirs, making a sudden rush, had overpowered and nearly destroyed the picquets immediately in their line of attack, holding the high bank above the camp ; here the greater mass stopped, while 500 of the bravest of them dashed into the camp sword in hand, the remainder keeping up a heavy fire from the ridge. As it happened, they were chiefly successful where the store godown and mounted levies were placed, but they also penetrated into a part of the Guide camp. Owing to the suddenness of the attack, considerable confusion at first prevailed, and the Wazirs did great mischief among the surprised mounted levies.

An in-lying picquet, consisting of a company of the Corps of Guides, was now placed on the ridge, to enfilade the slopes on the enemy's flank, and to check their advance. The confusion for a time was general, but Lieutenant E. E. B. Bond, of the Guides, and Lieutenant G. O. Lewis, 7th Fusiliers, attached to that corps, rallying a considerable body of men, drove back the Wazirs in front of them at the point of the bayonet. No sooner had the alarm been given, than the artillery under Captains G. Maister and T. E. Hughes, were in action, rendering the most valuable assistance in clearing the camp of the enemy.

In the meantime, Major O. E. Rothney had formed up the Hazara Gurkha Battalion on the ridge, supported by the 4th Sikhs, under Lieutenant F. H. Jenkins, the picquet of which regiment had not been driven in. After driving back the enemy, who were now pouring into that part of the camp, Major Rothney advanced on their flank, bearing down on the mass of Wazirs on the table-land above with great steadiness. After these two regiments had got clear of the right of the camp, they were joined by the Guides when the three corps pursued the enemy for fully three miles over the hills, inflicting severe punishment on them till they broke and dispersed,—a part going in the direction of Shingi Kot, and the rest over the ridges more to the eastward.

Our casualties were heavy, 63 killed and 166 wounded, for the attack had not only been sudden, but for a time was conducted with determined gallantry; indeed, it was a hand-to-hand conflict during the time the enemy were inside the camp, and the unarmed camp followers suffered much. The picquets, too, had greatly suffered; in the Corps of Guides alone there were the following casualties: in one piquet—one native officer, two non-commissioned officers, and ten sepoys killed, and six non-commissioned officers and thirty-eight sepoys wounded; in a second—one non-commissioned officer killed and three sepoys wounded; and in a third, three sepoys wounded. But the losses of the enemy were also very heavy; ninety-two of their bodies were found in and round the camp, and some forty more in a *nala* on their line of retreat.

To revert now to the movements of the main column, which was marching to rejoin Lieut.-Colonel Lumsden.

On the 24th the force marched to Turan China, and the following day to the western entrance of the Shahur gorge.

When the force had advanced, only such crops had been destroyed as were known to belong to the worst offenders; but after the attack on Palosin, and the evident attention of the Mahsuds to resist to the utmost, all the crops the troops passed were now destroyed.

Early on the 26th a move through the gorge was commenced; some attempt was made to harass the rear-guard, but all the heights have been crowned, and the picquets were withdrawn without any casualty on our side.

The camp was pitched at Mandanna Kach, where the main body was joined by Lieut.-Colonel Lumsden's force.

From the 27th of April to the 1st of May the force remained halted, to admit of the sick and wounded being sent back to Tank, and for the litters to rejoin preparatory to an advance upon Kaniguram.

On the 1st of May, as it was reported that the Mahsuds had occupied the Ahnai Tangi, nine miles beyond camp, it had been intended to move the next day to within easy range of the gorge, so as to attack it in the early morning; but late in the afternoon eleven Mahsud Maliks arrived in camp, deputed, they said, by the whole tribe to make terms.

The reasons for the force entering the hills were fully explained to the chiefs; the Government proclamation was read to them in Pushtu, and they were told there was yet time for them to make terms. These were either immediate payment of the value of the cattle stolen during the past eight years, calculated at a low estimate at Rs. 43,000, or giving security for its payment within a reasonable time, and hostages for their future good conduct; and they were further told there was not the slightest wish to meddle with their country, far less to annex any portion of it; all that was desired being that they should keep their tribe in order.

But the Wazirs had evidently no fancy for paying a fine, and the alternative proposal, namely, that they should give a free passage to the force to Kaniguram, the capital of the country, was equally unpalatable. The *malik* who acted as spokesman made great protestations of their anxiety for peace; but it was evident that they hoped for it without paying for the past, and that they were decidedly opposed to the march through their country. The question of security for the future never came actually under discussion, as the deliberation did not get beyond the first point.

Towards the end of this meeting there arose a point of difference as to whether the force should halt or move onward the next day. It was an object in every way to move on to Shingi; the ground occupied had become unhealthy, and supplies were getting scarcer every day. On the other hand, the *maliks* wished for a day's delay to consider the propositions; but after fully weighing the whole case, Brig.-General Chamberlain decided in favour of moving on, feeling convinced that if the *maliks* were sincerely bent on peace, this would not interrupt or mar their plan while it would save a day's supplies, and give the troops a health encampment.

General Chamberlain promised, however, that the force shoul only move to the better ground at Shingi, and should not advanc at all towards their position at Ahnai until the final decision of th council was received. On the other hand, the *maliks* undertool to go and consult their tribesmen, and to bring back an answer at Shingi on the evening of the following day.

When the force marched on the morning of the 2nd of May to Shingi Kot, the chiefs proceeded to rejoin their clansmen at the Ahnai Tangi; and as the advanced guard neared Shingi Kot, it was seen that the hills in its neighbourhood were occupied; but as their chiefs approached, the Wazirs descended and moved off with them.

Not even a message was received during the afternoon of the 2nd. The march was, therefore, continued the following morning. The Ahnai gorge was found abandoned, the Wazirs having fallen back to their next position, distant five miles, known as the Barari Tangi, which was said to be the more defensible of the two gorges. As there was no suitable ground for a camp between the Ahnai and Barari defiles, the force encamped for the day at Zeriwam, at the southern entrance to the Ahnai gorge, when the destruction of houses and crops was again carried on. During the afternoon 400 of the foot levies were brought up from Jandola, to assist in guarding the convoy of grain. The remainder of that garrison was then ordered to return to Tank.

Before any further advance was made it was thought right to make one last effort for a peaceful settlement with the Wazirs, and the Ahmadzai Wazir chief, who had been the bearer of the proclamation, was despatched to the Mahsud leaders to ask for the promised answer. So determined, however, were the Mahsuds generally for war, and so confidently did they count upon their numbers and position, that our messenger, though a Wazir, was insulted and threatened, and nothing was left, therefore, but recourse to arms.

The reason why the Wazirs had not stood at the Ahnai Tangi was obvious enough, for it was found to be the easiest defile the troops had passed through; whilst the Barari gorge was unquestionably the most difficult of any that had been seen. Moreover, from the Ahnai upwards, the passage is considerably narrower than it is below the gorge, and the hills on either side are steeper and higher. In short, above the Ahnai, the whole road (with the exception of the two *kaches*, one at the entrance to the Barari Tangi, and the other beyond it) is a defile until close to Kaniguram, where the hills become lower and rounder in form.

Soon after daylight on the 4th of May the force moved forward, and, after advancing four miles up the defile, entered a narrow, cultivated dell, at the further end of which, and distant about a mile, was the Barari gorge, which, it had been reported, the enemy was holding in strength. This was now confirmed by spies who met the column, as well as by the reports of the flanking parties; and as the force approached the position, the Mahsud picquets were seen retiring from their more advanced points.

The Barari Tangi is a narrow cleft cut by the Tank Zam through a chain of mountains crossing its course at right angles. Both sides of the passage are perpendicular cliffs of forty or fifty feet in height, from which the mountains slope upwards at a considerable incline.

A thick grove of trees concealed the actual mouth of the pass from the column, but it was conjectured, from seeing low lines of *sangars* immediately over it, that something difficult had been prepared there. This eventually proved to be a strong abatis, composed of large stones and felled poplar trees, forming a massive barrier, completely closing the pass.

The right of the enemy's position was very formidable. On the right of the mouth of the pass, and overhanging it, was a craggy, steep hill, surmounted by a tower; then came a short level interval, and then the foot of a lofty ridge, which, from its precipitous nature, was wholly unassailable by an attacking force; while, from the great distance of its chief peaks from the scene of action, it was only necessary for the defending force to occupy the spurs above their position to enable them to lend good assistance by their fire.

From the tower to the spur of the main hill stretched a double row of *sangars*, and for some distance up the spur of the ridge *sangars* were terraced one above the other, affording a flanking fire on a force attacking the main position. Above these again were the sharpshooters, whose fire would also tell on the ranks of a body advancing along the ledge between the main ridge and the ravine—the only line of approach by which an attack could be made on the *sangars* of the chief position. The precipitous ridge already described afforded also what most hillmen like—a safe line of retreat—enabling them to inflict injury on an attacking force up to the last moment, and then to retire without the fear being cut off.

The ascent to the left of the enemy's position was steep, but some of its spurs were practicable for infantry and mules. The most difficult feature to deal with was the ravine which joins the Zam just at the mouth of the pass; for it appeared that even if the heights on the left bank of this ravine were taken, little advantage would be gained, as probably this position was cut off from the heights beyond, which were very stiff, and were strongly occupied. The advanced position on the enemy's left was also strongly held, and when the Wazir leaders saw that it was intended to seize it as the first step, they lost no time in greatly strengthening it.

After a thorough examination of the position, Brig.-General Chamberlain rapidly formed his plan of attack, which was to gain possession at once of the heights on the enemy's left by a vigorous attack, and for a second column to ascend the hills on our left and threaten the right of the enemy's position, and await a favourable time to attack that also.

Two columns of attack were formed, as per margin, the right being under the command of Lieut.-Colonel G. Green, and the left under Lieut.-Colonel H. B. Lumsden. The guns of Nos. 2 and 3 Punjab Light Field Batteries and the 4th and 24th Punjab Infantry formed the support in the centre, under Lieut.-Colonel Wilde, and were about 900 yards from the gorge, with the Hazara Gurkha Battalion and the cavalry a little in their rear as a reserve, the baggage being massed behind, guarded by the 14th Punjab Infantry and foot levies, with the 4th Sikh Infantry as rear-guard.

Left Column.	Right Column.
Advanced body.	*Advanced body.*
6th Punjab Infantry, 300 bayonets.	3rd Punjab Infantry, 300 bayonets.
Support.	*Support.*
Guide Infantry, 250 bayonets.	2nd Punjab Infantry, 500 bayonets.
Peshawar Mountain Train Battery, 4 guns.	Hazara Mountain Train Battery, 4 guns.
Reserve.	*Reserve.*
Wing, 6th Police Battalion, 300 bayonets.	1st Punjab Infantry, 300 bayonets.

When the troops were in position, the column on the right advanced to the attack. A plateau, about 300 yards below the crest of the hill (on which the enemy had erected a strong line of breastworks), was reached without any loss. From this plateau three small spurs, with ravines between them, led to the crest of the hill, and the 3rd Punjab Infantry were ordered to advance, covered by the fire of the mountain guns.

Two companies were thrown into skirmishing order, the remainder being in support; but the fire from the breastworks being very heavy, the rear companies were pushed on to strengthen those in advance; at the same time the 2nd Punjab Infantry was ordered to move up in column of sections to the cover of the spur of a hill about two-thirds of the way up, to keep down the flanking fire on the left of the 3rd Punjab Infantry, and as a support to it. The 1st Punjab Infantry was halted as a reserve, and as a support to the mountain battery.

After a difficult advance, during which there were some twenty casualties, the leading men of the 3rd Punjab Infantry rushed to within a short distance of the breastworks, situated on the crest of a rugged, steep ascent, the last twelve or fifteen feet of which were almost inaccessible.

The ground was much cut up by ravines, and the attacking party was consequently dispersed and broken up into knots of men, so that there was not a sufficient body collected in any one spot to make the final rush. The men, to avoid the enemy's fire and the stones hurled down upon them from above, now sought shelter behind the rocks, whence they could only keep up a desultory fire on the breastworks.

The Wazirs, emboldened by the check, leaped their breastworks, and with a shout rushed down upon the 3rd Punjab Infantry, sword in hand, causing a panic, which became general. The 3rd Punjab Infantry were driven back upon the support, which also gave way, and the enemy continued their advance upon the mountain guns and the reserve.

Although many of the 1st Punjab Infantry, who were in reserve, got mixed up with the two lines which had been driven back, those on the right escaped the panic; and Captain C. P. Keyes, putting himself at the head of this party, quietly turned the tide of affairs. The Mahsuds, met by these men, and by the fire of the mountain guns, retreated up the hill, hotly pursued by the 1st Punjab Infantry, who took the main breastwork; and, the other troops now rallying, the right of the position was won.

Meanwhile, the column under Lieut.-Colonel Lumsden had advanced against the enemy's right, but the Wazirs, disheartened by the loss of their position on their left, and exposed to the fire of our guns from the right column, offered only a feeble resistance. Colonel Lumsden, after moving on the tower, ascended the eastern slope of the hill, when he cleared ridge after ridge with his mountain guns, with a loss of only two men. In the centre, as soon as the barricade at the mouth of the gorge had been removed, the 4th Punjab Infantry and the Gurkhas were sent up to clear the eastern ridges, as the hill ascended by Lieut.-Colonel Green's column was separated from these hills by the tributary to the Zam, before alluded to.

No further opposition was then offered, and the camp was pitched on the Bangiwala Kach, three miles beyond the defile.

Our loss had been thirty killed, and eighty-six wounded, while the enemy left thirty-five dead bodies on the ground, including some chiefs.

In the evening a deputation was received from the Mahsud chiefs, expressing renewed wishes for peace. The chief of Makin also sent to intercede for that place, and another leader sent a special messenger to beg that his property might be spared. Conciliatory answers were given, and all were assured that, if they would come in and make peace, there was no wish to injure them further.

On the 5th of May the force advanced, and, after a march of fifteen miles, halted near Kaniguram.

At Maidan, about four miles from Kaniguram, the force was met by the *saiyids* and the Urmur elders of the latter place, who were assured of protection, and who were told to return and recall the inhabitants, who had fled. On reaching Maidan, the country assumed quite a different aspect. The hills were generally low, and of easy slope, and in some places had the appearance of downs.

Hardly any Wazirs resided in the town of Kaniguram, but all the tribal meetings were held there. The inhabitants were composed principally of *saiyids* and Urmurs. As the latter had taken part in the defence of the Barari pass, and as they had furnished no supplies to the camp, it was thought proper that they should pay a fine of Rs. 2,000, in consideration of which the town was to be spared. This was immediately arranged for, and good security was given by the *saiyids*, who were the head of the society, and who had considerable mercantile and other connections with Tank.

Some of the townspeople now returned to their homes, but they were in too great awe of the Mahsuds to assist us with supplies, a little tobacco and some grass sandals being the extent of the aid afforded.

No further communication having been received from the Mahsud chiefs, a halt was made on the 7th, and messengers were sent to ascertain the intentions of the enemy. A most unsatisfactory reply was received, the only thing definite in it being that if the force would remain two or three days at Kaniguram, they would come in to arrange terms. They were aware of the unreasonableness of their request, knowing full well that the supplies were limited; and these once expended, there was nothing but starvation for the force until the plains were reached. The cavalry horses had already been put on half rations of grain. The General, however, determined to halt during the 8th, to give them no excuse for not coming in, when, in return for this forbearance, it was found the enemy were discussing where further opposition could best be made.

As no communication was received from the chiefs, the force moved back on the 9th five miles and-a-half to Do Toi, setting fire to everything that had been spared and protected on its upward march. To this an exception was made in favour of a small property opposite the camp, known to belong to the son of the Ahmadzai chief, Swahn Khan, famous as having, as far back as 1824, shown civility to the enterprising traveller Moorcroft, and as having subsequently rendered assistance to Lieutenant H. B. Edwardes, when that officer entered upon the settlement of the Bannu district in 1847.

On the march some attempt was made to annoy the rear-guard, but only two men were wounded, whilst the enemy suffered from the fire of our long range rifles.

On the 10th the force marched towards Makin; it was not known if the Mahsuds would oppose the force entering that valley, or if an attack would be made on the rear. The first part of the defile was difficult, but after about three miles the hills became lower, and opposite Makin the plateau was again reached. No attempt, however, was made to oppose the column; the picquets were skilfully withdrawn, and the rear-guard reached camp with only two men wounded. All Mahsud property passed on the march was destroyed.

The force was now approaching the boundary line that separates the Mahsuds from the Darwesh Khel Wazirs; and a settlement of the latter, located within the Mahsud border, was passed on the march. Relying on protection being afforded them, the inhabitants had remained in their homes, and safeguards had been placed over their property as the column passed. Unfortunately, however, one of the rear-guard flanking parties, not being aware of the circumstances, came suddenly upon some Wazirs, and taking them for Mahsuds, fired and badly wounded two of the Darwesh Khels. These men were brought into camp and their wounds attended to; but being unwilling to accompany the force, they were sent back to their homes, each with a handsome present.

The town of Makin was situated at the point where the mountains of Shuidar and Pir Ghal close in upon each other, a spur from each mountain forming its northern and southern face. It contained numerous smelting houses, and was the principal seat of the Mahsud iron trade. Next to Kaniguram, it was the most important and best built in the country. A small stream, having its rise within the gorge formed by the meeting of the Shuidar and Pir Ghal mountains, flowed through the centre of the valley, which was filled with villages of considerable size.

Earnestly desiring to come to a settlement, and to avoid having to commit further destruction, a last effort was made to induce the tribe to listen to reason, and to this end a Mahsud, who was in camp, was despatched by the Commissioner to inform the tribe of our wish to spare the place. But, though they had suffered so much, and were perfectly aware of their inability to withstand our arms, nothing came of the proposal.

The force accordingly halted the following day, the 11th, when the work of destruction went on. The ridges on the northern and southern sides were crowned by infantry and mountain guns, whilst a column moved up the centre of the valley. In this manner the few men inclined to offer opposition were driven back to the main ranges, where they were kept until the force retired. By evening the whole of the town and villages were in flames, and the towers burnt or blown up.

The state of the supplies now rendered it absolutely necessary to bring the operations to a close; and, as was previously intended, Bannu was the point on which the troops began to move. As they marched away from Makin on the 12th, two high towers, which guarded the entrance to the valley, and which had been occupied by our picquets, were blown up, and Makin was left in ruins.

A march of eight miles up the bed of the ravine was made to Razmak, whence descended the defile leading to the Bannu valley. Shortly after leaving Makin, the Mahsud boundary was passed, and the lands of the Mohmit Khel and Tori Khel Utmanzais were entered; but before crossing the boundary, the Mahsud village of Taoda China was destroyed.

On the 14th, the road down the pass having been made practicable for guns, the descent was begun. By nightfall the heights on either side of the pass were crowned, and everyone passed into camp, at Razani, in safety, though it was midnight before the rear-guard came in. Some shots were exchanged without loss to us.

From Razani the column marched, on the 15th, to Saroba, a Tori Khel village. The rear-guard was fired upon as it quitted the camping-ground at Razani, but after this the Mahsuds were left behind, and no further molestation was attempted.

On the 20th the force arrived at Bannu, where it was broken up.

Although the expedition did not result in the immediate submission of the Mahsuds, its success was great. A loss was inflicted on the tribe which it would take them years to recover. Whenever they had met our troops, although in difficult passes, they had been defeated. Their chief town, Kaniguram, had been occupied, and spared only on payment of a fine, whilst Makin, their next most important town, had been destroyed, and their hitherto unknown country surveyed and mapped.

The loss inflicted on the Mahsuds by this invasion was estimated by the Commissioner at not less than Rs. 1,40,000.

Information of the intentions and movements of the tribe proved for a long time during this campaign very difficult to obtain. At first it was only possible to work through the Bhittanis, and when the force entered the Mahsud lands, the Bhittani spies became nearly useless. A few Mahsud Wazirs were attached to the train of Nawab Shah Nawaz Khan, the chief of Tank, who accompanied the force, but these were not considered fully trustworthy. After a time matters improved; money, and possibly the growing belief in our ultimate success, enabled Shah Nawaz Khan to make use of men of respectability among the Mahsuds, who gave information concerning the chief movements and counsels and intentions of the tribe; and thus, latterly, the information was of a better kind.

Brig.-General Chamberlain, in his despatch on the operations, thus describes the services which the troops had rendered. The shortest marches took hours to perform, the safety of the followers, supplies, and baggage requiring the heights on both sides to be crowned and held until the arrival of the rear-guard. Though starting by sunrise, it was generally noon, and often later, before the new ground was reached; arriving there, day picquets had to be posted, and escorts for the surveyors, cattle, and foragers to be supplied. In the afternoon fatigue parties had to be turned out to construct breastworks for the night picquets. These had to be substantially built with stones collected from the hillsides, and to be palisaded, to prevent a sudden rush by overpowering numbers.[1] At sunset from 700 to 1,000 men occupied these works, their comparatively isolated position rendering support difficult, at dusk the tents were struck, and, in addition to in-lying picquets, half the men slept accoutred, and the whole in uniform.

The Indian Medal, with a clasp for the "North-West Frontier," was granted in 1869 to all survivors of the troops who took part in the expedition.

As no settlement had been come to with the Mahsud Wazirs before the force was withdrawn to British territory, the tribe was put under blockade, and as they traded largely with the plains, and lived in a great measure on the profits of their iron trade, their annual loss from exclusion was estimated at not less than Rs. 20,000.

More than a year passed away, but the Mahsuds would not submit. Being able to draw supplies from the valleys of Khost and Dawar, they were not pinched by famine, though they suffered

[1] The style of defence was to build an interior *sangar*, or breastwork of stones, and to surround it at a distance of some twenty-five or thirty paces with an abatis. When trees were not procurable, small thorny brushwood pegged down, or weighed down by massive stones when pegs would not hold, made a good substitute.

by the exclusion of their own and other commodities from British markets. During the whole of 1861 they lost no opportunity of making plundering raids. In June 1862, however, they agreed to the terms offered to them, and were again admitted to trade in our territories. The basis of the new engagement was, that each main section—Bahlolzai, Alizai, and Shaman Khel—should be responsible for any outrages committed by members of their sections. It was, moreover, ruled that six approved hostages should be given, two from each clan, and that three of these should be lodged at Bannu and three at Tank, receiving subsistence from Government.

The Mahsuds, however, had hardly concluded this treaty before they broke it; several thefts were committed, and five grass-cutters of the 3rd Punjab Cavalry were murdered by men of the Alizai and Bahlolzai sections. In consequence of this, all men of these sections found in our territory were seized, and their property confiscated; the Shaman Khels not being implicated, came and went without interruption, except when they used Alizai camels, which were then confiscated. The headmen subsequently professed their readiness to make good the fines due from them under the treaty, amounting in all to Rs. 4,500. Their camels, therefore, were sold, and the balance paid by a banker, who was to be repaid by the offending sections, with interest, by a toll on all their pack animals, till the debt should be liquidated.

Soon after, on the 17th of November 1862, a deputation of the principal men of each sub-division waited on the Commissioner at Dera Ismail Khan to ratify the treaty previously made. Lieut.-Colonel R. G. Taylor then advocated some of the Shingi and other sections being settled in the waste lands in the Dera Ismail Khan district, and employment in the militia being given to the tribe; but, although tried, this project failed.

Meanwhile they did not discontinue their raids. In 1862, on the Dera Ismail Khan border, there occurred many cases of cattle-lifting, and, in 1863 the Mahsuds in force attacked the Jatta outpost, which was then not quite finished, and did some damage. Five of the raiders were killed and thirteen captured.

As they gave no opportunity for reprisals, it was at last found necessary to exclude them from trading in the Bannu or Dera Ismail Khan districts. The instructions of the Commissioner, Colonel

J. R. Becher, C.B., on this subject, were issued in August 1863, from which date the Nana Khels and Shingis were prohibited from entering British territory. These sections continued to plunder whenever they found an opportunity, but at length, in April 1864, they sought for peace by sending deputations to the foot of the hills to ask permission for a *jirga* to come in and make terms.

The Nana Khel section having carried on their principal trade with Tank, their chief men sought and obtained an interview, through the Nawab, who forwarded them on to Dera Ismail Khan where they made terms, and promised to behave well in future.

The Shingi section would not, however, come to terms, either at Dera Ismail Khan or Bannu. A large *jirga*, who came into Bannu, to request that their clan might be forgiven and allowed once more to trade, were hospitably entertained for some days, but were told that they must make good all they had plundered, amounting to Rs. 2,272, and must besides pay a fine of Rs. 500, and give hostages for their good behaviour. They promised to do this, and went off in order to gain the consent of the rest of the tribe, who, however, refused.

Attempts were then made at reprisals, in order to obtain some compensation for our villages which had thus been robbed, and Rs. 1,359 were collected in this manner.

At last, in August 1865, Major S. F. Graham, then Deputy Commissioner of the Dera Ismail Khan district, despairing of doing anything with the tribe, recommended that service in the frontier militia should be given to twenty-five Mahsud horsemen, and that land should be granted to them within the border. The terms on which it was to be granted were a rent-free tenure for ten years, and then a demand of one-tenth of the produce; and an advance of Rs. 5,000 was to be granted by Government, to assist in bringing water to the land.

The preliminaries of this arrangement progressed but slowly. The Mahsuds demanded nothing less than 100 sowars for each section, and lands from Dabra to Tator; and they wished to make the release of some prisoners caught marauding the first condition of their assent to the proposal. Gradually, however, they gave in, and all sections agreed in February 1866, except part of the Shingis, who held out for more horsemen.

As soon as the terms were agreed to, the horsemen were enlisted, and in the cold weather of 1866-67 about twenty families of Mahsuds settled on the land, brought about sixty acres under cultivation, and reaped the produce—a sum of Rs. 2,000 out of the Government grant of Rs. 5,000 having been expended. The prisoners were detained pending the result of these measures.

During the year, from the 18th of February 1866 to the 18th of February 1867, the tribe was, on the whole, much better behaved, but towards the close of the year some heavy cases of plunder of camels occurred, which swelled the amount of compensation due from the tribe to about Rs. 8,000. As usual, the Shingi and Nana Khel sections of the Bahlolzai branch were the principal offenders, and, as usual, they were unable to pay up; the release of the prisoners, therefore, which was contingent on good behaviour, was held in abeyance, pending compensation.

But in order to show his scrupulous observance to the terms of the treaty, Lieut.-Colonel Graham caused the prisoners to be removed from the jail on the 18th of February 1867, and to be placed in a *serai* under a guard, with permission to see their friends freely, to resume their own dress, and to receive presents of food; their fetters were also removed.

In the meanwhile, a *jirga* of the tribe was summoned to Tank for the settlement of accounts previous to the release of the prisoners; and when matters looked sufficiently promising to warrant such a step, the prisoners were conveyed, still under guard, to Tank.

It soon, however, became apparent that no settlement of such heavy accounts could be hoped for, and when their inability to pay became clear, Lieut.-Colonel Graham determined to withdraw the prisoners from Tank to the jail as before, which was carried out without accident or outbreak of any kind.

Colonel Graham now summoned a special *jirga* of the tribe, and receiving the representatives of the three main clans separately, explained to the Alizais and Shaman Khels that, according to our old-standing treaty with them, each main section would be dealt with separately; that they had only a small amount of compensation to make good, and had no prisoners to be released; and that they should act up to their agreement with us, square their own accounts, remain on good terms with the Government, and leave the Bahlolzais to settle their own affairs. To this the delegates unhesitatingly agreed, and they were then dismissed. Colonel Graham then received the Aimal Khel and Band Khel sections, of the Bahlolzais, and suggested the same course to them, to which they also agreed.

Lastly, the Shingi and Nana Khel delegates presented themselves, and to them it was announced that their prisoners would be retained pending compensation for plunder during the year. The release of the prisoners was promised after another year on the same terms as before, *i.e.*, on the section refraining from plunder, or paying compensation for such plunder, etc., as might be committed, in which case their liabilities for the past year would be remitted as before.

At the same time they were given fully to understand that if they were determined to give trouble, their quota of horsemen (eight) would be discharged, that they would be ejected from their lands, and excluded from British territory, and from any further favours which might be extended to the rest of the tribe.

This occurred during April, and the delegates agreed to refer the matter to a conference of the whole tribe at their capital of Kaniguram, the result of which was that the Alizais and Shaman Khels elected to remain on good terms with the Government, while the whole of the Bahlolzais elected for mischief.

Amongst the murders committed by the Mahsuds in 1866 that of the agent of the Nawab of Tank was conspicuous. This act was committed by a party of Wazirs, numbering twenty-two, who came into the Gumal valley by the pass opposite the post of Murtaza.

In 1867 and 1868 there were many cases of murder, wounding, and cattle-lifting, and the state of this frontier was now deemed so unsatisfactory, that Brig.-General Wilde, commanding the Punjab Frontier Force, selected sites for new posts, near the Girni and Zam passes, the better to stop these raids.

The Girni post was begun in 1869 at a site three miles from the pass, but was abandoned on account of the failure to reach water, and the site was changed to the mouth of the pass; and in 1870 this post was completed and that of Kot Khirgi begun. On this the Mahsuds signalised their displeasure by making a treacherous, and, unfortunately, a successful, attack on the 13th of April 1870, on a guard of five bayonets of the 1st Sikh Infantry, proceeding to Tank, from Kot Khirgi. These men were joined in the Zam pass by a body of from twenty to forty Shingi Mahsuds, who represented themselves as servants of the chief of Tank, and being allowed to mix with the guard, suddenly disarmed and attacked them, killing two and wounding the remainder. It was afterwards ascertained that these men had come down for the express purpose of waylaying stragglers between Tank and Kot Khirgi.

On the 29th of October 1870, Lieutenant C. B. Norman, 1st Sikh Infantry, who had for some days been completing a survey of the Gumal valley on the Tank frontier, was attacked by a marauding party of some sixty Wazirs, whom he, however, succeeded in beating off with his escort.

During 1871 and 1872 the conduct of the Mahsuds on the Tank border continued to be most unsatisfactory. In the former year 108, and in the latter 78, offences were committed. The disorder, however, had rather a criminal than a political aspect, and the raids which were committed were few, and were not of a serious character.

In March 1873 the Shaman Khels, who had been guilty of numerous offences, made full submission to the terms offered by the British Government, *viz.*, that the clan should pay a fine of Rs. 3,000, be held responsible for the misconduct of individual members, and give twenty hostages as a guarantee of future good behaviour

Their example was followed by the Bahlolzais, and in February 1874 their representatives came in to Dera Ismail Khan, and agreed to the terms offered by the Government. These terms were payment of a sum of Rs. 5,585 as compensation for losses caused by them in British territory; payment of a fine of Rs. 3,000 in addition to this, and the giving of hostages for their future good behaviour.

While negotiations were still pending, a small party of the clan belonging to the Haibat Khel and Jalal Khel sections of the Nana Khels, aided by a few Bhittanis, made an attack, on the 31st of March 1874, on a party of travellers passing under escort through the Bain pass.

In consequence of this outrage, the Bhalolzai *jirga* were informed that the negotiations were at an end, unless they were prepared at once to prove their sincerity by bringing in the ringleaders of the offending party, and by making full reparation to the men who had been wounded on this occasion. The compensation money, according to Afghan custom, amounted to Rs. 1,500; and this sum the Bahlolzais agreed to pay in addition to the amount already imposed. They also produced the ringleaders as required. On the 26th of April 1874 a final settlement with them was effected.

They then paid into the Government Treasury the sum of Rs. 7,085 as compensation money, and they arranged that the fine of Rs. 3,000 should be recovered from a toll levied on their convoys entering British territory, and for their future good conduct they gave thirty-three hostages, to be located at Dera Ismail Khan. A satisfactory settlement was also made with the Bhittanis who had taken part in the Bain pass raid.

The Bhittanis, as already stated, had afforded some assistance to the British force in 1860, when operating against the Mahsuds, but after that they had relapsed into their old habits, and had committed numerous thefts and robberies on our border. In 1865 a settlement was made with them, and a portion of the tribe was located in the Dera Ismail Khan district, a tract of land being given to them on easy terms, in consideration of their being responsible for the passes.

The part taken by the tribe in the Bain pass outrage afforded a favourable opportunity for fixing the pass responsibility of the Bhittanis on the Bannu border, and in consideration of their accepting this responsibility, a small fine of Rs. 5,000 only was imposed on the tribe. In May 1874 they paid the fine, and entered into a formal agreement to be responsible for the border from the Kharoba pass to the Larzan inclusive. A militia force was enlisted from among them to hold selected posts, the higher appointments being in the nomination of the headmen.

In 1875, in order to prevent the Tank border from relapsing into its former unsatisfactory state, an entire reform in the administration of the Tank valley was introduced. This valley had hitherto been under the control of the Nawab of Tank, who, with the best intentions, had proved himself unable to keep in order the wild tribes on his immediate border; his circumstances were bad, and he was unable to provide a sufficiently large force, either military or police, to ensure order. The police administration was now taken over, and a new police organised. The

Nawab's position was in many respects ameliorated, and the revenue management of the *parganna* left in his hands. This reform, together with the acceptance of pass responsibility by the Bhittanis on the Tank, as well as on the Bannu border, and by the Mianis and Ghorazais on the skirt of the Gumal valley, and the enforcement among the Mahsud themselves of complete tribal responsibility for offences committed by any of their sections, led to a marked change in the character of this part of the frontier.

In August 1877, however, an offence was committed which led to the blockade for the first time of the tribe as a whole. On the night of the 12th of that month a Hindu child was carried off by a small party of malcontents, who refused to restore it except for a large ransom. Accordingly, on the 26th of August, tribal property to the value of Rs. 15,000 was seized, and the Bhittanis, acting up to their engagements, closed their passes; but it was not until the 18th of March 1878, that, driven by the pressure of the blockade, the boy was restored.

Operations in the Gumal valley against the Suliman Khel Powindahs and others, in January 1879.

In 1878 it was reported that the Tank border had never before been in such a satisfactory condition, nor life and property within the valley so secure as they had been during the last three years.

This peace was rudely broken by the raid on the town of Tank on the 1st of January 1879, which for audacity had been rarely paralleled in the history of the frontier. It was directly due to instigation from Kabul; Umar Khan, Alizai, having in December 1878, returned from that place with instructions from the late Amir Sher Ali to collect the Mahsud tribe, and endeavour to incite them to hostilities. It was only on the 25th of December that the district officer heard rumours of a probable raid, and he then took precautions against any attack which might be made on British territory. All the posts on the Tank border were doubled; at the same time their relief was deferred, so that in the important posts of Girni and Zam there was treble the usual number of troops, and by the 28th of December nearly half of the available force in the district was in the Tank valley; 210 bayonets and 150 sabres being in the Manjhi, Birni, and Zam posts. The villagers were also put on the alert in the usual manner, and the police and the Bhittanis, who were in charge of the passes, were properly warned. On the 1st of January the Bhittani posts and levies, failing to resist the enemy, or making common cause with them, the Mahsuds descended in a body, estimated at 2,000 to 3,000 strong, passing down the Zam, and in front of the military post of that name. After feeble and ineffectual efforts of the garrison to stop the raiders, the Mahsuds advanced on Tank, which they reached without further opposition, burning the *bazar* and many of the houses and carrying off such property as had been left behind by the Hindu population, who had taken refuge in an old fort adjoining the town. The Wazirs then retired with their women and children, who had formed part of the families of the hostages removed from Dera Ismail Khan to Tank some time previously, and regained the hills without molestation before any troops could intercept them.

The raiding party was joined by large numbers of *Powindahs*, who at this time were in the Dera Ismail Khan district, and who could not resist the temptation to plunder. The Bhittanis with everything to lose and little to gain by joining the Mahsuds, beyond the satisfaction of their religious fanaticism, made common cause with the enemy, while many British subjects belonging to the small Miani and Ghorazai tribes were equally culpable. The leader of the raiding party was Umar Khan, Alizai, the son of Jangi Khan, who had been the leader in the former attempt to surprise Tank in 1860, when he had been killed. The Mahsuds belonged chiefly to the Alizai clan although the Bahlolzais and Shaman Khels also joined in the raid.

On the 2nd of January the Extra Assistant Commissioner at Tank sent to request aid from the Zam post, and accordingly the whole of the cavalry detachment of the post proceeded to Tank and occupied the *tehsil* buildings.

The plunder and firing of Tank was the signal for general disorder; and lawless and predatory bands of Kharotis,[1] Suliman Khels, and even British subjects availed themselves of the confusion to plunder and destroy several border villages.

On the receipt of the report of the impending attack upon Tank, which reached Dera Ismail Khan on the morning of the 2nd of January, Colonel H. F. M. Boisragon, commanding at that place, at once gave orders for the available troops, consisting of about 100

1 These, like the Suliman Khel, are Ghilzai Powindahs.

sabres of the 4th Punjab Cavalry and 180 bayonets of the 4th Sikh Infantry, to move out at once to Tank. At the same time he telegraphed to the officer commanding at Edwardesabad to push on as rapidly as he could all available troops of his district towards Tank. Colonel Boisragon arrived at Hathala, at 2 A.M., on the morning of the 3rd, and was there met by Major C. E. Macaulay, the Deputy Commissioner. At 7 A.M. the 4th Punjab Cavalry pushed on from Hathala to Tank, and the 4th Sikh Infantry followed soon after. About four miles from Tank, the force came upon a Kharoti *kiri* in a strong position. On being summoned to surrender, these men refused to give up their arms or plunder, and the infantry was then ordered to advance in extended order, while the cavalry was sent round to the right flank. After a few shots had been fired, a *pagri* was waved as a token of submission, and the troops then entered the *kiri*, recovered the plunder, took about fifty prisoners, and arrived at Tank at 8 P.M., having marched nearly fifty miles.

On the 4th, at 8 A.M., the troops, as per margin, under the command of Captain B. E. Gowan, 4th Sikh Infantry, proceeded from Tank towards the frontier posts of Dabra, Jatta, and Girni. On arriving at Dabra, the Deputy Commissioner informed Captain Gowan that there was an encampment of Zalli Khel Wazirs near the hills, who had been plundering in British territory, and it was determined, with the assistance of some troops from the Girni post, to try and surround it.

4th Punjab Infantry	..63 sabres.
4th Sikh Infantry	..47 bayonets.

Captain Gowan accordingly, having sent orders to the troops at Girni to move out, proceeded to Jatta, and at 3 P.M. he left that post and made straight for the hills, meeting on the way the detachments of cavalry and infantry from the Girni post. On reaching the hills, the force moved along their base, but the encampments had in the meanwhile moved off across the frontier, and Captain Gowan, therefore, proceeded to Girni, which he reached after dark. On the morning of the same day, the 4th of January, the cavalry garrison of Girni, under Jemadar Amir Singh, had attacked a party of Zalli Khel Wazirs, who were making their way into the hills. Two Wazirs were killed and one severely wounded. They then surrendered, and the rest of the party, forty in number, were made prisoners.

On the morning of the 4th the Deputy Commissioner received information that a Suliman Khel *kiri*, which had been plundering in

British territory, was about to leave our territory by the Gumal pass. Arrangements were accordingly made to try and intercept it on the following morning.

At daybreak on the morning of the 5th of January the cavalry and infantry detachments moved out from the Girni post, under the command of Captain B. E. Gowan. The troops came upon the encampment at 8 A.M., about four miles from Girni, to the left of the Girni-Jatta road. The infantry and cavalry having advanced to within four hundred yards of the *kiri*, the headmen were summoned to surrender. Parleying went on for about an hour, but the *Powindahs* refused to submit. The position of the enemy was naturally a strong one, in the midst of a succession of low sand hillocks, which they had strengthened by throwing up shelter round them. Captain Gowan ordered the infantry to advance, and they rapidly moved forward by rushes, firing steadily, and taking advantage of any cover there was. Meanwhile half the cavalry, under Lieutenant W. Lambert, had moved round the enemy's right, to cut off the retreat and to prevent any aid being received from the ridge in rear, where some few men were seen collected. The fire of the enemy was well sustained, and they fought steadily from behind their cover.

After the attack of the infantry had lasted about half an hour the cavalry was ordered to charge in flank through the encampment; and the infantry making a final rush at the same time, the position was captured and destroyed.

The British casualties amounted to two killed and eleven wounded, while seventy of the enemy's dead were counted in and about the encampment.

After the termination of this affair, the troops marched to Manjhi, where they passed the night. On the night of the 6th they marched to Jatta, where they joined Colonel Boisragon and the headquarters of the 4th Sikh Infantry, which had come out from Tank that day.

On the 7th Colonel Boisragon, leaving fifty cavalry and fifty infantry at Jatta, returned to Tank with the rest of the troops.

On the evening of the 16th of January it was reported that 3,000 Mahsuds had collected at the mouth of the Zam pass. During the night they threw up stone breastworks round an old ruin called Aldad-ki-Kot on their left, and also round the base of the hill on their right, on the other side of the stream, and connected the two positions by a line of breastwork across the bed of the *nala.* The troops at Tank had now been reinforced by the 3rd Punjab Infantry from Dera Ghazi Khan. Lieut.-Colonel Bainbridge, commanding at Tank, accordingly moved out from this place early on the 17th with 245 bayonets and 95 sabres, and endeavoured to draw the enemy out of his position; but his efforts were of no avail, and, as it was getting late, the troops retired, not being strong enough to attack.

Early on the 19th Lieut.-Colonel Bainbridge, having received a small increase of strength, moved out again from Tank with 350 bayonets and 94 sabres. At 9 A.M. the troops arrived in front of the Zam pass, when it was seen that the enemy had left their position in the *sangars*, and were in great numbers on the low hills in rear. Major P. C. Rynd, commanding the 3rd Punjab Infantry, was then ordered to take his regiment and forty bayonets, 4th Sikh Infantry, and to turn the flank of the enemy by attacking the hill on the right of their position. At the same time the remainder of the 4th Sikh Infantry was extended to threaten a frontal attack. The cavalry was placed in rear of the 4th Sikh Infantry and in the bed of the *nala*.

Major Rynd's attack was entirely successful, and, almost as soon as his skirmishers opened fire the whole of the enemy fled. The 3rd Punjab Infantry then occupied the commanding position on the left, and the 4th Sikh Infantry advanced and occupied the main position, and remained there till the enemy had disappeared from the surrounding hills. With the small force at his command, Lieut.-Colonel Bainbridge did not consider it prudent to follow up, and at 1 P.M. he marched back to camp. There were no casualties on our side, but the enemy were said to have had seven men killed.

On the night of the 16th of March an attack was made by a body of about 100 Mahsuds on the village of Gumal. Warning of an intended raid had been received, and consequently the post at Jatta had been strengthened by fifty-five sabres. The attack was, however, beaten off by the villagers themselves before the troops arrived from Jatta and Manjhi. There were only about thirty men in the village at the time, and the raiders succeeded, in the first assault, in breaking open one of the gates, but were driven back by a volley from the defenders, and the gate was again closed. The raiders twice attempted to force it again, but the villagers defended the approach from the walls on both sides so well that they at last succeeded in beating off the attack; and the enemy, on hearing that the cavalry were coming, took to flight.

Order had now been restored on the Tank border; and the different tribes, with the exception of the Mahsuds, had received punishment for the part they had taken in the recent disturbances. Besides the punishment inflicted, as already shown, on the *Powindahs*, a sum of nearly Rs. 60,000 was levied as fine and compensation from these wandering tribes, whose settlements the necessities of trade placed within our grasp. The conduct of the *Powindahs* necessitated special precautions with regard to them for the future. All bands of these migratory tribes were to be disarmed on their entry into British territory; their arms were to be deposited in a military arsenal, and returned to their owners when they again crossed the border. No *Powindah* encampment was to be allowed within the immediate neighbourhood of the hill passes, but all were required to settle within a ring drawn at some distance from the hills.

The Bhittanis were punished by a fine of Rs. 10,000; and the ringleaders of the Mianis and Ghorazais were captured and sentenced by the ordinary tribunals of law to long periods of imprisonment: from the former, too, a fine of Rs. 3,000 was levied, and an allowance of Rs. 2,000 for service in the Murtaza post was withheld.

The Mahsuds alone, the principal offenders, remained unpunished. On them the Government had imposed the following terms:—

1st.—The surrender of all property plundered or payment of compensation for the value of it.

2nd.—The payment of a fine of Rs. 30,000.

3rd.—The surrender of six headmen, ringleaders in the disturbances of January 1879.

In the event of these terms being refused they were to be enforced by a punitive expedition as soon as a favourable opportunity should occur. In the meanwhile, a strict blockade was to be enforced against the tribe.

In April 1879 a large party of Mahsuds was seized in the Bannu district, and one hundred and sixty of their number were detained. On the 11th of the same month the Deputy Commissioner of Dera

Ismail Khan reported that seventy leading families of the Shaman Khel and Alizai Mahsuds had surrendered themselves unconditionally to Government. As it was impolitic to deal with anything but a full *jirga* of the tribe, a few of the principal men only were detained, and the rest sent back to their hills to endeavour to effect such agreement as would lead to compliance with the conditions of punishment imposed.

Affair with the Bhittanis of Jandola at the Hinis Tangi, in April 1880.

In March 1880 the excitement produced by the preaching of the fanatical priest, Mulla Adkar of Khost, extended to the Mahsuds. This man, as already mentioned, had been driven out of Khost by our troops in January 1879, and had taken refuge in Upper Dawar. At the end of March 1880 he visited Kaniguram, in the hope of rousing the Mahsuds to active hostilities against the British Government; but his ardour was temporarily checked by a fall from the roof of his house, resulting in injuries so serious that he had to be carried back on a litter to his home in Dawar. His visit to the Mahsuds was thus cut short, and he was frustrated in his purpose of superintending the proposed attack in person. He, however, left some of his disciples behind him to see that the tribe carried out his designs, and it is said that he distributed certain sums of money to the hostile tribal leaders as an inducement to them to lead their tribe in the proposed attack on British territory.

On the 5th of April the Deputy Commissioner received information that the Wazirs were gathering in small numbers at a place ten miles from our border up the Tank Zam, and that more would probably join them. He accordingly warned the officer commanding at Dera Ismail Khan (Lieut.-Colonel P. C. Rynd) that this border would probably require to be reinforced. Lieut.-Colonel Rynd thereupon ordered the troops, as per margin, from Dera Ismail Khan to Tank. A detachment of fifty bayonets was also ordered from Kulachi to Jatta. On the 6th information was received that the Wazir gatherings, which had largely increased in numbers, had collected near Jandola, and

No. 3 (Peshawar)) Mountain Battery.	3 guns.
4th Punjab Cavalry ..	50 sabres.
4th Sikh Infantry ..	150 bayonets.
3rd Punjab Infantry ..	150 „

were debating whether to come down by the Tank Zam, or to go up the Shahur Zam and descend on the Gumal valley. Umar Khan, Yarak, and Mashak were with them, but some of the main sections had declined to join the force, and owing to differences of opinion among those collected as to the direction they should take, and to their supplies running short, some of them began to return to their homes. The rest, chiefly Alizais, under Umar Khan and Yarak, determined to try what they could do on the Gumal border, and in the afternoon it was reported that they had begun to move in that direction. The posts in the Gumal valley were accordingly placed on the alert, and warned to expect an attack during the night. The Jatta and Manjhi posts were expressly entrusted with the protection of the Gumal town. After night had set in, a party of the enemy, some two hundred or three hundred strong, passing down the bed of the Gumal stream, and concealed by the high bank, got down close to the town, and then leaving the *nala*, made a rush at three of the gates. They managed to get into a deserted corner of the village, but the eighteen bayonets which had been placed in the town prevented their making any further progress, and the cavalry from the Manjhi post now coming up, compelled them to retire. After the failure of this attack, the Wazirs retired to their hills and the gathering dispersed to their homes.

In this affair the Bhittanis of Jandola, who were nominally friendly to the British Government, had failed in supplying information as to the movements of the Wazirs, and had given a passage to the enemy through their lands. Lieut.-Colonel Rynd, therefore, with the sanction of the Punjab Government, determined to attack Jandola. Accordingly, he advanced towards that place from Kot Khirgi on the morning of the 12th, with a force of 721 of all ranks.

Nothing of any importance occurred on the line of march till the troops approached to within half a mile of the Hinis Tangi, where it was reported that the enemy was holding the defile to dispute the passage. The force was, therefore, halted till daybreak.

At daybreak a company of the 4th Sikhs was sent ahead towards the mouth of the pass, and a company of the 3rd Punjab Infantry was ordered to crown the heights on the left. When the former company arrived within view of the defile it was seen to be held by the enemy in force. Lieut.-Colonel Rynd then advanced, and found that the pass was barricaded across the mouth, and was commanded by a *sangar*, on the hill on the right of the enemy's position. Another company of the 3rd Punjab Infantry was, therefore, ordered to reinforce, and the attack began. The guns were at the same time brought into action, and they made excellent practice, dropping several shells into the *sangar*. After a sharp encounter, the enemy began to retreat up the hill to the left, and the defile was carried.

As it appeared that all the inhabitants of Jandola had taken part in the engagement, orders were given for the place to be destroyed.

Lieut.-Colonel Rynd then returned to Kot Khirgi unmolested, which place was reached at noon. The troops were all back in Tank by 9 A.M., having marched forty miles in the twenty-four hours, over the stony bed of the Tank Zam. Our casualties during the engagement were only five men wounded.

At the end of May following the Bhittani headmen of Jandola came in and made their voluntary submission to the Deputy Commissioner. The three leading *maliks* were detained as hostages, and the rest were then allowed to return to Jandola.

Expedition against the Mahsud Wazirs by a combined force under Brig.-Generals T. G. Kennedy, C.B., and J. J. H. Gordon, C.B., in 1881.

To return now to the Mahsud Wazirs. As seen in the last chapter, this tribe was associated with the Darwesh Khel Wazirs, and with the Dawaris in 1880 in several serious outrages on the Thal-Kurram road. On the night of the 22nd April they were guilty of a further outrage on British territory, when, in company with a body of other Wazirs and Dawaris, they made an attack on the Baran post on the Bannu border.

On the termination of the operations in Afghanistan, the Government was able to take up the case of the Mahsud Wazirs. Since the commencement of the blockade, the general attitude of the tribe had been one of outward show of humility and desire to make terms; and at various times petitions to be forgiven had been presented by *jirgas* of different sections, but the tribe as a whole had not displayed any inclination to take active steps towards making the reparation required by the British Government, and had, moreover, been guilty of numerous acts of hostility, as shown above. Sanction was, therefore, asked to the movement of troops against the Mahsuds as the only measure which seemed likely to bring about the submission of the tribe. The spring was considered the best time of the year for the expedition. The proposal was sanctioned by the Government of India in March 1881, and arrangements were at once made for coercing the tribe.

A proclamation was published and widely circulated, which, after reciting the engagements under which this tribe had bound itself to abstain from raids and aggressions on British territory, offered to them a final opportunity for peaceable submission, and invited them to depute delegates to arrange for the terms of settlement and payment of the fine. Meanwhile orders were issued for the assembling of a force at Tank under the command of Brig.-General T. G. Kennedy, C.B., to whom was entrusted the command of the expedition. This force was to be composed of troops of the Punjab Frontier Force, to which were added a company of Sappers and Miners and the 32nd Punjab Native Infantry (Pioneers). At the same time a reserve brigade was to be formed at Bannu under the command of Brig.-General J. J. H. Gordon, C.B. Major C. E. Macaulay, who had been appointed Political Officer with the force, was told that the object of the expedition was to compel the Mahsuds to submit to the terms offered to them, which were the same as those originally imposed.[1]

No. 2 (Derajat) Mountain Battery.
No. 3 (Peshawar) " "
No. 4 (Hazara) " "
1st Punjab Cavalry.
4th " "
8th Company, Sappers and Miners.
1st Sikh Infantry.
4th " "
1st Punjab Infantry.
2nd " "
3rd " "
4th " "
6th " "
32nd Punjab Native Infantry (Pioneers).

On the 18th of April, the force, as per margin, consisting of 12 guns, 290 sabres, and 3,662 bayonets, under the command of Brig.-General T. J. Kennedy, C.B., commanding the Punjab Frontier Force, marched from Tank to near the Zam post. The force was accompanied by Major C. E. Macaulay, the Political Officer.

While arrangements for the assembling of troops were still in progress, several sections of the Mahsuds sent in their headmen,

[1] *Vide* page 396.

in the hope of making terms separately with the Government, and of thus avoiding punishment. Among these were the clans whose possessions were nearest to British territory, and whose headmen had for some time past been resident in Tank or Dera Ismail Khan. But many important sub-divisions of the tribe were still unrepresented, especially those whose homes were in the western and more inaccessible hills and whose leaders had been most closely associated with Umar Khan, and the faction for many years past opposed to peace with the British Government.

Shortly after the distribution of the proclamation, the question of submission to our demands had been discussed at a great council held at Kaniguram, where the leading men of the Shabi Khel Alizais, the Aimal Khel Bahlolzais, and the Shaman Khels urged unconditional surrender as the only means of rescuing the tribe from protracted suffering. The proscribed headmen consequently found that they had to pay the usual penalty of ill success, and that the majority of their fellow clansmen were not disposed to join them in armed resistance. Accordingly, Azmat (Shingi) and Boyak Khan (Aimal Khel), both of the Bahlolzai branch, surrendered at the Tank Zam post on the 18th of April, and on the following day Umar Khan and Matin (Alizais) gave themselves up with the son of Yarak, who was, or affected to be, prostrate with illness. The sixth ringleader whose surrender was demanded by Government, Mashak (Nana Khel), gave out that he would follow Umar Khan's example, and come down to Shingi Kot; but his resolution failing, he returned home. One of the three conditions, and seemingly the most stringent and hard of accomplishment, was thus nearly fulfilled at the outset; but the submission of the tribe was still incomplete. Several important sub-divisions, especially the Nana Khel section of the Bahlolzais, were still defiant, and while they remained unpunishsd, no negotiations for the payment of compensation and fine by the whole tribe were possible. Accordingly it was determined that the troops should advance into the Mahsud country with the object of coercing the Nana Khel section into submission.

On the 21st the force advanced to Kot Khirgi, and the following day to Jandola, where it was halted on the 23rd.

The instructions to the General Officer Commanding and to the Political Officer authorized them to destroy all fortified places visited by the troops, to seize the property of ringleaders and persons known to have been engaged in the raid on Tank, and to punish armed resistance by the seizure of cattle and of crops; while any village submitting in a body was to be kindly and considerately treated, the houses spared, and all supplies paid for.

The Shahur valley was the first portion of the Mahsud country visited by the British force. On the 23rd a reconnaissance of the Shahur pass was made, and the road was repaired. No opposition was met with, the force returning to camp the same day. The following day the column advanced to Haidari Kach, and on the 25th and 26th continued its march up the Shahur Zam, encamping successively at Turan China and Barwand.

On leaving Haidari Kach the rear-guard was fired on, and this was repeated more or less every day while the troops remained in the Wazir country.

Whilst the main body marched on the 26th from Turan China to Barwand, a strong force, under Lieut.-Colonel B. Chambers, 6th Punjab Infantry, was detached to visit the residence of Mashak, on the banks of the Aspalito Algad, about nine miles distant. The crops belonging to their chief were destroyed, and an attempt was made to destroy his residence, a large domed cave, but with indifferent success. The force then rejoined the main column at Barwand. A few stray shots had been fired at the column but no casualties occurred, and no opposition was offered by the Abdul Rahman Khels, whose headman, Taj, had already submitted at Haidari Kach.

The force now moved on towards the Khaisora valley, and encamped at the mouth of the Tangi Raghza, a narrow and difficult gorge leading into it from the Shahur valley. The gorge being found impracticable for camels, a mountain road was constructed over the hills to the north into the valley. Small parties of the enemy were observed on the hills, and some firing took place, but they did not venture to close quarters. A havildar and two sepoys amongst the troops covering the working-parties were wounded, and the enemy had one killed and four wounded.

It was probably hoped by the enemy that a demonstration on the hills might deter an advance into the Khaisora valley by so difficult a route, but Shah Salim, the principal Alizai headman of those parts, exercised his influence successfully as regards the people of his own clan, and prevented any of them joining the opposition. The Alizai headmen of the Khaisora valley also came into camp and submitted.

The opposition now exhibited chiefly proceeded from the Nana Khels of the Khaisora and Badar valleys, and other sections of the Bahlolzais who resided near Kaniguram. But it was quickly overcome and the force advanced on the 29th by the newly made road to Narai Raghza without any casualty, although the enemy showed on the right front and flank. On the following day the advance was continued to Kundiwan.

General Kennedy halted for two days at Kundiwan, and from there telegraphed to Brig.-General Gordon to advance with the reserve brigade into the Wazir country, so as to reach Razmak by the 6th of May, as he expected to reach Kaniguram on the 5th.

On the 3rd of May the force moved to Shah Alam, passing, on the way, the house of three of the leading Nana Khel chiefs who had refused to submit. Their towers, and a fort belonging to them, were destroyed, and their crops cut for the use of the troops.

On approaching Shah Alam, it was seen that the enemy was in force on the densely wooded hillsides to the right and right front. The 1st Sikhs were at once ordered to clear the front, which they did forthwith, and then, wheeling up half right, halted. The 3rd and 4th Punjab Infantry were, at the same time, moved out half right and halted. These three regiments, each covered by its skirmishers, then awaited further orders, while the General reconnoitred the enemy's position. Meanwhile, the guns had moved up, and had opened fire on bodies of the enemy moving in the open. 6th Punjab Infantry was in reserve. While thus halted the enemy, The with a shout, suddenly charged down on the 1st Sikhs. Seeing the state of affairs, the Brig.-General at once ordered up a wing of the 6th Punjab Infantry to support the 1st Sikhs, but they were not required, as the enemy had broken before the skirmishers alone, who, being joined by their supports under Lieut.-Colonel A. G. Ross, followed up the enemy, and cleared them out of their position on the crest of the hill. Here they halted until ordered to retire, which they did without any attempt being made by the enemy to molest them—a sure sign that they had been thoroughly beaten.

The casualties in the 1st Sikhs had been three killed and fourteen wounded, and the 3rd and 4th Punjab Infantry had each one man severely wounded. The enemy's loss could not be ascertained, but twenty bodies were counted over the line of advance of the 1st Sikhs, and it is known that there were some influential men among the killed and wounded. It was reported that the enemy numbered 3,000, but these numbers were not seen, and the party which attacked the Sikhs was not more than 50, with some 300 or 400 in second line. The gathering was headed by a chief named Madmir, who was killed while gallantly leading the charge against the 1st Sikhs, and by Mashak, and was composed chiefly of Bahlolzais, with a few bad characters from the other clans. They were also stimulated by the presence of Ali Muhammad, nephew of Mulla Adkar, and some of his bigoted followers. After the fight it appears that the enemy dispersed to their homes, and abandoned all idea of further resistance.

Mashak had not, like Madmir, distinguished himself by forward gallantry on the day of the battle, and had thus failed to inspire the further sympathy of his clan. His cause was deserted by all, and he crept back to his cave in the Aspalito ravine, and then on to Shingi Kot, where he intended to surrender as the force passed down the Tank Zam to the plains, had not new and unexpected prospects dawned on him during the last days of the expedition.

On the 5th of May the force reached Kaniguram. During this day's march a force was detached to punish four of the Nana Khel *maliks*, who lived about five miles up the Badar valley, and who had been engaged against us on the 3rd. Their towers having been blown up, this detachment returned and joined the main body the same day.

The column halted at Kaniguram during the 6th, but on the 7th the camp was moved to another site, about a mile to the east of the town, and was halted there during the 8th. Heliographic communication was opened with Brig.-General Gordon's column. On the morning of the 9th of May the force moved towards Makin by the Tank Zam, and encamped at Do Toi, and the following day marched to Makin, where supplies were received from the Bannu column, which was only seven miles distant at Razmak.

It is now necessary to turn to the movements of the Bannu column, originally designated the reserve brigade, which had been ordered to assemble at Bannu. On the 16th of April Brig.-General Gordon had moved from Edwardesabad and taken up a position on the right bank of the Tochi river, near the village of Miriam, commanding the entrance of the Khaisora, Tochi, and Shaktu valleys.

On the 4th of May, in compliance with the instructions received from Brig.-General Kennedy, the Bannu column, consisting of 8 guns, 326 sabres, and 3,380 bayonets, as per margin, marched for Razmak by the Khaisora route, to co-operate with the Tank column, and to take up a week's supplies for that force. Mr. R. Udny, C.S., Deputy Commissioner of Bannu, accompanied the force as Political Officer.

No. 1 Battery, 8th Brigade, Royal Artillery.
No. 1 (Kohat) Mountain Battery.
4th Battalion, Rifle Brigade.
18th Bengal Cavalry.
6th Company, Sappers and Miners.
14th Native Infantry.
5th Punjab Infantry.
20th Punjab Native Infantry.
21st " " "
30th " " "

At Saroba, which was reached on the 6th, the ground on which General Chamberlain's force had encamped in 1860 was found to have been washed away by floods. During the march up the Khaisora valley the force was accompanied by representatives of the Tori Khel and Mohmit Khel Waziris, who inhabit the valley.

On the 7th the force marched to Razani. Brig.-General Gordon halted the following day to allow the road up the Razmak pass to be improved; and from the summit of this pass heliographic communication was opened with the Tank column at Kaniguram. While halted at Razani, a private of the Rifle Brigade was shot dead whilst straying near the camp. For this offence, and for firing at the rear-guard when leaving Saroba, the Mohmit Khels, within whose limits both cases occurred, were fined. The offenders were supposed to be prowling Mahsuds or *talibs* from Dawar, who had accompanied Ali Muhammad, and, after the affair at Shah Alam on the 3rd, were returning to Dawar. After this the Mohmit Khels took precautions to prevent any further violation of their territory.

On the 9th the column marched to Razmak, and encamped at a height of 7,500 feet, where it halted during the 10th and 11th. On the morning of the 10th a convoy of 970 camels and six days' supplies were sent to Makin for the Tank column. This convoy had a skirmish with some Mahsuds on the hills along the line of march, in which one man of the Rifle Brigade was slightly, and one man of the 18th Bengal Cavalry was severely, wounded.

On the 12th of May the Bannu column began to retire, and the following day Brig.-General Kennedy broke up his camp at Makin and marched to Janjal. On the 14th Shilmanzai Kach was reached, and on the next day Kurghiband, one mile beyond Shingi Kot. The crops of the Nana Khel section along the route were used by the troops.

On the 16th the force marched to Jandola, the baggage keeping to the bed of the Zam, but the main body of the column taking a branch road to the east, crossing the open plain of Spin Raghza. On the 17th the march was continued to the mouth of the Tank Zam pass, and on the 18th to Tank, where the force was at once broken up. The return march had been almost entirely unmolested.

In the meanwhile, Brig.-General Gordon marched on the 12th to Razani by the Razmak pass, and the following day to Dosalli. On the 14th a short but difficult march of five miles brought the force out on to the open, grassy Sham plain, belonging to the Tori Khel Utmanzais. One of the advanced guard picquets was here fired on from the hills, but the enemy was soon cleared off by a party of riflemen and a few rounds from the artillery. While the force was halted at this place, most of the principal *maliks* of the Nana Khels inhabiting the Shaktu valley came into camp.

On the 15th the force again entered Mahsud territory, and, after a march of six miles, encamped at Waladin, a village on the Shaktu stream at the head of the valley of the same name.

The inhabitants of the Shaktu valley had hitherto held aloof from all negotiations, thinking themselves secure on account of the difficulty of penetrating to their settlements, and because they were left untouched in 1860. They had now submitted without a struggle, and the presence of their *maliks* in the camp reassured the people, most of whom had never before seen a European.

On the 16th the force marched down the course of the stream to Baramand, whence, after the road had been improved, they advanced to Mandawam. On the 19th Brig.-General Gordon marched to Karkanwam, and thence to the frontier post of Jan Khel, entering British territory after an absence of sixteen days

During the return march there had been no opposition to speak of, and only one casualty had occurred. The column reached Edwardesabad on the 22nd, and was then broken up.

The total number of casualties among the troops employed in the operations against the Mahsud Waziris was thirty-two.

The number of followers and transport animals which accompanied the two columns was 8,957 followers, 4,289 mules, 1,336 ponies, and 6,322 camels.

Although the expedition had been so far successful, and the boldest of the Mahsuds had been taught that no natural difficulties of their country could protect them from punishment, and although the tribe, as a whole, were eager to conclude peace, and to be relieved of the oppressive blockade, yet the demands of the Government had not been fully complied with, and the blockade was therefore ordered to be continued.

Even before the British troops had left their hills, some leading spirits among the party opposed to peace sought the intercession of the Amir. It was the news of this, as offering a loophole of escape, that deterred Mashak at the last moment from giving himself up, as he had determined to do.

Towards the end of May, Sardar Mazulla Khan, the Amir's agent, appeared at Kaniguram, where his presence and promises of assistance and intercession tended considerably to thwart the efforts of the party in favour of peace with the British Government.

Nevertheless, such was the pressure of the blockade that the welcome accorded to the Amir's emissary was but a cold one, and he departed suddenly for Khost, and thence to Kabul, accompanied by Mashak, Yarak, and a few other Mahsuds. The absence of these two proscribed chiefs, and the reaction consequent on hopes raised by interference from Kabul, naturally retarded a final settlement with the tribe; but ere long the Mahsuds discovered that papers had been sent to the Amir, purporting to offer to His Highness the allegiance of their clan and the sovereignty of their country; and that he wished to enlist troops from their hills. This discovery irritated and alarmed a people both proud and jealous of their independence. The feeling that their freedom was involved produced a reaction against the endeavour to profit by the Amir's interference, and in favour of concluding peace direct with the

British Government by submission to all its demands, in preferenc to the purchase of the assistance of Kabul by acknowledgments which the Amir or his successors might hereafter use against them. Accordingly, on the 10th of June, the leading men of the Mahsuds at Kaniguram sent a letter to the Amir, in which they disclaimed all connection with any offers of allegiance or admission of Kabul sovereignty over their hills.

It would seem that it was not long belore the Amir discovered that the deputation which accompanied Mazulla Khan to Kabul was one of small influence and importance, and the reception of Yarak and his companions was accordingly neither flattering nor satisfactory. In July they returned to their homes, dispirited and disappointed. On the 3rd of the same month four leading Nana Khel *maliks*, with the son of Mashak, were given up by the tribe as hostages and security for the surrender of Mashak himself, who had been detained in Kabul. In September he returned to the Mahsud country to find his fellow clansmen clamouring for his surrender. With this he refused to comply, trusting to the Afghan prejudice against delivering an offender up to punishment. Finally, it was necessary to resort to force. Mashak was seized by some leading men of the Bahlolzais at a council of the tribe, and delivered up to the British authorities at Tank on the 7th of September. This was followed by the voluntary surrender of Yarak, the last of the six proscribed ringleaders in the outrages of 1879. The Mahsuds having thus, by accepting a humiliation as great as a Pathan clan can suffer, proved their honest desire and intention to submit, the blockade which had been maintained against them for nearly three years was removed, and once more they were at liberty to renew trade and intercourse with markets in British territory.

The other conditions of settlement, however, the payment of fine and compensation, still remain to be fulfilled. The value of property plundered and destroyed in the Tank valley and in the villages in the neighbourhood of Kot Nasran, in January and February 1879, was at the time put down at Rs. 67,000, and the fine to be demanded was fixed by Government at Rs. 30,000. Subsequent offences by the Mahsuds during 1879 and 1880 raised the value of the compensation to be exacted to Rs. 74,948, making a total of Rs. 1,04,948. Against this had to be set off the value of such supplies, grain, and green crops, as were appropriated without payment for the use of the troops during the ex. pedition.

The amount was, however, still so large that it was quite beyond the power of a wild and semi-savage tribe to pay on the spot. Sanction was, therefore, obtained for the amount being liquidatec by a tax imposed on all goods imported by the tribe into British territory. To this arrangement the Mahsuds agreed.

In order to secure further guarantees for the future good behaviour of the Mahsuds, eighty selected hostages were taken from the tribe, and located at Dera Ismail Khan. Attempts were also made again to induce certain families of the tribe to settle in British territory, by giving them grants of land free of revenue for five years, on the condition of the responsibility for the safety of the general route being accepted by the tribe.

Our further dealings with the Mahsuds, and also with the Darwesh Khel Wazirs, up to the present time, are reserved for a new chapter.

APPENDIX A.

Genealogy of the Mahsud Wazirs.

MAHSUD.
(Main Division.)

- **Shaman Khel.**
  - **Upper or Hill Shaman Khel.**
    - **Khalli Khel.**
    - **Chahar Khel.**
    - **Badanzai.**
    - **Galeshahi.**
  - **Shahur Shaman Khel.**
    - **Khalli Khel.**
    - **Chahar Khel.**
- **Alizai.**
  - **Shabi Khel.**
  - **Manzai.**
    - **Abdur Rahman Khel.**
    - **Haibat Khel.**
    - **Jalal Khel.**
- **Bahlolzai.**
  - **Nana Khel.**
  - **Aimal Khel.**
  - **Shingi.**
  - **Band Khel.**

CHAPTER IX.

MAHSUD AND DARWESH KHEL WAZIRS—(continued).

AFTER the close of the expedition against the Mahsuds in 1881 their behaviour was almost uniformly good for the next ten years, during which time the most important events were the negotiations for the opening up of the Gumal pass.

In 1883 the Mahsuds escorted a native surveyor as far as Khajuri Kach, but the map then made, although supplying a certain amount of information, was very far from complete. The question of the survey of the pass again came up in 1888, and this time a party of three officers went up with a tribal escort. The behaviour of the tribesmen was, however, not good, and the party were obliged to withdraw.

In 1889 Sir Robert Sandeman, the Governor-General's Agent in Baluchistan, submitted proposals to Government for the extension of our protectorate over the Zhob valley and the country between the Gumal and Pishin; and at the same time the Lieutenant-Governor of the Punjab was asked to co-operate and open up the Gumal pass. These proposals were sanctioned, and Sir Robert started from Loralai on the 19th December 1889, with a strong escort, and reached Apozai on the 26th. Here he interviewed a combined *jirga* of Mahsuds, Zalli Khels, and Dotannis, who undertook, in return for certain allowances, to keep open the Zhob valley for traffic, and to be responsible for the safety of the Gumal. Sir Robert then marched through the latter pass as far as Nili Kach, whence he proceeded to Tank. After the successful termination of this march orders were issued for levy posts to be built in the Gumal, and for a military post at Mir Ali Khel. Allowances were also granted to the Wazirs of Wana, and additional allowances to the Mahsuds.

During the cold weather of 1890-91 a railway survey was carried out in the Gumal, and the Mahsuds behaved fairly well.

In February 1892, however, the Amir again began to intrigue with the Wazirs, and a party of *khassadars* was reported to have arrived in Gul Kach. The Wazirs who had accepted service were informed that they should have nothing to do with the Amir's emissaries. They, on the other hand, asked for an assurance from the British Government that they would be supported in the event of their rejecting the Amir's proposals; in reply to which they were told that provided they carried out their obligations, the Government was quite prepared to assist them.

In May 1892, Sirdar Gul Muhammad Khan arrived in Wana with a force of cavalry and infantry, and matters began to take a more serious turn. In July the Government of India addressed a warning to the Amir in regard to his dealings with the Wazirs, and he was clearly informed that the Government would not tolerate any encroachment on Wazir territory, pending a settlement of the frontier. The substance of this letter was communicated to the Wazirs in British service, and they were told to refrain from acts of aggression against the Amir, pending the settlement.

Owing to the attitude of Sirdar Gul Muhammad, whose apparent object was to embroil the Mahsuds with Government, several offences were committed by Mahsuds and Wazirs in the Zhob, and one Khalifa Nur Muhammad, who had accompanied the *Sirdar*, visited Mahsud country, and openly preached sedition against the British Government. In July the Mahsud *maliks* sent in a petition to the Government, stating that the *Sirdar* was trying to make trouble, and asking that the post at Khajuri Kach might be strengthened, so that the discontented men of the tribe could be kept in check.

In accordance with this request a small force was ordered from Dera Ismail Khan to Khajuri Kach; and, later, owing to the aggressiveness of the Amir's agents, another small force was sent from Bannu to Jandola.

On the 29th August the Viceroy addressed another note to the Amir requesting him to withdraw his troops from Wana and Gul Kach by the 1st October, otherwise the Government would be compelled to enforce their request.

From information received at this time, it appeared that the influence of the Amir was rapidly spreading among the Mahsuds and Wazirs; and in view of this the Lieutenant-Governor of the

Punjab asked that additional troops might be concentrated in Waziristan. Orders were, therefore, issued that the marginally noted troops should proceed to Khajuri Kach. On the 22nd September the Amir withdrew his forces from Wana and Gul Kach.

2nd Punjab Cavalry, 2 squadrons.
3rd „ „ 2 „
No. 7 Bengal Mountain Battery.
2nd Sikh Infantry.
5th Punjab Infantry.
22nd Bengal Infantry.

After this withdrawal the attitude of the tribesmen improved, and the Wana Ahmadzais asked Government to take over their country. Although several offences were committed in the early part of 1893, the troops at Khajuri Kach and Jandola were reduced to 200 rifles and a troop of cavalry, and 150 rifles and 50 sabres, respectively.

Fines for offences committed the previous year were paid both by Wazirs and Mahsuds, but the state of the border was still unsatisfactory. Owing to the intrigues of the Amir's agents numerous offences were committed in the hot weather, and on the 30th June 1893 Mr. Kelly, a subordinate officer in the Public Works Department, was shot by raiders near Mughal Kot. In August, owing to the presence of raiding parties, the posts of Mir Ali Khel and Mughal Kot were strengthened.

During the month of June a large *jirga* of Wana Darwesh Khel Wazirs had proceeded to Kabul and stayed there for about two months; after which they returned to their homes, having accomplished nothing.

In October a Mission under Sir Mortimer Durand went to Kabul, at the invitation of the Amir, and while there an agreement was signed by His Highness on the 12th November, by which he relinquished all claim to Waziristan and Dawar, with the exception of Birmal. In the meanwhile raiding had been carried on, and in October the Wazirs carried off a large number of camels, etc., from a Kharoti *kafila* near Khajuri Kach. In the beginning of 1894 Jemadar Kadir Baksh of the Border Police was murdered by Mahsuds in the Splitoi Algad, and many cases of cattle-lifting were reported during the first eight months of the year. In July three leading *maliks*, who had given great assistance in apprehending the murderers of Mr. Kelly, were murdered by the prisoners' relatives. The Punjab Government now wished to demand the surrender of the murderers under threat of an expedition, but the Government of India declined to sanction this course. About this time, owing to several raids having taken place, guards and escorts in the Zhob were strengthened, and the garrisons of the posts between Jandola and Khajuri Kach were increased by 300 rifles.

The Waziristan Delimitation Escort, and operations of the Waziristan Field Force, 1894.

In accordance with the settlement made by Sir Mortimer Durand in November 1893, preparations were made early in 1894 for demarcating the new boundary. As the attitude of the tribesmen in Waziristan was uncertain, the Government of India considered that, in order to avoid any risk of trouble with the Wazirs, a large force would have to be placed on the frontier during the delimitation. It also appeared an opportune moment to accept the invitation of the Wana Wazirs to take over their country.

It was finally agreed that the British and Afghan Commissioners should meet and start work at Domandi on the 15th October. In August a proclamation was issued to the Wazirs describing the line agreed upon, and informing them that the Government had no intention of interfering with their internal affairs, but only wished to establish peace. They were told that a Political Officer would proceed with the Commission, and would, in communication with the different sections of the tribe, settle all questions of entertainment of levies, etc. On receipt of this news large *jirgas* assembled to discuss the matter, and for the most part appeared to be prepared to receive the Commission in a friendly spirit.

The general objects of the arrangements which the Government of India wished to effect in Waziristan were thus stated in a despatch to the Secretary of State :—

> Our desire is to carry the tribesmen with us in whatever we do, and to interfere as little as we can with their internal affairs, provided only that our obligations are discharged in protecting our posts and the general caravan route, and in affording to those sections and leading men of the tribes who have thrown in their lot with us by co-operating in the coercion of turbulent characters and the punishment of murderers and robbers, that protection which they deserve and without which they cannot maintain their position.

In the meantime the Commander-in-Chief proposed that the escort, the main body of which should be located in Spin or Wana, should consist of the marginally named troops, and that the following regiments should be held in readiness to form a reserve brigade :—the 2nd Battalion, Border Regiment, at Mooltan, and one squadron, 1st Punjab Cavalry, No. 8 Mountain Battery, the 4th Punjab Infantry, and the 38th Dogras at Dera Ismail Khan.

	All ranks.
1 squadron, 1st Punjab Cavalry ..	129
No. 3 Punjab Mountain Battery..	265
No. 2 Sappers and Miners ..	189
1st Gurkha Rifles ..	748
3rd Sikh Infantry ..	744
20th Punjab Infantry ..	741
Nos. 16 and 23 Native Field Hospitals.	

He proposed that the force should be concentrated at Dera Ismail Khan under Brig.-General Turner by the 1st October and should be styled the Waziristan Delimitation Escort.

The above proposals were sanctioned by the Government of India, and on the 12th September the following civil officers were appointed :—Mr. R. I. Bruce, C.I.E., to be British Joint Commissioner, and to be accompanied by Mr. H. A. Anderson, Deputy Commissioner, Bannu, Mr. L. White King, Deputy Commissioner, Dera Ismail Khan, and Mr. A. J. Grant.

In addition a Survey party was attached to the Commission.

Mr. Bruce was instructed to explain fully to the Wazirs the object the Government had in view, and to inform them, that if they behaved well, that was all we wished to do, but that they would be held responsible if they behaved badly. He was further instructed to inform them that hereafter the Wana and Spin country and the trade routes to the border would be considered a protected area. Acts of retaliation and raids across the border were also forbidden.

On 13th September word was sent to the Amir that the British Commissioner would be ready to start work on the 15th October; and by the 1st of October the escort was concentrated at Dera Ismail Khan. On the 10th October the Ahmadzai (Wana) *jirga* came in and presented an unanimous petition that the British Government should take over Wana, and that they might become British subjects.

Owing to political reasons the escort did not leave Dera Ismail Khan until the 11th, 12th, and 13th October, in three detachments, concentrating again on the 18th at Khajuri Kach. Previous to this, reconnaissances had been carried out to Spin Tangi, Kutina, and Karab Kot to examine the water-supply.

On the 19th another reconnaissance was carried out in order to examine the routes by the Toi and by Spin, to Wana. The party returned to Khajuri on the third day, and it was then decided by General Turner to march *viâ* Spin and Karab Kot.

On the 22nd October the whole of the brigade except the 20th Punjab Infantry, who remained behind to bring on supplies, marched *viâ* the Karkana Kotal to the head of the Spin Tangi, whence they proceeded on the 23rd to Karab Kot.

On the 24th the brigade halted at Karab Kot and the General Officer Commanding proceeded to the Ughar springs to select a site for a camp. The road from Karab Kot to Wana was also reconnoitred and the construction of a post was commenced on a site about half a mile from the former place. A few shots were fired into the camp on this night.

On the 25th an advance was made to Wana, a company of Gurkhas and some Sappers being left behind to hold the new post and to complete its construction.

During the afternoon a large *jirga* of the Wana Ahmadzais came in. They appeared pleased at the arrival of the troops; but shots were again fired into the camp at night.

The camp at Wana was for political reasons pitched at the eastern end of the plain, which is about thirteen miles long and eleven broad, and is for the most part stony. On the 27th, the 20th Punjab Infantry marched into camp with supplies for the brigade. On the 26th and 27th, *jirgas* of the Nana Khel and Machi Khel Mahsuds came into camp and also some leading Mahsud *maliks*. On the 28th news was received that a certain number of Mahsuds, headed by the Mulla Powindah, were trying to create dissensions and prevent a representative *jirga* coming in.

Career of Mulla Powindah.

As Mulla Powindah played an important part in subsequent events, a few words about him will not be out of place. He is a Mahsud of the Shabi Khel section, and is between forty and fifty years of age. Twenty years ago he was well known in the Bannu district, where he used to wander about as a *talib-ul-ilm.*[1] In 1886-87 two of his associates were arrested as vagrants and imprisoned in the Bannu jail. On their liberation they apparently carried away with them a thirst for revenge on Allahdad Khan, the jail *darogha,* for the way they had been treated while in prison, and, shortly afterwards, they broke into Allahdad's house, murdered him, and made off with Rs. 600 worth of property, which it was said they made over to Mulla Powindah. There was, however, no proof against the latter, though he was strongly suspected of complicity in the murder. Mulla Powindah then fled to the hills, but the other two men surrendered on condition of a trial by *jirga,* and were awarded certain terms of imprisonment. On fleeing to independent territory, Mulla Powindah took refuge in Idak, in Lower Dawar, with Nazarband, an influential *malik* of the place. He now took to himself the title of "Badshah-i-Taliban" or head of the *talibs.* Shortly after this he became a *murid* of the well-known Mulla Gulab Din, who had also taken up his residence in Dawar, not far from Idak. While Gulab Din was alive Mulla Powindah's name was little known, and it is only since the death of the former that he has come into prominence. At the beginning of 1894 Mulla Powindah asked permission of the Deputy Commissioner of Bannu to be allowed to pass through British territory to visit the Mulla of Manki near Nowshera, himself a *murid* of the late Akhund of Swat, and this permission was granted. After his return he moved into the Mahsud country and settled down at Marobi, not far from Makin, and it was at his instigation that the *maliks* who had assisted in bringing to justice the murderers of Mr. Kelly and the sowar in the Zam pass were killed. He then became leader of the faction hostile to the *maliks,* which might be called the young Mahsud party, whose object was to embroil the *maliks* with Government, and to procure at all costs the release of the prisoners committed to the Peshawar jail.

On the 28th October news was received that the Mulla Powindah, with some Abdur Rahman Khels and Abdullais, had succeeded in collecting about 800 men, and intended going to Kaniguram.

1 The *talib-ul-ilms* of Bannu consist of a motley crowd who mostly live in the hills in the hot weather and wander about the Bannu villages in the cold weather, begging alms by day and committing offences by night.

He would then increase his force and proceed to attack the camp at Wana or harass convoys.

On receipt of this news the General Officer Commanding called in the detachment from Karab Kot, and also telegraphed for one battalion and two guns from the reserve brigade to be sent to Jandola.

On the 30th a reconnaissance was carried out up the Tiarza Nala towards Khaisora. The party met with no opposition going out, but when returning, a few shots were fired.

On the evening of the 1st November news was brought in that the Mulla, with about 1,000 men, was at Torwam in the Khaisora. Picquets were consequently doubled, and the troops were ordered to be under arms in their tents at 4 A.M.

On the 2nd a reconnaissance was carried out towards the Inzar Narai, during which a few shots were fired, but no damage done. The same day messengers came in from the Mulla; but they were informed by Mr. Bruce that no dealings could take place with him except through the *jirga*. Mr. Bruce further advised the Mulla to break up his following and return to his home. The camp defences were strengthened and the same precautions taken as on the previous night.

As has already been pointed out, the camp, the ground in the vicinity of which was much cut up by ravines, had been chosen chiefly on political grounds. The position of the civil camp was a source of great anxiety to the General, but he had consented to it being placed where it was on the urgent representation of the Commissioner, who thought it necessary that the *jirgas* should have free access to his tent. It should further be noted that, up to the end of October, the Political Officers had been persuaded that no large body of Mahsuds was likely to attack the escort.

Attack on Wana Camp.

The whole camp was surrounded by a chain of picquets, which were posted merely for observation purposes, and were not intended to hold their own in a serious attack. Nos. 1, 2, 3, 4, 5, and 6 picquets (*see* sketch) were furnished by the 3rd Sikhs, and of these Nos. 1 and 2 were ordered, in case of attack, to fall back on their supports, the whole then to rejoin the regiment; while Nos. 3, 4, and 5 were also to retire on their supports outside the civil camp, which they were to help to defend. About 100 yards to the north of the civil camp there was a detachment of forty rifles in a breastwork, whose duty was to protect the camp from an attack in that direction. No. 6 picquet had instructions to fall back on No. 7, which, with No. 8, was posted on Picquet Hill, and had a support about 200 yards in rear. This support, in case of attack, was to reinforce the two last named picquets, which, guarding a position of vital importance to the camp, were ordered to hold it at all costs. Both these picquets were furnished by the 20th Punjab Infantry. The 1st Gurkha supplied Nos. 8, 9, 10, the "Bogey," and No. 11; and of these the first two were to fall back on the Gurkha left, the last three on the right support, the whole were then to retire on the main body. No. 12, furnished by the 20th Punjab Infantry, was also to fall back on its support in case of attack, and to retire with it to camp.

To the north-east of the camp, about 500 yards distant, there was a deserted Darwesh Khel fort, which was held by a detachment of 100 rifles, 1st Gurkhas. The orders for this party were that, if the enemy made an attempt on the camp from that direction, they were to attack them in rear; if the attack was made on the left of the camp, they were to try and cut off any of the enemy retreating by the Toi valley.

The night of the 2nd November, which was very dark, passed quietly till 5-30 A.M., when the whole camp was suddenly roused by three shots, followed by wild yells and the beating of drums. At the same time a desperate rush of some 500 fanatics, supported by fire from the left front, was made straight on to the left flank and left rear of the camp, held by the 1st Gurkhas. So rapid was this rush that, before the Gurkhas could turn out of their tents, the leading men of the enemy had climbed over the defences, and penetrated into the middle of the camp.

It appears that, under cover of darkness, the enemy had crept up the two large ravines on the west, and rushing Nos. 9 and 10 picquets, one of which fired the three alarm shots, had charged straight down on to the camp. At the same time a large body of Mahsuds continued their course down the ravine past No. 9 picquet, and, checked by the left Gurkha support, had split up into two parties, one of which joined the main attack on the left flank, while the other, continuing down the ravine, broke up against the rear-guards. Many of this party made their way into camp behind the hospitals, where they did much damage among the transport animals, and some of them succeeded in reaching the cavalry lines, where they got to work freeing the horses, in the hope of causing a stampede.

In the meantime the Gurkhas had stopped the main rush from passing down the centre street; the reserve of the regiment, under Major Robinson, forming a rallying square in their camp and fighting hand to hand with the enemy. Colonel Meiklejohn, commanding the 20th Punjab Infantry, was now ordered to take two of his companies to reinforce the Gurkhas, and a company of 3rd Sikhs was despatched with the same object. This they did, clearing their way through the camp with the bayonet, but by the time they had reached the left flank, the enemy had already been driven out of that part of the position. The enemy now made two further but less determined attempts from the same direction, but these were steadily met; and, by the help of star shell, the infantry got in several effective volleys. Although the main attack was made on the left, large numbers of men were also seen on the hills to the right, evidently awaiting events.

At 6 A.M. the enemy's fire slackened; and, as it was evident that they were now retreating, orders were at once given for the cavalry to start in pursuit. Within a few minutes of receiving this order, the squadron, numbering sixty-one sabres, under Major O'Mealy, were making for the Inzar Kotal, and were almost immediately followed by the marginally named troops, under Colonel Meiklejohn, who was instructed to pursue the enemy as long as there was any chance of inflicting loss.

No. 3 Peshawar Mountain Battery.
1 company Sappers and Miners.
3rd Sikhs, 349 rifles.
20th Punjab Infantry, 200 rifles.

After covering about three miles, the cavalry came in sight of the enemy, but the ground was here so bad that it was impossible to move at a faster pace than a trot. On gaining better ground, however, they charged and re-charged the tribesmen with great effect. The squadron then retired until it met the main body of the pursuing column, when the whole force pushed on to the Inzár Kotal, and continued the pursuit for some three miles beyond. The column then retired to camp, which was reached about 4 P.M.

In addition to our losses in officers and men at Wana, which amounted to forty-five killed and seventy-five wounded, the enemy succeeded in carrying off a large number of rifles and Rs. 2,600 in cash. More than a hundred transport animals were also killed or wounded. The losses of the enemy were estimated at about 350 killed. With regard to the numbers of the enemy, it would appear that their total strength was about 3,000, but of these not more than half joined in the actual attack. They consisted principally of Mahsuds, with a few Darwesh Khels of Shakai and Baddar, and were commanded by twenty-nine leading men, of whom ten were killed.

Notwithstanding the gravity of the attack on the Wana camp, further endeavours were made to bring about a peaceable settlement. Mr. Bruce was directed to carry out the spirit of his original instructions, and was authorized to impose the following terms on the tribe :—

(1) The nineteen remaining leaders to be surrendered as hostages.
(2) Mulla Powindah to be expelled from the country until th edemarcation of the boundary was completed.
(3) All stolen property to be restored.

It was, however, determined that other steps would be taken if there were no signs of submission by the 1st December.

On the 5th November it was reported that the Mulla's gathering had dispersed to their homes, and that he himself had returned to Marobi. Subsequent report showed that he was again attempting to raise a following, and he was said to have sent messages to Dawar, Khost, and Urgun.

Consequent on this renewed activity, it was deemed advisable to strengthen the outposts on the Bannu border, and orders were accordingly issued for the Head-quarters and two squadrons, 3rd Punjab Cavalry, to move from Kohat to Bannu with all despatch. These orders reached the Officer Commanding at Kohat at 1-30 A.M. on the morning of the 15th. By 3 A.M. all necessary orders were issued, and at 6 A.M. the wing left Kohat, equipped for field service, and marched into Bannu at 10 A.M. on the 16th, the rear-guard and baggage ponies arriving by noon the same day. The distance marched was just eighty miles, which was accomplished in seventeen hours of actual marching.

This fine march, which won high praise at the time, is worthy of record.

On the 18th a large *jirga* came into camp. The terms having been explained to them they went away on the following morning, but returned on the 23rd, having accomplished nothing. They then asked that the Darwesh Khel and Dotanni *maliks* might assist them; and on the required permission being accorded, the combined *jirga* again left.

On the 27th the Mulla arrived in Shakai, where a large *lashkar* of from 2,000 to 3,000 men had assembled. Discussion regarding the Government terms then took place, but no agreement could be arrived at; and the *maliks* once more returned to Wana. They informed Mr. Bruce that they could not immediately carry out the terms; if they might be given till the 12th December all our demands should be met. The Government agreed to this request, but Mr. Bruce was told to inform the *jirga* that if all the terms were not fulfilled by the date named, British troops would at once enter their country; and that, in the meantime, all necessary preparations would be made for the advance.

On the 2nd December the Government of India ordered the formation of a punitive force, to be called the "Waziristan Field Force," under the command of Lieut.-General Sir William Lockhart, K.C.B. The force was to consist of three brigades, as shown in the margin. The Delimitation Escort was to be known as the 1st Brigade, the 2nd was to concentrate at Tank under Brig.-General W. P. Symons, and the 3rd at Mirian, near Bannu, under Colonel C. C. Egerton, C.B.

1st Brigade, Wana.

No. 3 Punjab Mountain Battery.
1 squadron, 1st Punjab Cavalry.
2nd Battalion, Border Regiment.
20th Punjab Infantry.
3rd Sikh Infantry.
1-1st Gurkha Rifles.
No. 2 Company, Bengal Sappers and Miners.

2nd Brigade, Jandola.

No. 8 (B) Mountain Battery.
1 squadron, 1st Punjab Cavalry.
1 „ 2nd „ „
33rd Punjab Infantry.
38th Dogras.
4th Punjab Infantry.
1st Battalion, 5th Gurkhas.
No. 5 Company, Bengal Sappers and Miners.
1 Maxin gun.

3rd Brigade, Mirian.

No. 1 Kohat Mountain Battery.
3rd Punjab Cavalry.
1st Sikh Infantry.
2nd Punjab Infantry.
6th „ „

Meanwhile more offences had been committed by the Mahsuds, and, on the 11th, the *maliks* asked for Mr. Bruce's confidential agent to help them in their endeavours to arrive at a settlement.

He went with them to the Khaisora, but returned next day with the *jirga*, who said that there appeared no hope of the tribe complying with our terms.

In the meantime the three brigades had moved to their respective stations, and on the 15th Sir William Lockhart took over supreme political control of South Waziristan, assisted by the following civil officers, who were attached to brigades as follows:—Mr. Bruce, to the 1st Brigade, Messrs. King and Grant, 2nd Brigade, and Mr. Casson, 3rd Brigade.

On the 16th orders were received by Sir William Lockhart that the advance into the Mahsud country was to be carried out as soon as possible. Orders were, therefore, issued for the 1st Brigade to advance from Wana by the Tiarza pass and the Sharawangi Kotal, with Kaniguram as its objective; the 2nd Brigade was at the same time ordered to advance from Jandola by the Tank Zam for Makin, and the 3rd Brigade to proceed by the Khaisora valley, in Darwesh Khel limits, to Razmak. The three columns were all timed to reach their respective places on the 21st December.

The movements of the 2nd Brigade will be described first. On the 16th a reconnaissance was carried out as far as Shingi Kot, without opposition. On the 18th the brigade accompanied by General Lockhart moved from Jandola to Marghaband, whence, marching *viâ* Shilimanzai Kach and Jangal, they reached Makin on the 21st, having destroyed the Mulla's village of Marobi *en route*. With the exception of a few shots fired into camp each night, no opposition was met with; the villages on the line of march had all been deserted, and the Mulla himself was reported to have fled to the Darra valley, north of Pir Ghal. Communication was now established with the other two columns, and Colonel Egerton was ordered to march his brigade into Makin the following day, while General Turner was directed to come in himself from Kaniguram for instructions.

To turn now to the movements of the 1st Brigade, the strength of which was, on the 14th December, increased by the arrival of the 1st Battalion, 4th Gurkhas. Previous to the advance from Wana, a fortified village near the camp was hired from the Khojal Khel Ahmadzais and converted into a military post, with a garrison of one regiment of native infantry, two guns, and twenty sowars.

Reconnaissances were, at the same time, made to the Tiarza and Inzar Kotals and the Wucha Tiarza Nala, the last of which was found to be the best road and was adopted for the advance into the Khaisora. Orders for the advance having been received on the 17th the brigade moved out the following morning, and marched to Jumai Kot. A halt was made here on the 19th, while a strong reconnaissance was pushed forward to the Sharawangi Kotal, the troops left in camp being employed in destroying the Shabi Khel houses of Torwam. Resuming the march on the following day, the column reached Kaniguram on the 21st, after encountering only slight opposition. The road had, however, been far worse than anticipated, and had so greatly delayed the baggage animals each day that it was invariably midnight before the rear-guard reached camp.

The Bannu column, meanwhile, marching on the 17th, reached Razmak on the 21st. The rear-guard was fired at from the Mohmit Khel village of Musakki, for which offence a fine of Rs. 400 was levied on that clan; in other respects the march was without incident.

On the evening of the 22nd, Colonel Egerton and General Turner having reached Makin as directed, General Lockhart explained to them that the object of the future operations would be to beat up the Mulla's party in the valleys round Pir Ghal, and that he intended to do this with six columns advancing simultaneously on Christmas day.

During the 22nd, a column, consisting of two guns and 600 men of the 1st Brigade, moved out from Makin and destroyed the village of Karram, belonging to Sinaband Garrarai. The troops were fired on during these operations, and two officers and four men were wounded.

On the 25th began the combined movements of the six columns, as mentioned above. Each column bivouacked out for two nights, and as a result of the operations, many towers and settlements of the Abdullai, Badanzai, Langar Khel, Garrarai, and Abdur Rahman Khel sections, all of which had joined in the attack on Wana, were destroyed; large quantities of forage were carried off; and over 1,000 head of cattle were brought back into camp. The only column which encountered any opposition was the one under General Turner, which, while operating in the Baddar valley, had a few shots fired at it, and sustained a loss of two men wounded.

On the 31st December, Colonel Egerton, with the troops noted in the margin, left Makin for the Shaktu valley, with the object of punishing the Shabi Khel, the Kikarai, and the Mar-sanzai sections. The rest of the Bannu column escorted a convoy of sick to Jandola, where they duly arrived without incident.

No. 1 Kohat Mountain Battery.
½ company, Sappers and Miners.
1st Punjab Infantry.
2nd " "
6th " "

Colonel Egerton's force marched *viâ* the Engamal pass and Waladin to Matwam, destroying several Kikarai and Shabi Khel towers *en route*. At Matwam the column was divided into two portions, one of which, under Major Sturt, visited Baramand and Khozhoba, in the Sheranna valley, while the other, under Colonel Egerton, moving up the Zardai Algad, crossed the Khwaja Khidr Ziarat Kotal, and eventually joined the first party on the Sammal Narai. The following day the whole column marched to the mouth of the Mariamana stream, destroying three Shabi Khel villages and an Abdullai encampment. From this place an advance was made to the junction of the Khaisora Nala with the Shuza, whence, after a party had been detached to a neighbouring village to capture a large number of cattle belonging to the Shabi Khel, the column set out for Jandola, which was reached on the evening of the 8th.

In the meanwhile news had reached the 1st and 2nd Brigades, who had been destroying towers in the neighbourhood of Kaniguram, that the Mulla had fled to Birmal, where he was trying, apparently with little success, to induce the Kabul Khel to join in a religious war.

On the 2nd January, in accordance with orders from General Lockhart, a flying column, strength as in the margin, under the command of Brig.-General Turner, marched from Kaniguram over the Zaterai range to Ahmadwam, in the Shinkai valley. The following day the Abdur Rahman villages in the Spli Toi Alga were destroyed by two small parties, and on the 6th a general advance was made to Bahadur Khel, whence, after destroying some more hamlets, the column proceeded to Jandola on the 9th.

No. 3 Punjab Mountain Battery.
1 company, Sappers and Miners.
2nd Border Regiment.
1st Gurkhas.
3rd Sikhs.
4th Gurkhas.

The 2nd Brigade, meanwhile, had evacuated Makin on the 5th January, and, accompanied by Sir William Lockhart, had marched to Jangal, from which place the Nargao, Tangai, and Janjara valleys were explored.

Up to this time the terms imposed upon the Mahsuds had been complied with to the extent that the Mulla Powindah had left the country, two hostages out of the eighteen demanded had been given up, and a few horses and rifles had been surrendered.

Sir William Lockhart now issued notices to all the leading *maliks* of the three sections, telling them to meet him at Kundiwam, in Khaisora, on the 19th January, when our final terms would be notified. These terms, which had been approved of by Government, were :—

(1) Partial disarmament of the tribe.
(2) Payment of all outstanding fines.
(3) Opening of the Shahar route from Jandola to Wana.
(4) The return of the Mulla not to be allowed until all the above terms were complied with and the delimitation completed.

On the 8th Sir William Lockhart continued his march *viâ* Shilimanzai Kach towards Jandola where the whole of the Waziristan Field Force now concentrated. Thus terminated the first phase of the operations.

On the 10th January orders were issued for the 1st Brigade to proceed to Wana, *viâ* the Gumal; for the 2nd Brigade to march on Kundiwam; and for the 3rd Brigade to proceed to Mirian in two parties, one, under Colonel Egerton, *viâ* the Shuza valley, and the other *viâ* Tank and the Bain pass. All these columns were to be at their respective destinations on or about the 19th January.

In accordance with these orders General Turner left Jandola on the 12th, and reached Wana on the appointed day without incident. The 2nd Brigade, after spending the 11th and 12th in improving the road through the Shahur Tangi, and in constructing a line of telegraph as far as Haidari Kach, marched on the 13th to the latter place, accompanied by Sir William Lockhart. The next day an advance was made on Barwand, whence a notice was sent to the Shakai *maliks*, to the effect that if they failed to surrender the five men demanded from their section, severe punishment would be inflicted on them. After a march of some difficulty, Kaniguram was reached on the 19th, when it was found that some of the head-men had already arrived, and that others were on the way. During this march the telegraph line was cut near Barwand; and in an affray which a party, sent back to repair it, had with the enemy, three Wazirs were killed. A post of 400 men was then established at Barwand to protect the line of communications.

The two columns of the Bannu Brigade, meanwhile, duly arrived at Mirian on the 20th January, having destroyed the defences of all Shabi Khel, Galeshahi, Abdullai, and Jelal Khel settlements met with *en route*, and having captured about 1,200 head of sheep and cattle.

On the 21st January General Lockhart announced the final terms to the assembled Mahsud *jirga* at Kundiwam, and on the next day he moved with Field Force Head-quarters to Wana, leaving General Symons and his brigade, with Mr. Bruce, at the former place, to see the terms complied with, or, if necessary, to bring further pressure to bear on the tribe.

This brigade remained at Kundiwam until the final withdrawal of troops from Waziristan.

Turning now to the doings at Wana, the 23rd January was spent in arranging for the despatch of the delimitation party to Domandi. It will be remembered that it had been arranged that the British and Afghan Commissioners should meet at Domandi on the 15th October 1894, but owing to the punitive operations this could not, of course, be carried out. After a good deal of correspondence between the two Governments, it was finally agreed that a British officer should carry out the demarcation of Waziristan without the co-operation of an Afghan official, but with the help of the local headmen; and it was added that His Excellency the Viceroy understood the Amir would accept the line laid down by the British Commissioner as completely as that of other portions of the frontier, where British and Afghan officers had acted together.

All preliminaries having been thus arranged, Mr. King left Wana for Domandi on the 24th January, with a strong escort, and started the delimitation, in company with the Suliman Khel and Kharoti *maliks*, on the 28th. It is unnecessary to follow his movements in detail, and will suffice to state that, having demarcated the boundary as far as Khwaja Khidr, he returned to Wana on the 14th February.

Meanwhile General Lockhart had selected a site for a post at Wana, and proposed to Government the construction of a fortified post of a less costly nature than that originally sanctioned. In his opinion Wana did not possess the strategical importance that had been attributed to it. These views were approved, and work was at once begun on the new post. About this time the Mahsuds began to comply with the British terms, and all except three of the hostages had been brought into Kundiwam by the 28th January.

On the 5th February the marginally named troops, under Colonel Gaselee, left Wana for Bannu, to form Divisional troops for the advance which was now to be made up the Tochi with the Delimitation party; and on the 12th General Lockhart also left for that place.

2nd Border Regiment.
1 company, Sappers and Miners.
2nd Punjab Infantry.
5th Gurkhas.

Meanwhile Mr. Anderson had summoned the leading Darwesh Khel and Dawari *maliks* to Bannu, and had written to the *hakim* of Khost, asking him to direct his *maliks* to be in attendance at Sheranni on the 3rd March. Large and representative *jirgas* also came into Bannu at this time, with whom the necessary arrangements were made for the advance up the Tochi.

General Lockhart joined Colonel Egerton's column at Saiadgi on the 24th February, and on the following day the whole force began the march up the valley to Sheranni, where the Afghan representatives were met as arranged.

On the 4th March the three remaining Mahsud hostages were surrendered, and as the Government account with the tribe was now held to be closed, Sir William Lockhart proposed to march the bulk of the troops back to India. At the same time he reported that, after seeing the Tochi, he was of opinion that a site for a military post could be chosen therein which would possess numerous advantages over Wana. Chief amongst these advantages would be its accessibility from Bannu; abandance of supplies; the strategical value of the valley, giving direct access to Ghazni; and the political value of the hold which such a fort would give over the Darwesh Khels.

On the 5th the Boundary delimitation party under Mr. Anderson, escorted by a force under Colonel Meiklejohn, moved out towards Charkhel and completed the demarcation from that place to Khwaja Khidr, whence they rejoined the rest of the force at Datta Khel on the 22nd. On the 26th the party again moved out to demarcate the remaining part of the boundary from Charkhel to Laram. The main body of the force remained at Datta Khel till the 27th, when they moved down parallel to the commission, who rejoined them, on the completion of their work, at Miramshah.

Meanwhile the Government of India having sanctioned Sir William Lockhart's proposals for the reduction of the troops in Waziristan, the 2nd Brigade was ordered to proceed to Tank, and Sir William Lockhart himself, with a part of his force, returned to Bannu. On the 30th March the Waziristan Field Force was broken up, the troops still remaining in the country being brought on to the strength of the Punjab Frontier Force. These troops consisted of a detachment of cavalry, a mountain battery, a company of Sappers and Miners, and four regiments of Native Infantry in the Tochi, under Colonel Meiklejohn, and a detachment of cavalry, a mountain battery, a company of Sappers and Miners and two regiments of infantry, under Brig.-General Turner, at Wana. There was also a wing of the 14th Sikhs at Barwand, and 100 men at Jandola.

The results of the expedition, thus terminated, may be said to have been completely satisfactory; all sections of the Mahsuds concerned in the attack on Wana, had been punished, the terms of Government had been fully complied with, and the demarcation of the whole boundary from Domandi to Laran successfully accomplished.

The Indian Medal of 1854, with a clasp inscribed "Waziristan 1894-95," was subsequently granted to all troops and public followers who took part in the operations.

During the month of May 1895 several murderous attacks on individuals took place. On the 13th Lieutenant Limond, 6th Punjab Infantry, was stabbed near Boya and died the following day; his syce and orderly were also dangerously wounded. On the 17th a lance-naick of the 2nd Punjab Infantry was shot at Miramshah. On the night of the 24th a party of Dawaris tried to enter the post at Miramshah, and one man succeeded in stabbing two sepoys. On the 31st July Lieutenant Campbell, 3rd Punjab Cavalry, was very severely wounded near Boya; and on the 2nd August a sowar of the 3rd Punjab Cavalry, on grass-cutting guard was shot dead about four miles from that place.

In August sanction was received from Her Majesty's Government to locate a military force in the Tochi valley permanently. The strength of the force was fixed at two battalions of native infantry, one squadron, native cavalry, and a mountain battery.

It is not necessary to go into the negotiations between the Political Officers and the tribesmen; and it will suffice to say that *jirgas* were assembled, and, in return for certain services demanded from the tribes, allowances were granted. By the end of 1896 the arrangements for carrying on the new policy in Waziristan were practically complete. In the autumn of that year both the civil and military head-quarters were transferred from Miramshah to Datta Khel; and in the following spring the permanent strength of the troops was reduced to four guns of a mountain battery, two Maxim guns, one squadron of native cavalry, and two battalions of native infantry.

But the establishment of these military garrisons had done little to counteract the natural lawlessness of the inhabitants. Crimes of violence were of frequent occurrence, in one of which the Political Officer in the Tochi, Mr. H. A. Casson, I.C.S., was dangerously wounded, and had to be replaced by Mr. H. A. Gee, I.C.S.

The Maizar outbreak, and the operations of the Tochi Field Force in 1897-98.

We now come to the circumstances that led more immediately to the Maizar outbreak. In June 1896 Honda Ram, the Hindu writer of the Sheranni levy post, was murdered in that village, and a fine of Rs. 2,000 was inflicted on the Madda Khels. The actual murderer escaped to Afghan territory. Some men suspected of complicity were surrendered for trial, but a number of tribesmen swore on the *Koran* that they were innocent, and in accordance with tribal custom they were released.

The Madda Khel who inhabit the lower part of the Shawal valley (in which Maizar is situated), and the upper portion of the Tochi, are known as the Ger Madda Khel to distinguish them from the Kazhawals, or Madda Khel, who inhabit the Kazha valley, north of the Tochi. It may here be mentioned that the distinction between the Ger Madda Khel and the Kazhawals is in no way ethnographic, as every sub-section of the clan appears to be represented both in the Tochi and the Kazha.

I B. Topo. Dy. No. 7.264.
Exd. C. J. A. March 1908.

SKETCH OF MAIZAR.

Looking W. from hill about 400 yards S.-W. of Kotal.

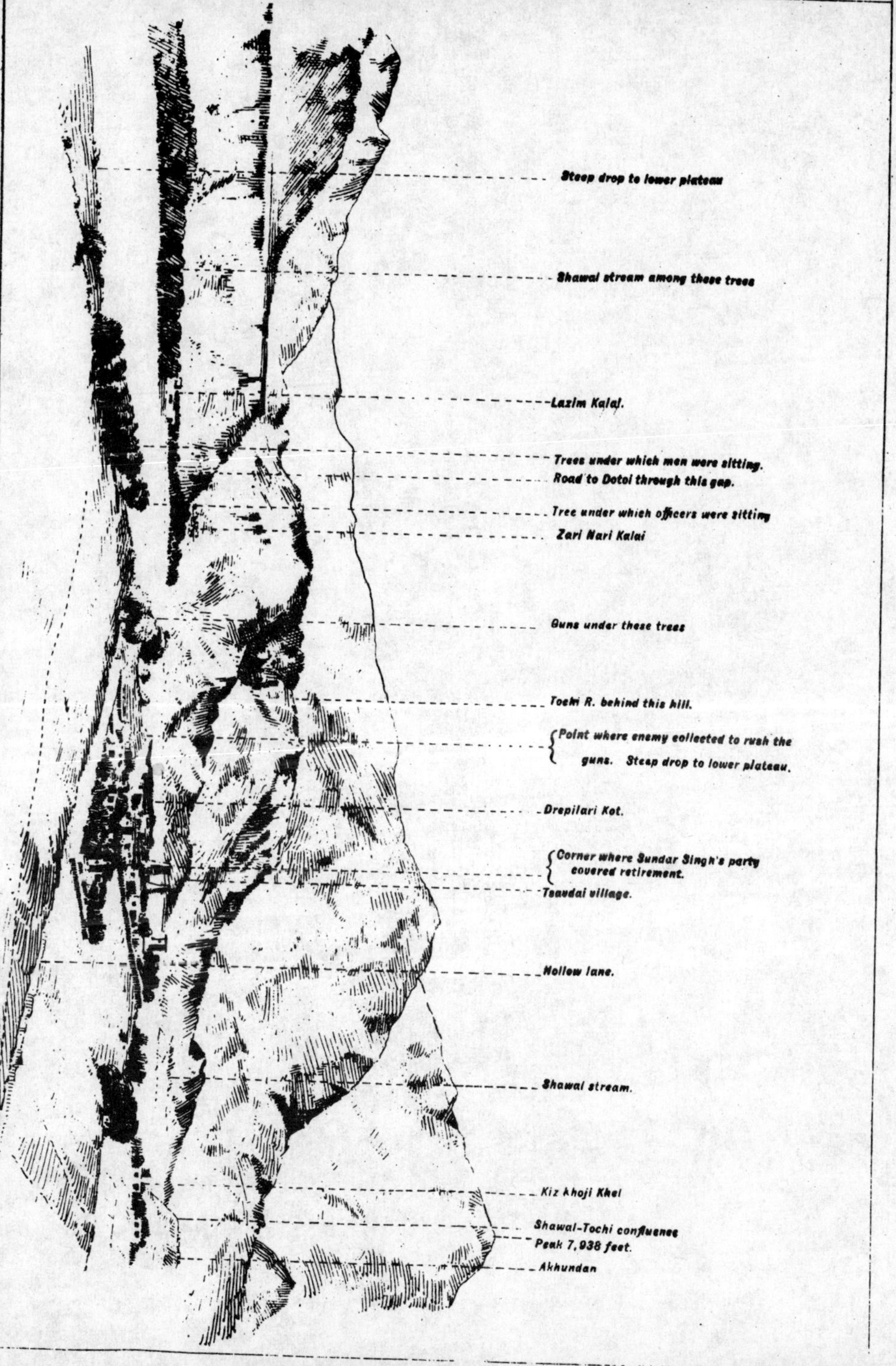

(Sd.) G. K. COCKERILL, *Lieut.,*
Field Intelligence Officer,
Tochi Field Force.

No. 4.368-I., 1908.

In recognition of the submission to authority shown by the Madda Khel, in surrendering for trial the men suspected of the murder of Honda Ram, the Government, in May 1897, reduced the fine of Rs. 2,000 to Rs. 1,200 (Kabuli), the blood-money due by tribal custom for the murdered man. The distribution of the fine was left to the *maliks* themselves, and it was on this point that dissensions arose. The sub-sections residing in Maizar objected to pay the share with which they had been assessed by Sadda Khan and his faction, contending that the offence was not a tribal one, and that the fine should be paid by Sadda Khan and the inhabitants of Sheranni, where the crime had been committed.

This Sadda Khan, a Ger Madda Khel of Sheranni, was the chief of the Madda Khel, and belonged to the Khazzar Khel branch of the Ali Khan Khel sub-section. The leader of the opposing faction was Alambe Khan, also a Khazzar Khel Madda Khel of Sheranni. On the 6th June the Political Officer, Mr. Gee, arrived at Datta Khel, and the next day the chief Madda Khel *maliks* came in, and some cases were settled. Before the Madda Khels were dismissed they were informed that Mr. Gee would visit Maizar and Dotoi with an escort, for the purpose of selecting the site for a levy post at Maizar, and of discussing the fine in Honda Ram's case.

On the 10th of June 1897, Mr. Gee, with an escort, as per margin, under the command of Lieut.-Colonel Bunny, 1st Sikhs, started at 6 A.M. from Datta Khel. On arrival in Maizar, the *maliks* appeared quite friendly, and, pointing out a site to halt at, offered to provide a meal for the Mussulman sepoys of the escort. The party were thus lulled into a false feeling of security.

1st Punjab Cavalry, 12 sabres.
1st Sikh Infantry, 200 rifles.
1st Punjab Infantry, 100 rifles.
No. 6 Bombay Mountain Battery, 2 guns.

The spot selected by the Maizarwals for the camp was close to the walls of a Drepilari (Madda Khel sub-section) village, and was commanded by several other villages from 100 to 400 yards distant. The guns unlimbered close to the walls, and the infantry drew up on the outer flank of the guns. Guards were posted facing outwards, and each sepoy retained his rifle, no piles of arms being permitted.

Directly after the arrival at Maizar, Mr. Gee and two other officers, with an escort of sowars, and accompanied by the *maliks*, visited Dotoi. They returned at midday, at about which hour the promised meal was produced from a neighbouring *kot*; and the whole escort had breakfast. After the meal the pipers of the 1st Sikhs began to play. Suddenly a hubbub began in the village, and the villagers, who had been listening to the pipes, drew off. A man was observed to wave a sword from the top of a tower; and two shots were fired in quick succession from the village, the second of which wounded Lieutenant Seton Browne. Firing now commenced from the villages to the south and east, and a hot fusillade was opened from the Drepilari village on the north, as a result of which Colonel Bunny was wounded.

The guns now opened with case, at 100 yards range, at a large number of men who were firing from the entrance of the Drepilari village and who were preparing to charge. Captain Browne and Lieutenant Cruickshank of the battery were quickly wounded, but continued pluckily to fight their guns till the enemy had been driven back into the village. As only sixteen rounds per gun, however, had been brought out with the escort, ammunition was now running short, and Colonel Bunny gave orders for a retirement to the ridge. At the commencement of the firing there had been a general stampede among the baggage animals, so that when the retirement was ordered most of the reserve ammunition and other equipment had to be abandoned.

The enemy now appeared on all sides in great force, but the retirement, which began under such very trying conditions, was carried out with great deliberation and in the most stubborn and gallant manner. At its very beginning Lieutenant Higginson and Captain Cassidy were hit, so that all the British officers were now wounded, two of them mortally; but they all continued to carry out their duties and lead their men.

The circumstances were trying in the extreme for the troops, and their staunchness is worthy of the highest praise. Subadars Narain Singh, 1st Sikhs, Sundar Singh, 1st Punjab Infantry, and Jemadar Sherzad, 1st Sikhs, behaved with the greatest gallantry. Getting together a party of their men, they made a most determined stand by the wall of a garden, whence they covered the first withdrawal, remaining themselves under heavy fire until the enemy closed with them. It was at this point that Subadar Sundar Singh was killed.

Under cover of this stand the wounded were carried and helped away, the guns withdrawing to a low *kotal* about 300 yards distant. Here a fresh stand was made, the guns firing blank to check the enemy, as the service ammunition had all been expended. Lieutenant Cruickshank now received a third, and this time a fatal wound, while Captain Browne, who had fainted from loss of blood, and had been fastened on to Mr. Gee's pony when the retirement began, was found to be dead on arrival at the *kotal*.

A further retirement was carried out by successive units, positions being held on the ridges stretching from south to north until the Sheranni plain was reached, about two miles further east; all this time the enemy was enveloping the flanks. Eventually, about 5-30 P.M., reinforcements began to appear, and the enemy was beaten off. With the ammunition now received, the heights around the village of Sheranni were shelled, with the result that the enemy finally retired, and the village was partially set on fire. The further withdrawal was unmolested, and the rear-guard reached camp at midnight.

Colonel Bunny died of his wounds on the road, and his body, with those of the other killed and wounded officers, was brought in with the retiring troops. Help was given by the Khidder Khel Mohmit Khel on the way back, and during the following days they brought in all the bodies of the killed.

The news of this fighting reached Colonel Gray at Miramshah at 11 P.M. on the 10th, and he arrived in Datta Khel the next morning and assumed command. Steps were then taken to reinforce the troops in the Tochi and at Datta Khel.

Immediately after the outbreak at Maizar the Madda Khel had despatched messengers to other sections of the Darwesh Khel for assistance, and they also approached the Afghan authorities. It was for a long time uncertain what effect the appeals would have; but on the 12th the Commissioner of Derajat wired that if there was any intention of our taking immediate action a strong force should be concentrated. On the 16th he again wired that not less than a brigade, with another in reserve, would be required to occupy Maizar.

1st Brigade.

Colonel C. C. Egerton, C.B., Commanding.

2nd Battalion, Argyll and Sutherland Highlanders.
1st Sikh Infantry.
1st Punjab Infantry.
33rd " "
1 squadron, 1st Punjab Cavalry.
No. 3 Peshawar Mountain Battery.
No. 2 Company, Bengal Sappers and Miners.

2nd Brigade.

Brig.-General W. P. Symons, C.B. Commanding.

3rd Battalion, Rifle Brigade.
14th Sikhs.
6th Jats.
25th Punjab Infantry.
1 squadron, 1st Punjab Cavalry.
4 guns, No. 6 (Bombay) Mountain Battery.

On the 17th June, it was decided that a punitive expedition, consisting of two brigades, should immediately be sent up the Tochi, under the command of Major-General Corrie-Bird, C.B. The composition of the force, which was designated the Tochi Field Force, is shown in the margin.

The point of concentration for the troops not already in the Tochi was Bannu. Supplies and transport were collected at that place, and on the 8th July, the concentration being practically complete, the Major-General marched to Idak. On the way he investigated an affray that had taken place at Saiadgi. It appeared that some unladen camels returning from Idak had taken a short cut down the river-bed through some fields below Saiadgi post. The levies in their ordinary clothes dashed down and drove off the camelmen with sticks and stones. The officer commanding the post at Saiadgi, under the impression that the convoy was being attacked by raiders, turned out and attacked the levies; and before the mistake could be discovered some fourteen of them had been killed and wounded. A sum of Rs. 5,000 was subsequently granted by Government as compensation.

On the 9th General Bird arrived at Miramshah and took over political charge of the valley. On the 13th, at Datta Khel he issued a proclamation in which it was stated that the intention of Government was to destroy Drepilari and all the fortifications of other *kots* in Maizar and Sheranni, in punishment for the affair at the former place.

The field force concentrated at Datta Khel on the 19th, and orders were at once issued for the 1st Brigade to advance to Sheranni the following day, and for the 2nd Brigade to remain in camp as are serve.

As regards the behaviour of the Madda Khel during this time, it was reported that the Ger Madda Khel had mostly fled to the hills, and were more likely to fly across the Afghan border than to offer any resistance. The Mulla Powindah was said to have been trying to raise the Mahsuds, but without success.

The 1st Brigade marched to Sheranni on the 20th, according to orders, and both that place and Maizar, which was visited by the cavalry, were found to be deserted. By the 5th August all the defences in the neighbourhood had been destroyed without more opposition than a little sniping into camp at night.

Notices were now issued to the Madda Khel, telling them to come in to hear the further terms of Government; and on the 17th in open durbar, the following terms were announced:—

(1) The tribe to make submission, and to surrender certain named leaders in the attack at Maizar.

(2) All stolen property to be restored, and outstanding fines to be paid.

(3) A further fine of Rs. 10,000 to be paid for their recent misbehaviour.

General Bird, accompanied by a small column, now made a tour through the Kazha valley, without meeting with any opposition, and returned to Sheranni on the 28th.

On the 3rd September the Maizar and Sheranni *maliks* definitely refused to accept the Government terms.

A few days later another column, under General Symons, was sent up the Kazha valley, and, marching *viâ* Ghazlamai, Isham, Pirakai, and Ismail Khel, reached Datta Khel on the 28th, having destroyed numerous defences *en route*.

Five days later a force under General Egerton visited the Upper Tochi, in search of fugitives. Beyond a skirmish on Charmina hill during the first day's march, little opposition was met with, and the columns returned to Datta Khel on the 17th, having carried out much useful survey work in Shawal, the Khina valley, and round Shindal.

On the 25th General Egerton took a third column into the Kazha to repair the boundary pillars from Dotoi to Mazdak. About the same time a small force was sent out from Miramshah to explore and survey the Mohmit Khel Tori Khel and Kabul Khel country.

During October there was a good deal of wire-cutting along the line of communications in the Tochi, and the camps were occasionally fired into at night; but the operations which were at that time being carried out against the Afridis and Orakzais did not cause any special restlessness amongst the tribes in Waziristan. Although the Madda Khel had still failed to make submission, there were signs that the tribesmen were getting uneasy at the approach of winter, and the prospect of losing their spring crops by further delay in coming to terms. On the 31st October Sadda Khan, the head of the clan, gave himself up, his life having been guaranteed; and, at his suggestion, Major-General Corrie-Bird despatched an influential *jirga* of the leading Darwesh Khel and Dawari *maliks* to explain to the Madda Khel generally the terms on which they would be allowed to return to their own country. In consequence of this step, a large *jirga* of Madda Khels arrived in camp on the 14th November, and formally submitted on the following day. During December the Madda Khel paid the first instalment of the fine imposed upon them for the Maizar outrage as well as the Rs. 1,200 long owing for the murder of Honda Ram.

On the 3rd January 1898 the General Officer Commanding started on his return to Bannu, and during that month the Tochi Field Force was gradually broken up, the command of the troops left in the Tochi valley devolving on Brig.-General Egerton.

The total casualties at Maizar had been, in addition to the officers already mentioned, twenty-one non-commissioned officers and men killed and twenty-eight wounded, while our losses in the subsequent operations up to 25th November were six men killed and two officers and six men wounded.

The most remarkable point in the campaign was the unusual amount of sickness amongst the troops. The climate of the Tochi valley is at all times trying, and in this instance the hurried march from Khushalgarh to Bannu, in the middle of the hot weather, had no doubt affected the constitutions of the men, and rendered them more disposed to contract disease, and less able to shake it off, than would usually be the case. The principal diseases were diarrhœa and dysentery, which eventually took an epidemic form and became very severe.

Blockade of the Mahsud Wazirs in 1900-01.

No sooner had the Government of India settled with the Madda Khel in the Tochi valley than the Mahsuds again began to give trouble, and eventually the punishment of this tribe had to be undertaken for the fourth time.

For some two years after the expedition of 1894, and the subsequent arrangements for the occupation and administration of Southern Waziristan, the Mahsuds had remained quiet, the *maliks* had kept their obligations, and the Mulla Powindah's influence seemed to have waned. In the summer of 1898, however, there was a recrudescence of outrages in British territory and within the protected area of Southern Waziristan, which was traced to the influence of the Mulla. During 1898 and 1899 raids were frequent, and, in January 1900, the levy post at Zam and the Public Works Department bungalow at Murtaza were both attacked.

In February a meeting took place between the Political Officer, Mr. Watson, and the Mulla Powindah; this being the first time that Government had recognized that chief. The Mulla, on this occasion, would not commit himself by consenting to receive any allowances; and his only petitions concerned the grievances of the Mahsuds, and of his own section, the Shabi Khel, in particular.

On the 21st March a Mahsud *jirga* assembled at Tank, many *maliks* coming in who would not have presented themselves if we had not first treated with the Mulla. A formal demand was made by Government for reparation due for outrages and crimes, but no complete settlement resulted; and subsequently Mr. Merk, the new Commissioner of the Derajat, reported that the amount of fines due from the Mahsuds reached the sum of Rs. 1,87,000.

Meanwhile there was no cessation of offences and raids, the most serious of which occurred on the night of the 22nd October, when the Border Military Police post at Nasran, eleven miles north of Tank, and in British territory, was surprised by Mahsuds. Two sepoys were killed on this occasion, and eight Snider rifles, two carbines, and two boxes of ammunition were looted. Lieutenant Hennessy, 4th Sikhs, commanding at Jandola, started at daybreak to intercept the raiders on their return up the Shuza valley. This he succeeded in doing at the cost of his own life; the Mahsuds on their side lost one man, and five rifles were recovered.

Mr. Merk now called in a Mahsud *jirga* to Tank, to settle accounts; and, at the same time, the Government decided that tribal allowances should no longer be paid to the *maliks*, who had proved themselves incapable of restraining their followers, but to the body of the tribe, who should themselves appoint the future recipients of the money. This change of system was announced by Mr. Merk to the *jirgu*, the *maliks* admitting that they were unable to restrain the tribesmen. A formal demand for the payment of Rs. 1,00,000 as a fine for past offences was then made, and the *jirga* was warned that, if half a lakh were not paid within fifteen days, a blockade would be imposed. They were further told that the amount of money really due from the tribe was nearly double the amount for which the Government now asked.

At the conclusion of the fifteen days' grace, the *jirga* returned and asked for a further period of two months, in which to consider the terms; and as there appeared no prospect of an early settlement, Mr. Merk was now authorized to proclaim a blockade, which came into operation on the 1st December 1900.

The following preliminary measures were taken to ensure the effectiveness of the blockade:—

On the eastern side two moveable columns were mobilized from Bannu (100 sabres, 300 rifles) and Dera Ismail Khan (200 sabres, 600 rifles), with head-quarters at Jani Khel and Zam, respectively; their duties were to form a cordon on the confines of the Bhittani country in conjunction with the Border Military Police posts to the north and south of the Bain Darra. The police posts of Khairu Khel and Mullagai were garrisoned by regular troops. On the southern side the Gumal line was reinforced by throwing military garrisons into Murtaza and Manjhi, and by forming two temporary posts at Toimanda and on the Khwuzhma Narai. Khajuri Kach was strengthened by half a company; Haidari Kach retained its usual garrison; and Jandola was increased by 50 rifles. Sarwakai post was considerably strengthened by the addition of 400 rifles, 35th Sikhs, and a new temporary post was established in the Spin plain. Ngandi Oba received a garrison of 20 sabres and 27 rifles; and the 23rd Pioneers were brought to Murtaza to carry on the construction of military works during the blockade. As far as possible all the posts were connected by telegraph.

South of the Gumal the Zhob district garrisons were increased by the addition of a new levy post at Shinbaz Kotal. The 23rd Bombay Infantry from Fort Sandeman, and a wing of the 24th Bombay Infantry from Loralai, were moved to Mir Ali Khel, and the posts of Mughal Kot and Kuchbina.

To provide the extra troops required for the blockade, the 28th Punjab Infantry, which was to be relieved by the 17th Bengal Infantry, was ordered to stand fast at Wana, and six companies of the latter regiment were divided between Jani Khel and the eastern outposts; while the 9th Bombay Infantry was brought to Dera Ismail Khan. The 1st Punjab Cavalry were moved up from Kohat, and were divided between the two moveable columns, besides providing detachments for posts north of Tank. The 5th Punjab Cavalry furnished detachments at Wana, Spin, Drazand, Khajuri Kach, and Sarwakai.

Shortly after the proclamation of the blockade the Mahsuds began to make overtures for the payment of the fine, and requested that it might be paid partly in kind. This concession was made, and for some time payment proceeded regularly, and until the middle of January 1901 there was a cessation of crime. In the latter part of January, however, several fresh offences were committed.

On the 1st of February Mr. Merk summoned another *jirga* to Jandola, and the *maliks* repudiated their responsibility for the outbreaks. By the beginning of April nearly half the fine had been paid, although offences still continued.

In May Mr. Merk again held a *jirga* at Jandola, and the *maliks* were clearly made to understand that neither would the blockade be removed nor would allowances be distributed until the fine was fully realized. They were also warned that offences committed meanwhile would be sharply punished by immediate reprisals on any section of the tribe within reach.

Meanwhile raids and offences continued. Among the more serious were the attack on the Border Police post on Baran, from which fourteen rifles were carried off, and the attack on the Kashmir Khar post, on which occasion the Mahsuds looted thirty rifles and five boxes of ammunition.

In September a party of clerks were attacked near the Chuhar Khel Dhana and the writer of the Zhob Agency office was killed. About this time the Mulla Powindah attempted to make overtures to Government regarding the recovery of the rifles looted at Kashmir Khar, but these were rejected.

The Government now decided that active retaliation should succeed the passive phase of the blockade. The proposals approved by the Viceroy in Council and concurred in by the Home

Government were that the blockade should be continued, but that it should be varied by sharp counter-attacks of three or four days' duration made by moveable columns. Secret preparations were accordingly made for retaliation on a large scale by punitive columns starting from different quarters.

The first series of operations was directed against the Mahsuds of the Khaisora and Shahur, combined with demonstrations from Jandola into the Takhi Zam, and from Datta Khel against the north-western portion of the Mahsud country. The general object was to destroy all defences, to capture as many prisoners and cattle as possible, and to carry off or to destroy all grain and fodder found.

On November the 23rd, at 9 P.M., No. 1 Column, consisting of 900 rifles, 3rd Sikhs, and 2nd Punjab Infantry, with two guns, under Lieut.-Colonel Tonnochy, 3rd Sikhs, left Datta Khel, and after marching due south halted at 3 A.M. below the Spina Punga Narai. The same day the column marched to Dodgul and halted for the night. The next day, having destroyed the defences of Dodgul, an advance was made down the Shuran Algad, no opposition being met with until the tower of Khandar, a noted outlaw, was reached. The tower was destroyed, one British officer and one sepoy being wounded. During the day the defences and towers of thirteen villages were destroyed, the force bivouacking for the night at a village called Bit Malikshai near the Razmak Kotal. On the 26th a reconnaissance of the head of the Shaktu valley was made; and, the following day, an escort of 160 rifles being left in Bit Malikshai, the force made a dash for Makin, the greater part of which was destroyed. On the 28th the column returned to Datta Khel *viâ* Mami Rogha. The enemy pressed the retirement over the Razmak Kotal, and some casualties occurred in the Rozani gorge. The total losses of the column during the raid amounted to two killed and sixteen wounded.

No. 2 Column left Jandola on the night of the 24th, and, consisting of 1,000 men of the 1st Punjab Infantry, 27th Punjab Infantry, 45th Sikhs, and 9th Bombay Infantry, was under the command of Colonel McRae, 45th Sikhs.

Advancing up the Tank Zam, Kot Shingi was reached about dawn, after some small villages had been destroyed *en route*. Heavy opposition was encountered at Kot Shingi, and, as the baggage coolies had stampeded, Colonel McRae retired to Jandola, followed by the enemy. Our total casualties during the day amounted to three killed and seventeen wounded.

Meanwhile No. 3 Column, consisting of 1,000 rifles of the 1st Punjab Infantry, 35th Sikhs, and 29th Punjab Infantry, under Colonel Macleod of the last named regiment, left Sarwakai early on the 25th and reached the Shahur Tangi without opposition. Two days were spent in destroying all the defences in the neighbourhood; after which the force returned to Sarwakai with seven prisoners and 500 head of cattle.

The 4th Column was under the command of Lieut.-Colonel Bunbury, and consisted of 1,250 men of the 17th Bengal Infantry, 23rd Pioneers, and 28th Punjab Infantry. Starting from Wana, and marching *viâ* the Inzar Narai, this force surprised the village of Torwam early on the 25th, being materially assisted by a detachment of all three arms, sent direct from Wana over the Tiarza Narai. On the 26th Colonel Bunbury bivouacked at the Tiarza post, whence, reinforced again by the detachment from Wana, he advanced into the Khaisora and destroyed several towers in the valley. The column returned to Wana on the 28th with 124 prisoners and a large number of cattle, having sustained a loss of about twenty killed and wounded.

Simultaneously with these operations both the Northern and Southern Waziristan Militia captured many prisoners and cattle.

The success of the first series of operations was largely due to the fact that it took the Mahsuds completely by surprise. They did not expect that any but the usual methods of coercion would be employed, and probably hoped that they would receive ample warning before an advance was made into their country.

As it was important that the blow they had received should be followed up as soon as possible by another, General Dening now submitted proposals for further operations, and at the same time asked for a reinforcement of two battalions of infantry.

General Egerton, commanding the Punjab Frontier Force, was ordered to direct the further operations against the Mahsuds, and five additional regiments and a mountain battery were sent to the front to take part in the second phase.

On the 4th December a force of 2,500 men and 4 guns, the whole under Brig.-General Dening, left Jandola, and again moved to Kot Shingi. The force was divided into two columns under

Colonel McRae, C.B., 45th Sikhs, and Lieut.-Colonel Gray, 1st Punjab Infantry.

Kot Shingi was occupied without opposition, and the British force, marching up the Tazar Tang, then crossed the Umar Raghza and bivouacked at Dwe Shinkai. On the 5th, after the defences of several villages had been destroyed, orders were given for a retirement on Guri Khel. During this movement, however, the rear-guard, under Colonel McRae, was so heavily pressed by the enemy across the Umar Raghza that that officer was compelled to storm the hills to the north and bivouac there for the night, whence he joined the main body at Guri Khel the next morning. His casualties during the retirement had been Captain McVean, 45th Sikhs, severely wounded, nine men killed and eleven wounded.

After a halt on the 6th, during the whole of which day frequent attacks were made on the picquets, a retirement was made on the morning of the 7th to Margha Band. The enemy followed up the column, driving their attacks home with great determination, but were in every case repulsed with loss; the casualties on the British side amounting to only two killed and two wounded.

The Mahsud's losses on this and the previous day must have been very severe, for they made no attempt to prevent the destruction of their defences in the Tank Zam on the morning of the 8th, or to molest the subsequent retirement on Jandola. This ended the second phase.

The third series of operations began on the 19th December, and consisted in two columns, starting from Jandola and Sarwakai, respectively, converging on Dwe Shinkai, in which quarter, as well as in the Spli Toi Algad, there were now known to be many Mahsud settlements.

The Jandola column, strength as shown in the margin, was under the command of General Dening, and leaving Jandola early on the morning of the 19th, marched *viâ* Kot Shingi to Umar Raghza without encountering any opposition. The following day the advance was continued past Ahmedwam, to a point near Paridai, a few miles up the Tre Algad; where the force bivouacked. On the 21st, after destroying the

Gujrat Mountain Battery, 4 guns.	
1st Pun. Cavy.	.. 13 sabres.
1st Pun. Infy.	.. 513 rifles.
27th „ „	.. 260 „
28th „ „	.. 461 „
35th Sikhs ..	.. 513 „
38th Dogras ..	.. 598 „
45th Sikhs ..	.. 416 „
South Waziristan Militia.	

defence of several villages, including Paridai, Biram Khel, and Darekai, the column retraced its steps to rejoin the Sarwakai force at Dwe Shinkai, where the whole force bivouacked that night.

The Sarwakai column, meanwhile, which was under the command of Colonel Hogge, and consisted of the marginally named troops, had left Sarwakai on the 19th and marched up the Shahur Nala to Badshah Khan. The following day they moved *viâ* the Nanu Narai into the Spli Toi Algad, whence, having punished the inhabitants of that valley, they proceeded across the Ghbargai Narai on the 21st and met the Jandola column as already narrated.

Gujrat Mountain Battery, 2 guns.
23rd Pioneers.
29th Punjab Infantry.
32nd Pioneers.

On the 22nd December, leaving the two Pioneer regiments as camp guards, the whole force raided up the Dwe Shinkai in three columns, whence, after destroying a number of towers and the defences of some villages, at the expense of only a few casualties, they returned to Jandola on the 24th.

In spite of the fact that all the defences in the Tre Shinkai and Wucha Khwar Nalas had been destroyed, the Mahsuds still showed no signs of submission, in consequence of which a fourth series of operations was now planned against them. The object of these new operations was the punishment of the Shabi Khel and other Mahsud sections having settlements in the Shaktu, Sheranna, and Shuza Algads, and the capture of a large number of cattle known to be grazing on the slopes of the Babaghar.

Three columns were ordered to take part in these movements. The first, about 2,500 strong, was under the command of General Dening, and started from Jandola; the second, 1,600 strong, was under Colonel McRae, and had Jani Khel for its base; while the third, commanded by Colonel Tonnochy, consisted of 1,400 men, and operated from Datta Khel.

To deal with the movements of these columns separately; General Dening moved out on the 1st January, and advancing up the Tank Zam reached Shilmanzai Kach without opposition. During the second day's march a large number of cattle were captured on the hills to the east of Zeriwam by a party sent out for this purpose. From Shilmanzai Kach the force moved up eastwards to the junction of the Shuza and Weshtanai Algads, whence it returned on the 7th to Jandola, marching *viâ* the Kani Narai to Marghaband.

Colonel McRae's column left Jani Khel on the 1st January and marched to Karkanwam, at which place the Northern Waziristan Militia, who formed part of the force, were detached with special orders to search all the country round Babaghar. The following day the main body marched up the Shaktu to Mandawam, and thence into the Sheranna, where the chief settlements of the Jelal Khel were destroyed. On the 4th an advance was made to Barawand, and the following day, having destroyed that place, the force swept over Khal Kach to Matwam, where a junction was made with Colonel Tonnochy's column. The militia, meanwhile, having captured a number of cattle round Babaghar, and destroyed some thirteen Jelal Khel settlements, marched to Datta Khel, *viâ* the Shaktu and Khaisora, where they rejoined their column.

Colonel Tonnochy, with No. 3 Column, left Datta Khel on the 1st January and moved to Wachfakiram and Waladin, whence he proceeded to Kikarai. On the 5th, he destroyed the defences of the Galeshahi villages of the Tank Zam, during which operation he sustained a loss of one man killed and two wounded. The following day No. 2 Column joined him as already described, and the combined forces then moved up the Shaktu and destroyed thirteen Tutia Khel towers. It was during the destruction of one of these towers that Captain Down, Political Officer, was mortally wounded, he having gone inside to look for a man who was hiding. On the 7th and 8th the whole force returned *viâ* Dosaki to Datta Khel.

The greater part of the troops in Waziristan had now been marching continuously since 24th November, and were badly in need of rest. General Egerton, therefore, decided to form standing camps at Zam, Miramshah, and Baran, from which places future operations might, if necessary, be resumed.

The Mahsuds had lost severely in men and cattle in the last operations, and the knowledge that we could penetrate into any part of their country now seemed to convince them of their inability to continue the struggle. As a result of this feeling, on the 16th January 1902, a deputation of *saiyids* was sent in to ask for a cessation of hostilities, until the tribe could hold a *jirga* and discuss matters among themselves. This proposition was agreed to, and the Commissioner further consented to receive the *jirga* on condition that the balance of the fine of one lakh was paid and that all rifles captured during the blockade were restored.

By the 26th February, these conditions had been complied with, and the *jirga* then asked that the blockade might be raised. The Government, however, insisted that before this could be done all outlaws must be surrendered and all cattle looted during the blockade must be restored. Finally, on the 10th March, as a result of further negotiations, into which it is not necessary to enter, the *jirga* promised to permanently exclude from Mahsud limits all outlaws who might escape arrest by flight, and gave up a number of *jirga* prisoners as hostages for the return of the cattle in one month. The blockade was raised the same day, and all restrictions in connection with it were withdrawn.

The total British casualties during the operations amounted to 32 killed and 114 wounded, while the losses of the enemy were roughly estimated at 126 killed and 250 wounded. In addition, 215 Mahsud prisoners were taken, 64 towers destroyed, 153 villages had their defences levelled, and 8,047 head of live stock were captured.

The punishment inflicted on the Mahsuds by the above blockade did not, however, impress all sections of the Wazirs, and, in the vicinity of Bannu, such constant trouble with the Kabul Khels continued to occur that another expedition had to be set on foot before the end of the year.

The Kabul Khel Expedition of 1902.

The Kabul Khel are a branch of the Darwesh Khel Wazirs, and inhabit the wedge of hilly country which lies between the Kohat and Bannu districts and east of the Kurram river.

From 1896 to 1899 many outrages were committed on the British border, the perpetrators of which were known to have taken refuge in the village of Gumatti, about 8½ miles from Bannu. This village was accordingly surprised and surrounded at dawn on the 6th February 1899 by a small column of troops from the Bannu garrison. The surrender of all outlaws resident in the village was then demanded, to which the men in question sent out the reply that they would resist to the last all attempts at capture. As it was only intended to punish the actual offenders, the rest of the inhabitants were now warned by the British officer in command of the party to leave the village, which they immediately proceeded to do. Seven of the outlaws, trying to escape by this means, were captured; the remainder of them took refuge in two strong towers from which it was found impossible to dislodge them. The mountain guns proved powerless against the solid masonry, and it was felt that a direct assault would have incurred a loss quite out of proportion to the result; and as the column had orders to return to Bannu the same day, it was now obliged to retire without effecting its object. The retirement was vigorously harassed by the tribesmen all through the Gumatti pass, the road through which is commanded on both sides by almost inaccessible hills, and, by the time Bannu was reached, the British casualties amounted to six killed and fourteen wounded. On the 9th February another column left Bannu, and, finding the village of Gumatti deserted, blew up the towers without encountering any opposition.

The outlaws, who had now lost all hope of pardon, continued to commit numerous crimes on the border until, in 1902, the state of affairs had become so intolerable that it was decided by Government to send an expedition into the district. A force of four small columns, the whole under the command of Major-General Egerton, was consequently organized, and concentrated at Thal, Idak, Barganatu, and Bannu, respectively. The composition of these columns is shown in the margin. The Idak column marched on the 17th November, and the Thal column, accompanied by General Egerton, one day later. The troops from Bannu and Barganatu also started on the 18th.

Thal Column.		
Kohat Mountain Battery.		
3rd Punjab Cavalry ..	151	rifles.
22nd Punjab Infantry ..	724	"
Kurram Militia	210	"
Idak Column.		
Derajat Mountain Battery ..	2	guns.
1st Punjab Cavalry ..	151	rifles.
5th Punjab Infantry ..	415	"
2nd " " ..	206	"
Northern Waziristan Militia.		
Barganatu Column.		
Gujrat Mountain Battery ..	2	guns.
5th Punjab Cavalry ..	42	rifles.
1st Sikh Infantry	271	"
4th Punjab Infantry ..	257	"
Bannu Column.		
Gujrat Mountain Battery ..	2	guns.
1st Punjab Cavalry ..	40	rifles.
3rd Sikh Infantry ..	311	"
4th " " ..	208	"

The Bannu column, on arrival at Gumatti, found itself confronted by a strong fortified enclosure, thickly surrounded by trees, and held by six outlaws, among them the well-known Silgai. The officer commanding, Colonel Tonnochy, determined to capture these men, and ordered the guns to try and make a breach in the walls. The guns, however, had no effect at 400 yards range, and the Colonel was ordering them to advance still closer, when he was mortally wounded.

Lieutenant C. M. Browne, R.E., now made two attempts to breach the walls with gun-cotton, but without success; and it was at last decided to carry the place by escalade. A storming party, led by Captain G. E. White, Captain C. H. Davies, and Lieutenant Airy, of the 3rd Sikhs, succeeded in this attempt, though Captain White was killed and both the other officers wounded. The whole of the outlaws were killed, while our total losses amounted to four killed and fifteen wounded.

Action at Gumatti.

On the 20th the Barganatu column joined the troops from Bannu, and the combined force, moving up the Zangara Nala, destroyed Sappari and Shakar, whence they returned to Bannu on the 25th.

Meanwhile the Thal and Idak columns had sent out small parties in various directions to harass the enemy and destroy his towers, and had returned to Bannu and Idak, respectively, with many prisoners and cattle, after encountering little or no opposition. The total losses sustained by the enemy amounted to 20 killed, 303 prisoners, 66 towers destroyed, and 5,288 head of cattle captured.

In connection with this expedition an incident occurred which, though it had no bearing on the course of the operations, deserves mention as affording a fine example of a forced march carried out at a very short notice.

It had been arranged that the whole of the prisoners and cattle collected by the Idak and Thal columns at Spinwam should, on the dispersal of the force, be taken to Idak; and in view of their large numbers the General Officer Commanding decided to order out 100 men from Idak to meet the Idak column on its return and assist in this task. A message was accordingly despatched, on the 22nd November, to the Officer Commanding at Idak, directing him to send 100 rifles to meet the Idak column about half-way from Spinwam on the following day; as it was not absolutely certain that the Idak column would be leaving Spinwam on the 23rd, the message contained the further instruction that, should touch with the column not be obtained by midday, the 100 rifles should return to Idak.

This message was sent from Spinwam by heliograph to Thal, from which place it should have been transmitted to Idak by telegraph, there being no direct heliographic communication between Spinwam and Idak. The address was, however, mutilated somewhere *en route*, with the result that the message was delivered to the Officer Commanding at Datta Khel, who received it at 3-10 P.M. on the 22nd.

In accordance therewith a detachment of the 2nd Punjab Infantry, strength as per margin, under the command of Lieutenant I. H. Gordon of that Regiment, marched out of Datta Khel fully equipped at 5-15 P.M., the same day, with orders to proceed as quickly as possible towards Spinwam and endeavour to join hands with the Idak column which, it was believed, was to leave Spinwam on the following day; if touch with the Idak column was not obtained by midday on the 23rd, the party was to proceed to Idak.

British Officer	1
Native Officers	2
Rank and file	101

The detachment marched all night and arrived at Miramshah, 25 miles, at 1-30 A.M., on 23rd November. At 7 A.M. the march was resumed towards Spinwam, the detachment now leaving the main road and proceeding over the Surghuluna Narai, north-east of Miramshah. At midday, when something over half-way between Miramshah and Spinwam, a halt was made, and Lieutenant Gordon ascended a hill near by, in the hope of getting a sight of the Idak column. Failing in this, he resumed the march at 2 P.M., making for Idak in accordance with the orders he had received on leaving Datta Khel. The detachment reached Idak at 5 P.M., on the 23rd November, having covered rather over 49 miles in under 24 hours. One man, a bugler, fell out during the march.

The Kabul Khel expedition of 1902 brings the history of our operations against the tribes of Waziristan up to date. While the Darwesh Khel have, on the whole, given little trouble since then, the Mahsud tribe have continued almost as turbulent as ever. Their chief offences have been the murder of three British officers, *viz.*, Captain Bowring, Political Agent at Wana, in 1904; Colonel Harman, D.S.O., Commandant of the Southern Waziristan Militia, in 1905; and Captain Donaldson, Brigade-Major at Bannu, in the same year. For these outrages the tribe has been heavily fined, all Mahsuds have been dismissed from the Southern Waiziristan Militia, and their enlistment in that corps has been stopped, at any rate for the present. There is every reason to believe that the Mulla Powindah was, if not the prime mover, at least largely concerned in all these outrages, and the most hopeful feature in the political outlook, as regards the Mahsuds, at the present day is that his influence in the tribe appears to be daily decreasing. The Mahsuds are beginning to realize that his advice invariably leads, in the end, to complications with Government and consequent loss to themselves, and it seems reasonable to hope that, should the Mulla Powindah either die or make up his mind to finally leave the country, as he has frequently expressed his intention of doing, the Mahsuds may at last settle down to a life of peace and friendship with the Government of India.

CHAPTER X.

THE DAWARIS.

Dawar is the name given to the valley which, watered by the Tochi, lies nearly due west of the point where that river, breaking through the Suliman Hills, enters the plains of Bannu. The valley is entirely surrounded by mountains, and is divided into two parts, known as Upper and Lower Dawar, by a narrow pass, some three miles long, called the Taghrai Tangi.

The inhabitants of this valley, although a Pushtu-speaking race, are not true Pathans, and have a very poor reputation for courage. A fanatical and priest-ridden people, they are said to number about 6,000 fighting men, but they have ever suffered much at the hands of the Darwesh Khel Wazirs who surround them, and have continually sought the protection of the British Government.

Expedition against the Dawaris, by a force under Brig.-General C. P. Keyes, C.B., in March 1872.

After the annexation of the Punjab, the first occasion on which we came into contact with the Dawaris was in 1851, when, in April of that year, a party of their tribe, conjointly with the Umarzai Wazirs, attacked a police guard in charge of some camels belonging to the Latamar outpost. They were driven off on this occasion with heavy loss, but not before they had killed two and wounded three of the small party who opposed them.

From this time to 1870 the Dawaris gave little trouble on our border. In 1858 they sent a deputation to ask the aid of the British Government against the Wazirs, but it was refused.

In 1870, however, they made themselves conspicuous by giving shelter and assistance to the Muhammad Khel Wazirs, who were then in open rebellion against the British Government. It is now well known that the recusant tribe, on leaving British territory, proceeded to Dawar; that the council at which hostile measures were determined on was held at the village of Haidar Khel on the 10th of June 1870; and that the measures then adopted were strongly advocated by the Dawari *maliks*, some of whom indeed took part in the cowardly attack on the guard of the 4th Sikh Infantry on the 13th of June. Throughout the defection of the tribe the Dawaris behaved in an underhand way; for while, in order to stand fair with the British Government, they constantly brought intelligence of the movements of the recusant tribe to the civil authorities, yet, to remain in the good graces of their Wazir neighbours, they gave them shelter and even land, distributing the families of the Muhammad Khels amongst the various villages of the valley. When the Wazirs submitted to the Government, on the 20th of September 1871, it was determined to fine all the tribes who had assisted them, and accordingly a fine of Rs. 3,000 was imposed on the two valleys of Upper and Lower Dawar. All the neighbouring tribes paid the fine demanded, and the men of Upper Dawar paid their share *viz.*, Rs. 1,500, of the tribal fine; but the men of Lower Dawar refused to do so.

All efforts to obtain reparation from these men were unsuccessful. A deputation sent to them, to summon their *jirga*, met with a most insulting reception; our messengers were abused and expelled from their villages, and were pelted with stones and clods of earth. Subsequently a written communication of the most insulting nature was addressed to the district officer and his assistant.

To submit tamely to such an insult would have been to endanger our prestige with all the tribes along the border; and orders were accordingly issued, on the evening of the 5th of March 1872, for the march on the following morning of all the available troops in garrison at Edwardesabad to the neighbourhood of the Tochi pass. Brig.-General C. P. Keyes, C.B., commanding the Punjab Frontier Force, was then at Edwardesabad, and was to direct the operations, which were on no account to extend beyond the period of twenty-four hours.

Further delay, in the opinion of both the Commissioner and Brig.-General Keyes, might have proved fatal to the accomplishment of the object in view within the time allowed for the operations and with the force then at Edwardesabad. Circumstances might so change that, within a few days, it might become imprudent, from a military point of view, to enter the hills with that force alone. It was known that the Dawaris had sent messages into Khost and the neighbouring hills for aid, and that certain priests and *saiyids* had been instigating them to resist. There were, too, rumours that the Ahmadzai Wazirs began to think that, if they had shown a bolder front and had offered more resistance, they might have escaped more easily in the settlement that had been made with those implicated with the Muhammad Khels.

Accordingly, on the morning of the 6th of March, leaving a force of 600 bayonets and 2 guns for the protection of the Edwardesabad fort and cantonment, Brig.-General Keyes marched with the troops, as per margin, towards the Tochi pass, and encamped about six miles from Edwardesabad, on ground where there was an abundant supply of water. Major A. A. Munro, the Commissioner of the Derajat, accompanied the force as Political Officer.

No. 3 Punjab Light Field Battery	2 howitzers.
1st Punjab Cavalry	.. 149 all ranks.
2nd „ „	.. 206 „ „
1st Sikh Infantry	.. 534 „ „
4th „ „	.. 424 „ „
1st Punjab „	.. 448 „ „

Arrangements had been made for two mule-loads of blasting powder to accompany the force, and also for fifty coolies, to repair the road if necessary. Cooked food was ordered to be taken by the troops.

The day previous to the march of the troops it was arranged that Muhammad Hyat Khan, Extra Assistant Commissioner, should proceed with 1,000 Wazir levies (supposed for the nonce to have been converted from bitter enemies into friendly allies) to seize the Tochi pass; but the number collected for this purpose were not so many as had been expected, and did not amount to more than 400, of which only 100 had matchlocks. The plan had been consented to, as Muhammad Hyat Khan had expressed himself confident of being able to carry it out, and also in order to spare no effort to effect the proposed object peacefully, and without coming into actual collision with the inhabitants of Dawar.

On the night of the 5th of March, Muhammad Hyat Khan proceeded with these levies, and occupied the Shinkai Kotal, at the western end of the pass, without opposition, at daybreak on the 6th, and also a *tangi* or defile, which was the narrowest part of the pass, about a mile on this side of the *kotal*.

On reaching the camp near the mouth of the Tochi pass, the Brig.-General proceeded to reconnoitre the pass itself. The road for the first few miles led along the left bank of the Tochi westward, and, taking then a more northerly course, followed the channel of the stream to the *tangi*, and thence to the *kotal*, over which the road passed at a height of 190 feet above the bed of the stream.

After the party had proceeded about four miles, reports were received from Muhammad Hyat Khan that the enemy had approached to within 300 yards; and that he required the assistance of a regiment. As it would have been quite dark long before a regiment could reach him, such support was utterly out of the question, and the General determined to push on and see matters for himself. It was about 4 P.M. when the party reached the *kotal*, and its occupants were found in a great state of excitement. There was a little firing, chiefly from the Wazir side, but it was manifest that the men who occupied the *kotal* had no intention of holding the place against opposition; they had, indeed, already begun to retire.

The attacking force did not exceed 150 men, led by a Hassu Khel *malik*, named Hussen, who was acting independently of the *jirgas* of the valley, and it had approached to within 200 yards of the Wazirs.

The Wazirs were assured that supports would be sent up as soon as possible; but General Keyes warned Muhammad Hyat Khan that he could not allow these supports to join him in the dark, and that, therefore, he need not expect them until the morning. General Keyes then started on his way back to camp; but before he had retired many yards, the Wazirs abandoned their position, and fled down the pass.

This conduct of the levies made a peaceful settlement more difficult, and it became a question whether it would not now be advisable to make a forced march by the longer and more open route through the Khaisora pass, in order to avoid loss of life, should the pass which had been abandoned by the Wazirs be occupied by the Dawaris. After due consideration, this plan was given up, on account of the length of the route, and of the difficulty of finding any one sufficiently acquainted with the road to lead the column in certainty on a dark night. There was also the probability that the Wazir *kiris*, of which there were several in the pass, would take alarm at the approach of the troops; on the other hand, the road and its difficulties by the shorter route were fully known; and, as the effect of forcing our way into the valley by this route would be so much greater and more lasting after what had occurred, it was resolved to carry out the bolder course.

At 4 A.M. on the 7th of March the camp was left standing, under the charge of Captain F. A. Bertie, 1st Punjab Cavalry, with 150 sabres of that regiment and the outlying picquets of the infantry corps, consisting of 40 bayonets each, while the remainder of the force, consisting of some 1,200 bayonets, 200 sabres, and 2 howitzers, marched towards the Dawar valley.

One hundred rounds per gun, and the same number per man, a day's rations in haversacks, and a hospital establishment accompanied the column. The usual precautions were taken to clear the heights which commanded the bed of the Tochi, but it was soon ascertained that the crest of the pass was unoccupied, and at 9 A.M. the Shinkai Kotal was reached without opposition.

It was said that the men of Dawar, knowing that the camp was at Tochi, and that no movement had been made to support the Wazirs, imagined that we would not attempt any further demonstration without endeavouring to negotiate, and, consequently, instead of securing the pass, they had returned to their homes, to assemble their people and hold counsel.

At the *kotal* the column halted, and a road practicable for guns was made. About 11 A.M. the road was reported ready, but it proved too steep for the horses to drag up the howitzers, and they had, therefore, to be dragged up the greater part of the ascent by the men of the battery and 4th Sikh Infantry. The descent on the Dawar side was comparatively easy.

The howitzers and ammunition waggons having been got over the *kotal* about noon, the Brigadier-General, accompanied by the Commissioner, pushed on with the cavalry, and after an hour's ride over the rocky bed of the river, ascending a slight rise, found himself at the end of a broad plateau with the three refractory villages of Haidar Khel, Hassu Khel, and Aipi in their front. Here he was met by two Hassu Khel *maliks*, who expressed a willingness on the part of the people of Dawar to agree to any terms which might be imposed. They were then informed by the Commissioner that the fines originally proposed would be levied, with an additional

Rs. 1,000 from Hassu Khel and Rs. 500 from Haidar Khel, as a mark of our further displeasure at their conduct. Blood-money at the usual rate would be demanded for a Bannuchi found dead in their pass that day; and two towers in each of the villages would be burnt for the previous day's misconduct of the Hassu Khel *malik*, as well as for the recusancy of the leading men of Lower Dawar, which had necessitated the march of a British force into the valley.

The *maliks* acquiesced in these demands, but they begged for time. It was, however, growing late, and, if the force was to return to camp that night, no time was to be lost. A quarter of an hour's delay was, therefore, granted to the villagers in which to collect the fine money, the cavalry remaining halted on the plain. A large body of the enemy was now seen assembling in front of the village of Haidar Khel, defiantly waving their swords, and apparently inciting to an attack.

On the arrival of the infantry and guns the assurances of submission were repeated, and the force advanced on the village of Haidar Khel, partly with the purpose of receiving the fine imposed, and partly to carry out the terms on which their submission was accepted, *viz.*, the burning of the village towers. In strange contrast with the submissive tone of the emissaries was the attitude of the great mass of the enemy, who, far from dispersing, still maintained their position in front of the village. The authorities were, however, so confident of the honesty of the Dawaris that the force, covered by the skirmishers of the 1st Sikh Infantry, advanced to within matchlock range of the enemy without firing a shot.

When the skirmishers had arrived within 200 yards of the Dawaris, a shot was fired, apparently as a signal, which was followed by a volley from the rest of the enemy, who at once took shelter behind the walls and in the ditches. The guns were promptly brought into action on the village, while the 1st Sikh Infantry made a spirited advance on the enemy. A wing of the 4th Sikh Infantry (the other wing having been left to hold the Shinkai Kotal) was, at the same time, sent round to the left flank of the village, and the cavalry to its right and rear, to cut off any attempt to escape. The 1st Sikh Infantry stormed the closed gates of the village and effected an entry, driving the inhabitants to the north corner, where for some time they made a stand behind some high-walled houses. The 1st and 4th Sikh Infantry having obtained entire possession of the left portion of the village set it on fire. The 1st Punjab Infantry was then brought up and sent to the right flank of the village to aid the cavalry in cutting off the retreat of the villagers. The fire and the determined bearing of the two Sikh regiments was soon too much for the defenders of the village, and, abandoning their position, they fled towards the plain, only to find themselves surrounded. The cavalry were speedily down upon them and sabred ten of their number, when the rest, seeing that all was lost, surrendered.

The cavalry and the 1st Punjab Infantry were then advanced to the adjacent village of Aipi, which was surrounded. Profiting by the severe lesson inflicted on Haidar Khel, the inhabitants at once gave security for the amount of the fine imposed, and the village was spared. It was now considered that sufficient retribution had been exacted, and that no further punishment was necessary. The more distant village of Hassu Khel was, therefore, spared, but, on the way back to camp, the Commissioner received the representatives of that village also, who had followed to surrender, and who yielded unconditionally to all demands. At about 4 P.M. the force commenced its return march; the Shinkai Kotal was cleared before dusk, and the troops arrived in camp at 10 P.M., having been eighteen hours under arms. No opposition of any sort was encountered during the return march.

Our loss had been trifling, while the loss inflicted on the enemy was forty-three killed and thirty prisoners. The result of these operations was satisfactory in a political as well as in a military sense; for a hitherto independent tribe had been compelled to recognize that even their secluded valleys did not protect them from just punishment. The fines imposed were subsequently paid in full, and the prisoners were then released.

After the above punishment of the Dawaris their conduct continued to be satisfactory until 1876. In March of that year the Haidar Khel, Hassu Khel, and Idak *jirgas* were summoned to Bunnu to answer for three burglaries which had been committed in the lines of the 5th Punjab Cavalry in January and February of that year by a band of robbers, headed by a Khostwal called Gul Azim. All three villages obeyed the summons, although it was the first time the representatives of Idak had attended as a body on any Deputy Commissioner. A large portion of the stolen property was produced by the *jirgas*, who paid a fine of Rs. 300 in compensation for the remainder.

This, it was hoped, would serve as a warning to the Dawaris for some time to come, but Gul Azim had sworn vengeance for the death of a comrade named Mir Salam, who had been shot dead by a sentry in one of the burglaries ; and, on the night of the 11th-12th August 1877, Gul Azim himself, with Mir Salam's brother and six other followers, made a savage attack on a guard of four policemen posted at the head of the Kuch Kot bridge, on the road leading to the Kurram outpost, within a quarter of a mile of cantonments.

The sentry on duty alone managed to escape, severely wounded, but the other three (who were asleep on *charpoys* at the side of the road instead of in the tower provided for their safety) were all killed, and their arms and accoutrements carried off.

Although only one of the murderers, a man named Kasim Gul, of Usuri, was actually a Dawari, their leader, Gul Azim, had always enjoyed an asylum in Idak and Musakai, and it was ascertained that the gang had not only assembled at Idak before the outrage, but had returned there afterwards. It was also impossible that the raid could have been effected without the connivance of the intermediate villages of Hassu Khel and Haidar Khel.

The surrender of the criminals was accordingly demanded, and, in order to enforce this demand, orders were issued that the whole of Lower Dawar should be blockaded, and traffic of every kind stopped. At the same time a seizure of all men and property of Lower Dawar was ordered, which resulted in the arrest of seventy men, and the capture of some cattle, from the sale of which a net balance of Rs. 275 was realized. Unfortunately the prisoners proved to be nearly all residents of Haidar Khel, and their detention had little influence directly on Idak, Musakai, and Usuri, which were chiefly implicated. The demand, too, for the surrender of the criminals was one which there was small chance that any tribe having pretensions to Afghan origin would comply with, except under more severe pressure than that of a blockade.

In the middle of November, the Dawaris having shown no signs of compliance with our demands for the surrender of the criminals, the Deputy Commissioner proposed that if it was inconvenient to move out troops, the case might be compromised by the infliction of a fine. This was approved by the Government, and the fine was fixed at Rs. 3,500.

In February 1878, as the Dawaris still held out, the Deputy Commissioner proposed that an attempt should be made to surprise, by the Baran pass, the village of Usuri, and to capture Kasim Gul, one of the raiders, who was known to be residing there. The Government would not, however, sanction this plan, and ordered the blockade to be continued. In the meanwhile the whole valley was feeling the effects of the blockade, and their long-continued exclusion from the Bannu market; but the realization of the fine was impeded by the want of unanimity which usually prevails in an independent border community, and by the absence of leading spirits to take the initiative.

The village of Haidar Khel went so far as to bring in Rs. 1,200; but they were sent back, as it was impossible to treat separately with a part of the tribe for the portion only of the fine imposed on the whole. Moreover, the greater part of this fine had been subscribed by the relatives of the Haidar Khel prisoners in our hands, so that it could not be received even as an earnest of submission on the part of the other villages.

In the month of May a reconnaissance of the Tochi pass was made by Lieutenant F. Mardall, 3rd Punjab Cavalry, and Lieutenant C. H. M. Smith, 3rd Sikh Infantry. As it was then the harvest season, the idea spread rapidly through the valley that the patience of the Government had at last become exhausted, and that this was only a preliminary to the employment of troops for sharper measures, or at any rate for the destruction of the ripening crops. The result was a scare almost amounting to a panic; this was soon followed by signs of submission on the part of the recusant villages, and in the beginning of June their *jirgas* came into Bannu and made their submission. The sum of Rs. 2,599 was realized from them in cash, and good security was furnished for the payment of the balance (Rs. 901) in three months. On the 11th of June the blockade was declared to be raised, and the *jirgas* were dismissed. At the same time orders were sent to Dera Ismail Khan for the Dawari prisoners detained in jail to be sent to Bannu, where they arrived a few days later, and were released. The balance of Rs. 901 was subsequently paid, and the whole of the fine demanded by Government was thus realized.

At the outbreak of the war in Afghanistan in 1878 the Dawaris did not at first show any open hostility to the Government, but when the British troops visited Khost in January 1879 the notorious Mulla Adkar fled from that valley, and took up his residence in the Mallakh villages of Upper Dawar. In the following month a series of raids and outrages were committed by the inhabitants of Dawar, aided by contingents from the different sections of the Wazir tribe, which were directly due to the instigation and encouragement of this man.

The residents of Upper Dawar, from Miramshah to Sheranni, were, more or less, concerned in every raid that occurred, and seem to have thought that their distance from our border quite put them beyond the reach of retribution. Upper Dawar also furnished the men who made themselves most conspicuous as leaders, *viz.*, Mauzamdin (a brother of Mulla Adkar), Ghulam Khan, son of Adam Khan, the Madda Khel *malik* of Sheranni, and Gulab Pir, a noted fanatic and freebooter, who lived with the Manzar Khel Wazirs, either at the village of Kanirogha itself, or in one of the neighbouring hamlets.

In Lower Dawar the village lying westward of Zerakki, *viz.*, Khadi, Idak, Hakim, Mubarakshahi, Tapiai, Palali, and Rasul Khel, were equally active in the raiding, and appear to have shared with their neighbours of Upper Dawar the idea that they were out of reach; but the rest of the population was less reckless. In a few cases, however, the eastern villages were implicated too; but it is worth remarking that Haidar Khel, which suffered so severely at the hands of Brig.-General Keyes's expedition in 1879, refrained altogether from participation in these raids. The outrages consisted for the most part of raids committed on the Thal-Bannu and the Thal-Kurram roads. The opening of the former route especially afforded them opportunities of plunder, of which they availed themselves with great pertinacity.

The month of April, 1880, saw an unusually audacious attack, led by Ghulam Khan, who, with a band of some 200 Dawaris and Wazirs, assaulted and occupied the Baran militia post, on the Bannu frontier, about five miles from Edwardesabad.

This post was occupied on the night of the 22nd-23rd of April when the raid was committed by a party of eight men of the militia. About 10 P.M. some of the raiders, having placed roughly-made ladders against the wall of the post, effected an entrance, all the occupants, even the sentry, being asleep. On being awakened by the raiders, the militia begged for their lives, saying they were all Mussulmans, and that they had been forced to take service and garrison the post. They then showed the raiders where the ammunition and other things were, after which they were allowed to go into the tower at the west angle of the post, where they remained the whole time the raiders were in the place. The marauders then looted the post, taking away five horses, three carbines, three matchlocks, three swords, and other property.

For their cowardly conduct in this affair the militia-men occupying the post were dismissed.

The Dawaris were also implicated in the attack on the Chapri post on the 1st-2nd of May 1880, already described, in which Lieutenant O. B. Wood, of the Transport Department, was killed.[1] The leader in this raid was a favourite *talib* of Mulla Adkar, named Wazir Khan.

In addition to the above, the people of Dawar were guilty of several minor raids, and the total value of the property plundered by them, excluding many items which, by common frontier custom, would be charged against them, amounted to no less than Rs. 45,000.

It was, therefore, proposed, in order to exact reparation from the inhabitants of Dawar for their many offences, to take advantage of the assembling of the force at Bannu in April 1881 to act as a reserve against the Mahsud Wazirs (*see* Chapter VIII), to visit the Dawar valley and to realize a fine of Rs. 50,000 from its inhabitants. This fine it was proposed to allot as follows :—

		Rs.
Lower Dawar	.. ..	15,000
Upper Dawar	Dawaris	25,000
	Manzar Khel and Hasan Khel Wazirs	5,000
	Madda Khel Wazirs of Sheranni ..	5,000

The people of Dawar, conscious of their guilt, and alarmed at the preparations against the Mahsuds, had already begun to make overtures to avert the retribution which they dreaded. Adam Khan himself, the Wazir *malik* of Sheranni, was reported

[1] See Chapter VII.

to have sent word of his readiness to purchase, by the payment of a fine, immunity from punishment for the inveterate hostility shown towards us since the days when he harboured the murderers of Captain Mecham, and for the part taken in these later raids by his son, Ghulam Khan.

The plan of operations proposed was that Brig.-General Gordon's force, after advancing to Makin by the Khaisora pass to open communications with the main column from Tank, under Brig.-General Kennedy, should, instead of returning to British territory by the same route, cross the Loargai Sar from the Khaisora valley into the Upper Dawar valley by the Darrevasta. After visiting Sheranni and the Wazir settlements at the western end of Upper Dawar, and exacting the fines demanded, the force was to march down the Tochi and realize the fines due from the Dawaris proper from Tindai eastward, which it was expected would be attended with little difficulty.

The Lieutenant-Governor advocated these measures, and considered that, to ensure the permanent peace and tranquillity of the Bannu border, it was necessary to prove to Dawar, which for many years had been a hot-bed of disaffection and fanaticism, that British territory could not be attacked, or British subjects murdered, with impunity.

The Government of India, however, refused to sanction the proposed expedition, on the ground that all the offences recorded against the Dawaris, with the exception of the attack on the Baran post, were committed beyond the frontiers of British India during the time the British forces were engaged in military operations beyond the border, and that the offences in question were more or less connected with these operations. The Governor-General in Council was of opinion that these offences did not afford ground for extending operations, which, for general reasons of policy, it was very desirable not to prolong.

In May 1882, as already mentioned, the notorious priest, Mulla Adkar, whose harangues had been chiefly instrumental in inciting the people of Dawar to acts of hostility, died.

In later years, with the exception of a treacherous attack made in 1903 on a party of British officers returning from a game of hockey, the conduct of the Dawaris has been fairly satisfactory and has given little cause for complaint.

END OF VOLUME II.